The CHRISTIAN EDUCATOR'S

Kenneth O. Gangel and
Howard G. Hendricks, editors

HANDBOOK ON TEACHING

A
BRIDGEPOINT
BOOK

Baker Books

A Division of Baker Book House Co
Grand Rapids, Michigan 49516

©1988 by Kenneth O. Gangel and Howard G. Hendricks

Published 1996 by Baker Books
a division of Baker Book House Company
P.O. Box 6287, Grand Rapids, MI 49516-6287

BridgePoint Books is an imprint of Baker Book House Company.

First published 1988 by Victor Books, a division of Scripture Press Publications Inc., Wheaton, Illinois.

Printed in the United States of America

Library of Congress Cataloging-in-Publication Data

Recommended Dewey Decimal Classification: 268

Suggested Subject Heading: CHRISTIAN TEACHING

Library of Congress Catalog Card Number: 88-60199

ISBN: 0-8010-2122-7

Unless otherwise noted, all Scripture quotations are taken from the HOLY BIBLE, NEW INTERNATIONAL VERSION®. NIV®. Copyright ©1973, 1978, 1984 by International Bible Society. Used by permission of Zondervan Publishing House. All rights reserved.

Scripture quotations marked NASB are from the New American Standard Bible, © the Lockman Foundation 1960, 1962, 1963, 1968, 1971, 1972, 1973, 1975, 1977.

Scripture quotations marked TLB are from *The Living Bible*, copyright © 1971 by Tyndale House Publishers, Wheaton, Illinois 60189. All rights reserved. Used by permission.

Scripture quotations marked KJV are from the Authorized King James Version.

For information about academic books, resources for Christian leaders, and all new releases available from Baker Book House, visit our web site:
http://www.bakerbooks.com

CONTENTS

LIFELINE GIVING

Your gift to the Northwest Bible College goes a long way. But you can help it go even further by joining our Monthly Giving Plan. It ensures a reliable income that helps us plan our long-term strategies. It also lowers administrative costs so even more of your gift can be used to help where it is needed the most.

It's convenient for you -- just check the box on the enclosed remit form indicating the monthly amount you wish to contribute. Enclose a voided cheque and the amount will be debited from your chequing account OR submit your credit card information to make a monthly credit card gift.

For immediate donation, simply call (780) 452-0808.

We'll send you a tax receipt of the total of your year's contribution at the end of the calendar year.

Thank you. If you have any questions, please call us.

www.nwbc.ca

INTRODUC
CHRISTIAN TEACH....
APPOINTMENT FROM GOD
Howard G. Hendricks

> He seems to do nothing of Himself which He can possibly dele-
> gate to His creatures. He commands us to do slowly and blun-
> deringly what He could do perfectly and in the twinkling of an
> eye. . . . Perhaps we do not fully realize the problem, so to call
> it, of enabling finite free wills to coexist with Omnipotence. It
> seems to involve at every moment almost a sort of divine abdi-
> cation. (*The World's Last Night.* New York: Harcourt, Brace,
> Jovanovich, 1952, p. 9)
>
> *C.S. Lewis*

A cartoon once appeared depicting a Mr. Brown and Miss Smith. The
lady was obviously applying for a teaching position, armed with test
scores and interview results.

"I'm awfully sorry, but we can't use you. We note that you are a
recent graduate of a school of education, and we require a teacher with
at least five years classroom experience. Also, you have only a bache-
lor's degree and we prefer someone with master's level qualifications."

The reader's eye then shifts to the next frame where Mr. Brown
is now interviewing as Sunday School superintendent, Miss Smith resist-
ing his plea for a teacher: "Mr. Brown, I'm a recent convert and really
don't know the Bible that well."

"Oh, that's no problem," he replies. "The finest way to learn the
Bible is to teach it."

"But, Mr. Brown, I've never taught junior high pupils," she
demurs.

"Oh, don't let that be a barrier, Miss Smith. All we require is a
willing heart," comes the response.

The scenario is more than a cartoon; it's a commentary on our low level of discernment regarding teaching. If you are planning to teach that $2 + 2 = 4$, you may need five years teaching experience. If you expect to teach children to say, "I don't know anything," rather than, "I don't know nothin'," a master's degree may be required. But to teach the curriculum of the Christian life, anything is good enough for God.

What a contrast with the design for teaching presented in the New Testament. Second Timothy 2:2 informs us that teaching is not a ministry of mediocrity but a ministry of multiplication. No human being is fully aware of the power resident in teaching. Every time one teaches he launches a process which, ideally, will never end.

Two reasons conspire to build a convincing case: the church must teach. It is not an option but an essential; not nice but necessary. The church that ceases to educate ceases to exist as a New Testament church. Christianity, to be perpetuated, must be propagated.

JESUS CHRIST COMMANDS IT

Matthew 28:19-20 focuses the Holy Spirit's zoom lens on the Great Commission, the last words of the risen Head of the church to His disciples. Five appearances of the Great Commission in the New Testament (vv. 19-20; Mark 16:15-16; Luke 24:46-48; John 20:21-23; Acts 1:8) indicate it is not peripheral but pivotal to our Lord's strategy.

The mandate, "Make disciples," essentially includes teaching. But we must note that the teaching called for is of a particular stripe; namely, "to obey everything" Christ commanded. In other words, His teaching is designed to produce both information *and* transformation. That brand of instruction is very demanding and incredibly difficult to accomplish.

Luke 6:40 further supports Christ's objective for His teaching when He says, "But everyone who is fully trained will be like his teacher." God's truth was not revealed to satisfy our curiosity but to conform us to Christ's image.

THE EARLY CHURCH PRACTICED IT

The New Testament unmistakably commands the church to teach. But did the early church obey that command?

THE ILLUSTRATION.

In Acts 2:41-47 we have a portrait of the early church which apprizes us that "they devoted themselves to the apostles' teaching" (v. 42). This was their persistent pattern, not an exception.

THE IMPLEMENTATION.

Ephesians 4 confirms a commitment to teaching. The ascended Christ gave gifts to men and gifted men to the church. Among them, "Some to be pastors and teachers" (v. 11). The purpose? "To prepare God's people for works of service, so that the body of Christ may be built up" (v. 12), further evidence that gifted men are called to a ministry of multiplication, not addition.

To the Jew there was no higher rung on the societal ladder than that of a rabbi. Therefore, when the first-century church was taught the doctrine of spiritual gifts they were confronted with a problem. People were clamoring for the "gift of teaching" with all the privileges pertaining thereto. As a result James had to issue this warning: "Not many of you should presume to be teachers, my brothers, because you know that we who teach will be judged more strictly" (James 3:1). Since the teacher is compelled to speak and the tongue is the last member to be mastered (v. 2), one should be very careful in aspiring to such a sobering responsibility.

The above biblical evidence should be compelling enough to attract the serious and to abort the superficial.

This book has been written by a group of Christian education specialists, each of whom is desperately concerned that the reader be equipped for the awesome and eternal privilege of teaching. A potpourri of principles and practices are outlined including valuable insights for the beginning teacher as well as the veteran.

Foundations are laid, patterns are presented, varieties of teaching are revealed, and crucial roles in Christian teaching are exposed—all with a view to providing *The Christian Educator's Handbook on Teaching.* Keep it on your desk—at arm's length—for ready reference and repeated reading.

In the second century, while resting in the course of his arduous campaigns against the German barbarians, the Roman emperor, Marcus Aurelius set down his famous *Meditations.* My favorite passages are contained in the opening book in which he offers up thanks to those teachers who in his youth arranged for him to grow not into a mere emperor but into Marcus Aurelius.

I too have had good teachers, and perhaps three or four great ones. That this realization should strike me forcibly forty-plus years after my graduation is not strange, anymore than it was strange for Marcus Aurelius to record his gratitude in his fifties.

It takes at least a couple of decades for a person to discover that he was well taught. All true education is a delayed-action bomb, assembled in the classroom for explosion at a later date. An educational fuse forty years long is by no means unusual.

The authors of this book pray that in future generations—perhaps long after the readers are in heaven—a substantial corps of men and women will rise up and call their teachers "blessed." Our interest is more than professional; it is deeply personal.

Teaching is only work if there is something else one would rather do.

Part One

FOUNDATIONS
for Christian Teaching

1. FOLLOWING
THE MASTER TEACHER
Howard G. Hendricks

INTRODUCTION

Jesus was the quintessential Teacher. He provides the teaching template, the paragon of pedagogy. He was the ultimate authority and prototype for teaching though He never discussed the subject. His actions modeled the discipline.

Though more has been written about Jesus as a Person than about anyone else in history, His role as a Teacher has been somewhat minimized, perhaps because of a negative reaction to the portrait of a teacher which characterized nineteenth-century liberalism. Herman Harrell Horne calls this neglect "an unworked mine." (*Jesus the Master Teacher,* Preface, p. ix.)

In the New Testament more than forty epithets describe the person and work of Jesus Christ. For example, He is Lord, Messiah, Saviour, Son of God, Son of man, *et al.* Frequently there is a tendency to emphasize one over the other.

Within the Gospels one of the most frequently used designations is Teacher; it occurs forty-five times. Fourteen times He is referred to as Rabbi.[1] So it is obvious that one of the prominent functions of our Lord during His public ministry was teaching.

Students of Scripture often study the content of the Gospels but tend to overlook the methodology of the Gospels. We need to remind ourselves that what Christ said and what He did were equally inspired by God. He could say in every scene and circumstance of His life, "I always do what pleases Him" (John 8:29).

This study aims to be suggestive, not exhaustive. It is committed to the proposition that, in teaching, the process is often greater than the product. Therefore, the student reader is urged to use the material presented as a stimulus for further personal inductive study. It is designed to provoke, not paralyze, thinking.

How can a housewife, truck driver, computer programmer, beautician, or physician become a master teacher, perhaps for only one hour a week? That's a Herculean task. But we can all profit from the example of the greatest Teacher, whom Nicodemus perceptively called "a Teacher . . . come from God" (3:2).

THE MAN

The Lord was distinctive as a Person. His birth, life, death, and resurrection were all unique. This uniqueness pervades His pedagogy as well.

JESUS WAS CONGRUENT.

What Christ said and did were one. He never did anything that contradicted what He said. This congruence provides the consistent model because He fulfilled all righteousness.

> The teaching of Jesus is great only if the content of His teaching conforms to reality. A creative teacher who teaches falsehood is not a great teacher. A poor teacher who deals inadequately with truth is not made great just because she or he tries to confront great issues. But a great teacher who brings pure perspectives on reality—ah, there is the seedbed for real teaching! There is the teaching of Y'shua!
>
> If Jesus were not who He claimed to be, then He was not a good teacher. He would have been a charlatan and a deceiver. In Israel a false teacher, like a false prophet, was to be condemned, not indulged.
>
> In classical Protestant theology we have been encouraged to think of Jesus Christ as having three principal offices. These are Prophet, Priest, and King. That is, as Prophet, Jesus is superior to Moses. As Priest, He is grander than Aaron. As King, He is more excellent than David.
>
> It is time to add to our understanding of the offices of Christ. There is a neglected office of Christ. *He is also Teacher.* Y'shua is the Wise whose wisdom surpasses Solomon. Jesus is the Sage whose wisdom was anticipated by the imagery of Lady Wisdom in Proverbs 1–9. Jesus is the great Rabbi, the Master Teacher of the ages, who came to explain very God: "No one has ever seen God, but God the only Son, who is at the Father's side, has made Him known" (John 1:18). The Apostle Paul affirms that in Christ "are hidden all the treasures of wisdom and knowledge" (Col. 2:3).[2]

In His teaching and lifestyle He realistically links knowing and

14

doing (cf. Matt. 5:36; 7:24-27). To know and not to do is not to know at all. To Jesus, all learning relates to doing the will of God (John 7:15-17) and we reinforce knowing through the process of doing.

As LeBar succinctly states:

> Christ Jesus was the Master Teacher par excellence because He Himself perfectly embodied the truth . . . He perfectly under- stood His pupils, and He used perfect methods in order to change people. He Himself was "the way, the truth, and the life" (John 14:6). He knew all men individually and He knew human nature, what was in man generically (2:24-25).[3]

Ronald Allen underscores Christ's uniqueness with these words:

> We tend to link a great teacher with a great institution. Jesus had no such ties.
> We tend to think of a great teacher as one who makes difficult things less complex. Jesus seemed to show new com- plexities even in simple things.
> We tend to anticipate that a great teacher helps us face life more independently. Jesus kept insisting that life must be lived in full dependence on another.
> We tend to associate a great teacher with technical language of his or her field. Jesus used simple language and everyday things.
> We tend to link a great teacher to his or her brilliant, erudite students. Those who learned best from Jesus were the poor, the lonely, the simple.
> We tend to think of a great teacher in the setting of a classroom. Jesus' classroom was a hillside overlooking the Sea of Galilee, a corner of a living room, a walk along a path, a small space in a little boat.
> Today we tend to look for a teacher to use multimedia tools. Jesus' tools were the heavens, the fields, mountains and birds, storms and sheep, a vineyard, a well, and a banquet. In short, whatever was around He would use as a teaching tool.[4]

JESUS WAS REALITY-ORIENTED.

He was maladjusted to the status quo. Studying the life of Christ, therefore, always returns us to reality. Reality—not ritual—was His main concern.

Subjects such as life and death, heaven and hell, money, prayer, anxiety, and children were all a part of His curriculum. He offered no classes in which the students were told to "take this down, because someday you will need it." All His teaching took place in the settings of everyday life.

From His birth in a manger to His death on a cross, the Saviour was always extraordinary. In the realm of His morals He was totally predictable; in the realm of His methods, totally unpredictable.

He was never unpredictable just to *be* different but because He *was* different. He was exasperating. Wherever He went He produced a crisis. He compelled individuals to decide, to make choices. Dorothy Sayers, in her characteristically trenchant manner, comments:

> The people who hanged Christ never, to do them justice, accused Him of being a bore—on the contrary; they thought Him too dynamic to be safe. It has been left for later generations to muffle up that shattering personality and surround Him with an atmosphere of tedium. We have very efficiently pared the claws of the Lion of Judah, certified Him "meek and mild," and recommended Him as a fitting household pet for pale curates and pious old ladies. To those who knew Him, however, He in no way suggested a milk-and-water person; *they* objected to Him as a dangerous firebrand. True, He was tender to the unfortunate, patient with honest inquirers, and humble before heaven; but He insulted respectable clergymen by calling them hypocrites; He referred to King Herod as "that fox"; He went to parties in disreputable company and was looked upon as a "gluttonous man and a wine-bibber, a friend of publicans and sinners"; He assaulted indignant tradesmen and threw them and their belongings out of the temple; He drove a coach-and-horses through a number of sacrosanct and hoary regulations; He cured diseases by any means that came handy, with a shocking casualness in the matter of other people's pigs and property; He showed no proper deference for wealth or social position; when confronted with neat dialectical traps, He displayed a paradoxical humor that affronted serious-minded people, and He retorted by asking disagreeably searching questions that could not be answered by rule of thumb. He was emphatically not a dull man in His human lifetime, and if He was God, there can be nothing dull about God either.[5]

There is a direct correlation between one's predictability and one's impact. The higher the predictability, the lower the impact.

Watch Him in action, for example, in Mark 12:13-17. The Pharisees are teamed up with the Herodians—a strange and diabolical melding. They thought they had Jesus impaled on the horns of a dilemma with their question, "Is it right to pay taxes to Caesar or not? Should we pay or shouldn't we?" Either way He chose to answer they were convinced they had Him trapped. But He slipped up on their blind side, compelling them to wonder, "Who thought up this dumb question anyway?"

The Gospels tell the stories of the holiest Man who ever lived, and yet it was the thieves, the lepers, and the prostitutes who adored Him while the religious hated His presence. He stands invariably the controversial Christ, the Divider of men. He may be rejected, but He can never be ignored.

JESUS WAS RELATIONAL.

His heart beat for individuals as well as ideas; for people as well as tasks; for change, not merely concepts. Jesus knew that the greatest relay for truth was relationships.

Christ's teaching took the form of a traveling classroom with maximal interaction between teacher and student. He asked and was plied with questions.

He performed miracles in the disciples' presence. They observed as He coped with the opposition of religious leaders.

He started right where His pupils were and spoke to them in terms of their immediate and often unperceived needs. Take the case of the disabled man at the pool of Bethesda (John 5:1-15). Jesus asks, "Do you want to get well?" (v. 6) What a startling and apparently foolish question for one who had been an invalid thirty-eight years! No such person would choose to remain sick.

But as Merrill Tenney suggests:

> A closer examination of Jesus' address to the victim shows that He was probing his inner heart, "Have you the will to be cured?" The reply revealed that the man was placing the blame for his condition on what somebody else had not done for him. He was bound by his circumstances and could rise no higher than a futile complaint. The paralysis of body was accompanied by a partial paralysis of will. Jesus' selection of this man from the large number of invalids at the pool indicated His interest in restoring those who have been reduced to utter helplessness both in body and spirit.[6]

Christ's relationships invariably focus personal needs at the deepest level. Study our Lord's instructive process of building bridges rather than walls with the Samaritan woman (John 4). A prostitute becomes a missionary in one significant and sensitive encounter.

It appears that there was something about the way Jesus lived that invited imitation. Listen to LeBar's summary of her studies:

Just about half the teaching incidents in the Gospels were initiated by the learners themselves. As people became captivated by His person, by the authority of His words and the marvel of His works, they came to Him with personal needs of all kinds. How much easier it is to teach when our pupils begin a lesson! When they begin, we may be assured of their interest, attention, and personal involvement.[7]

Consider our Lord's prayer life. He prayed about everything. Study the Gospel of Luke for the details. Why did the disciples ask Jesus to teach them to pray? (11:1) It's the only thing the disciples ever asked Him to teach them because every time they went to find Him they observed He was engaged in prayer and concluded, "This must be essential to life and ministry." Would anyone ever ask you as a teacher to teach them to pray because they found you so frequently in prayer?

There were times when He consciously set an example and urged invitation (e.g., John 13—the washing of the disciples' feet).

Numerous personal qualities attracted people's attention to our Lord: His approachability, appearance, love, gentleness, firmness, sensitivity, courage, vitality, determination.

It's hard to imagine any teacher securing the attention of his potential leaders unless he is infectious with a strong sense of mission in his personal life and commitment. Jesus clearly demonstrated that. In fact, He even went public right at the outset of His ministry in the synagogue at Nazareth (Luke 4:16-30), declaring His measurable objectives.

THE MESSAGE

Jesus *is* the greatest Teacher, but He can never be divorced from His great teaching. Donald Guthrie, in his helpful chapter, "Jesus," spells out the relationship between teacher and teaching:

Christianity has historically stressed religious teaching since Jesus Himself was the supreme exponent of the art. His influence on education in the church cannot be overstressed, yet caution is needed in one respect: Jesus was more than an educator. Although He may be regarded as an Illuminator of the mind, His mission was more basic. He came to bring redemption, and that redemption was the key to His teaching. Even if He had not come as Redeemer, His teaching, in both its content and its method, would be unique. His real claim to preeminence, however, rests in the fact that the practicability and relevance of His teaching depend on His work of atonement.[8]

18

There are seminal characteristics of His teaching.
HIS MESSAGE WAS REVEALED.

Jesus said, "I speak nothing of Myself. I do exactly what My Father has commanded Me." Examine the following passages: Matthew 11:27; John 3:27; 5:19; 8:28. In each Jesus becomes the conduit for the communication of divine truth while affirming a continuity between Himself and the Father: "I and the Father are One" (10:30).

Becky Pippert capsulizes the concept scripturally:

He informed people that knowing Him was the same as knowing God (John 8:19), seeing Him was the same as seeing God (John 12:45), believing in Him was the same as believing in God (John 12:44), and receiving Him was the same as receiving God (Mark 9:37).[9]

People constantly clashed with Jesus, mostly because of His unabashed claims. In His address at the synagogue of Nazareth He read from Isaiah and said, "Today this Scripture is fulfilled in your hearing" (Luke 4:21). In other words, "You are looking at the fulfillment." While at first they spoke well of Him and were amazed at His gracious words, on reflection they became so outraged they tried to kill Him.

C.S. Lewis has warned against the claim that Jesus was merely a *good* teacher but not who He claimed to be—the Son of God. How could He be good if He lied about the major subject of His teaching—namely, *Himself?*

"I'm ready to accept Jesus as a great moral teacher, but I don't accept His claim to be God." That is the one thing we must not say. A man who was merely a man and said the sort of things Jesus said would not be a great moral teacher. He would either be a lunatic—on a level with the man who says he is a poached egg—or else he would be the devil of hell. You must make your choice. Either this man was, and is, the Son of God: or else a madman or something worse. You can shut Him up for a fool, you can spit at Him and kill Him as a demon; or you can fall at His feet and call Him Lord and God. But let us not come with any patronizing nonsense about His being a great human teacher. He has not left that open to us. He did not intend to.[10]

He healed on the Sabbath because He was the Lord of the Sabbath. He said He was God and He acted like Him. He informed the religious leaders He was greater than Jonah and Solomon and He demonstrated it by His resurrection.

Because Jesus was the God-Man He taught by His works as well as His words. Spiritual meanings were embedded in spiritual acts.

Mark the extensive use of imperatives in His teaching: "Watch and pray." "Be ready." "Come." "See." "Go tell." He compels commitment.

HIS MESSAGE WAS RELEVANT.

Because His message was revealed, it was relevant. He never answered the questions no one was asking. He scratched where people were itching.

But He was no mere theoretician. The writer to the Hebrews informs us, "For we do not have a high priest who is unable to sympathize with our weaknesses, but we have one who has been tempted in every way, just as we are—yet was without sin" (Heb. 4:15). He also explains, "Because He Himself suffered when He was tempted, He is able to help those who are being tempted" (2:18).

Reaching the core of a student's life demands contact with the whole person as he/she thinks, feels, and wills. That is why Jesus so frequently shared His own emotions of compassion, judgment, love, hate, joy, sorrow, gratitude, and sympathy.

All of these were magnetic to a hungry, hurting world. He was relevant as no other.

HIS MESSAGE WAS AUTHORITATIVE.

One of the most striking features of Jesus' teaching lay in the authority with which He gave it. He never spoke tentatively, timidly, or apologetically. He knew His message and never stuttered in declaring it. It is this that impressed people so much.

In fact, at the conclusion of the Sermon on the Mount, His teaching generated a unique response "because [in sharp contrast with His contemporaries] He taught as one who had authority, and not as their teachers of the Law" (Matt. 7:29). He *had* authority; they quoted authorities.

While there were many similarities, one profound difference rises between Jesus and the religious leaders of His day. The linchpin is one of authority. Mark 11:27-33 makes this transparent.

We also see His authority in the demands He made on people (Luke 14:25-35). In each case Jesus makes a threefold repetition: "cannot be My disciple." The categoric finality of those words! Truth must surely involve exclusions but because we are fallen and proud human beings, men find this part of discipleship very distasteful.

John Stott convincingly concludes:

> Though but a peasant from Galilee, carpenter by trade and preacher by vocation, He claimed to be the Teacher and the Lord of men, He said He had authority over them to tell them what to believe and to do. It is an evident (if indirect) claim to

Deity, for no mere man can ever exercise lordship over other men's minds and wills.[11]

The crowd was correct for a change: "Nothing like this has ever been seen in Israel" (Matt. 9:33). The Pharisees' explanation: "It is by the prince of demons that He drives out demons" (v. 34). They were critical of Him but He was even more outspokenly critical of them. The gauntlet had been thrown down.

HIS MESSAGE WAS EFFECTIVE.

Mark the results of Christ's teaching: amazement, fear, silence, belief, and violent opposition, but never indifference or neutrality. Lives changed because His teaching objective provided not merely information but transformation.

People brought their friends to Jesus, followed Him, spread abroad His fame, and ministered to Him. They dropped everything and followed Him (cf. Mark 1:18 and 2:14 for two examples).

In the Great Commission one of Jesus' stated goals for the process of discipleship was "teaching them to obey everything I have commanded you" (Matt. 28:20). Eager for insight and change on the basis of His teaching, He did not expect that knowledge would automatically result in action.

What kinds of results must we work for in our teaching? "Sin isn't God's brand of humanity: perfect obedience is."[12]

THE MOTIVES

True teaching emanates from within. There is an experience of resonation between teacher and pupil without which the process of learning is sterile and, not infrequently, aborted.

Several motives surface in our study of the Gospels. The following are basic.

THE MOTIVE OF LOVE.

Jesus always had the best interests of the one loved paramount in His relationship. John, the apostle of love, says, "Having loved His own who were in the world, He now showed them the full extent of His love" (John 13:1).

But it was no sentimental slush; it was tough love. For example, He rebuked His disciples, not for superficial reasons but for substantive ones. "Why are you so afraid?" He asked, "do you still have no faith?" (Mark 4:40)

Notice the context. Jesus, the greatest Teacher, had just been lecturing on faith (vv. 1-34). After the explanation He gives them an examination. He had said, "Let us go over to the other side" (v. 35).

They concluded on the basis of their experience, "Teacher, don't You care if we drown?" (v. 38) He had not said, "Let's go to the middle of the lake and drown!" They flunked the hearing test. "He who has ears to hear, let him hear" (vv. 9, 23-24).

Again, He rebuked James and John when they desired to call fire down from heaven to destroy the Samaritans (Luke 9:54-55). He even severely rebuked Peter, the leader of the disciples, in the presence of the entire group. " 'Out of my sight, Satan!' He said. 'You do not have in mind the things of God, but the things of men' " (Mark 8:33).

Rebuke always depends on the basis of relationship; He loved the disciples as they were, but He loved them so much He would not allow them to remain as they were without intervention. He rebuked but never rejected them.

Regardless of His demanding statements regarding the cost of discipleship, He never demanded a fully developed faith at the beginning of one's spiritual pilgrimage. He never rejected anyone because of his incomplete, faltering faith or failure to live up to God's laws.

He was true to Isaiah's prophecy of the Messiah (Isa. 42:3) quoted in Matt. 12:20: "A bruised reed He will not break, and a smoldering wick He will not snuff out."

C.S. Lewis reflects on Christian love with his customary lucidity:

> If I am sure of anything I am sure that His teaching was never meant to confirm my congenital preference for safe investments and limited liabilities. . . .
>
> Love anything, and your heart will certainly be wrung and possibly be broken. If you want to make sure of keeping it intact, you must give your heart to no one, not even to an animal. Wrap it carefully round with hobbies and little luxuries; avoid all entanglements; lock it up safe in the casket or coffin of your selfishness. But in that casket—safe, dark, motionless, airless—it will change. It will not be broken; it will become unbreakable, impenetrable, irredeemable. The alternative to tragedy, or at least to the risk of tragedy, is damnation. The only place outside heaven where you can be perfectly safe from all the dangers and perturbations of love is hell.[15]

THE MOTIVE OF ACCEPTANCE.

Acceptance is the first step of effective teaching. Notice His crowd: prostitutes, unscrupulous tax collectors, sinners, the hurting and helpless, lepers. Certainly not a Madison Avenue public relations collection!

Mark His reputation. "Here is a glutton and a drunkard, a friend of tax collectors and 'sinners' " (Matt. 11:19). Jesus' primary concern was not His reputation but His responsibility.

"When the teachers of the Law who were Pharisees saw Him eating with the 'sinners' and tax collectors, they asked His disciples: 'Why does He eat with tax collectors and 'sinners'?" indicating the kind of people with whom Jesus spent time (Mark 2:16). Jesus' answer is highly instructive. "It is not the healthy who need a doctor, but the sick. I have not come to call the righteous, but sinners" (v. 17). *What* Christ was determined *where* He was. He could companion with sinners without being complicated by their sins. He hated sin but loved the sinner. Acceptance cannot be equated with approval.

The intrinsic worth of the individual was paramount in His choices. He permitted no discrimination for any reason or any individual.

THE MOTIVE OF AFFIRMATION.

Andrew T. LePeau, in his excellent book *Paths of Leadership*, provides this insight:

> There are few leaders who, while needing affirmation, require less of it than most. Their self-esteem is lifted by simply knowing they have done a good job. They tend to assume that others are like them and also need little affirmation; consequently, they give little. They pay little attention to the concerns of others and bury themselves in their work, their source of esteem.
>
> Both these extremes—the insecure, distant leader and the task-oriented leader—result in the same behavior: no affirming of others. They also arise from the same cause: self-concern. The first group continually compare themselves with others, wondering how they are coming across. They have little time to consider the needs of others. The second group continually focus on their jobs and how to do them better. They have little time to consider the needs of others.[14]

Jesus frequently affirmed people by issuing a challenge: "Come, follow Me . . . and I will make you fishers of men" (Matt. 4:19). Statements like that have a Pygmalion effect on people. "You follow Me. I'll make you." That involves a mutual responsibility in the teaching-learning process.

In the midst of a group of troubled hearts Jesus said, "I tell you the truth, anyone who has faith in Me will do what I have been doing. He will do even greater things than these, because I am going to the Father" (John 14:12). What a confidence booster!

While recognizing that He had more to say to His disciples and they had more to learn, that constituted no pressure on His part. He had implicit confidence in the Holy Spirit's continuing ministry in them.

"When He, the Spirit of Truth, comes, He will guide you into all truth" (16:13). He affirmed them by assuring them of the Holy Spirit's personalized ministry to them. Jesus would not leave them to fend for themselves as orphans.

In his characteristic manner Peter says, "We have left everything to follow You! What then will there be for us?" (Matt. 19:27) Jesus assured Peter He had positions and rewards and eternal life in store for them. In fact, the sacrifice would bring a guaranteed 100 percent return on their investment.

When our Lord sent His disciples out two by two He gave them both authority and specific instructions, assuring them that they had no need to be afraid (Matt. 10; Mark 6:6-13). Though a group of sheep among wolves, they were protected and productive in their mission.

Perhaps Christ's greatest means of affirmation was prayer. He informed Peter, "Satan has asked to sift you as wheat. But I have prayed for you, Simon, that your faith may not fail. And when you have turned back, strengthen your brothers" (Luke 22:31-32). In our Lord's High Priestly Prayer recorded in John 17 Jesus prayed, "I am not praying for the world, but for those You have given Me, for they are Yours" (v. 9). What a double security knowing that God gave them to Jesus and that Christ was praying for them.

In Matthew 28:16 the disciples had just come off the biggest fiasco of their involvement with the Saviour. He never found fault with their failures. Instead He said, in effect, "Now, men, let's go and take the world. I'm giving you My authority and My presence." What more could they ask for?

THE METHODS

John Gardner surfaces the fact that this kind of teaching is desperately lacking today:

> Much education today is monumentally ineffective. All too often we are giving your people cut flowers when we should be teaching them to grow their own plants. We are stuffing their heads with the products of earlier innovation rather than teaching them how to innovate. We think of the mind as a storehouse to be filled rather than as an instrument to be used.[15]

Another component that made Jesus a great Teacher is frequently evaded by evangelicals. That is the HOW, or the exciting manner in which Jesus taught.

He used methods but was not bound to any one method. He

moved comfortably from the known to the unknown; from the simple to the profound; from the concrete to the abstract. A remarkable freedom appears in His methodological skills and with a clear-cut objective. He is not an entertainer but an educator. He desires more than gaining attention; He is committed to changing lives.

No one could ever accuse Jesus of a truncated educational philosophy. He understood that all learning involves a process. He not only knew *what* He wished to teach, but He also knew *how* to teach. Learning was more than listening; teaching more than telling. How did Jesus become so effective without bells and schedules, a fixed classroom, and an overhead projector or flannelgraph?

Here are some clues to His effectiveness. Jesus' teaching had distinguishable and transferable characteristics.

JESUS' TEACHING WAS CREATIVE.

There is nothing stereotypical about the patterns of Christ's teaching. It's difficult to find Jesus ever doing the same thing in the same way. One reads the Gospels with fascination to discover what Jesus will do and say next. We see His creativity in the following:

In His use of questions. These form the heart of His teaching method. The four Gospels record over a hundred different ones. Some of His questions were direct and simply intended to secure information; some clarified uncertainty in the minds of His hearers and some invited expressions of faith. For example, "Do you believe that I am able to do this?" (Matt. 9:28) He said to a sick man.

Robert Stein, in his book *The Method and Message of Jesus' Teaching,* says:

> He used questions in a variety of ways and in a variety of situations. One way in which Jesus used questions was by drawing from His audience the correct answer He sought. By being drawn out from the listeners rather than by simply being declared by Jesus, the correct answer was more convincingly and permanently impressed upon their minds. The turning point of His entire ministry centered around an incident in Caesarea Philippi, where Jesus asked His disciples:
>
> " 'Who do men say that I am?' And they told Him, 'John the Baptist; and others say, Elijah; and others one of the prophets.' And He asked them, 'But who do you say that I am?' Peter answered Him, 'You are the Christ.' And He charged them to tell no one about Him.
>
> "And He began to teach them that the Son of man must suffer many things, and be rejected by the elders and the chief priests and the scribes, and be killed, and after three days rise again. And He said this plainly" (Mark 8:27-32).[16]

25

Frequently His indirect questions required the learners to compare, examine, recall, and evaluate.

Hypothetical questions placed problem-solving situations before His hearers. As in Matthew 21:31, "Which of the two did what his father wanted?" Or as in Luke 10:36, "Which of these three do you think was a neighbor to the man who fell into the hands of robbers?"

Jesus was remarkably adept at handling the questions which came to Him, even when they were intended to trap Him. In Mark 12:13-34 He discusses three subjects: (1) taxes to Caesar; (2) marriage in the resurrection life; and (3) the priority of the commandments. Each question was fielded differently and the listeners received so much to explore that they had nothing more to ask at that time.

In His use of parables. Jesus was the Master Storyteller. His teaching provoked thinking; it did not paralyze. Parables were His most famous characteristic form of involving people creatively in the process of learning. Mark notes that Jesus "taught them many things by parables" (Mark 4:2).

Archibald Hunter claims that 35 percent of Jesus' teaching in the synoptic Gospels can be found in parabolic form.[17]

A critical question asks, "Why did Jesus teach so extensively in parables?" Again, Robert Stein has a masterful chapter on "The Parables of Jesus" in which he sets forth three reasons: (1) to conceal His teaching from those outside (cf. Mark 4:10-12; Matt. 11:25-27); (2) to illustrate and reveal His message to His followers (Mark 4:34); and (3) to disarm His listeners (12:1-11; Luke 15:1-2).[18]

Jesus employed a variety of creative methods such as overstatement (Mark 5:29-30); proverb (6:4); paradox (12:41-44); irony (Matt. 16:2-3); hyperbole (23:23-24); riddle (11:12); simile (Luke 13:34); pun (Matt. 16:18); allusion (John 2:19); and metaphor (Luke 13:32).

JESUS' TEACHING WAS UNIQUE.

Every lesson was hand-tooled and chosen to fit the demands of the situation and the needs of the learner. Every encounter was distinctively different because He knew what was in man generically and individually (John 2:24-25). The three interviews that follow (Nicodemus, the Samaritan woman, and the nobleman of Capernaum), demonstrate His ability to deal skillfully and uniquely with three different types of personalities. The goal was identical—to bring them to faith. The methodology was different.

He dispensed truth "as much as they could understand" (Mark 4:33). As LeBar notes: "Learning is a process, usually gradual, but marked sometimes by high moments of rapid advance."[19]

Jesus did not resort to a storage-tank approach to education: "Take this down because someday you will need it." He was under no compulsion to teach His disciples everything they needed to know right then, even though He was the personification of truth (John 14:6). We never see Him rushing to cram spiritual content down people's throats. He never asks people to memorize and repeat answers back to Him. He was content to trust the Holy Spirit to guide them into all truth (16:13).

The Saviour always began where people were—with their questions, needs, hurts, and concerns. He knew how to listen to people and to key off their comments. He tuned in to their channel; He could adapt to the issue of the moment; He could mesh with their gears without stripping them.

Christ never disengaged from His culture. His language always stood tangent to the person's experience—his occupation, social problems, customs, family life, nature, religious concepts.

Note Jesus' use of the element of surprise with the Samaritan woman (asking for a drink, John 4:7-9); that which was at hand (a child in Matt. 18:2; a coin in Mark 12:15; and fishing nets in Luke 5:4).

LeBar observes:

> He usually started on a personal level because then the pupils connected His eternal truth with their own lives. The few times when He started on a content level, He continually related that content to the lives of His hearers.[20]

JESUS' TEACHING WAS ENGAGING.

People do not think unless led to do so. A problem-solving mentality pervades the pages of the Gospels. Jesus does not merely solve problems *for* people but *with* people; they are always involved in the process.

He engaged people by presenting a problem, by asking an appropriate question, by using repetition, by telling a story or simply by maintaining silence.

To be flexible in his methodology one dare not only know his subject thoroughly, he must also have in mind the direction in which he wishes to guide his learners. Our Lord proceeded informally but not aimlessly.

Luke 10:25-37 (the Parable of the Good Samaritan) offers a classic case of the greatest Teacher involving a lawyer in exploring truth for himself. Instead of answering his questions Jesus questioned his answers.

JESUS' TEACHING WAS DEVELOPMENTAL.

Our Lord's goal was to take people from where they were to where they ought to be.

The conversation Jesus had with the woman of Samaria is an object lesson in the Saviour's incredible skill in this art (John 4).

27

Jesus tears down every barrier—cultural, social racial, sexual, and religious—and turns her into an evangelist in her community. That's change.

But *how* did this radical change come about? Becky Pippert incisively observes:

> The Samaritan woman had had five husbands and was currently living with a sixth man. The disciples took one look at her and felt, "That woman? Become a Christian? No way, why just look at her lifestyle!" But Jesus looked at her and came to the opposite conclusion. What Jesus saw in her frantic male-hopping wasn't just looseness. It wasn't her human need for tenderness that alarmed Him, but rather how she sought to meet that need. Even more, Jesus saw that her need indicated hunger for God. He seemed to be saying to the disciples, "Look at what potential she has for God. See how hard she's trying to find the right thing in all the wrong places."[21]

This is the result of seeing people with an entirely radicalized set of eyes (cf. John 4:34-35).

He challenged the Pharisees, "Go and learn what this means: 'I desire mercy, not sacrifice' " (Matt. 9:13). Jesus never forced decisions but He encouraged people to make them. Patiently He paced the learning experience of His disciples and those with whom He interacted.

From our Lord we learn that good teaching involves helping the learner to assume responsibility for his thinking and living. He was forever encouraging and enabling people to make the best possible choices.

To guide a person in the name of Jesus is a great privilege and a sobering responsibility; to misguide an individual is no minor matter to Him (Matt. 18:6).

CONCLUSION

Herman Harrell Horne, in his classic *Jesus the Master Teacher,* enumerates the essential qualifications of a world-teacher:

1. A vision that encompasses the world.
2. Knowledge of the heart of man.
3. Mastery of the subject taught.
4. Aptness in teaching.
5. A life that embodies the teaching.[22]

Jesus fleshes out every one of those qualities and more with distinction.

If teaching is causing people to learn—to alter their thinking, feelings, and behavior—then the Saviour qualifies as the ultimate Teacher. He changed His generation and every one since.

Hopefully the reader's appetite has been whetted to engage in further personal study of the world's greatest Teacher—to master the Master's model.

No wonder Kenneth Scott Latourette, eminent historian and former chairman of the department of religion at Yale Graduate School, launches his provocative chapter "Jesus and the Gospel: the Foundation of Christianity" with these words:

> Christianity had what looked like a most unpromising beginning. The contemporary observer outside the little inner group of the disciples of Jesus would have thought it impossible that within five centuries of its inception it would outstrip its competitors for the religious allegiance of the Roman Empire and become the professed faith of the rulers and of the overwhelming majority of the population of the realm. Still less would he have dreamed that within less than two thousand years it would become worldwide, with a more extensive geographic spread and a greater influence upon mankind than any other religion.[23]

ENDNOTES

1. Robert H. Stein, *The Method and Message of Jesus' Teachings.* Philadelphia: Westminster Press, 1978, p. 1.

2. Ronald B. Allen, *Lord of Song: The Messiah Revealed in the Psalms.* Portland, Ore.: Multnomah Press, 1985, pp. 59–60.

3. Lois E. LeBar, *Education That Is Christian.* Old Tappan, N.J.: Fleming H. Revell Co., 1958, p. 51.

4. Allen, pp. 57–58.

5. Dorothy Sayers, *Creed or Chaos?* New York: Harcourt, Brace and Company, 1949, pp. 5–6.

6. Merrill C. Tenney, *John: The Gospel of Belief.* Grand Rapids: Wm. B. Eerdmans Publishing Co., 1948, p. 104.

7. LeBar, p. 81.

8. Elmer L. Towns, ed., *A History of Religious Educators.* Grand Rapids: Baker Book House, 1975, p. 15.

9. Rebecca Manley Pippert, *Out of the Salt Shaker and Into the World.* Downers Grove, Ill: InterVarsity Press, 1979, p. 42.

10. C.S. Lewis, *Mere Christianity.* New York: The Macmillan Co., 1952, p. 41.

11. John R.W. Stott, *Christ the Controversialist.* Downers Grove, Ill: InterVarsity Press, 1970, p. 209.

12. Pippert, p. 30.

13. C.S. Lewis, *The Four Loves.* New York: Harcourt, Brace and Word, Inc., 1960, pp. 168–69.

14. Andrew T. LePeau, *Paths of Leadership.* Downers Grove, Ill: InterVarsity Press, 1983, p. 57.

15. John W. Gardner, *No Easy Victories.* New York: Harper and Row, 1968, p. 68.

16. Stein, p. 23.

17. Richard A. Batey, ed. *New Testament Issues.* New York: Harper and Row, 1970, p. 71.

18. Stein, pp. 41–42.

19. LeBar, p. 71.

20. LeBar, p. 82.

21. Pippert, p. 119.

22. Herman Harrell Horne, *Jesus the Master Teacher.* Grand Rapids: Kregel Publications, 1964, pp. 184–85.

23. Kenneth Scott Latourette, *A History of Christianity.* New York: Harper and Brothers, 1953, p. 33.

BIBLIOGRAPHY

Batey, Richard A., ed. *New Testament Issues.* New York: Harper and Row, 1970.

Gangel, Kenneth O. and Warren S. Benson. *Christian Education: Its History and Philosophy.* Chicago: Moody Press, 1983.

Gardner, John W. *No Easy Victories.* New York: Harper and Row, 1968.

Highet, Gilbert. *The Immortal Profession.* New York: Weybright & Talley, 1976.

Horne, Herman Harrell. *Jesus the Master Teacher.* Grand Rapids: Kregel Publications, 1964.

Latourette, Kenneth Scott. *A History of Christianity.* New York: Harper and Brothers, 1953.

LeBar, Lois E. *Education That Is Christian.* Old Tappan, N.J.: Fleming H. Revell Co., 1958.

LePeau, Andrew T. *Paths of Leadership.* Downers Grove, Ill: InterVarsity Press, 1983.

Meye, Robert P. *Jesus and the Twelve.* Grand Rapids: Wm. B. Eerdmans Publishing Co., 1968.

Pippert, Rebecca Manley. *Out of the Salt Shaker and Into the World.* Downers Grove, Ill: InterVarsity Press, 1979.

Sayers, Dorothy. *Creed or Chaos?* New York: Harcourt, Brace and Company, 1949.

Stein, Robert H. *The Method and Message of Jesus' Teachings.* Philadelphia: Westminster Press, 1978.

Stott, John R.W. *Christ the Controversialist.* Downers Grove, Ill: InterVarsity Press, 1970.

Tenney, Merrill C. *John: The Gospel of Belief.* Grand Rapids: Wm. B. Eerdmans Publishing Co., 1948.

Towns, Elmer L., ed. *A History of Religious Educators.* Grand Rapids: Baker Book House, 1975.

2. THE ROLE OF THE HOLY SPIRIT IN CHRISTIAN TEACHING
Roy B. Zuck

Christian education is unique because of its *subject matter*—the Bible, God's written revelation; because of its *goals*—spiritual transformation of lives; and because of its spiritual *dynamics*—the work of the Holy Spirit.

To neglect the Spirit's ministry in teaching is to overlook one of the most important aspects of Christian education.

THE NEED OF THE HOLY SPIRIT IN EDUCATION

Why should the Holy Spirit be necessary in Christian education? Is it not enough to place the Bible in the hands of Christian teachers, encouraging them to follow proper pedagogical principles and use appropriate methods and materials? What can the Holy Spirit bring to the teaching/learning process in the Christian realm that is unique to Him? Why is the Holy Spirit necessary in the educational process?

REASONS FOR THE SPIRIT'S ROLE IN TEACHING.

One reason the Holy Spirit is necessary in Christian education is that the Christian teacher needs divine enabling. Only by the Holy Spirit can teachers be guided and enabled to teach the Bible and related subjects effectively. A spiritual task—involving spiritual truths to meet spiritual needs—requires spiritual power. Effectiveness in service demands salvation and yieldedness to the Holy Spirit. Seeking to serve the Lord in one's own strength apart from dependence on the Holy Spirit avails little by way of lasting results.

Purity of life, stemming from submission to the Spirit's control, contributes to effective teaching. Conversely, failure to model the truth makes a teacher ineffective. Students are not drawn to truths taught by a teacher who "mouths" them without modeling them. Inconsistency between "lip" and life turns students off and turns them away.

Another reason the Holy Spirit's work is necessary in the teaching/learning process is that the Spirit makes the Word of God effectual in the students' lives. Bible knowledge and comprehension of spiritual truths, essential as they are, do not of themselves guarantee spiritual change and growth. Not all who hear the Word believe or respond (John 10:25; 12:47-48; Acts 7:57-59; 17:5, 32). As the Word of God regenerates (Ps. 19:7; Rom. 10:17; James 1:18; 1 Peter 1:23), the Holy Spirit must be on hand to remove spiritual blindness and give eternal life (John 3:5-7; Titus 3:5).

Believers too must be open to the ministry of both the Word and the Spirit. The Word sanctifies (John 17:17-19; Acts 20:32; Eph. 5:26; 1 Peter 2:2), and so does the Spirit (2 Thes. 2:13; 1 Peter 1:2). The Word enlightens (Ps. 119:105, 130; 2 Tim. 3:16), and so does the Spirit (John 14:26; 16:13; 1 Cor. 2:10-15). The written Word, to be effective in the lives of unbelievers and believers, requires the ministry of the Holy Spirit. Changed lives require both the Word and the Spirit. And since Christian education focuses on bringing about spiritually transformed lives, the teaching/learning process requires both the Holy Scriptures and the Holy Spirit. One without the other is inadequate.

FALSE CONCEPTS OF THE SPIRIT'S ROLE IN TEACHING.

Some educators, consciously or not, neglect the work of the Holy Spirit. Committed to high standards in educational theory, programs, and personnel, committed to the need for a proper learning environment, and to the importance of well-defined educational goals and learning objectives, some creative and well-meaning teachers tend to operate "on natural grounds without the aid of the Spirit."[1] This overlooks the frailties of man's fallen nature, and "elevates man's creativity and methods over God's and fails to realize that only the Spirit can accomplish the spiritual goals of Christian education."[2]

Teaching is more than "dispensing the truth." Helping students understand Bible facts falls short of the spiritual dimension of Christian education. The goal is to help students come to know God and love Him, not just know *about* Him. It involves helping them walk in accord with His will, growing in spiritual maturity and Christlikeness—and that requires the ministry of the Holy Spirit.

Others stress the work of the Holy Spirit to the neglect of human teachers. They suggest that education is the enemy of spirituality, that education is a work of the flesh and conflicts with and opposes the work of the Spirit. This view, however, overlooks the fact that in Bible times God used human teachers (Matt. 28:19-20; Acts 5:42; 15:35; 18:11, 25; 28:31; 2 Tim. 2:2), and that God has given the gift of teaching to some believers (Rom. 12:6-7; 1 Cor. 12:28; Eph. 4:11). Human teachers, as instruments of the Holy Spirit, can stimulate and challenge students, guiding them into a proper understanding and application of God's Word.

Stressing the role of the Holy Spirit in the teaching process does not suggest that teachers need not study and prepare. Far from it! "Only the teacher who is well prepared can do the most efficient task while at the same time relying on the Holy Spirit to work *through* him and his students."[3] Since teaching is a divine-human process, a ministry involving the Holy Spirit and teachers jointly, preparation makes the teacher a better instrument, a sharper tool in God's hands. Depending on the Holy Spirit in one's teaching does not mean being unprepared and "simply letting the Holy Spirit speak through me," as if preparation competed with spirituality. Just the opposite is true. Unpreparedness is *not* a sign of being "more spiritual." Sometimes, however, the Holy Spirit has seemed to use poorly prepared teaching efforts and has apparently accomplished much. How can we account for this fact? While it is true that the Spirit can and does override a teacher's bungling, lack of preparation is nowhere encouraged in the Bible.

Paul's words in 1 Corinthians 3:6, "I planted the seed, Apollos watered it, but God made it grow," make it clear that human effort is accompanied, not substituted, by the divine working of God Himself. Rather than an excuse for laziness or ignorance, the role of the Spirit in the educational process provides a challenge to excellence.

However, 1 John 2:27 seems to suggest that human teachers are not necessary: "As for you, the anointing you received from Him remains in you, and you do not need anyone to teach you." The "anointing" is a reference to the Holy Spirit because the anointing "teaches." In a metonymy, the effect (the anointing) is substituted for the cause (the Holy Spirit).

Various explanations have been given of this verse: (a) No outsider needs to teach you.[4] (b) You only need to be reminded, not taught.[5] (c) You do not need to be taught repeatedly because you are not ignoramuses.[6] (d) No human teacher, including the Gnostics, is your ultimate authority.[7] (e) You need be taught only by the Holy Spirit, not by false teachers or antichrists, because you are spiritually mature.[8]

Whichever view is correct, all properly imply that ultimately learners are independent of humans and that God the Holy Spirit is the Teacher of spiritual truth. In danger of following man-made teachings of Gnosticism, the initial readers of 1 John needed reminding that the Holy Spirit, not man, was their Teacher. This does not rule out the need for human teachers for even the Apostle John was teaching through his writings. Though God uses human teachers, the learners must be sure their teachers are not counterfeit or false, and must remember that their divine Teacher is the Holy Spirit. "The Spirit of God, who lives in each believer, is [his] private tutor."[9] Human teachers (Eph. 4:11-12) are in addition to the Spirit, not a substitute for Him.

Another false concept of the relationship of the human to the divine in teaching is that the Holy Spirit somehow suddenly "zaps" the teacher or learner with spiritual insight in a mysterious work that is unexplainable or unpredictable. In this view, learning comes by sudden impulses of the Holy Spirit, by some unknown force or mysterious work beyond verification or validation. This, however, places the teaching/learning process in a subjective, mystical realm, neglects the place of the Scriptures, and overlooks other elements involved in the normal learning process. Lee opposes this view, [10] but he goes too far in ruling out the Holy Spirit altogether,[11] as if dependence on the Spirit is to "spookify" religious instruction as a "nonterrestrial affair which is beyond the regular workings of nature."[12] Again balance is needed. The Holy Spirit must not be overemphasized nor neglected. Both represent dangerous extremes.

THE TITLES AND FUNCTIONS OF THE HOLY SPIRIT IN TEACHING
TITLES.

Some of the titles and ministries ascribed to the Holy Spirit in the Scriptures make it clear that He is related to and involved in the work of teaching. As the "Spirit of Truth," a title Christ used of Him three times in the Upper Room Discourse (John 14:17; 15:26; 16:13), He is the Source of truth, the Revealer of truth, and the Applier of truth, the One who subjectively applies the objective Word, God's truth (17:17).

"Paraclete," another title of the Holy Spirit, is used, like "Spirit of Truth," only in John—in 14:16, 26; 15:26; 16:7. The various renderings of this word in English Bible versions reveal the difficulty in translating its range of meanings. In the *New International Version* it is "Counselor," the *King James Version* has "Comforter," and the *New American Standard Bible* renders it "Helper." Advocate, Supporter, Ally, Consoler, Encourager, Strengthener, and Adviser are all ideas in the Greek word *paraclētos,* literally "one who is called alongside." The Holy Spirit is "another" Helper, along with Christ. As the believer's "Helper," which is perhaps the best rendering,[13] the Holy Spirit, according to the four verses that use the word *paraclētos,* (a) was sent by the Father in response to the Son's request, (b) teaches believers all things, (c) reminds them of Jesus' teachings, and (d) testifies about Christ. Without His help, believers would be unable to understand all things or to recall all Christ taught. The fact that the Paraclete is twice identified with the "Spirit of Truth" (John 14:1-17; 15:26) shows that the Paraclete's ministry includes teaching.

The title "Spirit of wisdom and revelation" in Ephesians 1:17 suggests that the Holy Spirit provides wisdom for believers and reveals God's will to them. This seems preferable to the rendering "spirit of wisdom and revelation," as in the *King James Version* and the *New American Standard Bible,* as if Paul prayed for an attitude of wisdom and revelation on the part of believers. For, how can one have an attitude of revelation?

In the Ephesians' day, when Scripture was not yet complete, revelations were still being given. Now that the New Testament canon is complete, "the Spirit's job is to give us wisdom concerning what has already been revealed in the Scriptures."[14] In Isaiah 11:2 the Holy Spirit is also called "the Spirit of wisdom and understanding," a title used prophetically of Christ to point to the Spirit as the Giver of wisdom and understanding (or "discernment") to the Messiah.

FUNCTIONS.

Jesus said the Holy Spirit would give instruction in "all things" (John 14:26); recollection of what He had taught (v. 26); guidance into "all truth" (16:13); and declaration of future events, "what is yet to come" (v. 13). The promise that the Holy Spirit would "teach you all things" and "remind you of everything I have said to you" (14:26) refers primarily to the apostles. The Spirit enabled them to recall what Christ had taught them as they (at least some of the Twelve, though not all of them) wrote the New Testament Scriptures under the Spirit's inspiration. However, the promise may relate secondarily to all believers, to whom the Spirit brings to remembrance the recorded sayings of Christ.[15]

In what sense would the Spirit "guide you into all truth," as Jesus said? (16:13) The "all truth" seems to refer to the same as the "all things" in 14:26. "All truth" should probably be understood as all truth about Christ;[16] that is, all spiritual truth relating to the person and work of Christ, all revealed truth about God and His ways recorded in His Word. Paul called this the "deep things of God" (1 Cor. 2:10), and John referred to the Holy Spirit (God's "anointing") as teaching believers "all things" (1 John 2:27). After Christ's ascension the apostles were guided by the Spirit to comprehend spiritual truth, some of which they could not comprehend before the Cross (John 16:12).

Christ said the Spirit would also "tell [or declare to] you what is yet to come" (v. 13). Expositors suggest this refers to (a) New Testament books dealing with eschatological themes, (b) the gift of prophecy, (c) events at Christ's second coming, (d) Jesus' death and resurrection, or (e) things to come in the age of grace—things both near and distant to the disciples. If the fifth view is taken, which seems preferable, then this statement of the Spirit's ministry is applicable to all believers. As Jesus said, the Spirit would "take from what is Mine" (vv. 14-15) and "make it known to you" (v. 15). The Spirit glorifies Christ (v. 14) by communicating about Christ and announcing or making it known to believers.

The Holy Spirit's teaching ministry is necessary if believers are to understand spiritual truth. Paul makes this clear in 1 Corinthians 2:9-14. "What God has prepared for those who love Him" (v. 9) is "what God has freely given us" (v. 12). Just as no one person can fully fathom the thoughts of another person, so God's thoughts are known only by the Holy Spirit (v. 11). These thoughts, recorded in Scripture, are thus part of God's revelation to man (v. 10). These truths are then communicated by believers in Spirit-taught words (v. 13), which Paul said is "a message of wisdom" (v. 6). "Spiritual truth revealed by the Spirit (2:10) is spoken in spiritual words taught by the Spirit (2:13)."[17]

An unregenerate person, "the man without the Spirit" (v. 14), cannot receive (lit., does not welcome) the things of God, regardless of his intellectual abilities (1:20). Since he is spiritually dead (Eph. 2:1), spiritual truths "are foolishness to him" (1 Cor. 2:14; cf. 1:18), and he has no ability by which to comprehend them. Initially he needs regeneration for spiritual life which then opens his heart to the illuminating ministry of the Spirit (Eph. 1:18).

THE RELATIONSHIP OF THE HOLY SPIRIT TO THE TEACHERS
A COOPERATIVE VENTURE.

Christian education is a cooperative process, a venture involving both the human and the divine. Human teachers communicate and exemplify truth; the Holy Spirit seeks to provide guidance, power, illumination, and insight to the teachers.

Human teachers must depend on the Holy Spirit to work through them, to use them in reaching their students with the truth, and the Holy Spirit desires to fill and control the human instruments. In expounding the truth, teachers should help students see how the truth can be applied to their lives, and the Holy Spirit seeks to motivate and enable students to appropriate the truth.

Teachers are to encourage their students to understand the Word of God and to relate it to themselves, and the Holy Spirit seeks to encourage students to appropriate it personally. Without the work of the Holy Spirit in the teaching/learning process, the educational goal of spiritual transformation cannot be accomplished.

To be effective, human teachers must exemplify the truth they teach, being models of Christlikeness and growing in spiritual maturity. This requires obedience to the Word of God, dedication to the will of

God, and submission to the Spirit of God.

The relationship of the human to the divine is clearly demonstrated in 1 Corinthians 2. Paul wrote that his message was not communicated with mere human eloquence, wisdom, or persuasion, but with inner spiritual power (vv. 1, 4). He was involved in giving a message of God's wisdom, but the Holy Spirit was involved in enabling him to understand God's wisdom (v. 12) and to have insight into God's ways (v. 16). Paul spoke (v. 13) what he had been taught by the Holy Spirit (v. 13). Teachers are also responsible to learn how God made people to learn, then to teach accordingly. Since teaching helps others learn, teachers must know the ways in which students of various ages best learn (see chap. 6) and teach accordingly (see chaps. 7–13). In doing so they are cooperating with the Holy Spirit.

THE SPIRITUAL GIFT OF TEACHING

Another area of cooperation between the human and the divine teachers pertains to the spiritual gift of teaching. The Scriptures reveal several facts about spiritual gifts in general. (1) Every believer has a spiritual gift (Rom. 12:6; 1 Cor. 12:7, 11; Eph. 4:7; 1 Peter 4:10). (2) Spiritual gifts are divine enablings sovereignly given by God in His grace (Rom. 12:6; 1 Cor. 12:11, 18). (3) They are to focus on Jesus Christ, to glorify Him. (They are enrichments received from Christ.[18]) (4) Spiritual gifts are given so that believers in Christ may edify other believers (1 Cor. 12:7; 14:4-5, 17-26; Eph. 4:12). Gifts are not for the outward display of one's abilities. Edification, not self-aggrandizement, is the purpose. Edification means "growing in the depth and fullness of one's understanding of Christ and all else in relationship to Him and in the quality of one's personal relationship with Him."[19]

The gift of teaching is mentioned in each of the three major New Testament passages on spiritual gifts (Rom. 12:7; 1 Cor. 12:28; Eph. 4:11). It ranks first after the gifts of apostleship and prophecy (1 Cor. 12:28) and since those gifts were temporary,[20] the gift of teaching has a prominent role in the church. This underscores the importance of the educational ministry of the church. The gift of teaching is the supernatural, Spirit-endowed ability to expound (explain and apply) the truth of God. All believers in fellowship with the Lord are taught by the Holy Spirit, and all believers are responsible to teach others. All teach to some degree, but not all believers have the ability to teach others as effectively as those who have the teaching gift. It seems to be a special endowment.

Since the gift of teaching, like other spiritual gifts, is given at salvation, does this suggest no relationship exists between the natural ability to teach before and after salvation and one's spiritual abilities? Oholiab's natural ability as a craftsman, designer, and embroiderer (Ex. 38:23) was followed by his (and Bezalel's) being enabled by God to teach others (35:34). Apparently Paul's natural abilities along with his training under Gamaliel (Acts 22:3) made him a capable teacher. And in keeping with his natural abilities as a teacher God gave him the spiritual gift of teaching (along with other gifts, 1 Tim. 2:7). How then does the spiritual gift of teaching differ from the natural ability to teach? The former seems to be a sanctifying, enhancing, or channeling of natural abilities into the spiritual realm.[21] Packer suggests that "the most significant gifts . . . (preaching, teaching, leadership, counseling, support) are ordinarily natural abilities sanctified."[22] As I have written elsewhere:

> The fact that spiritual gifts are bestowed at the time of salvation does not rule out the fact that God may be preparing a person before salvation along certain lines, in keeping with the spiritual gifts that God plans for him to possess and exercise after salvation. This may often be true of the gift of teaching. Believers who possess the teaching gift may often be those whom God has been preparing, before their salvation, in areas related to a teaching ministry. But this is not *always* the case.[23]

One should not assume, therefore, that every Christian schoolteacher has the spiritual gift of teaching. This may or may not be true.

How then does a believer determine if he has the spiritual gift of teaching? Several things may be done. (1) If he has a natural ability in teaching, he should consider whether that ability may be enhanced by the Lord for edifying the body of Christ with the spiritual gift of teaching. (2) He should minister in various ways in the local church to see if teaching is an enjoyable experience. (3) He should see if God's blessing on his teaching seems evident to him and others. McRae suggests that the process of discovering one's spiritual gift should be initiated by prayer, enlightened by study, indicated by desire, confirmed by ability, and accompanied by blessing.[24]

Having discovered if he has the spiritual gift of teaching, a teacher is then responsible to develop that gift. Paul wrote to Timothy, "Do not neglect your gift" (1 Tim. 4:14) and "fan into flame the gift of God" (2 Tim. 1:6). A spiritual gift is "fanned into flame" (a good translation of *anazōpyrein,* a word that occurs only here in the New Testament) when it is exercised or used. To let it lie dormant or unused signals a shortcoming in good stewardship. Developing the gift of teaching can be done by (a) exercising or using the gift, that is, by teaching others, (b) observing others who are effective teachers, (c) reading books on teaching, (d) getting training in the principles and practice of teaching, (e) having someone observe one's teaching and make helpful evaluative comments afterward, and (f) attending Christian education conferences and workshops.

While every believer in one sense is a teacher, it is also true that effective Bible teaching calls for those whom God has gifted to teach.

LOVE FOR STUDENTS.

One of the ways in which a teacher's relationship with the Holy Spirit is to be manifested is in his love for his students. Along with the knowledge of the content to be taught, an effective teacher also has a concern for those he teaches.[25] Being lovingly sensitive to their needs and interests enables him to cooperate more effectively with the Holy Spirit in the teaching process. As he prepares his lessons, an awareness of their needs helps him be directed by the Spirit in seeking to relate the truth to those needs.

In Galatians 5:22-23 love heads the list of nine characteristics of a Spirit-filled life. As a Christian is "filled with the Spirit" (Eph. 5:18), he evidences the character of Christ, whom the Spirit honors (John 16:13-15). This love is a selfless, self-sacrificing, other-oriented concern, an attitude of genuine interest in the well-being of the other person. Students know if a teacher is genuinely concerned for and interested in them. They know if he loves them; if he, like the Lord, has compassion for them and their needs. Teachers who reveal this kind of interest are obviously working in cooperation with the Holy Spirit and are more effective than those whose love or care is not evident.

In fact a teacher's compassion sparks student interest and motivation. As Hendricks has written:

> It's your *compassion* that produces the learner's *motivation*. If I sense you love me, I'll be eager to do all kinds of things you want me to do.
>
> Why did the disciples follow Jesus? It's simple: He loved them. . . . "When Christ saw the multitudes, He was moved with compassion for them." Men and women and youth and children are all drawn to a person who loves them.[26]

Effective, Spirit-directed communicators are those "who have a great heart,"[27] who communicate from their souls with inner concern and genuine compassion. This is the fruit of the Spirit.

EDUCATIONAL METHODOLOGY.

A teacher working in tune with the Holy Spirit will seek to use the best educational techniques and tools available. Having studied the Word, seeking to interpret it properly under the Spirit's guidance,[28] he then designs his teaching time to enable him to teach in the most effective way. Far from being incompatible with or contrary to the Holy Spirit, educational methods are the means by which the Spirit works in the teaching/learning process. "Methodicalness involves a description of how the Spirit works through the mind and how one may cooperate with the Spirit so that he may function freely."[29] As a teacher discovers, experiments with, and improves his use of pedagogical procedures relevant to the given age-group, he is working with the Holy Spirit, desiring to be an effective teacher in the hands of *the* Teacher. "As teachers consciously depend on the Spirit in prayer and seek to be creative and effective in their teaching, He will guide them in choosing appropriate teaching techniques."[30]

Methods are simply ways of teaching, ways to link content with experience, means by which learners are brought into contact with God's Word and God's Son. And is that not the goal of the Holy Spirit?

EDUCATIONAL GOALS.

Christian teaching concerns itself with spiritual transformation, with maturation in the lives of the students. Teachers want their students "to accept Christ as their personal Saviour, and walk with Him, grow in Him, know Him, serve Him, obey Him, worship Him, and enjoy Him."[31] These goals cannot be accomplished apart from the power and the ministry of the Holy Spirit. Spiritual goals require the spiritual Teacher.

Accomplishing these goals, however, also calls for cooperation on the part of the learners. If a teacher is cooperating with the Holy Spirit but the learners are not, then the teaching/learning process is stifled. On the other hand, if students and teachers are open to the Holy Spirit's ministry and submit to His proddings to apply the truth where it is needed in their lives, learning takes place. In other words, true learning requires three persons working together: the human teacher, the Holy Spirit, and the learner. Being receptive to the work of the Holy Spirit in understanding and applying God's Word contributes to genuine learning. A prayerful attitude, an open and obedient heart, and a yielded spirit ready to appropriate biblical content—these are essential if students are to become learners.

CONCLUSION

Teaching spiritual truths is a supernatural task, a ministry calling for the work of the Holy Spirit. The Spirit adds a unique dimension to Christian teaching, including (a) Spirit-filled and Spirit-guided teachers, who with the gift of teaching are well-prepared, depend on the Holy Spirit, teach creatively in accord with the way God made people to learn, and give evidence of loving concern for their students; (b) the Holy Spirit, the divine Teacher who "guides" into truth; and (c) learners who learn to the extent they open their hearts to the Word and cooperate with the Holy Spirit in appropriating and living out God's truth.

This dynamic work of the Holy Spirit makes Christian education distinctive and dynamic, glorious and noble. In the final analysis, teaching, like any ministry, is, "'not by might nor by power, but by My Spirit,' says the LORD Almighty" (Zech. 4:6).

ENDNOTES

1. C. Fred Dickason, "The Holy Spirit in Teaching," in *Introduction to Biblical Christian Education,* ed. Werner C. Graendorf. Chicago: Moody Press, 1981, p. 112.

2. Dickason, p. 112.

3. Roy B. Zuck, *The Holy Spirit in Your Teaching,* rev. ed. Wheaton, Ill.: Victor Books, 1984, p. 75.

4. Abraham Kuyper, *The Work of the Holy Spirit.* Grand Rapids: Wm. B. Eerdmans Publishing Co., 1956, p. 185, and F.F. Bruce, *The Epistles of John.* Old Tappan, N.J.: Fleming H. Revell Co., 1970, pp. 71–2.

5. A.T. Robertson, *Word Pictures in the New Testament.* Nashville, Tenn.: Broadman Press, 1930, 6:218.

6. R.C.H. Lenski, *The Interpretation of the Epistles of St. Peter, St. John, and St. Jude.* Minneapolis: Augsburg Publishing House, 1966, p. 442.

7. Kenneth S. Wuest, *In These Last Days.* Grand Rapids: Wm. B. Eerdmans Publishing Co., 1957, p. 138.

8. Zane C. Hodges, "1 John," in *The Bible Knowledge Commentary—New Testament,* ed. John F. Walvoord and Roy B. Zuck. Wheaton, Ill.: Victor Books, 1983, p. 892.

9. Bob Smith, *Basics of Bible Interpretation.* Waco, Texas: Word Books, 1978, p. 37.

10. James Michael Lee, "The Authentic Source of Religious Instruction," in *Religious Education and Theology,* ed. Norma H. Thompson. Birmingham, Ala.: Religious Education Press, 1982, pp. 194–97.

11. Lee, pp. 193–94.

12. James Michael Lee, "Toward a New Era: A Blueprint for Positive Action," in *The Religious Education We Need,* ed. James Michael Lee. Mishawaka, Ind.: Religious Education Press, 1977, p. 130.

13. See Zuck, *The Holy Spirit in Your Teaching,* p. 30, for reasons in support of this rendering.

14. Dickason, p. 115.

15. James I. Packer, *Keep in Step with the Spirit.* Old Tappan, N.J.: Fleming H. Revell Co., 1984, p. 65, and Zuck, p. 40.

16. Packer, p. 65.

17. Zuck, p. 39. Some, however, say the Spirit-taught words refer to inspiration of Scripture by the Holy Spirit (e.g., Dickason, p. 120). However, in verse 13 Paul said, "We speak . . . in words taught by the Spirit," not "we write . . . in words taught by the Spirit."

18. Packer, p. 82.

19. Packer, p. 83.

20. On the temporary nature of some spiritual gifts see Joseph Dillow, *Speaking in Tongues*. Grand Rapids: Zondervan Publishing House, 1975; Robert G. Gromacki, *The Modern Tongues Movement*. Nutley, N.J.: Presbyterian and Reformed Publishing Co., 1973; Robert P. Lightner, *Speaking in Tongues and Divine Healing*, 2nd ed. Schaumburg, Ill.: Regular Baptist Press, 1978; and John F. Walvoord, *The Holy Spirit*. Grand Rapids: Zondervan Publishing House, 1958, pp. 173–88.

21. R.C.H. Lenski, *The Interpretation of St. Paul's First and Second Epistles to the Corinthians,* Minneapolis: Augsburg Publishing House, 1963, p. 49.

22. Packer, p. 30.

23. Zuck, p. 87.

24. William McRae, *The Dynamics of Spiritual Gifts*. Grand Rapids: Zondervan Publishing House, 1976, pp. 111–19.

25. Robert W. Pazmiño, "Curriculum Foundations," *Christian Education Journal 8.* Autumn 1987, p. 32.

26. Howard G. Hendricks, *Teaching to Change Lives*. Portland, Ore.: Multnomah Press, 1987, pp. 107–8.

27. Hendricks, p. 108.

28. For a discussion on the relationship of the Holy Spirit to biblical interpretation, see Zuck, pp. 136–46.

29. Robert A. Traina, *Methodical Bible Study*. Grand Rapids: Zondervan Publishing House, 1980, p. 19.

30. Zuck, p. 175.

31. Zuck, pp. 152–53.

BIBLIOGRAPHY

Chadwick, Ronald. *Teaching and Learning: An Integrated Approach to Christian Education.* Old Tappan, N.J.: Fleming H. Revell Co., 1982.

Ford, LeRoy. *Design for Teaching and Training.* Nashville: Broadman Press, 1978.

Gangel, Kenneth O., and Warren S. Benson. *Christian Education: Its History and Philosophy.* Chicago: Moody Press, 1983.

Gangel, Kenneth O. *Building Leaders for Church Education.* Chicago: Moody Press, 1981.

Hendricks, Howard G. *Teaching to Change Lives.* Portland, Ore.: Multnomah Press, 1987.

Joy, Donald M. *Meaningful Learning in the Church.* Winona Lake, Ind.: Light and Life Press, 1969.

LeBar, Lois E. *Education That Is Christian.* Westwood, N.J.: Fleming H. Revell Company, 1958.

Richards, Lawrence O. *A Theology of Christian Education.* Grand Rapids: Zondervan Publishing House, 1975.

————. *Creative Bible Teaching.* Chicago: Moody Press, 1970.

Schreyer, George M. *Christian Education in Theological Focus.* Philadelphia: Christian Education Press, 1962.

Zuck, Roy B. *The Holy Spirit in Your Teaching.* Rev. ed. Wheaton, Ill.: Victor Books, 1984.

3. DESIGNING
BIBLICAL INSTRUCTION
David L. Edwards

> If we want to educate a person in virtue we must polish him at
> a tender age. And if someone is to advance toward wisdom he
> must be opened up for it in the first years of his life when his
> industriousness is still burning, his mind is malleable, and his
> memory still strong.
>
> Johann Amos Comenius
1592–1670
The Great Didactic

This exhortation from a champion of Christian education rings as true
at the conclusion of the twentieth century as it did 300 years earlier.
His emphasis on the protective benefits of early nurture squares well
with a conception of Christian education as proactive rather than reme-
dial. To raise children from their earliest years in paths of righteousness
is surely more desirable than to rescue them later from the ravages of
deviance.

But this statement echoes reality as well in its focus on concepts too frequently neglected in contemporary Christian education—
the issues of virtue and wisdom. In a surge toward cognitive credibility,
our teaching of the Bible has often centered on the "knowing" rather
than the "being," and in so doing, has opted for programs that inform
the mind without forming the character. This is especially true in our
contemporary age where we are saturated with data from many
sources.

The church possesses a clear biblical mandate for engaging in
direct instruction. Even the cursory reader finds Scripture replete with
admonitions to communicate the truth of God's revelatory activity
among men. Chadwick has identified at least twenty-five distinct Hebrew and Greek words used by the canonical authors to describe some

aspect of the teaching/learning process.[1] Such diversity in terminology implies something of the complexity of the learning process, but it should also convey a sense of priority and urgency. Any ministry addressed in the Word of God with such fervor must hold genuine significance for the people of God.

While English provides nothing like the semantic diversity with which the biblical languages describe teaching and learning, even these few terms require a measure of definition. We speak for example of "teaching," "training," and "instructing," as well as "counseling" and "disciplining," all under the rubric of "educating." Setting aside the guidance functions, not as unimportant but as beyond the scope of this chapter, the didactic functions implicit in the first three terms still require clarification.

Lee has defined education as "the broad process by which a person learns something" and instruction as the activities by and through which learning is "caused" in an individual.[2] Instruction then may take the form of teaching or training. One aspect of distinction is suggested by the difference between "learning that . . ." and "learning to. . . ."

Teaching focuses on informing and training on enabling; teaching stresses content and training capacity; teaching tends divergently with many practical applications possible, while training tends convergently toward the "one best way" to do something. Effective biblical instruction incorporates both teaching and training in fulfilling different aspects of the educational mandate of Scripture.

Instruction (both teaching and training) occurs in a variety of contexts with consequent impact on instructional design. Different strategies are invoked when educating learners as individuals, in defined groups, or as a mass audience. We also undertake to teach in organizational settings ranging from the highly structured to the very informal. Teacher and learner may be disparate in age, understanding, or authority, or they may be virtual peers.

Among the many valid possibilities, however, in this chapter we address education in the institutional context, "schooling," defined as "a system of complex, planned, organized, systematic, purposive, deliberative, and intentional learning experiences which in concept bring about behavioral changes in the person."[3]

This intentional quality in institutional education makes instructional design a legitimate concern. The model proposed here (Fig. 1) is hierarchical: those elements specifically pertinent to providing effective learning experiences for students are increasingly within the domain of teacher choice. These elements rest, however, on philosophic and policy decisions derived from Scripture, elaborated and clarified by the institutional leadership.

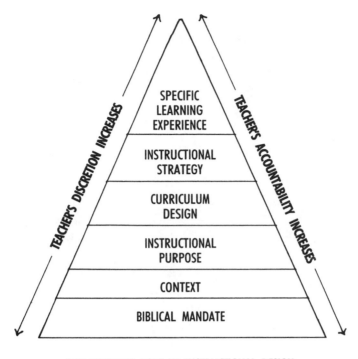

THE TEACHER'S ROLE IN INSTRUCTIONAL DESIGN
Figure 1

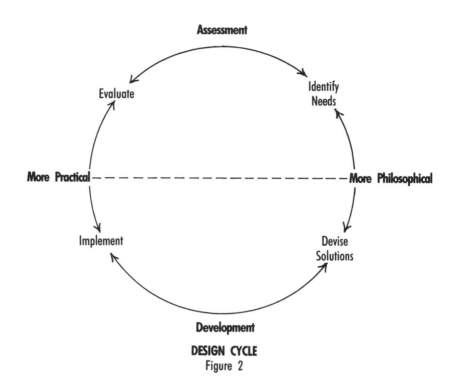

DESIGN CYCLE
Figure 2

INSTRUCTIONAL PURPOSE

Design implies purpose, and instructional design demands clear articulation of the mission for which it is intended. In a general sense we have been addressing purpose indirectly while discussing both mandate and context. However, we need to examine in greater detail the process of defining concrete institutional aims, for they establish the foundation on which the entire instructional edifice will stand.

As visualized in Figure 2, instructional design cannot be viewed as a discrete event, accomplished once for all time. The process is cyclical, spiraling through successive iterations of four key steps. Breaking into the cycle for analysis, we might begin with "identifying needs." Educational goals not anchored to an accurate comprehension of existing needs within the population become sterile and ineffective. Those needs form the link to reality, indeed the rationale for whatever the institution decides to do educationally. Having identified the need, concern shifts to possible solutions, providing effective biblical teaching to satisfy the deficiency. Determining a feasible proposal leads to the implementation stage where proposals become reality. The final component in the cycle is evaluation, where evaluation is not restricted to the product, learning achievement, but also considers factors such as resources, staff support, and overall program efficiency. Mutual interaction among the steps is indicated by the ease with which the cycle can be divided into linked segments along either of the two diameters.

ESTABLISHING GOALS

An initial task in planning effective learning experiences for students involves specifying aims. Learning goals are defined at the macrolevel by statements of mission or philosophy, formulated by boards and administrative leaders as they recognize needs within a given community. Goals establish the general parameters for the institution and flow into policies to guide the actual day-to-day operations. At the microlevel of the classroom interaction with students, those plans become more specific and personal as the teacher translates institutional goals into instructional objectives. Clear, frequent communication between leaders and teachers helps maintain consistency in practice.

Distinctions between goals and objectives become fuzzy at times. As a rule, however, goals are broader and less specific: they establish direction and intent, not means or methods. It may help to reserve the use of certain auxiliary verbs to goal statements such as:

1. Each student should know how to use a concordance.
2. Children should demonstrate a reverential attitude during worship.
3. Visitors to our church will experience a friendly welcome.

Note that goals do not indicate details about teaching process, materials, or even degree of proficiency. Goals are painted with broad strokes, realizing that fine detail will be added through more specific statements of objectives. Both goals and objectives are essential to good instructional design: they differ in the scope and precision with which they define anticipated outcomes.

INSTRUCTIONAL OBJECTIVES

Educational aims are generally established at leadership levels where direct teacher input may be either substantial or totally lacking. The formulation of detailed objectives, however, becomes a teacher task. Prospective teachers can anticipate expending considerable time and effort in the pursuit of well-stated aims to guide their teaching. Even where an institution uses a prepared curriculum with course and lesson objectives included, it anticipates adapting and modifying those objectives to meet the specific needs of this class. The professional skill and personal understanding of a teacher intervenes to make those broad intentions relevant to the students she teaches.

In a bit of classic wisdom, Edge[4] advised making objectives (1) brief enough to remember, (2) clear enough to write down, and (3) specific enough to achieve. These remain commendable standards, but teachers often find it easier to recall the advice than to put it into practice, especially with regard to specificity.

Earlier we defined "schooling" in terms of changed behavior. This conception of what learning entails has strongly influenced the process of clarifying instructional aims; teachers are encouraged to define "performance objectives" as a guide to planning effective learning experiences. In other words, an objective describes what a student will be able to do once he has mastered this particular aspect of instruction. Within the context of instructional objectives "behavior" encompasses more than just overt physical activity: it also can describe mental processes like remembering and forming preferences. All learning aims seem, however, to fit within three broad categories or "domains": the cognitive domain of knowledge and understanding; the affective domain concerned with attitudes and values; and the psychomotor domain focusing on skill development.[5]

Developing skill in defining performance-oriented objectives doesn't come easily, but help is available. One recommended model[6] for writing objectives suggests four components to include in a complete statement: audience, behavior, conditions, and degree.

"Audience" specifies the learner(s) for whom the instruction is designed. The planner takes into account age, developmental level, scholastic experience, and other relevant details which might affect ability to achieve the teaching aim. When writing objectives consistently for the same class one may simply refer to "the student(s)," but don't permit that generic rendering to mask the distinctions among individuals in the class. Having defined learning in terms of behavioral change, we ought to specify objectives similarly. The "behavior" component emerges from answers to a question like, "What will a student be able to do once he has mastered this lesson?" Some behavior from among the three taxonomies—cognitive, affective, or psychomotor—should be identifiable as an appropriate outcome.

"Conditions" refers to two elements, either or both of which may require elaboration for a particular lesson aim. In order for a student to perform as expected, he may need some materials, resources, or equipment provided; anything that must be accessible for achievement to be demonstrated can be incorporated into a phrase such as, "Given a map showing Israel and Judah during the reign of Solomon. . . ." A second type of condition establishes the parameters of performance: will the behavior be evidenced through written response? Orally? By demonstrating a skill?

For some kinds of instruction the purpose is clearly either fulfilled or not. In other instances degrees of attainment are possible, and the teacher may choose to specify in the objective a level consistent with satisfactory achievement. Adding the provision that Juniors in Sunday School recite the books of the New Testament in order "with no more than two errors" would be an example of specifying the level of performance. Considering factors like student age and background, ability, whether the concept or skill is essential, and if it will be reviewed later in the curriculum will help the teacher decide if something less than 100 percent mastery is acceptable.

To some people, making behavioral objectives a prerequisite part of lesson planning is questionable, perhaps even counterproductive. Arguments commonly advanced against reliance on such rigidly formulated statements include:

1. Trivial outcomes are easy to specify; really significant learning goals are difficult to define in behavioral terms. Teaching thus focuses on less important issues.
2. Written objectives constrain a teacher's ability to take advantage of "teachable moments" that arise unexpectedly during class.
3. Effective teaching isn't merely a matter of doing all the steps by the book; many intangibles impact the learning process.
4. Tightly defined objectives turn students into objects: they don't "learn," they "get taught."

Certainly teachers must exercise caution that objectives don't become an end in themselves rather than a means toward effective instruction. Popham responds to criticisms like these by advocating refinement of practice and not abandonment. With effort, *any* learning goal can be translated into one or more performance-linked statements. Finally, objectives should never restrict a teacher's freedom to alter a plan in order to capture an unanticipated lesson; only clear statements of priority, however, can prevent wandering down each interesting byroad that appears.[7]

CURRICULUM DESIGN

In the continuing quest for effective learning experiences for students we look next at curriculum. In the original Latin *curriculum* meant, among other things, a racecourse or prescribed path. Transliterated the word retains considerable diversity: educators use it for (1) a prescribed academic program, as in defining a "core curriculum" of collegiate studies; (2) a set of documents that outline content in a specific area, such as a school's math or language arts curriculum; or (3) the specific printed materials actually used in the classroom. Each educational institution and agency deals with all three aspects, but the latter two are of most direct concern to the classroom teacher.

ASSESSMENT.

Impetus for modifying a school's curriculum can come from a number of sources. Identified deficiencies or overlap among courses, organizational restructuring, creation of new programs, or even new institutions all demand careful reflection of instructional content. The process of institutional accreditation commonly poses questions about the validity and quality of program elements for colleges and schools, but every educational context needs some systematic process for periodic review and revision.

The primary motivation for improving Bible curriculum is to increase its impact on students. While the declarative content of Scripture is changeless, the specific needs of learners are not. If curriculum is to help students learn and apply principles by which the Spirit of God directs their lives toward righteousness and truth, it must meet critical standards of attractiveness, relevance, and clarity in addition to accuracy of presentation. Assessing the needs of specific students and choosing materials that will optimize their opportunities for learning challenges the professional skill of each teacher.

DEVELOPMENT.

Curriculum decisions emerge at various levels. Policy decisions establishing the parameters of choice come from boards or committees as an aspect of their duty to oversee. Administrators issue directives and communicate guidelines for implementation. At some point, written documents, such as curriculum guides are developed in order to maintain fidelity to institutional goals. Still, teachers exercise considerable discretion in the actual selection of both content and methods for their own classrooms.

A fundamental decision in program development is whether to adopt an existing curriculum or devise one unique to a specific locale. For most church agencies, the variety and quality of materials available from established publishers makes adoption an attractively viable choice. Christian schools also have several sources of ready-made curriculums, offering a full range of teaching materials including textbooks. Deciding to select or create represents a policy option to be determined at the board level.

The decision to use an instructional program prepared elsewhere should demand the same kind of involvement locally as if the program were being developed in-house, however. Curriculum is necessarily localized, and the materials chosen for use should be fitted into a scheme for fulfilling the goals and objectives of this school or this church. An inherent danger in adopting a full curriculum from any source is that local implementation succumbs to a program designed to satisfy a different set of needs.

Developing a strong curriculum plan entails organization. In his rationale for designing effective learning experiences for students, Tyler suggested four questions for educators to ask in the process:

1. What educational purposes should the program seek to attain?
2. What educational experiences can be provided that are likely to attain these purposes?
3. How can these educational experiences be effectively organized?
4. How can we determine whether these purposes are being attained?[8]

The middle two questions focus attention on the basic process of curriculum development: selection and organization.

Curriculum theorists suggest a variety of principles to govern content selection. Tyler himself argued that three primary sources should determine content: *society, subject,* and *student.* The societal matrix surrounding an educational enterprise makes certain expectations, as that students will possess common skills of communication and will become good citizens. The students' need to mature personally and spiritually as well as academically imply other content. Proficiency in the curriculum subject requires that essential facts, concepts, theories, and skills be included.

Teachers contribute to the process as they share evidence of student deficiencies in mastery of necessary skills or information. Parent questionnaires or interviews might surface other needs. Research into curricular programs offered elsewhere frequently results in solid recommendations. A curriculum consultant familiar with the age-level and institutional philosophy can assist too.

Once content has been determined it must be organized into some framework. Selection of content determines curriculum "scope," but the related issue of "sequence" requires some additional coordinating principles. Curriculum specialists commonly use one of the following as an organizing principle: chronological order (historical studies); complexity (simple concepts lead to more complicated ones, as in math); thematic (literature); or pedagogical theory (moving from personal experience to more remote events, or from concrete to abstract).[9] Similar rationale should be applied in arranging biblical studies into an effective instructional sequence.

Selection and organization of content are commonly documented in forms such as a "scope and sequence chart" which provides an easily comprehensible summary of a particular course of study or of a broader segment. More detail on both content and resources is included in the curriculum guide which elaborates on goals and objectives, content, resources, and the institutional plan for evaluating learning.

EVALUATION.

Ultimately curriculum is evaluated in the actual experience of the learners: only then can those responsible for designing instruction be assured that they have succeeded in equipping students to fulfill God's unique purposes for them. But this should not deter leaders from assessing the *apparent* quality of the curriculum design even before implementing it. An effective plan should pass muster in three significant areas.

First, is the curriculum consistent with the mission and philosophy of the institution? There should be strong, evident correlation between the purposes emanating from a statement of philosophy and those reflected in the curriculum documents. In particular, curriculum developed for Christian education should provide thorough integration of biblical principles into all other subjects taught. A second concern is pedagogy: are valid concepts of instructional theory incorporated into the curriculum plan? Does the curriculum accommodate the developing capabilities of children? Do topics and skills facilitate transfer of learning? Finally, will teachers find this a functional tool, understandable and relatively easy to translate into effective plans for classroom instruction?

INSTRUCTIONAL STRATEGY

In our overall conception of instructional design (Fig. 1, p. 47) we include a component called "instructional strategy." Strategy is a military term: it invokes an image of leaders poring over charts, maps, and facts as they plot a master campaign. Their overall plan clearly in mind, commanders issue orders for the tactical maneuvers that will poise personnel and resources in position for victory. Effective strategy leads to accomplished objectives. The analogy holds for teachers as well. Good strategy in the classroom improves the probability that learning objectives will be accomplished, and that students will find the experience enjoyable as well as productive.

The link between the organized curriculum and a specific learning activity is a well-written lesson plan. In nearly every formal teaching context, supervisors expect teachers to prepare a lesson plan that indicates such elements as specific lesson aims, materials and methods to be used, and the follow-up learning activities to be assigned.

Some new teachers fret under the demand and view lesson-planning as an exercise in tedium, a chore to be endured in order to get to the real challenge of teaching. In other instances teachers mistake end for means, and spend so much time writing and revising their plans that little time or energy remains for implementation.

ASSESSMENT.

A written lesson plan should not stifle creativity or inhibit spontaneity between teacher and class. In fact, a good lesson plan should become the most liberating device in his practioner's repertoire. With the elements of a good learning session clearly defined in writing, the teacher can concentrate on making the lesson come alive for the students.

The first element is, of course, a list of specific objectives related to the lesson topic. Teaching the Bible for the purpose of changing lives requires a clear recognition of what changes are necessary. Think carefully about individual students in the class: what do they need to know and understand about this topic? What attitudinal changes are appropriate? What skills must they develop to live out consistently what they learn? Visualizing and then verbalizing the needs of specific class members improves the practicality of instruction.

A good plan also includes a list of potential class activities. Learning is never passive: not what the teacher does but what students do achieves genuine learning. While planning activities, consider the resources available to the class, such as, texts and reference materials, visual aids, audio materials like tapes and records, and the living resource of class members themselves. Combining methods with resources, several options probably stand out as preferable. Finally, your plan should provide some way of ascertaining if students learned what you intended them to learn. Evaluation may be as simple as a few questions asked, or as elaborate as a lengthy written assignment.

DEVELOPMENT.

Though we recognize student activity as the essential ingredient, teacher behaviors influence learning very directly. Gage identifies four components of learning that correlate with teacher behaviors; in this paradigm, learning results from a sequence that includes (1) motivation; (2) perception; (3) response; and (4) reinforcement.[10] Student motivation typically mirrors teacher attitudes like enthusiasm and appreciation for the subject. Perception occurs best when teachers provide clear cues to focus attention on significant ideas and match methods to content. Providing students with opportunity for interactive response over the material, with both teacher and with peers improves retention, as does the teacher's skill in reinforcing and affirming so that achievement becomes pleasurable.

A group's readiness to learn is frequently determined within the first few minutes of a class session. During that time a "psychological set" is established that often persists through the entire period. Happily, that set may be positive as well as negative. Reflecting on some of your own experiences may help you avoid these common pitfalls:

> Consuming too much time with administrivia (taking roll, making announcements)
> Offering "dead time" with no expected activity (gathering materials, waiting for others to arrive)
> Stifling interest with a hackneyed introduction ("Please open your Bibles to . . .")

Instead, look for techniques that offer currency (a recent news article), reality (interesting physical objects linked to the lesson), drama (role play, audio tape) or vividness (pictures, slides) as a stimulus for attention. A brief review and summary of the goals for the current lesson are effective transitions from introduction to the body of the lesson. Having clarified objectives, resources, and methods in the written plan, the teacher can concentrate on the moment-to-moment factors that generate learning.

TIME.

One variable that consistently differentiates high-achieving classes is time spent on learning. A recent study reported variation of over 50 percent in the total number of weekly hours devoted to actual instruction among selected public elementary schools.[11] The potential for increased learning by simply cutting down on the time lost within a class session is enormous. But time allocation within the hour is of equal import: good lesson strategy allows adequate time for each instructional segment and plans in advance for making smooth transitions from one phase to the next.

VARIATION.

Monotony discourages involvement, and uninvolved students don't learn. Variation of activities helps prevent boredom, but it also makes learning easier in other ways. Research on children's learning styles suggests that individuals differ markedly in their ability to receive and process information presented through any one of the senses. Teaching that consists largely of talking to students helps some; pictorial images are more readily received by others. For the most benefit to the largest number of students, variation in methods and in the types of learning materials used should be built into each lesson.

TAXONOMIC HIERARCHY.

Keeping in mind that each of the three areas of instructional concern forms a hierarchical structure, teachers should strive to challenge students toward the higher levels. In the cognitive area, for example, it becomes easy to remain at the "knowledge" level, focusing on factual data only unless a conscious effort is made to press upward. One effective technique is through questioning. Questions can encourage students to think beyond the what? when? where? to the more significant issues of how? why? and if?

EVALUATION.

Just as a good lesson strategy provides for an effective beginning and middle sections, closure is also important. Good closure not only summarizes the lesson just completed and anticipates the lesson to follow, it should also provide some clue about student learning. Student responses to a few prepared questions, their ability to summarize key points, even their facial and bodily reactions offer insight into their understanding. Specific technique matters less than intention: it should be deeply etched into each lesson plan that evaluation of student achievement and of the entire learning activity must occur if teaching is to be improved.

CONCLUSIONS

Our biblical mandate has not been completed. The challenge of providing learning experiences for children, youth, and adults that impact their lives truly and deeply, evidenced in lifestyles conforming more and more to the image of Christ—that challenge remains. Despite substantial progress in clarifying our purpose, in establishing programs to extend Bible teaching beyond the Sunday School walls, and in developing quality teaching materials, some persistent problems still lie ahead. Here are a few.

EXCEPTIONAL STUDENTS.

Since 1975, when Congress enacted PL94-142 ("Education for All Handicapped Children Act), public schools across America have responded with an impressive infusion of time and talent aimed at providing an equitable education for handicapped children. We have not addressed with comparable vigor provision for their *Christian* education. Curriculum publishers who offer materials devised specifically for the mentally and emotionally impaired don't sell them in any quantity. Few churches, and fewer Christian schools, could with integrity invite parents of these special children to consider enrolling them.

Most of our middle-class evangelical institutions are ill-prepared to serve the ethnic minorities concentrated in major metropolitan centers. Although these minorities represent together less than 20 percent of the total U.S. population, an estimated 30 percent of incoming first-graders in 1986 were either black or Hispanic.[12] We have before us the challenge of devising Bible teaching programs that reach exceptional children not as a missionary foray but as an integral component of our efforts to serve the present church community.

APPLICATION AND INTEGRATION.

It has been observed that "the end of life is not knowledge, but action" *(Technical Education, 1977).* The American educational enterprise generally is at risk of failure to maintain appropriate balance between the importance of knowing and the drive toward doing. The seductive lure of a completely utilitarian expectation for education must be resisted. But the challenge to those who teach the Living Word is that understanding should result in action. Change as the evidence of incorporated learning should be the touchstone by which we gauge success.

RESOURCES.

Perhaps never in the history of Christian education have we observed such disparity among ministries. Some churches enjoy magnificent facilities while others struggle to provide even minimally adequate space for teaching. Bible colleges struggle for survival against the tide of declining enrollments and diminished financial support. Christian schools and parachurch educational programs experience similar patterns: some have thrived while others are deprived. Nor is the issue solely a question of finance; the need for capable and committed people to serve poses an even greater threat to many of these institutions.

Evangelicals are committed to a philosophy premised in the unity of truth, that "all truth is God's truth." By implication we accept the challenge of excellence in the study of any and every discipline in order to achieve an integration of truth discerned with truth revealed. And that entails thorough knowledge of the Bible. Even more than adequate funding we desperately need a corps of men and women well-trained in the Scriptures and committed to teaching them faithfully to the glory of God.

ENDNOTES

1. Ronald P. Chadwick, *Teaching and Learning: An Integrated Approach to Christian Education.* Old Tappan, N.J.: Fleming H. Revell Co., 1982.

2. James Michael Lee, *The Shape of Religious Education.* Mishawaka, Ind.: Religious Education Press, 1971, pp. 7–8.

3. Lee, p. 7.

4. Findley B. Edge, *Teaching for Results.* Nashville: Broadman Press, 1956.

5. For a popularly written introduction to the topic see LeRoy Ford, *Design for Teaching and Training.* Nashville: Broadman Press, 1978.

6. Kathleen M. Wulf and Barbara Schave, *Curriculum Design: A Handbook for Educators.* Glenview, Ill.: Scott, Foresman and Co., pp. 57f.

7. W. James Popham, "Probing the Validity of the Arguments against Behavioral Objectives" in *Current Research on Instruction,* ed. by Richard C. Anderson, *et al.* Englewood Cliffs, N.J.: Prentice-Hall, Inc., 1969, pp. 66-72.

3. Ralph W. Tyler, *Basic Principles of Curriculum and Instruction.* Chicago: University of Chicago Press, 1949, p. 1.

9. Peter F. Oliva, *Developing the Curriculum.* Boston: Little, Brown and Co., 1982.

10. N.L. Gage, ed. *Handbook on Research on Teaching.* Chicago: Rand-McNally and Co., 1963.

11. John I. Goodlad, *A Place Called School.* New York: McGraw-Hill Book Co., 1984.

12. Richard D. Lamm, "The Melting Pot: Half-Empty?" in *The Christian Science Monitor,* September 19, 1985, p. 16.

BIBLIOGRAPHY

Block, J.H. *Mastery Learning: Theory and Practice.* New York: Holt, Rinehart & Winston, 1971.

Bruner, Jerome. *The Process of Education.* Cambridge, Mass.: The Harvard University Press, 1960.

Chadwick, Ronald P. *Teaching and Learning: An Integrated Approach to Christian Education.* Old Tappan, N.J.: Fleming H. Revell, 1982.

Cornett, Claudia. *What You Should Know about Teaching and Learning Styles.* Fastback No. 191. Bloomington, IN: Phi Delta Kappa Educational Foundation, 1983.

Joy, Donald. *Meaningful Learning in the Church.* Winona Lake, Ind.: Light and Life, 1969.

Joyce, Bruce and Martha Weil. *Models of Teaching.* 3rd Ed. Englewood Cliffs, N.J.: Prentice-Hall, Inc., 1986.

LeBar, Lois. *Education That Is Christian.* Old Tappan, N.J.: Fleming H. Revell, 1958.

LeFever, Marlene. *Creative Teaching Methods.* Elgin, Ill.: David C. Cook Publishing Co., 1985.

Lockerbie, D. Bruce. *Asking Questions: A Classroom Model for Teaching the Bible.* Milford, Mich.: Mott Media, 1980.

Mager, Robert F. *Preparing Instructional Objectives,* 2d Ed. Belmont, Calif.: Fearon Publishers, 1975.

Morris, Lynn Lyons, ed. *Program Evaluation Kit.* Beverly Hills, Calif.: Sage Publications, 1978.

Richards, Lawrence O. *A Theology of Christian Education.* Grand Rapids: Zondervan Publishing Co., 1975.

Sanders, Norris M. *Classroom Questions: What Kinds?* New York: Harper & Row, 1966.

Tyler, Ralph W. *Basic Principles of Curriculum and Instruction.* Chicago: University of Chicago Press, 1949.

Wilhoit, Jim. *Christian Education: The Search for Meaning.* Grand Rapids: Baker Book House, 1986.

Willis, Wesley. *Make Your Teaching Count!* Wheaton, Ill.: Victor Books, 1986.

Zuck, Roy B. *The Holy Spirit in Your Teaching.* Rev. ed. Wheaton, Ill.: Victor Books, 1984.

4. BIBLICAL FOUNDATIONS FOR A PHILOSOPHY OF TEACHING

Michael S. Lawson

A Christian philosophy of teaching begins in the Bible and forms part of the larger concept of Christian education. The Word of God offers more than the content of Christian teaching; it provides the essential philosophical framework as well. Fundamental questions, such as, "Why should we teach?" "What results should we expect?" "Who mediates Christian teaching?" "How should we teach?" and "Who should we teach?" find provocative answers in the Bible. A clearly defined mandate and goal mesh precisely with the Bible's remarkable insights into the teacher, student, and God to form a stable superstructure. Each Christian teacher constructs a personal philosophy of teaching by correctly or incorrectly understanding the biblical framework. Therefore, the lifelong challenge to build a truly Christian philosophy correctly starts by examining each component part furnished by the Scripture.

THE MANDATE FOR CHRISTIAN TEACHING

Christian teaching traces its roots back to the earliest days of man on the earth. God began teaching when He placed a restriction on man's behavior in the Garden of Eden. After the Fall, the need for teaching increased. Godly parents passed down crucial spiritual information from one generation to the next till God formalized parental responsibility by commanding them to teach their children (Deut. 6). Because the Law functioned within a theocracy, spiritual training largely depended on the family but received reinforcement from the whole social, economic, political, and religious system. Though prophets were occasionally sent to other lands (cf. Jonah), the focus of teaching during the Old Testament remained on the people who lived in the land of Israel. Jesus Christ would first articulate the idea of teaching *everyone everywhere.*

61

The Great Commission in Matthew 28 is at once one of the most familiar and most underrated passages of the New Testament. In the history of the world, no one ever seriously commissioned or attempted universal education. Yet Jesus expects His followers to make disciples of ALL NATIONS. If taken seriously, this passage should overwhelm Christian teachers with the lack of a rigidly defined curriculum, professionally trained teachers, or extraordinary education budgets. Amazingly enough, the history of this mandate determines the history of the church. Where Christian teaching flourishes, the church flourishes.

The most significant feature of the Great Commission for Christian teachers revolves around the learner. The phrase "make disciples" actually means to make or develop learners.[1] The very mandate for Christian teaching which Christ gives involves more than dispensing information. Based on this passage, the Christian teacher must develop learners. Christian teachers struggle with their task until their students become students of Jesus Christ.

Hardly anyone seriously questions the Christian community's call to teach its constituents. But we fiercely debate how to accomplish that teaching. Christianity's ability to survive under almost every kind of educational philosophy may speak more highly of its God than of its teachers. But the superintending hand of God does not relieve us from the divine mandate. Precisely how should we develop learners? Do we train them in monasteries? Do we raise them in agricultural communes? Do we instruct them in large groups or employ primarily interpersonal communication?

Christian teachers should stop long enough to consider how creatively God gave His revelation. Too much teaching methodology copies traditional models which may or may not reflect a Christian (not to mention creative) perspective. Because the Bible is largely a propositional document, some Christian teachers primarily present propositional and verbal explanations of biblical truth. But consider the incredible variety of methods and extremely diverse ways God used to communicate His Word.

1. He spoke directly and audibly from heaven.
2. He wrote on tablets of stone.
3. He became flesh.
4. He revealed Himself in supernatural beings.
5. He gave vivid dreams and visions.
6. He drew on walls of palaces.
7. He made animals talk.
8. He voiced truth through human prophets.
9. He composed poetry.
10. He provided visual reminders of promises.

The list could be expanded. Obviously God communicated cre-

HOW THE WORD COMES TO US

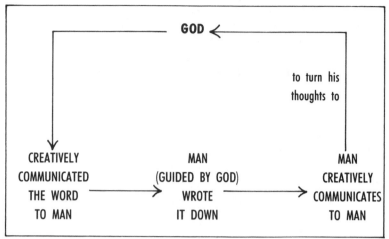

atively to the original recipients. Should modern students receive less? The simple diagram illustrates how God's truth should come to modern students.

While God's creativity cannot be completely duplicated, teachers can and should imitate His approach.

Ultimately, of course, the mandate for Christian teaching includes more than creativity on the part of the teacher. The student must respond. The follower of Christ must obey His commands. Unlike other forms of education which stress content, command of the material, skill acquisition, and other data base requirements, Christian teaching includes the necessity of a change in living habits. We teach the Word of God not to satisfy curiosity but to transform lives.

Throughout the Bible, men and women are called on to respond to the teaching from God. People have been required to do such things as:

1. Kill animals
2. Set up markers for reminders
3. Sprinkle blood on their doorposts
4. Wash in rivers
5. Burn their best products
6. Change vocations
7. Die
8. Suffer immensely.

All of these occurred as people responded appropriately to the explicit teaching of God.

The mandate challenges us to teach everyone everywhere. While God paces our creativity with His own example, we measure our success in changed lives. But what exactly should be accomplished in the lives of persons who become Christ's disciples?

THE GOAL OF CHRISTIAN TEACHING

In one sense the mandate for Christian teaching assumes a goal. Those who learn about God must respond positively to Him. Almost invariably, when the goal of Christian teaching is raised, the word *maturity* surfaces. We seem to assume a common definition for this key word but such an assumption produces confusion.

Scripture uses at least three different words as both goals for teaching and measures of maturity. Maturity should manifest itself in *relationships, morality,* and *theology.* First Timothy, Hebrews, and Ephesians state these marks of maturity clearly. As themes, we find them everywhere in the Bible. But the clarity of expression in these particular passages makes them ideal summaries.

FIRST TIMOTHY 1:5: "The goal of this command is love, which comes from a pure heart and a good conscience and a sincere faith." For our purposes, the substance of the verse is really straightforward and hardly astonishing. Paul intends his teaching to produce LOVE in the life of the student. Until that was accomplished, the goal for his instruction was not achieved. This simple verse ties vast amounts of the New Testament together. Note how the following passages focus on love:

1. The first commandment (Matt. 22:37-38)
2. The second commandment (v. 39)
3. The distinguishing mark of a disciple (John 13:35)
4. The fruit of the Spirit (Gal. 5:22-23)
5. The fruit superior to the gift (1 Cor. 13:1)
6. The way to tell if a man loves God (1 John 4:20)
7. The question Peter answered three times (John 21:15-18).

In other words, until a student produces love, the task of teaching is not complete. But what is love?

Modern English largely ignores the biblical definition by using love to cover so many different experiences. But because of its central position, love receives extensive and precise treatment in the New Testament. Unfortunately, the crucial passage frequently fails to tease our thinking. When we mention it people say, "Oh, yeah," and then proceed to ignore its teaching.

In order to avoid that trap, see if you can recognize the passage from the following list of statements which reflect the truth of the passage but use different words to describe it.

1. The Holy Spirit does not produce impatience. Can I really love God and be impatient?

2. The Holy Spirit does not produce unkindness. Can I really love God and be unkind?

3. The Holy Spirit does not produce jealousy of someone's strength, beauty, intelligence, success, money, power, possessions, relationships, or person. Can I really love God and be jealous?

Though we could study thirteen more words like these which define love quite precisely in behavioral terms, you probably have enough to recognize the passage as 1 Corinthians 13. Imagine what would happen if Christians lived out even the first three definitions each day and simply measured their success or failure in each relationship based on impatience, unkindness, and jealousy!

As teachers, we can never be satisfied until we see love generously produced in the lives of our students. Judging from the divorce rate among Christians, the innumerable personality conflicts in churches, and the frequent alienation between Christian leaders, we have a lot of work to do in this area alone. But love is not the only criterion for maturity mentioned in the New Testament.

HEBREWS 5:14: "But solid food is for the mature, who by constant use have trained themselves to distinguish good from evil."

The author of Hebrews notes two things which describe mature disciples. First, they are able to take in "solid food," and second, they are able to distinguish between good and evil because over time they have exercised their moral senses. "Solid food" and "exercised senses" are strategically connected in this verse. After all, the Word of God must radically affect our thinking so we literally think God's thoughts. As we "think God's thoughts" our judgments on matters become more "godly." As our thoughts become more "godly," we grasp the difference between good and evil, enabling us to make correct moral choices.

Just like the love principle, moral choices govern our behavior toward both God and others. But, in the final analysis, all moral choices relate directly to God since all sin is ultimately against God (Ps. 51). Even though Christian maturity suggests the capacity to make correct moral choices, it does not guarantee immunity from wrong ones.

Again, we do not achieve the goal for Christian teaching until Christ's disciples consistently make correct moral choices; until they become interested enough to test their life choices against scriptural standards. People should not be judged immature because they do not enjoy listening to hours of tedious lectures on the Bible (even if the subject is somehow considered "solid food"). On the other hand, mature disciples need to be curious and interested in talking about the more intricate aspects of the Bible and its implications for their lives. In the final analysis, maturity should be measured by good moral choices, and making good choices requires practice. If the current moral crisis among church *leaders* reflects a general condition in the church at large, the task looms large indeed!

In spite of their significance, love and morality still leave an incomplete picture of the goal for Christian teaching. Love and morality help us think about our behavior toward one another and God. But *theology* helps us think about God Himself. Christian maturity requires theological stability.

EPHESIANS 4:11-14: While avoiding disservice to the text, let me quote the following portion of the passage with deletions not directly pertinent to the goal of teaching. "It was He who gave some to be . . . pastors and teachers, to prepare God's people for works of service . . . until we all . . . become mature. . . . Then we will no longer be infants, tossed back and forth by the waves, and blown here and there by every wind of teaching and by the cunning and craftiness of men in their deceitful scheming."

Though considerably longer than the other two, this passage does talk about teachers, maturity, and teaching (theology). Paul's words seem to suggest both a goal and a result. In other words, when we achieve the goal of maturity, we also reap the result of theological stability. This whole idea coincides nicely with the Hebrews passage which suggests that mature believers are able to deal with solid food. Have we any reason to believe that solid food and theology are different concepts? No longer should disciples be victimized by articulate, persuasive, self-serving teachers. Instead, they should be able to see through such deceitful schemes and their false ideas about God. The job seems impossible considering how many self-promoting teachers there are on television, radio, and in our communities everywhere. Nevertheless, good teaching requires a degree of theological sophistication that immunizes students to such teachers and their false doctrine.

The apostle also suggests *service* as another result of maturity. Is it too trite to say we are taught to serve? Though not a prerequisite for service, true maturity eludes us apart from service to Christ's body.

If maturity is the goal how can we measure progress? How are we doing? Have we achieved maturity? If the followers of Christ are willingly serving the body of Christ, we should assume from this behavior that some progress has been made. Interestingly enough, pastors, youth workers, directors of Christian education, and other staff members continually struggle to recruit enough workers for Christian service. The ministry of teaching, therefore, needs constant emphasis.

As the goal for Christian teaching, maturity seems clear enough when measured by love, morality, theological stability, and service. These ideas are hardly new in the Christian community. Yet after almost 2,000 years of church history, we have certainly not achieved the goal. The need for Christian teaching remains as great today as ever.

This will always be the case. Each generation, each new convert must start with little or no information and begin his walk with Christ afresh. Even growing Christians need reminding and encouraging as they move toward maturity. Our advanced technological society has not reduced the need. The disciples of Jesus still require teaching and teachers!

THE PARTICIPANTS IN CHRISTIAN TEACHING
THE HOLY SPIRIT.

We have devoted an entire chapter to the role of the Holy Spirit in teaching. Yet, we cannot overemphasize His importance as a participant in the process of Christian teaching. Whatever we say about the other two participants (the teacher and the student) must always be understood in light of the overall superintending work of the Holy Spirit and His interaction with teacher, student, and the Word of God.
THE TEACHER.

How are teachers different in Christian teaching? Frequently we assume we know precisely what teachers should do because we have spent so much time under their supervision. Twelve of the best years of our lives elapse under formal education where teachers have tremendous influence (both consciously and unconsciously) on our development. Yet much of what they do may or may not be effective or worth imitating. Carefully examining the role of the teacher from a Christian perspective clarifies our understanding.

Are there conflicting notions about the role of a Christian teacher? Two groups of words conjure up completely different thoughts about teachers. Note the mental images stimulated by the following words:

1. Expert
2. Authority
3. Professional
4. Genius
5. Intellectual
6. Master
7. Specialist
8. Brilliant.

All these words seem to reflect excellence in the personal knowledge of the teacher. Yet, they say absolutely nothing about one's ability to teach. Frequently students describe their favorite teachers with another set of words and complain when these are missing from a teacher's style. Note the difference in the mental images stimulated by this group:

1. Guide
2. Coach
3. Facilitator
4. Model
5. Encourager
6. Motivator
7. Stimulator
8. Mentor.

These words seem to describe something about the teacher's relationship to the student. Teachers of Christian truth must do more than simply accumulate and dispense vast amounts of information about the Bible; they must help the disciples of Jesus grow in their relationships, morals, theology, and service. Necessary teacher assistance will be more welcomed by the student when a class reflects the second set of words.

Do teachers have other responsibilities? Let us borrow the managerial model from business to explain how a teacher deals with major components in the teaching process.

Motivation. Whether intrinsic or extrinsic, motivation remains one of the real keys to learning. Cornelius Jaarsma makes the insightful comment, "Pupils learn what they set out to learn, not necessarily what a teacher tries to teach."[2] Therefore, when teachers sense their students are not intrinsically motivated to learn the material at hand, they should take every appropriate measure to motivate the student extrinsically. Unfortunately, many teachers resort to fear, guilt, or academic pressure to promote extrinsic motivation or they simply grumble about the poor quality of students these days. Too few attempt to stimulate interest or relate their teaching to immediate life needs. Understanding and managing student motivation stands as a major component in teaching.

Time. Though the amount of time devoted to teaching is usually fixed and predictable, many teachers fail to manage it very well. Many teachers fail to prepare enough interesting activities for students. They assume that listening equals learning and talk the whole time. To move students through time so that the lesson neither drags nor appears too rushed requires good planning. Even for adults, three or four changes of activity are certainly appropriate within an hour.

Content. If any phrase should be stricken from the terminology of teaching, "covering the material" qualifies! This phrase provides a lame excuse to make students responsible for the failure of teachers to plan carefully and realistically. The abilities of the students should govern the specific plan. Age, familiarity with the Bible, and spiritual development are only a few of the factors to consider. We dare not dump the Word of God on students and assume they will automatically make an application to their lives. Time must be taken to think about the Bible, talk about it, speculate about its impact, and pray for help to implement it in our lives.

Jesus set the perfect example for His disciples when He said in John 16:12, "I have much more to say to you, more than you can now bear." Jesus realized the limitations on human beings to respond to His teaching. Amazingly, Jesus usually revealed tiny pieces of information in His lessons while allowing large blocks of time for consideration and reflection with His disciples afterward.

The Bible itself is the primary text of Christian teaching. But the Bible contains different levels of material. Some teaching is considered "milk of the Word" while some other is considered "solid food." Jesus condemned the Pharisees for tithing spices and neglecting more important matters such as justice, mercy, and faithfulness (Matt. 23:23). The teacher must select how much and which kind of material the student can realistically digest and integrate into life in any teaching situation. Simultaneously, the content of a lesson must move students toward service, theological stability, moral integrity, and love for God and one another.

Space. All teaching occurs somewhere. Yet many Bible teachers do not consider themselves managers of space. Teaching situations vary widely—from excellent to horrible. Some of the finest Christian education buildings ever designed have been built during the last two decades. Frequently the flexibility and creativity that this excellent space affords goes unnoticed (and, therefore, unused) by too many teachers. The following charts graphically illustrate how to creatively rearrange space. Each arrangement serves a different purpose even if only for a short period of time during the hour. Note how the focus of attention shifts with each new configuration. The interest stimulated by constructive change affects motivation in a wholesome way.

Participation. A teacher must manage and encourage participation. Jesus sets the pace in a fascinating way. He accepted numerous invitations from people who wanted to have Him over for dinner to discuss theology. His habit of eating with sinners brought criticism from other teachers. Obviously, Jesus set a tone which invited questions about God. Not only did He welcome questions, He asked them as well. His listeners often left puzzled rather than content.

A good teacher manages the tone of a class in such a way that

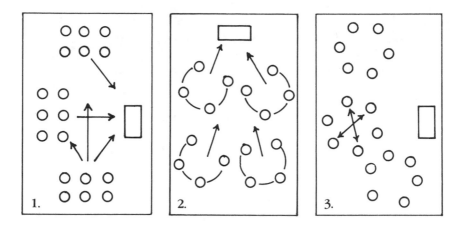

1. Note how the room arrangement focuses on the teacher but enables students to look at one another.

2. Note how the focus shifts from the teacher to a few people but still enables students to see the teacher.

3. Note how the focus is exclusively on the members of the group but the teacher facilitates the group work when necessary.

students feel physically, emotionally, and spiritually secure enough to think and wonder out loud. Unless the teacher assumes responsibility for class atmosphere, students will, and they may not have everyone's best interest in mind.

Dispensing information appears simple when compared to balancing complex factors such as motivation, time, content, space, and participation. Like Jesus, Christian teachers must control more than their academic field; they must skillfully organize, plan, and manage.

THE LEARNER.

Philosophies of education and theories of learning have existed for hundreds of years. But the question of how people learn remains largely unanswered today. There are many theories in the colleges of education, but no one has comprehensively solved the puzzle. Several theories offer insights into individual facets of learning.

One educational psychologist addresses the question by dividing learning theory into two major camps.[3] Developmentalists stand in one camp while stimulus-response devotees stand in the other, bristling at each other's thinking. Both make contributions to our understanding of how people learn. But neither completely synthesizes our understanding of the learning process. For the students' benefit, teachers should cooperate with the learning process for best results. But in Christian teaching, to some degree, results will always remain unpredictable.

For the Christian, many questions about spiritual truth complicate the theories of learning even further. Is spiritual truth by nature different from other truth? Does spiritual truth need to be apprehended by a mechanism different from the normal senses? Certain passages suggest that problems await those who intend to teach spiritual truth, and two passages seem to address the issue rather directly.

FIRST CORINTHIANS 2:14-15: Whatever else is true, a difference exists between the natural man and the spiritual man where the things of the Spirit of God are concerned. Some suggest depravity corrupted man's ability to comprehend spiritual truth.[4] Others propose that the natural man understands spiritual truth but is unable to respond in a spiritual way to it.[5] In the first case, the Spirit of God must illuminate the biblical information for the truth to make any sense to the student. In the second case, the Spirit of God must activate the will for the student to make a spiritual response. In either case, spiritual truth ordinarily seems to come to the student through one of the five senses.

But depending on the position adopted, the teacher needs to anticipate trouble either with comprehension or application of the truth. Questions about the student's fundamental spiritual condition become crucial.

HEBREWS 5:13-14: In this passage, the author distinguishes among "spiritual" people. Some are apparently able to take in "solid food" while others are still consuming "milk." Because maturity requires some amount of time, teachers should expect some students to be further along than others. Frequently a teacher confronts a mixed audience. That lesson should balance between meat and milk (so the young do not become discouraged) and solid food (so the mature do not become bored).

The Holy Spirit, the teacher, and the student gather around the Word of God in Christian teaching. Each contributes uniquely to the process. Paradoxically, the Holy Spirit and the student often operate independently of the teacher. But a Christian teacher needs both students and the Holy Spirit to fulfill his mission.

SUMMARY

Several fundamental questions confronted us as we opened this chapter. The lifelong challenge to construct a Christian philosophy still awaits. But the Bible furnishes a sufficient framework to teach in while we build our philosophy. Review the questions to pull the framework together.

1. "Why should we teach?" Christ commissions our attempts while God challenges our communication to be creative.

71

2. "What results should we expect?" Love, morality, theological stability, and service combine to forge the goal of Christian teaching.

3. "Who mediates Christian teaching?" No other kind of teaching furnishes a divine enabler like the Holy Spirit.

4. "How should we teach?" Christian teachers develop as they creatively manage motivation, time, content, space, and participation.

5. "Whom should we teach?" For the Christian teacher, students come in a variety of packages composed of natural men and two kinds of spiritual men.

Great rewards await those teachers who serve faithfully and build on a solid foundation.

ENDNOTES

1. A.T. Robertson, *Word Pictures in the New Testament*. Nashville: Broadman Press, 1930, p. 245.

2. Cornelius Jaarsma, "The Learning Process," in *An Introduction to Evangelical Christian Education*, J. Edward Hakes, ed. Chicago: Moody Bible Institute, 1964, p. 82.

3. Morris L. Bigge, *Learning Theories for Teachers*. New York: Harper and Row, 1964.

4. J. Dwight Pentecost, *Pattern for Maturity*. Chicago: Moody Press, 1966, p. 42.

5. Daniel P. Fuller, "The Holy Spirit's Role in Biblical Interpretation," in *Scripture, Tradition and Interpretation*. W. Ward Gasque and William Sanford LaSor, eds. Grand Rapids: Eerdmans, 1978, p. 192.

BIBLIOGRAPHY

Bushnell, Horace. *Christian Nurture*. Grand Rapids: Baker, 1861, 1979.

Daniel, Eleanor, *et al. Introduction to Christian Education*. Cincinnati: Standard, 1980.

Ericksen, Stanford C. *The Essence of Good Teaching*. San Francisco: Jossey-Bass Publishers, 1985.

Gaebelein, Frank E. *The Pattern of God's Truth*. Chicago: Moody Press, 1968.

Geisler, Norman L. and Paul D. Feinberg. *Introduction to Philosophy: A Christian Perspective*. Grand Rapids: Baker Book House, 1980.

Grawbs, Jean D. and L.M. McClure. *Foundations of Teaching*. New York: Holt, Rinehart and Winston, 1964.

Green, Thomas F. *The Activities of Teaching*. New York: McGraw-Hill Book Company, 1971.

Kuhlman, Edward. *Master Teacher.* Old Tappan, N.J.: Fleming H. Revell Company, 1987.

LeBar, Lois E. *Education That Is Christian.* Old Tappan, N.J.: Fleming H. Revell Company, 1958.

Miller, R.C. *The Theory of Christian Education Practice.* Birmingham: Religious Education Press, 1980.

Richards, Lawrence O. *Creative Bible Teaching.* Chicago: Moody Press, 1977.

_____. *A Theology of Christian Education.* Grand Rapids: Zondervan, 1975.

Schaeffer, Francis. *Escape from Reason.* Downers Grove, Ill.: InterVarsity Press, 1968.

5. BIBLICAL INTEGRATION:
THE PROCESS OF THINKING LIKE A CHRISTIAN*
Kenneth O. Gangel

As the twentieth century draws to a close, the survival of the world seems tenuously dependent on the rationality of its leaders. Yet, it is a world in which the rationality of some of those leaders is increasingly being called into question, and with no small amount of evidence. It is also a world in which Christianity stands wrongly accused of irrationality by those who misunderstand the essence of biblical faith.

The premise of this book rests on a twofold presupposition: that the Christian teacher is our best hope for rationality in an irrational age; and, that those Christian teachers must have highly developed and thoroughly consecrated minds in order to meet the challenge of leadership in such an age. Such minds are tuned to the process of constant biblical integration of faith and learning, a spiritual and academic commitment which stretches far beyond the boundaries of content transmission.

The process of Christian mind-building begins at regeneration. T.F. Torrance spells it out:

> At the end of the day that was the test I used to put to my students, as I read their essays and examinations or listened to them in the chapel. "Has this person a genuinely theological instinct or not? Is his or her thinking spontaneously and naturally governed by the mind of Christ?" That is much more important than being theologically learned, much more important than being able to offer a formal academic account of some doctrine or historic debate in the church. What really counts in

---

*Adapted from "Thinking Like a Christian: An Evangelical Analysis of Rationality," by Kenneth O. Gangel in *Christian Education Journal,* Vol. 3, No. 1, © 1987 Scripture Press Ministries. Used by permission.

the end is whether a person's mind is radically transformed by Christ and so spiritually attuned to the mind of Christ, that he thinks instinctively from the depths of his mental being in a way worthy of God.[1]

WHY MUST OUR STUDENTS DEVELOP THEIR MINDS?

This first question of our chapter seems almost primitive, certainly elementary, and I fear my answers may not be sufficiently profound. But surely those of us who stand before students with regularity are consistently called on to affirm the kind of Christianity which gives back to God all of what He has produced by grace in us, including intellectual capacity. Therefore, the first reason why our students must develop their minds is *because God has commanded it.* Indeed, the first commandment according to its affirmation by the Lord Himself is, "Love the Lord your God with all your heart and with all your soul and with all your mind" (Matt. 22:37).

This summary of the first table of the Law is expanded slightly in Mark's version by adding "strength" (12:30). The passage emphasizes the worship of God with all aspects of the human being and the text stresses the comprehensive nature of serious Christian commitment. It is not enough to love only with heart; nor even with heart and soul; nor yet with heart, soul, and strength. Serious Christian teachers emphasize the importance of worshiping God with the mind.

In the 1985 Griffith Thomas Lectures at Dallas Theological Seminary, D. Bruce Lockerbie reminded the students that after the eternal soul, the most Godlike attribute of man is the mind, and he warned that "Christians may underrate the mind and overrate the heart and therefore have no stomach for the fight."[2]

Oliver Barclay explains why the concept of worshiping God with one's mind seems so out of step.

> This appears such an alien idea [because] our concept of love is becoming increasingly different from that of the New Testament . . . it may or may not involve emotion. The Bible when it talks of the mind, is not asking us to develop a philosophy (useful as that may be in its place), but to allow revealed truth to control us. It is the truth that sets us free, it is the truth as it is in Jesus that we are to consider, believe, and act upon . . . thinking is part of what it is to be a human being. The alternative is to be "a fool" (Prov. 18:2).[3]

The second reason why Christians must develop their minds is

75

because thinking Christians are called on to construct an evangelical world and life view. Here again the role of the Christian teacher at all levels remains foundational. According to James Sire, a worldview is "a set of presuppositions (or assumptions) which we hold (consciously or unconsciously) about the basic make-up of the world."[4] How essential, therefore, for every Christian to learn how to interpret his culture "Christianly." But what does that mean? How can it be achieved?

How does one actually practice thinking Christianly about surrounding culture? And how does one teach one's students to do so? Such an integrated exercise requires analytical synopsis of society enlightened by God's revelation. At least three steps are involved.

KNOW THE SCRIPTURES INTIMATELY.

Integration of any kind can never rise from theological ignorance. This has long been a major problem in Christian elementary and secondary schools as well as in Christian colleges. While requiring adequate credentials in a particular age-level or content specialization, we require only the most rudimentary biblical instruction. Schools often hire faculty with little or no formal training in biblical and theological studies, expecting that strong church affiliation and personal devotions will fulfill that side of the requirement. Such teachers can no more construct an evangelical world and life view than a practicing pastor can integrate Scripture and astronomy from watching several episodes of "Nova." The problem is exacerbated because the administrators who do the hiring and requiring do not themselves know the Scriptures intimately and, therefore, find that quality a less-than-demanding issue among their subalterns.

STUDY THE CULTURE DILIGENTLY.

For years I have been asking students to sort out and articulate the differences among secular humanism, religious humanism, and Christian humanism. Recent popular literature in the evangelical camp has been no ally in this campaign. Secular humanism is tangled in the swamp of human intellect and will rather than divine guidance. Christian humanism, by contrast (exemplified historically by Desiderius Erasmus and in greater modernity by C.S. Lewis), grounds itself in a commitment to God's revelation, both natural and special. Religious humanism takes a middle road, repudiating denial of God while at the same time refusing a commitment to the exclusiveness of Christian theism. All three are found in the current culture, and thinking Christians must be wary of maladroit use of terms.

Notice how the exercise of studying the culture depends on knowing the Scriptures.

One cannot bring his study of culture to any kind of fruition without running that evaluation through a distinctly biblical grid, an impossibility if he or she has too frail a familiarity with the Scriptures.

This then leads us to yet a third step.

ANALYZE EVENTS AND ISSUES THEOLOGICALLY.

As Christians live in the world they are bombarded constantly with ideas and issues in direct experience or through the instrumentality of the media. Five practical questions form powerful lines in the straining net of theological analysis through which all experience must pass.

Does the Bible speak to this issue? An obvious example here is the late twentieth century question of *homosexuality.* Some argue it is merely an alternative lifestyle; others, a genetically caused physical state. Still others place it within the arena of sin, dramatically condemned by any historic orthodox explanation of the Bible. When there are texts which apply, the serious Christian must find them; but sometimes there are not and the second question must be applied.

Are there general Christian principles which apply? Another cancer on the skin of contemporary life is *drug abuse* in multitudinous forms. One could argue that no specific Scripture condemns the use of drugs. But surely the principle of "body control" provides an appropriate standard for dealing with drug and alcohol abuse: " 'Everything is permissible for me,—but I will not be mastered by anything" (1 Cor. 6:12).

Have Christian scholars, past or present, dealt with this issue? The cabals of *pro-abortionists* include few evangelicals, but one could imagine a beginning integrationist, a college student struggling with relating faith to learning, thrown off balance by the less-than-dramatic body of Scripture which can be directed at this issue. Yet a part of God's gift to His church comes in the forms of those gifted individuals able to go beyond the boundaries of average thinking, to probe the depths of difficult and controversial issues. In this particular illustration, the work of Schaeffer and Koop provides strategic value and example.

Does this position or theory defy absolute standards of morality or value? Presumably when we discuss "absolute standards" with students, we are prepared to defend that claim with specific passages drawn from special revelation. The inveterate tendency of the church, however, from ancient heresy trials to modern hyper-separationism, classifies the relative interpretation of man as the absolute standard of God and, therefore, codifies rubrics of behavior.

Meanwhile, relativism offers us the other extreme, burning all absolute standards on the altar of expedience and existential situationism. *Premarital sex,* for example, has always been condemned by biblical Christians, who affirm the absolute value of chastity. The shifting standards of society offer no measure of morality for the Christian, for the "times are always a changin'."

The attitude of the younger generation toward sexuality shifted in advance of their parents. Pollster Daniel Yankelovich noted that in 1969, 77 percent of college students believed extramarital sexual relations were morally wrong; in 1971, 57 percent; that in 1969, 42 percent of college students believed that relations between consenting homosexuals were morally wrong; in 1971, 25 percent; and that in 1969, 34 percent of college students believed that casual premarital sexual relations were morally wrong; in 1971, 25 percent. A sexual revolution appeared to be in full swing.[5]

The Christian teacher has committed himself to thinking in a context which defines morality in terms of biblical absolutes and subjects all conclusions to Lord and Word.

Is the Holy Spirit leading me to a definitive viewpoint on this matter? Quite possibly, even after activating the first four rubrics, the Christian student still holds only a vacuous interrogative. Consider the questions of *war* or *personal self-defense.* The Bible truly speaks to these issues, but intelligent and committed believers down through the centuries have differed on how that biblical information should be interpreted. We struggle with the endless flow of what seem to be conflicting values. If forced to the unpleasant choice, should I protect my family at any cost or refuse to take a human life? Should I fight for the freedom and safety of my homeland or place myself into a non-military situation allowing others to preserve my safety? Such issues we must finally decide on how the Holy Spirit teaches us with quiet but firm inner assurance. Assuming we subject our own selfish minds to both text and principles of God's Word, such decisions can be made.

ADOPT A SET OF DISTINCTLY CHRISTIAN
PRESUPPOSITIONS.

One could expound indefinitely on how those presuppositions might look and what they might include. The following list directs attention to areas which require attention, without expecting the wording to be comfortably adopted by all teachers.

Ultimate reality resides in the personal, sovereign, Triune God.

Absolute truth comes to man in the form of God's self-initiated, inerrant revelation, the Bible.

The nature of human beings is declared by God to be in His image, fallen through sin, but redeemed by the Cross.

Value is not determined by society or majority vote, but ascertained as a part of God's revelation. In short, Christian axiology (values) depends on Christian epistemology (knowledge).

The meaning of history centers in the plan and power of God. As Groothuis puts it, "His ordering of all events is leading to the consummation of His intent for man and the universe. The tragedy of rebellion in the Fall is followed by the drama of redemption—God pursuing man. History is not the meaningless reign of chance or impersonal necessity, but the unfolding of divine government most clearly seen in the invasion of God into time and space in Christ (John 1:18)."[6]

Our students must also develop their minds *because the structure of unbelief is more militant in our day.* Consider the knowledge explosion, the raw paganism in much of what passes for education in the public domain, and the obtuse irrationalism evident in the influence of leading educators. Marching alongside traditional paganism we also hear the occult tattoo evidenced in everything from advanced graduate classes in voodoo to documented cases of satanism.

Rejection of the disciplines of Scripture leads to the kind of loose morality commonplace in today's world. Governor Charles Robb of Virginia claims that 1.25 million teens are "disconnected" from school, work, family, and the values these traditional agencies promote. He asserts the proportion of children in poverty has risen from 16 percent in 1970 to 22 percent today; that drug and alcohol abuse among the young is up sixtyfold since 1960; that teenage homicide, suicide, and crime have climbed steadily since 1950, and that in this most educated of nations, the number of school dropouts has risen dramatically to the point that, in some major cities, fewer than half the young people who enter high school actually graduate.[7]

Christian teachers storm the arena precisely because much of this cultural ennui can be attributed to wrong thinking, as Paul reminded the Ephesians.

> So I tell you this, and insist on it in the Lord, that you must no longer live as the Gentiles do, in the futility of their thinking. They are darkened in their understanding and separated from the life of God because of the ignorance that is in them due to the hardening of their hearts. Having lost all sensitivity, they have given themselves over to sensuality so as to indulge in every kind of impurity, with a continual lust for more (Eph. 4:17-19).

Finally, our students must develop their minds *because Christian leadership in any form requires disciplined thinking.* The disciplined Christian thinker does not replace faith with reason; he integrates the two by bowing before a reasonable faith. Stott quotes Martin Lloyd-Jones in support of such a concept.

> Faith, if you like, can be defined like this: It is a man insisting upon thinking when everything seems determined to bludgeon and knock him down in an intellectual sense. The trouble with the person of little faith is that, instead of controlling his own thought, his thought is being controlled by something else, and as we put it, he goes round and round in circles. That is the essence of worry . . . that is not thought; that is the absence of thought, a failure to think.[8]

Christianity invites investigation, as Thomas learned when he confronted the risen Lord (John 20). Feeling is not enough; it is never enough. But such talk of defending the faith may quickly become too militant and the thinking Christian must be reminded to avoid unwarranted dogmatism.

Too much of what passes for Christian teaching today is nothing more than monarchial dogmatism wrapped in the robes of academic success. We must resist the sacred/secular paradox so that a total unified lifestyle can result from disciplined thinking. The believer's mind must be continually renewed (Rom. 12:2) as he exercises his freedom to think on virtuous things (Phil. 4:8). Woodbridge properly attacks false compartmentalization.

> Though evangelical Christians affirm that the Bible is an infallible rule for faith and practice, many of them compartmentalize their faith in such a manner that biblical teachings do not much affect the way they live on a daily basis. They profess sound evangelical doctrine but betray those confessions by their deeds. They do not consciously seek each day to live under the direction of biblical ethics.[9]

HOW CAN A CHRISTIAN STUDENT BLOW HIS MIND?

The ways seem numerous and widely variant in severity. One is reminded, for example, of that now infamous phrase which has come back many times to haunt its author—"benign neglect."

A CHRISTIAN STUDENT CAN BLOW HIS MIND THROUGH CARELESSNESS.

Shoddiness in study habits, procrastination in responsibilities, rationalization of sloth—all these and a host of other common practices trick us into "blowing" this wonderful gift from God. Thousands graduate from Christian schools and colleges every year never to appear again in the ranks of Christian leadership, however severe the need.

Completing some phase of one's education merely provides

certain tools. Using those tools effectively beyond the boundaries of classroom and institutional regimentation more closely relates to wisdom than to knowledge. Nevertheless, Christian students at all levels must see their present tasks in biblical perspective—they are engaged in ministry, they are doing the work of the Lord.

A CHRISTIAN STUDENT CAN BLOW HIS MIND
THROUGH PRIDE.

By positing the mind at the center of all life, one traps oneself into the error of Platonic idealism, the heresy of the Cartesian imperial self. The Bible teaches that spiritual pride is a horrible sin, but those who have enjoyed the privilege of serious learning may be prone to yet another pitfall—mental pride.

Perhaps the most humbling act, both intelligent and purposeful, is the cultivation of an attitude of worship. Surely that is what Jesus had in mind when He said, "Love the Lord your God with all your mind." When the thinking Christian allows intellectual success to go to his head, he may very well discover that it "blows his mind." And a mind blown on one's own achievements is no longer a mind capable of bowing before Jesus Christ.

Second Corinthians 10:5 serves as compass and lodestar for Christian teachers: "We demolish arguments and every pretension that sets itself up against the knowledge of God, and we take captive every thought to make it obedient to Christ." Many of the great minds of history were humble Christians who knew that mind-bowing in no way appeals to ignorance or shoddy anti-intellectualism.

A CHRISTIAN STUDENT MAY BLOW HIS MIND
THROUGH SIN.

Here the Scriptures offer repeated warnings but perhaps none more poignant than the words of Paul, "The mind of sinful man is death, but the mind controlled by the Spirit is life and peace; the sinful mind is hostile to God. It does not submit to God's law, nor can it do so" (Rom. 8:6-7).

Some Christian scholars maintain fortresses of faith which Satan can never besiege with temptations of drunkenness, debauchery, thievery, murder, or lust. With such his tool may have to be a sharpened spear of mental pride, forcing them to stand as modern models of Nebuchadnezzar and Herod, pointing out to an admiring world the great thoughts they have thought and the great words they have written.

God's Word, meanwhile, continues to talk positively about the man whose mind is stayed on God (Isa. 26:3); who shares the unity of mind with other believers (Rom. 12:16); who possesses a willing mind (2 Cor. 8:12); who treasures a humble mind (Phil. 2:3); and who allows God to produce in him the Spirit of a sound mind (2 Tim. 1:7).

81

THE CHRISTIAN STUDENT CAN BLOW HIS MIND THROUGH DOGMATISM AND RIGIDITY.

Renewal requires a process of change. The Scriptures attest to the progress involved in moving toward spiritual maturity (Rom. 8:28-30; 2 Cor. 3:17-18; 2 Peter 3:18). The word *dogmatic* is not in and of itself derogatory. We speak of a study in dogmatics as related to the pursuit of systematic theology. But modern usage has made the adjectival form almost parallel to the word "rigid," and the epithet "uncompromising" would be a welcome panegyric in the eyes of some Christian leaders. Nancy Barcus points up the confusion in such thinking.

> Sometimes we may detect an error of assurance so totally serious that it is disarming. That very sound of self-assurance should put a person on guard. Is there room for any attitudes or interpretations other than this one? If the speaker is convinced, and masterful, we will be left with the feeling that there are only two ways to view an issue: the right way and the wrong way, the good way and the foolish way. Giving you the impression of fairness and rationality, a thinker may actually be very unfair, suggesting that anyone with a clear mind would reach no other conclusions than these. If you detect such a stance, beware. This is likely to be dangerous ground.[10]

The Spirit-filled teacher then seeks a balance of law and Gospel, of Word and Spirit. Douglas Moo reminds us that "the new pattern of thinking that begins with conversion must undergo a constant process of renewal. In the building of this Christian mind, the commands of God and Scripture provide a basic blueprint, while the redeemed, Spirit-filled mind itself applies those commands in certain situations."[11]

HOW CAN A CHRISTIAN STUDENT KEEP FROM BLOWING HIS MIND?

Quite obviously the way to stay healthy is to avoid disease—in this case, notably those mentioned above. But there is a positive dimension too in which the thinking Christian takes definitive steps toward mind-bowing as an alternative to mind-blowing.

A CHRISTIAN STUDENT CAN AVOID BLOWING HIS MIND BY RECOGNIZING THE DEPENDABILITY OF BIBLICAL AUTHORITY WITH WHICH TO COMBAT THE IRRATIONALITY OF THE AGE.

In more than a quarter century of teaching I have frequently seen how difficult it is for students to grasp the appropriate relationship

between natural and special revelation. Some are so biblically committed that they fail to see the reality and significance of God's revelation
in means other than the Scriptures. Others, more inclined toward scientific research, struggle with the application of faith principle to the
learning process.

The Christian thinker, however, must rise to the level at which
he can integrate faith with learning in any form. We must view natural
revelation through the eyes of special revelation. Such a process puts us
on our way toward Christo-centric thinking.

> The more we see the biblical account as a reliable base, the
> more willing we become to test other experiences and ideas by
> its precepts. We find an even sanity, a respect for personhood,
> an undaunted realism, and, too, the possibility that restoration
> and redemption provide a surer foundation for goodness and
> idealism than the roads other thinkers have proposed. Nowhere
> else is there such a delicate balance between unblinking recog-
> nition of evil and commitment to human moral responsibility,
> such undaunted hope, such promise of goodness and
> restoration.[12]

A CHRISTIAN STUDENT CAN AVOID MIND-BLOWING BY
LEARNING TO LINK REASON AND FAITH.

This is apposite to the former discussion, but so crucial I offer
it as a separate step. There is an unenlightened faith of which Paul once
spoke: "For I can testify about them that they are zealous for God, but
their zeal is not based on knowledge" (Rom. 10:2). Christianity is indeed rational, but it is not rationalism; it is intellectual, but it is not
intellectualism.

The mind is a tool of faith and the Christian leader allows
reason and faith—the little boy and the strong man—to begin the hike
together. But he must expect that somewhere down the road, perhaps
in the difficult climb through mountainous terrain, the strong man
(faith) may have to carry the little boy (reason) on his back. The
process of believing/thinking and thinking/believing, writes Groothuis,
"is the preoccupation and conviction of the Christian mind. One need
not be an 'intellectual' to apply the Christian worldview concretely to
all of life and thus 'give a reason for the hope that is in you' (1 Peter
3:15) to a doubting world."[13]

A CHRISTIAN STUDENT CAN ESCAPE THE DANGER OF
MIND-BLOWING BY CREATING A WORD-CENTERED
ENVIRONMENT.

The reality of environmental conditioning and the impact of
one's surroundings stand as fact. How many times we remind impres-

sionable teenagers that the television programs they watch, the music they listen to, the movies they attend, and the friends with which they surround themselves all make indelible impressions on their lives. Yet somehow we behave as though that influence is no longer significant in the adult years. The courts are full of cases clamoring for freedom of "consenting adults" to engage in all manner of activities, many of which corrode both mind and body.

Against this pattern the Apostle Paul offers a now familiar refrain: " 'Everything is permissible'—but not everything is constructive" (1 Cor. 10:23). Moo argues that the surroundings in which the Christian voluntarily places himself offer the most important single factor in developing a renewed mind.

> How can a Christian facilitate the process of training a renewed mind, the mind of the Spirit? The key would seem to be environment. What are the influences, the atmosphere in which his mind is being formed? What is determining the direction of his thinking? How ironic it is that many Christian parents who are concerned about the kind of school environment in which their children are being trained are completely unconcerned about or even unconscious of the environment that affects their own way of thinking. A mind that is exposed constantly to a barrage of secular television, secular advertising, secular literature, and secular ideas is probably going to turn out to be a secular mind.[14]

A CHRISTIAN STUDENT CAN AVOID MIND-BLOWING BY SUBMITTING TO THE HOLY SPIRIT'S CONTROL IN ALL THINGS.

This is neither late medieval mysticism nor contemporary charismatic theology. Control of the mind by the Spirit is a theme melody running through the music of both Testaments, as old as God's relationship with His creation.

Earlier in this chapter I alluded to the negative paragraph from the fourth chapter of Ephesians, a warning to reject the darkness of the past. The paragraph immediately following offers the positive corrective, reminding Christian thinkers to live as children of light.

> You, however, did not come to know Christ that way. Surely you heard of Him and were taught in Him in accordance with the truth that is in Jesus. You were taught, with regard to your former way of life, to put off your old self, which is being corrupted by its deceitful desires; to be made new in the attitude of your minds; and to put on the new self, created to be

84

like God in true righteousness and holiness (Eph. 4:20-24).

Grant Osborn draws a parallel between the Ephesians passage and Romans 8 and sees "the new mind as sharing the outlook and assumptions of the Spirit, fully committed to the Spirit rather than to the flesh."[15]

Christian teachers laboring to reproduce students committed both to mind-building and mind-bowing offer up with meaning the prayer contained in a familiar hymn:

> May the mind of Christ my Saviour live in me from day to day,
> By His love and pow'r controlling all I do and say.
> May the Word of God dwell richly in my heart from hour to hour,
> So that all may see I triumph only through His pow'r.[16]

Christian integration rests on spiritual-mindedness. It reveres not dogmatism but tolerance; not shouting but reason. And perhaps teachers should never view it as an accomplished ideal. At best, we can point to some position along the journey and trust by God's grace that it will be more advanced than positions at previous points of evaluation. Integrating faith and learning falls within the boundaries of that magical word *liturgy*—it is both worship and service. Perhaps that is what Charles Wesley had in mind when he wrote:

> To serve this present age my calling to fulfill,
> O may it all my powers engage to do my Master's will.

ENDNOTES

1. T.F. Torrance, "The Reconciliation of Mind," in *TSF Bulletin*. January—February 1987, p. 6.

2. D. Bruce Lockerbie, Griffith Thomas Lectures, Dallas Theological Seminary, 1985.

3. Oliver Barclay, "Loving God with All Your Mind," in *Christian Arena*. June, 1985, p. 17.

4. James W. Sire, *The Universe Next Door*. Downers Grove, Ill.: InterVarsity Press, 1976, p. 17.

5. John D. Woodbridge, ed., *Renewing Your Mind in a Secular World*. Chicago: Moody Press, 1985, p. 13.

6. Douglas Groothuis, "The Christian Mind," *CSSH Quarterly*. Winter 1984, p. 17.

7. Charles S. Robb, "We Can't Write Off 1.25 Million Teens," *USA Today*. November 8, 1985, p. 10A.

8. John R.W. Stott, *Your Mind Matters*. Downers Grove, Ill.: InterVarsity Press, 1973, p. 38.

9. Woodbridge, p. ix.

10. Nancy Barcus, *Developing a Christian Mind*. Downers Grove, Ill.: InterVarsity Press, 1977, pp. 16–17.

11. Douglas Moo, "Putting the Renewed Mind to Work," in Woodbridge, *Renewing Your Mind in a Secular World*. p. 150.

12. Barcus, p. 93.

13. Groothuis, p. 17.

14. Moo in Woodbridge, p. 158.

15. Woodbridge, p. 61.

16. Kate B. Wilkinson, 1925.

BIBLIOGRAPHY

Barcus, Nancy. *Developing a Christian Mind*. Downers Grove, Ill.: InterVarsity Press, 1977.

Blamires, Harry. *Where Do We Stand?* Ann Arbor, Mich.: Servant, 1980.

Davis, John. *Evangelical Ethics*. Philipsburg, N.J.: Presbyterian and Reformed, 1985.

Grounds, Vernon C. *Revolution and the Christian Faith*. Philadelphia: J.B. Lippincott Company, 1971.

Hoffecker, W. Andrew and Gary S. Smith, eds. *Building a Christian World View*, vol. 1. Philipsburg, N.J.: Presbyterian and Reformed Publishing Co., 1986.

Lockerbie, D. Bruce. *The Cosmic Center*. Grand Rapids: Eerdmans, 1977.

Schaeffer, Francis A. *How Shall We Then Live?* Old Tappan, N.J.: Revell, 1976.

Stott, John R.W. *Balanced Christianity*. Downers Grove, Ill.: InterVarsity Press, 1975.

————. *Your Mind Matters*. Downers Grove, Ill.: InterVarsity Press, 1972.

Strauss, Richard. *Win the Battle for Your Mind*. Wheaton, Ill.: Victor Books, 1980.

Woodbridge, John, ed. *Renewing Your Mind in a Secular World*. Chicago: Moody Press, 1985.

Zylstra, Henry. *Testament of Vision*. Grand Rapids: William B. Eerdmans Publishing Co., 1968.

6. AN EVALUATION
OF CONTEMPORARY LEARNING THEORIES
David L. Edwards

How should we define the essence of teaching? For many educators teaching qualifies as "science." There are facts to gather, concepts to clarify, principles to discover. The research tradition of the physical sciences which spawned first a better comprehension of fundamental principles and then led to improved technological application provides the necessary model. For advocates of the "teaching-as-science" approach, the classroom provides a laboratory for developing and implementing strategies grounded in empirical research.

Alternatively we could view teaching as an "art," noting that two teachers working with similar groups of students on comparable materials often experience very different results, even when using the same instructional methods. If there are such elusive factors involved, surely a better way to improve capability lies in observing the work of master craftsmen plying their pedagogic skill. Understanding instructional principles is of secondary import compared to the value of pragmatic effect. For supporters of "teaching-as-art," the classroom becomes a studio for perfecting of the teacher's unique tutorial skills.

Skinner distinguished between "the science of learning and the art of teaching." He labored throughout his career, however, to demonstrate how teaching could become more "scientific" and encouraged the use of instructional technology as the means to improving student achievement.[1] More accurately, teaching might be described as a craft that requires artistry in practice, grounded on a solid scientific base.[2] Life in the classroom becomes a continuing challenge to utilize the findings of research, but apply them creatively to the specific demands of each unique teaching-learning context.

In this chapter we want to examine in overview what research has disclosed about the learning process and how we can use this understanding to improve classroom instruction. Recognizing that all research involves assumptions and interpretation, the Christian teacher must seek always to assess the findings of scientific studies against the declarations of Scripture. Perhaps it will help if we understand how theories develop.

LEARNING THEORIES

According to one standard definition, a theory consists of:

> A set of interrelated constructs, definitions, and propositions that present a systematic view of phenomena by specifying relations among variables with the purpose of explaining and predicting the phenomena.[3]

Theory development begins with a question. With learning theories, that question concerns how the human mind acquires and retains knowledge. From available data a researcher formulates a possible explanation or hypothesis; experimental testing is devised to either substantiate or deny the validity of the hypothesis. If repeated studies provide additional confirmation, this conceptual answer to the research question gains strength, and eventually may take on stature as an accepted theory. The quality of any learning theory depends ultimately on its ability to (1) provide explanations for what occurs during the learning process, and (2) predict which instructional practices most effectively enhance the acquisition of knowledge.

Over the course of several decades a number of learning theories have been proposed, each with its set of assumed "constructs, definitions, and propositions." Some have enjoyed only temporary acceptance while others have endured and continue to influence educational practice and policy to some degree. In reviewing them, our attention will focus on identifying the premises which underlie the theory as well as the experimental evidence offered in its support. At the risk of oversimplifying issues, we consider two fundamental elements in learning theory directing special attention to the extremes of what is really a continuum of possible variations.

PERSONAL DEVELOPMENT.

"Learning" occurs internally, but its effects are evidenced in external behaviors. More specifically changes in the way an individual acts are taken as evidence of changed understanding. In Hilgard's classic definition, "Learning refers to the change in a subject's behavior potential to a given situation brought about by the subject's repeated experiences in that situation . . . [which] cannot be explained on the basis of . . . native response tendencies, maturation or temporary states (such as fatigue, etc.)."[4] The development of an individual from infancy to maturity is thus seen as the consequence of progressive learning.

The relative strength of *external* and *internal* forces as influences on personal growth represents one major dichotomy in learning theory. Is individual behavior a consequence of environment and experiences, or does human development follow some common inherent pattern? Is learning essentially a process of molding and shaping, or do children merely "unfold" in time, developing capacities independent of outside influences? Both possibilities draw adherents quick to adduce the evidences of science. We look first at these two alternatives.

Behaviorism received a major impetus from the studies of Edward L. Thorndike near the end of the nineteenth century. Based on extensive studies with animals, Thorndike interpreted learning as an acquired ability to form relatively permanent connections between discrete events in one's experience. Animals confined in cages were required to perform specific actions, which they discovered by trial-and error, to escape. Repeated trials on the same problem took less time, suggesting that the animals had learned to connect an appropriate response (action) to the initiating stimulus (confinement).[5]

Thorndike's "laws of learning" represented an early attempt to relate research findings to educational practice. His "Law of Exercise" encouraged teachers to use drill exercises to strengthen learning, since repetition of an activity increases the probability of eliciting the desired response in the future. His "Law of Effect" proved even more influential: linking achievement to the relative satisfaction experienced by the learner, suggesting that reward and motivation are essential to learning. Most significantly Thorndike's studies lent support to the belief that learning works from the outside in, that external stimuli prevail.

Still more support derived from the well-known studies of the Russian physiologist Ivan Pavlov who demonstrated that even instinctive behavior patterns could be modified through training. The principles of "conditioning" seemed to provide an explanation for the process of learning, a process applicable across the boundaries of species. Potentially, if human development is but a product of environment, then any child could achieve anything. Watson summarized his euphoric expectations this way:

> Give me a dozen healthy infants, well-formed, and my own specified world to bring them up in, and I will guarantee to take any one of them at random and train him to become any type of specialist I might select—doctor, lawyer, artist, merchant, chief, and yes, even beggar man and thief, regardless of his talents, penchants, tendencies, abilities, vocations, and race of his ancestors.[6]

The behaviorist thus anchors one end of a continuum with his reliance on external forces as the predominant influence in human development.

From birth onward, learning is a continual component of maturation. Infants learn to recognize sights and sounds, and later to walk and talk. Social mores are assimilated, basic skills developed; formally organized or informally achieved, learning continues. If behaviorism is correct, we would anticipate considerable variation in the sequence and rate at which these new behaviors appear. Reflecting their particular experiences, children from diverse backgrounds should exhibit highly individual patterns of developmental maturation. Comparative studies of children, however, demonstrate relatively minor differences attributable to culture, race, home environment, and other external factors.

Clinical observations compiled by Arnold Gesell[7] and others at Yale led to the publication of behavioral norms describing remarkable consistency in patterns of mental, social, and physical growth. External influences varied greatly; thus Gesell theorized the existence of some common internal factor to guide the developmental process and effectually limit the impact of environmental diversity. Maturation might be compared to the unfolding of a flower according to some inherent timetable. According to this view, learning demands, in addition to effective instructional technique, the appropriate level of individual readiness.

Between the extreme positions of the behaviorist and his developmentalist counterpart an array of intermediary concepts have been proposed. Most contemporary theories attempt to accommodate the findings of both sides, synthesizing the evidence into learning approaches accounting for both internal and external factors. It is important for our purpose simply to note the tension that exists.

ACQUISITION OF KNOWLEDGE.

The operative mandate in all education is the transmission of information from teacher to learner. But learning theories diverge not only in their conception of "how": the nature of knowledge itself is an issue. As indicated in Figure 1, a second dimension to our continuum is necessary, a dimension describing how knowledge is acquired. At one end we will locate the premise that learning incorporates existing knowledge into the individual from the outside. Call this the "infused model." At the other pole resides the conviction that significant learning is actually "created" within the learner. Denote this alternative as the "devised model."

Knowledge infused. The work of B.F. Skinner applies behaviorism to classroom practice. More specifically his intent was to transfer the principles of classical conditioning studies, like those of Pavlov, to applications affecting human learning. Pavlov effectively altered instinc-

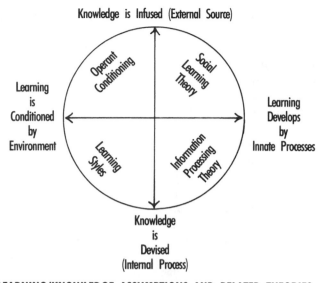

LEARNING/KNOWLEDGE ASSUMPTIONS AND RELATED THEORIES

Figure 1

tive behavioral traits; would the same techniques work in helping people learn or adapt information? *Operant conditioning* theory advances
from the premise that they do.

In operant conditioning the researcher (or teacher) will not
know in advance precisely how a learner will respond to a particular
stimulus. But when the desired behavior is observed among a variety of
"operants" (random responses), the teacher can reinforce that response
by manipulating its consequences. Subjects responding in the desired
way receive a reward ("positive reinforcement"), increasing the probability of similar behavior when presented again with the same stimulus.
Skinner devised reinforcement schedules to maximize formation of links
between the stimulus and the learner's operant response.

Classroom application requires that a teacher identify and develop a repertoire of rewards attractive to students, things like verbal
praise, token awards, even candy or treats. When a student reacts to an
initiating stimulus with an appropriate response, as in giving a correct
answer or handling provocation on the playground without retaliation,
that behavior is reinforced *immediately*. A teacher may also influence
learning through "negative reinforcement," not punishment, but the
removal of an unpleasant condition as a consequence of good behavior.
A class might, for example, be allowed a time of physical activity following a period of intense, productive seat-work.

Punishment also has an effect on behavior. Many conditioning

91

theorists deplored the use of intentionally hurtful responses by an adult to children's misconduct as "inhumane." Application of unpleasant consequences in some research studies appeared less effective than reinforcement techniques in producing durable behavioral change. More recent studies would suggest that under appropriate conditions punishment can be very effective.[8] Alternatively, punishment *removes* something desirable when a student misbehaves; teachers invoke this type of punishment when they keep a child in from recess to complete a homework assignment. Figure 2 illustrates the relationship among reinforcement and punishment modes.

Operant conditioning also offered theoretical support for programmed instructional techniques. Skinner's advocacy of teaching machines assumed that students receiving immediate feedback on their answers should achieve faster and more permanent gains. Early studies failed to demonstrate consistent benefits for programmed learning; however, computer-assisted instructional techniques show considerable promise, and function from similar assumptions about shaping behavior through motivation and feedback.

Learning through conditioning requires time, time for exploratory activities, time for teacher recognition and response, time for reinforcement to induce enduring behavioral effect. Experience suggests that some learning occurs more quickly, even instantly, in a "no-

Figure 2
REINFORCEMENT AND PUNISHMENT

		Attractiveness of the Response to the Student(s)	
		Positively Valued	Negatively Valued
What Happens in Response to the Student's Behavior	Something Presented	Positive Reinforcement (Praise rewards, tokens)	Punishment I (Spanking, scolding)
	Something Removed	Punishment II (Loss of privilege, "time-out" techniques)	Negative Reinforcement (Changed environment)

trials" fashion not explicable by Skinnerian theory. Albert Bandura's proposal focused on the social impact of instructional groups: both practice and reinforcement might be achieved vicariously as well as personally. Social learning theory suggests a four-step sequence. To profit from instructor demonstration or peer example the learner must: (1) pay attention to a stimulus, such as a command or instruction, and the appropriate response by a model; (2) encode and retain the pertinent cues in memory; (3) accurately reproduce the desired action when the stimulus is repeated; and (4) be motivated to carry through all the steps.[9] Social learning represents another approach to the transmission of knowledge from outside into the mind of the learner.

Knowledge devised. The conclusions of Pavlov's research which defined learning as the formation of stimulus-response links did not long remain unchallenged. In his own studies with primates Kohler observed instances where the animals solved problems without resorting to random activity. Instead they seemed able to reason through the task. Kohler interpreted this capacity for insight as evidence for the mind's direct participation in the learning process.[10] When several pieces of data were mentally integrated into a coherent whole, the solution emerged; learning was achieved.

Adherents of *Gestalt* theory, from the German for "pattern" or "form," offer no simple mechanisms. Learning involves complex processing of a multitude of sensory data in order to produce a clear conception of reality. Recollections of past events could be stored as memory traces and later retrieved like items from a file. These memories might either assist or inhibit the formation of accurate insights. The educational tasks of teachers grew more complicated and less amenable to control. How is it possible to plan instruction effectively if learning depends largely on internal processes, probably unique to each individual student?

The descriptive work of Swiss psychologist Jean Piaget provides some insight. Based on decades of personal observations meticulously recorded and analyzed, Piaget concluded that learning capacity in children develops in sequential stages roughly paralleling chronological age.[11] The stages are approximately constant for all children, essentially unaffected by culture or experience. Each of the four (or five) stages represents a discrete step toward cognitive maturity. The ability to organize and structure information during infancy is limited but the acquisition of language leads to expanding capacity for complexity. Use of all the power of human reasoning is typically attained by adolescence (see Fig. 3).

According to Piaget's theoretical model, the human mind functions by forming *schema* or networks of knowledge. Learning occurs as these schema are built and extended by two fundamental processes.

93

Figure 3
PIAGET'S STAGES OF COGNITIVE DEVELOPMENT

Stage	Approximate Age	Characterized By . . .
Sensorimotor	Birth–2 yrs.	Simple perceptual and motor skills: progresses from simple reflexive actions to more organized activity
Preoperational: Preop'l phase	2–4 yrs.	Uses language to aid in concept development; learning to classify and categorize
Intuitive phase	4–6 yrs.	Forms conclusions from general impressions; less dependent on language to form concepts
Concrete operational	7–11 yrs.	Uses logic related to manipulation of concrete objects; can visualize or imagine results
Formal operational	11–14 yrs.	Capable of abstractions and propositional thinking; can handle deductive as well as inductive reasoning

Assimilation fixes new information within existing schema. A youngster may, for instance, form a schema for "kitten" based on experience with a household pet. Other animals are frequently called "kitten" because of superficial similarities: four legs, fur, a tail. Eventual realization that all furry four-legged creatures with tails are not identical with the criteria for "kitten" triggers *accomodation.* Now a new and larger schema develops, perhaps one for "animals"; "kitten" becomes one subschema along with those for "dog" and "squirrel." Knowledge has been acquired as a primary correlate of mental processing, organizing, and structuring, rather than by transmission intact from the environment.

Brain research. As a correlate to learning theory, investigations designed to extend our comprehension of the human brain and its role in learning require some attention. Several million nerve cells, or neurons, comprise this remarkable organ. Neurons, all essentially alike, are grouped into several substructures of the brain, each having a distinct function. Largest of these segments is the *cortex,* the locale of memory and where most intentional cognitive learning occurs. The cortex itself consists of two sections separated by a central fissure running from front to back. The two halves, or hemispheres, process knowledge dif-

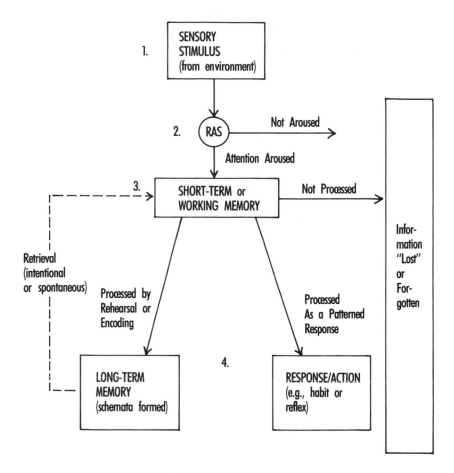

Figure 4
A MODEL FOR MEMORY FUNCTION (COGNITIVE PROCESSING)

ferently. The left hemisphere "thinks" logically, analytically, and sequentially; handles language and symbols effectively; it functions within a temporal context. The right hemisphere, by contrast, thinks experientially, synthetically, and artistically; deals with images and pictures; it creates and intuits.

Unless damaged, the two hemispheres readily exchange information. People tend, however, to demonstrate hemispheric preferences for mental processing just as they develop right- or left-handedness in physical pursuits.[12] Such preferences appear as differential aptitudes. Relative facility in reading and math skills characterizes the left-brained person while right brain dominance reflects in artistic or musical proficiency or in getting correct answers without understanding the process.

Memory, according to brain research, emerges as considerably more complex than the mere retention of stimuli. "Remembering" occurs not as a single event but the net result of a sequential system as outlined in Figure 4. Of all the external stimuli impacting our senses each moment, only a fraction actually engage our conscious attention. This discriminatory function belongs to another neural structure, the *reticular activating system* or RAS. Sensory impressions passing through the RAS filter enter short-term memory.

Short-term memory, limited in both duration and capacity, may evoke a reflexive physical response if required, or pass the information into long-term memory. Irrelevant data can be discarded. Short-term memory serves as a mental worktable for sorting incoming sensations, holding perhaps a dozen bits of information or less for only a few seconds. For the learner to retain instruction, the sensory stimulus must, therefore, (1) arouse attention; (2) pass from short-term to long-term memory; (3) engage one or more mental schema for effective retrieval. By implication teaching method and context of presentation strongly influence both memory and hemispheric processing.[13]

DEVELOPING A BIBLICAL PERSPECTIVE

A teacher committed to biblical orientation for life and ministry assumes a perpetual obligation to the integrity of truth. God as the ultimate Source of all truth has endowed the created universe with intimations of that truth, and the operation of common grace enables fallible and even unregenerate men to disclose elements of that truth. For that reason Christians must not arbitrarily dismiss the possibility of valid conclusions emerging from empirical studies of human behavior. The believer also comprehends that truth is more explicitly declared in Scripture; consistency demands that truth from general revelation be conformed to that provided through special revelation.

In seeking to integrate truth we must avoid two equally peril-ous tendencies. The first is to assume "nothing-but" Scripture as a guide to forming a coherent approach to educating. The Bible speaks often and strongly about the compelling role of teaching in bringing people to faith and spiritual maturity, but is largely silent concerning effective methods. An opposite danger lies in unquestioned acceptance of scien-tific findings without examining them in the light of biblical truth. Since we have devoted considerable attention to the verdicts of behavioral science, we turn now to address the scriptural elements.

Speaking of Christian teaching, Mark Fakkema urged primary focus on what he termed the "three foundation stones" of a biblical orientation to education: creation, sin, and salvation.[14] Each of these fundamental doctrines contributes to an overall conception of learning theory from a biblical perspective.

Man, throughout the biblical record, is presented not as the product of random evolutionary forces but of direct creation by divine intent. The earliest chapters of Scripture explicitly refer to man's like-ness to God (Gen. 1:26), a semblance that includes both spirituality and rationality with capacity to think, know, and will. The mind of man finitely reflects the infinite mind of God, but in that reflection resides the *implication* that the human mind transcends potentially the physi-cal plane of nonrational creation.

The conception of man's mind as a mere appendage to his body is incompatible with the tenet of creation in God's image. We reject categorically Watson's apt summary of his own position: "The behaviorist recognizes no dividing line between man and brute . . . [he] finds no mind in his laboratory, sees it nowhere in his subjects."

The Apostle Paul by contrast emphasizes the essential agency of the mind in spiritual transformation (Rom. 12:2) and consequently in-vests the teaching duty of the church with priority.

Sin represents an inescapable reality since the Fall, a reality which negatively impacts the mental as well as the spiritual capacity of man. This inherent imperfection affects knowledge both in its acquisi-tion and its retention, and most particularly with respect to the knowl-edge of God (1 Cor. 2:14-16). The prime directive in Christian educa-tion necessarily addresses evangelism before nurture: salvation precedes spiritual understanding. Apart from God's grace in redemption and the restorative work of the Holy Spirit, any capacity for perceiving truth remains impaired.

What are some biblical implications for learning theory? First, the integrity of human personality reminds us that man is not mind *or* body, flesh *or* spirit, but a unified being. That the learning process enables both physical and nonphysical dimensions is clearly implied by scriptural emphasis on this unity. Detailed disclosure of that process is not a priority for revelation, however, a model of mind informed solely by reaction to external stimuli correlates poorly with man's creation bearing the image of a self-existent God. Scriptural references to teaching and training imply gradual development: several passages emphasize progressive capacity to learn and profit from instruction (e.g., Deut. 6:5-8; Luke 2:52; 1 Cor. 13:11). Finally, we recognize the legitimate role of reward and punishment in training, a role that Proverbs makes fundamental to effective discipline and training.

None of the learning theories we have discussed claims any special merit of orthodoxy when subjected to the light of biblical scrutiny. Those elements of truth in each are admixed with assumptions and implications inconsistent with biblical revelation. The Christian educator must maintain constant vigil in order to sift wheat from chaff. But learning theories do contribute to the science orientation of the teaching craft; in the artistic implementation thereof rests instructional effectiveness.

INSTRUCTIONAL IMPLICATIONS FROM LEARNING THEORIES

Learning and teaching are not identical: either can occur independently of the other and frequently does. A teacher's approach to instruction will reflect in great measure, however, his conception of the functioning of the human mind. Especially where the instructional purpose is to incorporate truth issuing from God's self-revelation, we require effective instructional methods to encourage learning.

All methods are not equivalently effective for all teachers: part of the artistry in teaching lies in discovering those strategies most appropriate to a specific context of teacher, student, and lesson. Instructional intent, physical environment, resources—these and many other factors enter into the decision to use a particular teaching approach. Some research-based suggestions follow.

TASK ANALYSIS.

Early attempts to discover the mechanisms of learning were frequently frustrated by a fixation on finding the one way to teach. Whether the task was learning to tie one's shoe, solve word problems in arithmetic, or write a collegiate term paper, educators assumed that "how" was largely independent of "what."

Gagné found that different instructional methods should be invoked according to the demands of varied learning challenges.[15] He categorized distinct purposes common to educational endeavors: clarifying desired outcomes should help in the choice of effective methods. He listed five distinct "varieties of learned capabilities," summarizing purposes for which teachers provide instruction:

1. to impart basic intellectual skills ("procedural knowledge"),
2. to extend verbal information ("declarative knowledge"),
3. to facilitate development of cognitive strategies,
4. to develop attitudes,
5. to enhance physical motor skills.

From clarified objectives teachers can better select teaching strategies.

Cognitive learning, encompassing the first three varieties in the list, comprise a hierarchy. At the lowest level, students acquire information by processes akin to classical conditioning. Following directions and learning the names of letters and numerals represent what Gagné calls "signal learning" in which specific stimulus-response associations form between the visual or aural cue and a specific behavior. Combining or "chaining" several simple actions represents the next level; the result may be either a verbal chain, linking words, or a procedural chain of sequential actions to perform. Reciting the pledge of allegiance and following a set of instructions to start a car involve chaining. For these simpler tasks teachers find elements of behaviorism, such as drill and reinforcement techniques, appropriate.

Much school learning involves more complex demands. Students must be able to classify groups of items or facts; form concepts; deduce rules to link concepts; and apply these rules to solve problems or evaluate issues. Use of demonstration and similar elements of social learning theory may prove effective, and students may begin to initiate their own strategies for achievement.

MEANINGFUL LEARNING.

Learning theorists often disparage instruction aimed at direct impartation of knowledge. This aversion to "telling as teaching" has empirical grounding; studies indicate material learned by rote is quickly forgotten.[16] David Ausubel's theory of verbal learning suggests, however, that retention improves when material becomes meaningful to the learner.[17] Ausubel's strategy stresses the use of "advance organizers" to enhance meaning. Advance organizers consist of information provided in advance of a lesson to help students store and retrieve learned material. This preliminary information might include definitions for concepts and terms in the lesson; analogies, anecdotes, or clarifying visual devices; or generalizations to provide a framework for the detail which follows. Ausubel's strategies implement the cognitive developmental approach of Piaget's theory: advance organizers facilitate both assimilation and accommodation of lesson content. In Ausubel's words:

> If I had to reduce all of educational psychology to just one principle, I would say this: the most important single factor influencing learning is what the learner already knows. Ascertain this and teach him accordingly.[18]

99

LEARNING STYLES.

Brain research reinforces the fact that learning is a highly individualized activity. Each of us develops certain unique strategies for incorporating knowledge, strategies that reflect innate tendencies, experience, and perhaps the ways in which instruction has been received in the past. The inclusive term "learning styles" encompasses a variety of approaches each purposing to make instruction more effective by matching it to the specific ways different students learn.

Learning typically requires passage of information from the environment through one of the five senses; people differ markedly in relative sense perception ability. Some studies indicate that younger students, in particular, evidence strong sensory "modalities." Among elementary school pupils an estimated 30 percent performed better with visual input, while 25 percent have auditory strengths. Fifteen percent, those demonstrating kinesthetic preference (learning by touching), need special attention in most look-talk dominated classes. The remaining 30 percent evidenced no clear modality, and probably function well with many kinds of sensations.[19]

Learning style research has also considered impact of physical environment on student achievement. That discomfort detracts from attention is no revelation. What recent research discloses is that discomfort is not always specific: students tend to be differentially affected by the levels of light and sound in a room, temperature, even time of day. Preferences in social context (learning alone vs. learning in groups) also vary. Effective teachers seek to recognize and cooperate with the variety of personal tendencies present in each class.[20]

CONCLUSIONS

Teaching methods derive from convictions about the nature of human mentality. To understand what behavioral research discloses represents one vital component of good pedagogy. Effective teachers incorporate significant learning principles in the artistry of their ministry. But in deciding what to teach as well as how to teach it the Christian teacher relies on a biblical perception of human personality. Empirically derived theories become appropriate only as the teacher applies their constructs within an integrated philosophy of teaching.

The demands of Christian teaching never prove easy. Our sacred mandates of evangelism and discipleship demand that use of maximally effective methods. Maturity in this profession is evidenced by increasing ability to devise instruction that facilitates the learning process cooperating with the creative uniqueness with which God invested each student. This is essentially the art of teaching.

ENDNOTES

1. B.F. Skinner, "The Science of Learning and the Art of Teaching." *Harvard Educational Review,* 24 (2), 1954. pp. 86–97.

2. N.L. Gage, *The Scientific Basis of the Art of Teaching.* New York: Teachers College Press, 1978.

3. Fred N. Kerlinger, *Foundations of Behavioral Research,* 2d ed. New York: Holt, Rinehart & Winston, 1973, p. 9.

4. Gordon H. Bower and Ernest R. Hilgard, *Theories of Learning,* 5th ed. Englewood Cliffs, N.J.: Prentice-Hall, 1981, p. 11.

5. Edward L. Thorndike, *Experimental Study of the Associative Process* (Doctoral dissertation, 1898).

6. John B. Watson, *Behaviorism.* Chicago: University of Chicago Press, 1925, p. 82.

7. Arnold Gesell and Frances L. Ilg, *Infant and Child in the Culture of Today.* New York: Harper, 1943.

8. N.L. Gage and David C. Berliner, *Educational Psychology,* 3rd ed. Boston: Houghton Mifflin, 1984, pp. 290–93.

9. Albert Bandura, *Social Learning Theory.* Englewood Cliffs, N.J.: Prentice-Hall, 1977.

10. Wolfgang Kohler, *The Mentality of Apes.* New York: Harcourt, Brace & World, 1925.

11. Bärbel Inhelder and Jean Piaget, *The Growth of Logical Thinking from Childhood to Adolescence.* New York: Basic Books, 1958.

12. R.H. Bailey, *Human Behavior: The Role of the Brain.* New York: Time-Life Books, 1975.

13. Ellen D. Gagne, *The Cognitive Psychology of School Learning.* Boston: Little, Brown and Co., 1985.

14. Mark Fakkema, *Christian Philosophy: Its Educational Implications.* Chicago: National Union of Christian Schools, 1952.

15. Robert M. Gagné, *The Conditions of Learning and Theory of Instruction,* 4th ed. New York: Holt, Rinehart & Winston, 1985.

16. Gage and Berliner, pp. 305–09.

17. Paul D. Eggen, Donald P. Kandiak, and Robert J. Harder, *Strategies for Teachers: Information Processing Models in the Classroom.* Englewood Cliffs, N.J.: Prentice-Hall, Inc., 1979, p. 277.

18. David P. Ausubel, Joseph D. Novak, and Helen Hanesian, *Educational Psychology: A Cognitive View,* 2nd ed. New York: Holt, Rinehart & Winston, 1978, p. 163.

19. Walter B. Barbe, R.H. Swassing, and Michael N. Milone, Jr., *Teaching through Modality of Strengths: Concepts and Practices.* Columbus, Ohio: Zaner-Bloser, 1979.

20. See James W. Keefe, ed., *Students Learning Styles: Diagnosing and Pre-*

scribing Programs. Reston, Va.: National Association of Secondary School Principals, 1979; or Claudia E. Cornett, *What You Should Know about Teaching and Learning Styles*, Bloomington, Ind.: Phi Delta Kappa Educational Foundation, 1983.

BIBLIOGRAPHY

Ausubel, David P., Joseph D. Novak, and Helen Hanesian. *Educational Psychology: A Cognitive View,* 2nd ed. New York: Holt, Rinehart & Winston, 1978.

Barlow, Daniel L. *Educational Psychology: The Teaching-Learning Process.* Chicago: Moody Press, 1985.

Beechick, Ruth. *A Biblical Psychology of Learning.* Denver: Accent Books, 1982.

Boivin, Michael J. "Behavioral Psychology: What Does it Have to Offer the Christian Church?" *Journal of the American Scientific Affiliation 37* (June 1985).

Bruner, Jerome. *Toward a Theory of Instruction.* Cambridge, Mass.: Harvard University Press, 1966.

Carter, John D. and Bruce Narramore. *The Integration of Psychology and Theology: An Introduction.* Grand Rapids: Zondervan Publishing Co., 1979.

DeJong, Norman, ed. *Christian Approaches to Learning Theory: A Symposium.* New York: University Press of America, 1984.

Dunn, Rita. *Teaching Students through Their Individual Learning Styles: A Practical Approach.* Reston, Va.: Reston Publishing Co., 1979.

Eggen, Paul D., Donald P. Kandrak, and Robert J. Harder. *Strategies for Teachers: Information Processing Models in the Classroom.* Englewood Cliffs, N.J.: Prentice-Hall, 1979.

Gagné, Robert M. *The Conditions of Learning.* New York: Holt, Rinehart & Winston, 1965.

Kilpatrick, William K. *Psychological Seduction: The Failure of Modern Psychology.* Nashville: Thomas Nelson, 1983.

Mager, Robert F. *Developing Attitude toward Learning.* Palo Alto, Calif.: Fearon Publishers, 1968.

Novak, Joseph D. and D. Bob Gowin. *Learning How to Learn.* Cambridge, Mass.: Cambridge University Press, 1984.

Piaget, Jean and Bärbel Inhelder. *Memory and Intelligence.* New York: Basic Books, 1973.

Wlodkowski, Raymond J. *Motivation and Teaching: A Practical Guide.* Washington, D.C.: National Education Association, 1978.

Part Two

PATTERNS AND PROCESS
of Christian Teaching

7. TEACHING CHILDREN
Robert Joseph Choun, Jr.

INTRODUCTION

The Scriptures mandate the teaching of God's children.[1] Today's children will become the parents of tomorrow and the leaders of the church in the twenty-first century. Consider the words of three educators who feel strongly about children's ministry. Reading what they have to say is both challenging and stimulating to us as we prepare to teach children.

> As we approach the end of the twentieth century, I see a greater emphasis being placed on the importance of children and their education by both secular and Christian leaders. Parents demand excellence for their children in the church and the school. I also see a great importance in the strengthening of the home, the basic unit for Christian education. At our church we feel that it is much better to "build" a child correctly than to "repair" a man later on.[2]

> I've read a statistic published by Campus Crusade for Christ which says that 85 percent of all believers trusted Jesus Christ before the age of 18. At our church our goal is to train children to become a part of the body of Christ. Our desire is to see each child trust Jesus Christ as Savior and Lord and grow in Him, bearing fruit that will lead him to teach others (2 Tim. 2:2).[3]

> The Bible gives parents the responsibility of teaching their children (Deut. 6:4-9; Ps. 78). The church must assist in this task by training parents in what to do and how to do it. Placing them in the Sunday School classroom is one excellent way to equip

105

them for the ministry at home. We find that parents will give their time, talents, and finances to sports programs, day care centers, and leisure activities. Are they willing to invest these same resources in their family? It is a high calling![4]

In considering the scriptural mandate and our three pastoral interviews, the question arises, "How can I effectively teach children in a God-pleasing way?" There is a plan which can help teachers and parents to accomplish this task.

THE EDUCATIONAL CYCLE FOR TEACHING CHILDREN
The educational cycle provides direction by which an effective teaching ministry can be planned and programmed.[5]

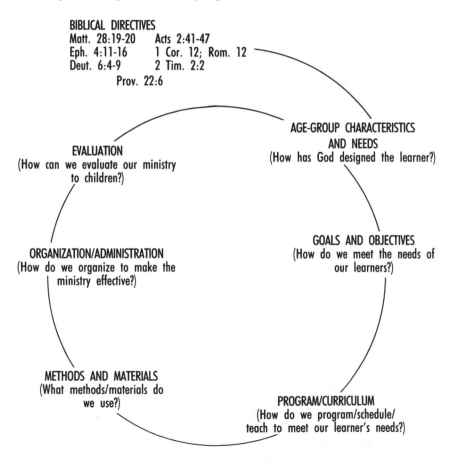

BIBLICAL DIRECTIVES
Matt. 28:19-20   Acts 2:41-47
Eph. 4:11-16   1 Cor. 12; Rom. 12
Deut. 6:4-9   2 Tim. 2:2
        Prov. 22:6

EVALUATION
(How can we evaluate our ministry to children?)

AGE-GROUP CHARACTERISTICS AND NEEDS
(How has God designed the learner?)

ORGANIZATION/ADMINISTRATION
(How do we organize to make the ministry effective?)

GOALS AND OBJECTIVES
(How do we meet the needs of our learners?)

METHODS AND MATERIALS
(What methods/materials do we use?)

PROGRAM/CURRICULUM
(How do we program/schedule/teach to meet our learner's needs?)

BIBLICAL DIRECTIVES

God's revelation demands a response from each of His children. What is Scripture telling us to do in our children's ministry?

MATTHEW 28:19-20: The imperative in this passage is clearly to "make disciples." As we go, we are to teach all people—children included—the Word of God. The implications from this passage are (a) evangelism (sharing the Good News with all people) and (b) discipleship (helping each person grow in Jesus Christ to become a disciple-maker). This can be done effectively with children if they are nurtured in the correct way.

DEUTERONOMY 6:4-9: Moses commanded parents (a) to teach the Word of God diligently to their children (b) in a very casual and natural way, (c) using their lifestyle as the main method. This guided conversation will help nurture each child as well as present a model of a godly adult.

PROVERBS 22:6: This short proverb or truism gives us a brief insight into teaching children. Teachers of children should desire to (a) "train up"—create a taste or desire in the child for the things of God; (b) "in the way"—according to his way. Instruction should take into account his individuality and his mental and physical development. (c) "He will not depart"—if the child has been correctly nurtured in the things of God his eventual desire will be to cling to them. An expanded version of this proverb might look like this: "Dedicate to the Lord and create a taste for the things of the Lord in a child in accordance with his age-level; and even when he becomes mature he will not depart from his spiritual training."

ACTS 2:41-47: This is a brief account of the coming of the Holy Spirit and the beginnings of the church. We can see the results of Pentecost in four major factors operative in the life of that New Testament community: (a) Worship—the believers prayed, broke bread together, sang, and worshiped their Lord. (b) Instruction—the believers devoted themselves to the apostles' teaching. (c) Fellowship—the believers fellowshiped with one another for the purpose of spreading the Gospel message. (d) Expression—the believers expressed themselves to the body of Christ through edification and encouragement and to the world through evangelism. These four ingredients should be included in a children's ministry.

EPHESIANS 4:11-16; 1 CORINTHIANS 12; ROMANS 12: These three references reveal God's methods for implementing the ministry to children—through the gifts of the Holy Spirit.

In Ephesians 4:11-16, we learn Christ has given His church those who teach, evangelize, and pastor. He bestowed them for the purpose of the unity of believers, maturity of the body, and conformity to Himself. These leaders equip the saints to do the work of the ministry—including ministering to children in the home, church, and school!

First Corinthians 12 and Romans 12 show us that it is not enough to seek and find the lost. They must also be tended, fed, and led into becoming mature Christians. Where do we get the resources? These two passages give us the answers. The Holy Spirit empowers God's people to minister—helping develop others into Christlikeness.

2 TIMOTHY 2:2: Paul describes the ministry of multiplication that must take place during each generation so that the Christian faith will be taught until Jesus comes again. Christian leaders must equip teachers and parents in every facet of children's ministry so that correct teaching will take place on the level of each learner. Thus, the cycle of evangelism will be complete—the disciple now becomes the disciple-maker.

AGE-GROUP NEEDS AND CHARACTERISTICS
How has God designed the child?

Ministry to children demands an understanding of age-level characteristics and needs. How did God design the child? What are our children like? Luke 2:52 reveals that Jesus grew in wisdom (intellectually); and stature (physically); and in favor with God (spiritually); and with man (socially and emotionally). The following age-level characteristics describe early childhood (birth to five years) and childhood (grades 1 through 6). Remember that these represent typical characteristics and needs. Children develop at different rates in different areas and must always be treated as individuals.

BIRTH-ONE-,
TWO-, AND THREE-YEAR-OLDS[6]

CHARACTERISTICS		NEEDS

PHYSICAL

1. Continually active.	1. Opportunity & space for activity.
2. Hungry senses.	2. Use materials which child can see, hear, touch, smell, taste.
3. Spontaneous, impulsive reaction.	3. Interest centers. Use all five senses.
4. Sensitive nervous system.	4. Avoid all causes of hurry & strain—calm & unhurried program.
5. Health frail, endurance limited.	5. Good health conditions, periods of rest and refreshments.
6. Difference in maturation.	6. Program geared to individuals.
7. Small muscles not coordinated.	7. Utilize large muscles—crayons, paper, etc.
8. Shorter legs in proportion to body—about 2 ft. tall.	8. Size chairs—play toys, etc., within reach.

MENTAL

1. Love for repetition & routine.	1. Use familiar.
2. Imaginative & suggestible.	2. Use stories, suggest ways & means.
3. Narrow experience, concrete conceptions, literal-minded.	3. Broaden experience, avoid abstractions & symbolism.
4. Limited knowledge & vocabulary.	4. Use objects, pictures frequently, use child's adopted vocabulary.
5. Undeveloped musical ability.	5. Program of music.
6. Short attention span (2 ½-3 min.)	6. Varied program of activities.
7. Unreliable memory.	7. Repeat essentials often—simple statements of directions.
8. Curiosity.	8. Provide materials to arouse.
9. Asks innumerable questions	9. Answer questions simply—avoid detailed explanations.

SOCIAL	1. Individualistic & self-centered.	1. Give individual care, provide time for free play, develop social consciousness.
	2. Dependent & demand attention.	2. Child needs constant watching, recognition of fact that child is *not* responsible.
	3. Imitative.	3. Proper examples of conduct, importance of attitude, consistency of life and word.
	4. Negativistic, eager to please "No" learned first.	4. Positive, acceptance of his activity, some conformity, recognition of contribution. (Don't ask—but *TELL!*)
	5. Strong play interests.	5. Furnish room with equipment for meaningful play.
EMOTIONAL AND SPIRITUAL	1. Timid & emotionally sensitive.	1. Create permissive & secure atmosphere.
	2. Affectionate.	2. Direct to the Lord, develop a consciousness of God & His love for them.
	3. Awakening spiritually, natural trust.	3. Individual feeding, place trust in a Person.
	4. Capable of worship.	4. Direct to the Lord, never underestimate ability.
	5. Filled with awe & wonder.	5. Arouse the sensory experiences, appreciate color & beauty, develop prayer habits.
	6. Fearful.	6. Counteract with concept of the protecting God; stories of children who have overcome fear.
	7. Sensitivity to spiritual atmosphere.	7. Calm, Christlike atmosphere, sensitivity to their needs & responses.
	8. Plastic, impressionable, teachable.	8. Tell truth, teach nothing which has to be unlearned.
	9. Growing sense of right & wrong.	9. Distinguish between right & wrong, reward right, standards set by God.

FOUR-, FIVE-, AND SIX-YEAR-OLDS

	CHARACTERISTICS	NEEDS
PHYSICAL	1. Rapid growth, extreme activity.	1. Constant change, alternate program of activity and rest.
	2. Small muscles, motor skills incompletely developed.	2. Provide large, sturdy, creative materials, paints, crayons, clay, etc. Sufficient room.
	3. Learning health habits, growing responsibility for self.	3. Challenge with Christian responsibility. Don't baby, assist.
	4. Health delicate, fatigued easily, eyes & ears easily strained, susceptible to disease.	4. No strain or overstimulation. Sanitary conditions. Precautions: isolate by inspection. Explain health standards to mothers.
	5. Active sensory processes.	5. Large, durable pictures. Firsthand experiences. Opportunity to learn by seeing and doing things.
	6. Spontaneous motor reactions.	6. Direct activity; do not repress it.
MENTAL	1. Short interest span (5–10 min.)	1. Keep in mind when planning games, stories, programs, etc.
	2. Mental immaturity, wants to do more than is capable of, vocabulary small but rapidly increasing.	2. Furnish things to do that they are able to understand. Explain slowly & clearly. Clarify understanding. Simple, clear routine. Limited choices.
	3. Inquisitive, asks countless questions for information, initial thinking challenged.	3. Answer *all* questions honestly. Seek reasons behind questions. Encourage them to think for themselves.
	4. Limited concepts of space & time. "Eternal now."	4. Refrain from referring to history or chronology. Emphasize present. Explain in terms of known. Increase their experience.
	5. Thinking is concrete & literal. Making mental pictures of things.	5. Use concrete terms. Avoid symbolism.
	6. Highly imaginative.	6. Encourage imagination as essential. Distinguish between fact & fantasy.

SOCIAL

1. Individualistic, negativistic.	1. Teach obedience & the joy of doing right. Accept necessary limits & restraints.
2. Imitative: language, manners, habits, etc. Conformist: what teacher is like is very influential.	2. Be a consistent example to them. Learn acceptable behavior. Guidance & a proper pattern of behavior to follow.
3. Group awareness, extremely social: want to be & do things with people.	3. Promote opportunities for group activities. Teach give-and-take responsibilities. Circle games, not relays. Cooperative play.
4. Learning to lead in activities & adjust to others. Increasing independence. Widening scope.	4. Allow & encourage leadership activities. Tactful guidance. Service projects.
5. Thoughtful, mothering instinct.	5. Lessons on Christian virtues. Provide dolls & animals to play with. Illustrate Bible stories with stuffed toys.
6. Strong play interests.	6. Provide variety of cooperative games.
7. Strong desire to please. Wants adult approval.	7. Mediate to them God's approval.
8. Conversationalist.	8. Give opportunity to talk (learning activities). Allow place for his thinking (test teaching). Use as teaching clues.

EMOTIONAL AND SPIRITUAL

1. Intense, but transient emotions.	1. Avoid arousing negative emotions, approve positive emotional expression.
2. Strong desire for love.	2. Stress God's love & care for them. Security of love & affection from parents.
3. Credulous.	3. Teach the truth. Teaching nothing that must be unlearned. Encourage trust in the Lord.
4. Full of wonder.	4. Stimulate their desire to worship. Build reverence for prayer, Bible, the house of the Lord, etc.
5. Eagerness to be taught & learn.	5. Watchful of readiness of learners to receive spiritual truth. Requires time, patience, understanding & genuine interest of adult leaders.

PRIMARY
GRADES 1–3
AGES 6–8 YEARS

CHARACTERISTICS	NEEDS

PHYSICAL

1. Growth slower, small hand muscles not completely coordinated, but improving.
2. Energy & vitality fluctuate. Tend to overdo.

3. Susceptible to disease, resistance greater, period of contagious disease.
4. Activity level high, restlessness.

5. Keen senses.

1. Use large muscles. Assign simple tasks, easily completed. Use regular crayons.
2. Guard against overdoing. Balanced program. Opportunity for excess energy & restlessness to find an outlet.
3. Protect, observe & exclude suspicious cases at the door. Avoid overcrowding.
4. Program providing ample opportunity for varied activities. Exploration methods.
5. Provide objects to see & handle which teach. Firsthand acquaintance.

MENTAL

1. Wide range of reading ability, varied interests.

2. Widening experience, increasing ability & accuracy, developing reasoning power.

3. Concrete & literal thinking, beginning concept of abstract thought.
4. Learning greater self-control, employing more self-evaluation.

5. Attention span increasing (7–15 min.)
6. Memory improving, though unreli-

1. Graded materials. Divided classes. Teach to read the Bible. Supply good reading materials. Enjoy songs, rhythms, nature and true stories, comics, radio, movies, etc. Employ varied teaching techniques.
2. Furnish varied experience, confront & grapple with issues, exercise reasoning power in solving their own problems.
3. Avoid symbolism which is beyond their understanding. Multiply illustrations.
4. Teach joy of self-control (fruit of the Holy Spirit), & to rely on it. Establish basis of standards, minimum of interference.
5. Challenge thinking; do not tax it.
6. Meaningful memory program. Under-

113

able. Growth from interest in present & immediate reality to interest in the past.

7. Extremely conversational and increasingly communicative.
8. Eager (more enthusiasm than wisdom) & curious. Desirous of learning.

standing what & why they memorize. Acceptance at their own level of development with understanding of nature & interests. Teach from past experiences.

7. Promote self-expression and conversational opportunities.
8. Learns best through active, direct participation & concrete learning situations. Respond with eagerness & enthusiasm.

SOCIAL

1. Continuing growth from dependence to independence. Assuming greater responsibilities.

2. Imitative & inventive. Enjoy dramatic play.

3. Make friends quite easily. Concerned about group status.

4. Sympathy easily aroused. Highly sensitive, emergence of class & race prejudice.
5. Desire to please & do well. Sensitive to adult feeling. Resent being told what to do.

6. Emotional immaturity, egotistic, individualistic.

7. Friendly & cooperative. Wholehearted approach.
8. Strong sense of fairness. Demands own turn & rights. Highly competitive.

1. Give opportunity for responsibility through supervised group work. Encourage proper combination of independence and dependence.
2. Play situations. Imitate great Bible characters & their characteristics. Write own words and music for songs. Set Scripture to music.
3. Encourage Christian fellowships. Learn to work out group plans & to cooperate with members of a group.
4. Be careful about expressing opinions. Direct sympathy in scriptural channels.
5. Help in gradual development of acceptable manners & habits. Wants & needs adult approval. Encouragement, ample praise, warmth, and patience from adults.
6. Do not teach beyond their ability to respond. Foster group ideas. Centrality of the Lord in all of life.
7. Encourage their working together. Contagious enthusiasm.
8. Equity & justice in all decisions. Encourage them to make their own rules.

---

1. Emotions easily aroused & played on.

1. Train emotions to love & hate appropriate things. Employ discrimination.

<table>
<tr><td rowspan="7" style="writing-mode:vertical-rl">EMOTIONAL AND SPIRITUAL</td><td>2. Concerned about right & wrong. Differences are black & white.</td><td>2. Apply the Bible to real-life situations to aid decision-making. Faithfulness in exposing error. Reward the right. Firmness with wrong.</td></tr>
<tr><td>3. Credulous & yet uncertain due to conflicting voices.</td><td>3. Direct belief to the Lord. Walk & rely on the Lord, the constant Friend & Confidant. Basis of authority.</td></tr>
<tr><td>4. Salvation-conscious because sin-conscious.</td><td>4. Present Christ for individual response. "After class" approach.</td></tr>
<tr><td>5. Fascinated with heaven & God.</td><td>5. Teach spiritual truth in the reality of their own experience.</td></tr>
<tr><td>6. Appreciation of supernatural.</td><td>6. Stress strange things that really happened. Miracles.</td></tr>
<tr><td>7. Growing desire for love & security.</td><td>7. Teach God's care & love for them.</td></tr>
</table>

JUNIOR
GRADES 4–6
AGES 9–11 YEARS

CHARACTERISTICS	NEEDS

<table>
<tr><td rowspan="5" style="writing-mode:vertical-rl">PHYSICAL</td><td>1. Abounding energy, rapid growth, loves to do things, acts first & thinks afterward.</td><td>1. Provide a variety of constructive things to do: crafts, shop work, active & dramatic play; encourage to think about consequences of their actions.</td></tr>
<tr><td>2. Strong & healthy.</td><td>2. Expect regular attendance. Let him do "difficult" jobs; develop good health habits. Urge plenty of rest and good food at regular intervals.</td></tr>
<tr><td>3. Noisy, loves to fight.</td><td>3. Arrive before he does. Give something to do; encourage poise and calm by providing quiet activities & atmosphere.</td></tr>
<tr><td>4. Loves the out-of-doors.</td><td>4. Take on hikes, camping, nature walks, tours.</td></tr>
<tr><td>5. Appreciates doing the difficult & competitive, manifesting individual differences & abilities.</td><td>5. Challenge ability with projects. Bible learning activities in which they can compete and excel, training in game skills.</td></tr>
</table>

6. Interested in babies, somewhat curious about sex.	6. Considerate answers to questions concerning the coming of physiological changes. Wholesome sex education on an appropriate level.

MENTAL

1. Strong geographical & historical sense, factual (not fantasy) studies.	1. Teach chronology & geography in the Bible. Trace journeys, make & use maps, time lines, models.
2. Collector	2. Interest in a worthwhile hobby. Collections related to missions, stamps, coins, curios.
3. Inquisitive, varied interests, daydreaming common.	3. Help answer questions. Encourage interest in varied areas, confront with reality.
4. Likes to read, write, and talk. Varying ability.	4. Provide good reading material (biographies recommended). Use Bible studies that require some writing.
5. Critical, especially of adults.	5. Set example of thoughtfulness & kindness. Listen to & talk with them.
6. Logical reasoning power developing. Increasingly aware of other ideas and beliefs.	6. Reasonable explanations, provide opportunities to make behavior choices, various teaching approaches, evaluation of different viewpoints.
7. Rote memory at its best.	7. Promote memorization of Scripture.
8. Literal-minded, symbolism difficult to understand.	8. Avoid using object lessons which confuse rather than clarify thinking.
9. Desires to do well but loses interest if discouraged or pressured.	9. Encourage attempt at new activities as well as finish ones already started. Challenge & praise constantly.

1. Can accept responsibility.	1. Organize classes with officers who have special duties and specific responsibilities, committee, and group planning.
2. Does not like authority over him, strong sense of justice and honor, will argue over fairness in clubs and play, patriotic.	2. No threats or ultimatums. Be a guide, not a dictator. Opportunities to discuss respect for property and others, consistency in life & discipline, Christian citizenship & loyalty.

SOCIAL

3. Strong "gang" instinct, clubs, teams.	3. Let class be a club, give sense of belonging and personal attention.
4. Scornful of opposite sex, close friendships with same sex.	4. Separate classes for boys & girls.
5. Hero worshiper, impressionable.	5. Be an example, present Christ as his Hero.
6. Undisciplined, unwise in spending.	6. Develop disciplined habits, provide an opportunity to earn and manage an allowance, teach to assume responsibility for personal dress & grooming.

EMOTIONAL AND SPIRITUAL

1. Has few fears, but many problems.	1. Teach what to fear and what not to. Learn how they feel about things, personal counseling.
2. Quick-tempered, self-centered.	2. Avoid causes of flare-ups, life to be centered on Christ.
3. Dislikes outward display of affection, distaste for sentimentality in religion.	3. Avoid such display, private counseling on spiritual matters.
4. Keen sense of humor, much noise & giggling.	4. Challenge and channel humor. Teach evaluation of what is, and what is not funny.
5. Recognizes sin as sin.	5. Teach Christ as Saviour from penalty & power of sin. Praise good work & commendable behavior.
6. Has questions about Christianity.	6. Answer truthfully, help them find the answers in their own Bibles.
7. Emotions feature little in religion.	7. Avoid emotional stories & appeals.
8. Sets high standards for himself but his ideals are not fixed.	8. Meet high standards in your life. Set biblical standards.
9. Intensely practical, needs encouragement and spiritual motivation.	9. Doer, not a hearer. How does Christianity work? Correlation of teaching and everyday life, activities in which he will develop spiritually, provide devotional helps.
10. May express concerns about home life, especially when separation or divorce takes place or in his relationships with stepparents.	10. Be sensitive to & understanding of the child's situation. Do not ridicule or be judgmental. Show God's unconditional love. Support each child as a special person.

117

Aside from these very specific characteristics and needs, children have six very general needs. These must also be considered when teaching God's Word.

A child needs love.
- ☐ be pleasant, call child by name
- ☐ use touch, hug, pat to convey love
- ☐ listen when the child talks
- ☐ get on the child's eye level
- ☐ offer specific praise/encouragement often

A child needs security.
- ☐ be positive
- ☐ be consistent in discipline
- ☐ use familiar activities with child
- ☐ guide conversation toward God's constant care

A child needs acceptance.
- ☐ allow children to make choices of activities
- ☐ accept children even if they have negative feelings
- ☐ accept the child even if you can't accept his behavior
- ☐ guide the conversation toward God's love of the child

A child needs discipline (self-control).
- ☐ be realistic and consistent in expectations in class/home
- ☐ give consistent and specific praise and encouragement
- ☐ model the behavior that you expect of your children
- ☐ allow children to experience logical consequences of misbehavior (consequences should fit misbehavior)

A child needs independence.
- ☐ provide several learning activities from which to choose
- ☐ place all materials and equipment on their level
- ☐ don't do for the child that which he can do for himself
- ☐ ask questions, guide conversation to help child do it alone

A child needs recognition of worth.
- ☐ talk to child directly, on his eye level
- ☐ do not label a child
- ☐ be courteous to each child ("please," "thank you")
- ☐ deal with a behavior problem one-on-one, never in front of the entire group
- ☐ encourage proper teacher/learner ratios to ensure spending time with each child

By meeting these needs, teachers and parents not only talk about God's Word, they also model what it says, and modeling is one very important method for teaching children God's truth.

GOALS AND OBJECTIVES
How do we meet the needs of the child?

How do we meet these needs in our teaching ministry within the church, home, and school? Our goals for children's ministry fall into two categories: (1) goals for the child and (2) goals for the institution (church, home, or school) to facilitate teaching.

One exciting way to develop goals is for church leaders and key teachers to devote a weekend to planning. Brainstorm goals and objectives for each area (spiritual, mental, emotional, social, and physical) and each age/grade level. These goals will give leaders and teachers direction for the coming year. They will also provide a basis for evaluation of teacher performance and achievement in the lives of learners at the end of the year.

Here are twelve goals for the school, church, or home.

1. Introduce each child to the Bible as God's holy Word.
2. Lay a foundation for the major biblical doctrines on the child's mental and spiritual level.
3. Lead each child to Jesus Christ.
4. Provide a balanced program of worship, instruction, fellowship, and expression.
5. Provide opportunities for quality teaching of God's Word—both content and application.
6. Know and understand the characteristics and needs of children at every age-level.
7. Provide a continual training program for all teachers and parents.
8. Provide a staff of teachers with proper ratios: nursery—1:3, 2–5 years—1:6, grades 1–6—1:8-10.
9. Provide adequate facilities and equipment.
10. Encourage variety in the selection and use of creative methods and materials in all children's ministries.
11. Maintain records for follow-up of visitors and absentees.
12. Encourage leaders, teachers, and parents to evaluate their ministries, noting strengths and weaknesses with specific goals for improvement.

CHRISTIAN EDUCATION OF CHILDREN—GOALS & OBJECTIVES[7]

	Birth–3 Years	4–5 Years	Grades 1–3	Grades 4–6
GOD	1. He loves me. 2. He made everything. 3. He cares for me. 4. I can talk to Him.	1. He is loving and good. 2. He has all wisdom. 3. He has all power.	1. He is strong and reliable. 2. He is holy. 3. He is the forgiving Father. 4. I can pray to Him. 5. He cares for me.	1. He is the King and we are loyal to Him. 2. He is the Lawgiver and Authority. 3. He is the Judge of sin. 4. He has a plan and purpose for me.
JESUS	1. He was the Christmas Baby. 2. He is my Friend. 3. He grew to be a Man. 4. He is God's Son. God sent Him. 5. He is God.	1. He is my Helper in daily life. 2. He is the One who helps me do what I cannot do.	1. He is God, Jesus, and Christ—the same Person. 2. He is the Saviour for individual acceptance. 3. He is the children's example. 4. He is to be relied on for daily life.	1. He is the Supreme Hero. 2. He is my Saviour. 3. He is my Lord. 4. He is to be confessed publicly.
THE BIBLE	1. It is God's Book. 2. It is a special Book to be loved. 3. It tells us how to please God. 4. It has good stories.	1. It has many good stories. 2. It speaks to me. 3. It is to be learned in my language.	1. It has miracle stories. 2. It is my authority for life. 3. It is the place where I find solutions to my problems. 4. It is to be memorized.	1. It presents God's standards. 2. It has chronology, history, and geography to be learned. 3. It has the answers to my problems. 4. It is to be used for my daily devotions.
OUR CHURCH	1. It is God's house. 2. It is where we learn about God. 3. It is the place where I meet my friends. 4. It is my church, the place where I belong. 5. It is a place where I have a happy time.	1. It is a big family and I have a part. 2. It is a place where I have responsibilities. 3. It is supported through my gifts.	1. It is a family in which I have responsibilities. 2. It has forms which I want to learn. 3. It has ordinances which I must understand.	1. It is a church where I should become a member. 2. It has responsibilities for me. 3. It is a place where I introduce my friends to the Lord and His Word. 4. It is a place of worship.
MY LIFE	1. I want to please God. 2. I want to share with others.	1. God loves me and always will even if I am disobedient. 2. We don't want to displease the Lord. 3. Growth in thoughtfulness, sympathy, and sharing.	1. Seeking of God's help in my problems. 2. Interpreting life in terms of God's will and Word. 3. An attitude of sorrow for sin.	1. Living according to God's standards. 2. Consideration of others. 3. God has a plan for my life. 4. Problems solved by God's Word.

PROGRAM AND CURRICULUM
How do we program, schedule, and teach to meet our learners' needs?

Programming based on our *view of the child* meets the needs of the learners. The child is not a miniature adult, but a unique individual with special characteristics and needs at each age-level. Programming based on *how children learn* will achieve the biblical directives already mentioned.

The Scriptures describe the two foci as (1) evangelism—reaching out to children, leading them to a commitment to Jesus Christ as Saviour and Lord; and (2) discipleship—leading them to grow in the Word of God and equipping them to share their faith.

Effective programming for children includes these guidelines:

1. *Love and acceptance.* Children need to see God's unconditional love modeled by caring, encouraging leaders, teachers, and parents. An environment of love and acceptance sets the tone for teaching.
2. *Building relationships.* Children learn biblical and theological truths in the context of deep, personal relationships. Programming can be fruitless without teacher/student relationships. Meaningful relationships can be cultivated when teacher:student ratios are small.
3. *Active involvement.* Children learn best by doing—using all five senses. Learning demands active involvement in the lesson. Children involved in making their own discoveries experience greater retention. Participation leads to attitude changes that in turn motivate learners to apply the Bible to life.
4. *Application to life.* It is essential for teachers and parents to teach for application in the lives of their students and children. James 1:22 says, "Do not merely listen to the Word, and so deceive yourselves. Do what it says." Through guided conversation and active involvement in the learning process, God's Word can be put into action in the lives of our children and students.
5. *Guided conversation.* Guided conversation is informal but planned dialogue that can take place during learning activities, worship, or anytime. This method conveys attitudes along with biblical content.
6. *Choices.* Allowing children to make choices of activities helps them to think independently, be motivated, and interested in that learning activity. When all activities in the room point to the same aim from God's Word, the child can choose any activity and still learn the Bible content,

121

the proper attitudes, and application to life. Not all children learn in the same way. Some may enjoy the challenge of a Bible dictionary search in preparation for the lesson. Others may enjoy an art activity. Still others may enjoy using a Bible memory game to learn the verse for the lesson. Giving choices allows children the freedom to learn.

7. *Total session teaching.* From the minute the first child walks into the classroom until the last child leaves, everything taught and experienced should point to the aims of the lesson from God's Word. The music, art, memory verse, story, activities, and guided conversation, should all point to those stated lesson aims. With children, in particular younger children, we need to teach one concept and teach it well. This single-concept approach enables children to assimilate a Bible truth and apply it to their own lives as they go through the week.

8. *Large and small groups.* Children's ministry usually lacks workers. Consequently, classes are large and the teaching staff small. The ratio of teacher to learners should be 1:5-6 in early childhood and 1:8-10 in older children's classes. Large groups can be used for Bible sharing, worship time, games, etc. Small groups can be used for telling the Bible story, learning activities, and developing those crucial teacher-learner relationships.

9. *Lessons divided into units.* Each lesson taught to children should be part of a larger group of lessons called a unit. These lessons all focus on one theme or aim from God's Word. It is important that lessons be grouped into units because children learn best by having one theme taught through many different methods.

10. *The teaching-learning process.* Understanding how children learn determines our teaching ministry. Children learn through direct experiences, active involvement, and discovery. In the 125 teaching situations recorded from Jesus' ministry, over two thirds of the time the learner asked a question in response to what Jesus had done or said. The Master Teacher knew that words had to be linked with actions if learning was going to take place. He asked His learners, the disciples, and others to become active participants in the learning process. For Jesus, learning was a process of construction, not solely transmission.

Our programming for children should be scheduled to meet their needs and accomplish biblical goals.

EARLY CHILDHOOD SCHEDULE—BIRTH THROUGH FIVE YEARS
When young children are to be taught, we follow a schedule similar to this one, though it may vary in length or purpose, because the principles remain the same.

Step 1—Bible learning activities (approx. 30–45 minutes). Bible learning activities begin when the first child walks into the classroom. He chooses one of two or three activities that focus the aim from God's Word. The activity linked with the guided conversation provides real learning for the child as well as building readiness for the rest of the session. Each activity takes place in a small group with an adult leader.

Step 2—Worship time (approx. 10–15 minutes). During the worship time children come together in one large group for music, memory verse, offering, and review of the session thus far. At the end of worship time children divide into the same small groups each week for the Bible story and activity time.

Step 3—Bible story and activity time (10–15 minutes). The Bible story, told in a small group, uses a different method each week. The activity time allows each teacher to review and reinforce the Bible story and application.

Step 4—Wrap-up time (10 minutes). Wrap-up time provides the extra minutes till parents arrive or till the staff reports for the second hour session. This conclusion usually consists of music, reviewing the memory verse, and cleanup time.

ELEMENTARY CHILDREN'S SCHEDULE—GRADES 1 THROUGH 6
Step 1—Bible study time (30–40 minutes). Bible readiness activity: Provide two or three readiness activities for immediate involvement. Design these activities to prepare the child for the rest of the lesson (dictionary search, geography search, art activity, Bible memory verse games).

Bible story: Let the children experience the Bible story. Methods vary from week to week. The Bible story time incorporates Bible readiness activities, allowing learners to share their discoveries, thus creating interest and motivation for the study.

Bible application: Discuss the aim or central truth from God's Word and encourage learners, by the power of the Holy Spirit, to apply it to their lives. Each child should be challenged to make a change based on what God's Word has said to him or her. "What will I do now that I've learned this lesson from the Bible?"

Step 2—Bible learning activities (15–20 minutes). Bible learning activities (1) review what has been learned in the Bible study time and (2) reinforce the truths that need to be lived. Use methods such as art and drama. This opportunity for repetition is essential for learning and application to take place.

Step 3—Bible sharing. In a larger group, encourage children to share what they have learned from God's Word. Music, memory verses, testimonies from both teachers and children, and sharing what took place during Bible learning activity time can bring the teaching session to a close on a positive note.

Step 4—Until parents come. Teachers can review music, memory verses, and build relationships through conversation.

Our programming for children must provide variety and balance. Here are suggestions for a year-round ministry for children:

1. *Sunday School* provides both evangelism for the non-Christian and discipleship through the teaching of the Word of God.

2. *Church time* provides an opportunity for children to worship on their age-levels and includes many of the same activities used in Sunday School. For early childhood and elementary children, the second hour should be coordinated with the first to provide the continuity and repetition needed for effective learning.

3. *Midweek club programs* provide an informal time of building relationships with peers and leaders, evangelism, discipleship, recreation, Bible memory, and service projects. Summer camps and special trips can be included.

4. *Weekend retreats* are a time for getting away with parents and leaders to focus on one topic or theme.

5. *Day camping* can provide an exciting camping program without the high cost of a resident camp. Informal in nature, camp provides opportunities to develop new relationships and new skills. When taught in natural surroundings, the Bible can come alive with excitement and meaning.

6. *Resident camping* can give children a week-long experience of building relationships and living in a community setting—seeing Christian principles being put into practice each day by leaders and peers. Campfires, treasure hunts, Bible stories told in the woods, swimming in the lake, and canoeing are just a few of the exciting events that can take place during a child's week at camp.

7. *Vacation Bible School* can be an effective outreach tool. VBS offers perhaps as much teaching time in one week as an entire Sunday School quarter.

8. *Group counseling sessions* should be planned as a regular part of the ministry to children. With the high rate of separation and divorce among adults, and stress in the lives of children, a regular program of counseling should be available. Lay counselors could be

used to talk and listen to children. Providing Christian guidance and direction is crucial.

9. *Children's Sunday* focuses all of the church's activities on the children's ministry. Slides shown in the worship service, Bible learning activities displayed in the church narthex, and testimonies given by teachers and parents excited about their ministry can help the congregation catch the vision for children's ministry.

10. *Music programs* give children an opportunity to use their talents for our Lord. Children's choirs, musical groups, handbell choirs, and even a puppet team can have a ministry in the adult and children's church time.

Programming for children needs to be designed to minister to their characteristics and needs. Leaders and teachers should be involved in the planning, implementing, and evaluation of programs. Is the educational ministry accomplishing the goals set out for each program?

METHODS AND MATERIALS
What methods and materials do we use?

Children learn actively, think concretely, love to get involved and make discoveries. Because children are like this, the Bible teaching ministry must provide firsthand experiences—using all the five senses. The more involvement and interaction a child has with God's Word and the teacher, the more effective the lesson will be.

We use teaching methods as a vehicle. The activity, linked with guided conversation focusing on God's Word, can contribute to the child's understanding and application. Several principles apply when choosing and using methods and materials for children:

1. All methods, materials, equipment, conversation, and directions should be on the child's age-level.

2. Give choices as often as possible. When we allow a child to choose an activity he will be motivated to begin and complete that activity. Focus all of the activities offered during one teaching session on a single theme.

3. Variety is key to using methods and materials. The worst method a teacher could use this Sunday is the same method that was used last Sunday. Vary the learning activities. Use different methods in telling the Bible story. Keep the element of surprise alive.

4. Give clear instructions for each learning activity. When children can read, write the directions on the board. Teachers should circulate throughout the classroom, making sure each child understands what to do.

5. Planned questions help children think through what they are doing. It is not enough for children to know and understand a concept. They must be able to apply it as well. Skillfully phrased questions help children arrive at their own conclusions.

6. Guidance and encouragement keep children motivated during a learning activity. Some activities may take 20 to 30 minutes to complete. Remember the child's short attention span. Keep guiding and encouraging with specific praise for work under completion.

At least seven categories or methods can be used with children of all ages.

1. *Art activities.* These activities provide an exciting and enjoyable way for children to learn God's Word. In using art, the thought processes that the child goes through are more important than the final product. Specific praise and encouragement is needed throughout these activities.

2. *Drama activities.* Link up the child's imagination, feelings, and actions to produce a very successful learning experience. Drama can put a child into the shoes of Daniel as he stands before the handwriting on the wall. It can even take children to the crossing of the Red Sea. Such exciting role playing makes the Bible come alive!

3. *Oral communication.* Most children enjoy talking and sharing their ideas and experiences. It can help children develop their skills in Bible memory, listening, problem-solving, and sharing needs and requests.

4. *Creative writing.* This excellent method helps children crystallize their thoughts. Writing accounts of Bible events can encourage children to research the customs, historical background, and even some of the archeological findings.

5. *Music activities.* Psalm 150 says, "Praise Him with the sounding of the trumpet . . . harp and lyre . . . tambourine and dancing" (vv. 3-4). Children can worship and praise the Lord with their voices and with simple musical instruments. Music can be used during times of worship so that children are encouraged to respond to God for His Word and mighty works.

6. *Research activities.* These activities assist children in developing research skills in order to understand and apply Bible truths. Bible dictionaries, Bible handbooks, maps, atlases, and books on archeology can help children with this task. Research activities work best with older children who can read.

7. *Bible games.* Children love to play and learn. Bible games assist children in learning content and remembering specific truths. Games are available from various publishers and can be used to review and reinforce the Bible lesson.

Creative methods and materials are valuable tools to help children know, understand, and apply God's Word. It is crucial that teachers and parents be trained in the effective use of the various methods and materials available.

ORGANIZATION AND ADMINISTRATION
How do we organize to make the ministry effective?

Organization and administration is often the forgotten area of children's ministry. Without proper administration, our resources, equipment, curriculum, and facilities may lack proper attention and hinder the teaching ministry.

Certain specific areas of organization must have the attention of leadership if a children's ministry is to be effective:

1. *Recruiting and training of teachers and parents.* Recruiting and training are continuous processes. Programs always need leadership and teachers. Having adequate staff for each age-group demands a proper perspective on the importance of recruiting. Nine steps can help in the recruiting process.

a. *Everyone gets involved in recruitment.*

b. *Publicize the educational ministry.* At specific times during the year the congregation should be made aware of the children's ministry—what it is doing and how people can help.

c. *Provide job descriptions for each position.* Letting people know the expectations helps alleviate the fear of the unknown. Job descriptions help workers see requirements, lines of authority, and the extent of their own responsibilities.

d. *Finding the prospects.* Collecting lists of classes of adults and senior and junior highers can initiate recruitment. Surveys provide information on past ministry experience and current availability and interest.

e. *Approving prospects.* Once names have been screened, they would be taken to the church board or Christian education committee. Get names approved before people are asked to serve.

f. *Interview potential workers.* This is a very important step in the recruiting process. Sitting down with the candidate will help both of you understand each other, the ministry, and the requirements. Allow the candidate at least a week to think and pray about a commitment.

g. *Allow time for observation.* Ask the candidate to sit in on the class or ministry.

h. *Follow-up for the decision.* When the person says yes, praise God for that commitment. If the person says no, praise God that he was honest instead of taking the ministry only to resign two or three weeks into the quarter. Above all, allow the decision to be a spiritual commitment to the Lord Jesus Christ.

i. *Training for ministry.* Leaders must provide adequate training to prepare new recruits to meet the needs of their students.

2. *Facilities for effective learning.* Programming should determine your facilities instead of the reverse.

Early childhood classes need approximately 35 square feet of space per child. Elementary-aged children need 20 to 25 square feet of space. Having too many children in a room will make everyone feel cramped and squeezed. Discipline problems arise and it becomes harder to retain teachers.

Facilities should focus on the child in the learning situation and should also provide space for involvement in active learning.

3. *Curriculum that will meet the needs of children.* Children's ministry requires professionally prepared curriculum. There are many excellent published curriculums available. A local bookstore can provide samples.

Ask these questions when evaluating and choosing curriculum:
   a. Does it center on the Bible as the Word of God?
   b. Does it promote evangelism?
   c. Does it focus on the learner—keeping in mind age-group characteristics and needs?
   d. Does it provide for active learner involvement and participation?
   e. Does it work toward changed lives?

In the organization of a children's ministry many areas must be considered. If a church or school works on these three it will effect change in the life of each child.

EVALUATION

How can we evaluate our ministry to children?

The following twenty questions will help you evaluate your ministry to children. These can be used by a teacher for self-evaluation or by a leader for evaluation of teachers on an annual basis.

1. How much did I motivate each child?
2. Did I make the lesson personal and meaningful?
3. Did I pray? Did I expect results in my learners' lives?
4. Did I plan for all of the events that took place?
5. Did I meet the needs of my learners—in each area?

6. Did I respond to each child in a loving, warm manner?
7. Did I prepare for my ministry today? How could I improve?
8. Did I balance unconditional love with discipline?
9. Did I use Bible learning activities? Did I vary methods?
10. Did I plan for my transitions? Were they meaningful?
11. Did I get my learners to actively participate today?
12. Did I get to know my learners better today?
13. Did I use the session to emphasize the aim from the Bible?
14. Did I use music? Did I teach the words accurately?
15. Did I prepare for extra time at the end of the session?
16. Did I accomplish the aims for the session? Was I flexible?
17. Did I build on last week's session? Did I review?
18. Will I apply the Bible truth to my life this week?
19. Will I have my quiet time each day this next week?
20. When and how will I prepare for next week's session?

Your children's ministry can be challenging and rewarding as you see children become more like the Lord Jesus Christ. Teaching children is strenuous, especially after extended service, but seeing them involved in the Word of God is exciting.

Remember the story of our Lord Jesus Christ in John 13? Jesus actually took water in a basin and a towel and washed His disciples' feet. He modeled humble service for the Twelve—even the one who was about to betray Him! He gave His disciples this object lesson and then asked a question: "Do you understand what I have done for you?" (v. 12) The truth of the passage is found in verses 14 and 15, "Now that I, your Lord and Teacher, have washed your feet, you also should wash one another's feet. I have set you an example that you should do as I have done for you."

As teachers or parents, we must take our high calling seriously. The learners of today are the leaders of tomorrow. Will they base their lives and decisions on God's Word? May God help us to be committed to the great task at hand—ministry to His children!

ENDNOTES

1. Deuteronomy 6:4-9; Psalms 78:1-8; 119; Proverbs 22:6; Matthew 28:19-20; 2 Timothy 2:2; 3:14-15.

2. Pastor Mark Chittwood, Pastor of Childhood Education, University Baptist Church, Fayetteville, Arkansas.

3. Pastor Jerry Hull, Minister of Christian Education, Faith Bible Church, DeSoto, Texas.

4. Pastor Pat Muro, Minister of Christian Education, Fellowship Bible Church, Dallas, Texas.

5. Adapted from Kenneth O. Gangel, *Building Leaders for Church Education.* Chicago: Moody Press, 1981, p. 42.

6. Age-Group Characteristics and Needs Chart adapted from unpublished materials developed by Scripture Press Ministries, Wheaton, Ill.

7. Christian Education of Children Goals and Objects Chart adapted from unpublished materials developed by Scripture Press Ministries, Wheaton, Ill.

BIBLIOGRAPHY

Aarons, Trudy and Francine Koelsch. *One Hundred and One Language Art Activities.* Tuscon, Ariz.: Communication Skill Builders, 1980.

Ames, Louise Bates and Frances L. Ilg. *Your Five Year Old.* New York: Delta Books, 1979.

————. *Your Four Year Old.* New York: Delta Books, 1976.

————. *Your One Year Old.* New York: Delta Books, 1982.

————. *Your Seven Year Old.* New York: Delta Books, 1985.

————. *Your Six Year Old.* New York: Delta Books, 1980.

————. *Your Three Year Old.* New York: Delta Books, 1976.

————. *Your Two Year Old.* New York: Delta Books, 1976.

Biehler, Robert F. *Child Development.* Boston: Houghton Mifflin Company, 1981.

Bolton, Barbara and Charles T. Smith. *Creative Bible Learning Activities for Children—Grades 1–6.* Ventura, Calif.: Gospel Light Publications, 1977.

Bolton, Barbara. *How to Do Bible Learning Activities for Grades 1–6.* Ventura, Calif.: Gospel Light Publications, 1982.

Broman, Betty L. *The Early Years in Childhood Education.* Boston: Houghton Mifflin Company, 1982.

Brown, Catherine Caldwell, ed. *The Many Facets of Touch.* Skillman, N.J.: Johnson and Johnson, 1984.

————. *Play Interactions.* Skillman, N.J.: Johnson and Johnson, 1985.

Brown, Lowell E. *Sunday School Standards.* Ventura, Calif.: Gospel Light Publications, 1986.

Chance, Paul. *Learning through Play.* Skillman, N.J.: Johnson and Johnson, 1980.

Clark, Robert E., Joanne Brubaker, and Roy B. Zuck. *Childhood Education in the Church.* Chicago, Ill.: Moody Press, 1986.

Coles, Robert. *The Moral Life of Children.* Boston: Houghton Mifflin Company, 1986.

Crystal, David. *Listen to Your Child.* New York: Penguin Books, 1986.

Dykstra, Craig and Sharon Parks. *Faith Development and Fowler.* Birmingham, Ala.: Religious Education Press, 1986.

Elkind, David. *Children and Adolescents.* New York: Oxford University Press, 1970.

_____ . *The Hurried Child.* Reading, Mass.: Addison-Wesley Publishing Company, 1981.

_____ . *A Sympathetic Understanding of the Child.* Boston: Allyn and Bacon, 1978.

Fowler, James H. *Stages of Faith.* San Francisco: Harper and Row Publishers, 1981.

Harrell, Donna and Wesley Haystead. *Creative Bible Learning for Young Children—Birth through 5 Years.* Ventura, Calif.: Gospel Light Publications, 1977.

Haystead, Wesley. *Teaching Your Child about God.* Ventura, Calif.: Gospel Light Publications, 1974.

Hendricks, William L. *A Theology for Children.* Nashville, Tenn.: Broadman Press, 1980.

Kesler, Jay, Ron Beers, and Lavonne Neff, eds. *Parents and Children.* Wheaton, Ill.: Victor Books, 1986.

Ketterman, Grace and Herbert Ketterman. *Baby and Child Care.* Old Tappan, N.J.: Fleming H. Revell, 1982.

Klein, Karen. *How to Do Bible Learning Activities for Ages 2–5.* Ventura, Calif.: Gospel Light Publications, 1982.

Montessori, Maria. *The Secret of Childhood.* New York: Ballantine Books, 1966.

Mussen, Paul H., John A. Conger, J. Kagan, and Aletha Huston. *Child Development and Personality.* New York: Harper and Row Publishers, 1984.

Newell, Arlo, ed. *Fun and Learning.* Anderson, Ind.: Warner Press, 1983.

Phillips, Mike. *Building Respect, Responsibility and Spiritual Values in Your Child.* Minneapolis: Bethany House Publishers, 1981.

Richards, Lawrence O. *A Theology of Children's Ministry.* Grand Rapids: Zondervan Publishing House, 1983.

Striker, Susan. *Please Touch.* New York: Simon and Schuster, 1986.

Stuart, Sally E. *Teaching and Reaching Junior Resources.* Anderson, Ind.: Warner Press. 1984.

_____ . *Teaching and Reaching Kindergarten Resources.* Anderson, Ind.: Warner Press. 1984.

_____ . *Teaching and Reaching Primary Resources.* Anderson, Ind.: Warner Press, 1984.

8. TEACHING YOUTH
Robert Joseph Choun, Jr.

INTRODUCTION

God commands us to teach youth. Today's teenagers *are* tomorrow's leaders. They set goals, make choices, and live life in the light of their decisions. The teaching ministry to youth must be one of excellence.

> Youth are at a crossroads. People who are in touch with kids today have an ominous sense of an accelerating and compounding crisis. Something must be done. There is an urgency about youth ministry, and those who feel it are a giant step ahead of those who assign it a low priority.[1]

> Teaching youth is important for our church because of where these kids are in life. Crucial decisions are being made as they move into adulthood. We teach them, not only to help them as youth, but also to help them become godly adult leaders. We seek to build into them qualities and characteristics of Christian adulthood. Our deepest desire is that their Christian walk might become a lifestyle, growing in God's Word and sharing Christ.[2]

> Youth look for answers and respond, for the most part, to leaders. They are both encouraging and excitable. In our youth ministry, we're laying a foundation for the choices and decisions of the next few years. We're teaching them how to build an exciting relationship with God, family, peers, and themselves!
>
> We work to salvage youth damaged by the world. Kids have been raped, physically and mentally abused. Thousands of youth from broken homes live in our city. We point them to the God who loves and cares for them, One who will never

forsake them. Teaching youth is exciting, but also a tremendous challenge and responsibility.[5]

In considering these three pastoral interviews, the question naturally arises, "How can I effectively minister to youth in a God-pleasing way?" There is a plan which can help both teachers and parents accomplish this task.

THE EDUCATIONAL CYCLE FOR TEACHING YOUTH

The educational cycle (chap. 7, p. 106) provides the direction by which an effective teaching ministry can be planned and programmed.

BIBLICAL DIRECTIVES

The biblical directives for youth ministry remain the same as those for children's ministry. Teachers and parents are called to make disciples; model the truth in everyday life; move learners toward godliness; involve them in activities of worship, instruction, fellowship, and expression; and lead them by the gifts God has given to them as teachers and parents. For an expanded discussion of each Scripture reference please refer to the section "Biblical Directives" in chapter 7.

AGE-GROUP CHARACTERISTICS AND NEEDS

How has God designed the teenager?

Ministry to youth necessitates an understanding of their characteristics and needs. How has God designed the teenager? What are young people like? Luke 2:52 states that Jesus grew in wisdom (intellectually), and stature (physically) and in favor with God (spiritually) and man (socially and emotionally).

The following age-level characteristics describe junior high (grades 7–9) and senior high students (grades 10–12). Remember that these represent only typical characteristics and needs. All teenagers develop at different rates in different areas and deserve treatment as unique individuals.

It is easier for a teacher or parent to understand teenagers once they know adolescent characteristics. Paul, in Acts 17, knew his audience very well. In his teaching session on Mars Hill, Paul proved that he knew his audience, their background, culture, and their literature. He

133

CHARACTERISTICS OF A JUNIOR HIGHER—GRADES 7–9

PHYSICAL

1. He is growing rapidly.
2. Girls grow more rapidly than boys.
3. He is undergoing many internal bodily changes.
4. He is usually awkward.
5. He has boundless energy alternated with periods of fatigue.

MENTAL

1. He has a keen memory.
2. He is interested in adventure and discovery.
3. He is capable of real thinking (moving toward the abstract).
4. He often will question authority.
5. He will make quick judgments.
6. He has an active imagination.
7. He has a strong sense of humor.

SOCIAL

1. He wants to be an adult.
2. He desires to be independent of adults.
3. He wants to belong to a "group."
4. He has a strong sense of loyalty.
5. He is usually self-conscious.
6. His social problems reflect his sexual development.
7. He is looking for a model—a hero.

EMOTIONAL

1. He often feels misunderstood by adults and peers.
2. His emotions fluctuate—extreme joy to sadness.
3. He lacks self-control of emotions.
4. His emotions are very intense.

SPIRITUAL

1. He wants a faith that is practical—here and now.
2. His spirit is ripe for the Gospel message.
3. He has a vision for service—being needed to serve.
4. He can have many doubts about Christianity.
5. He is looking for the ideal (in thoughts and in people's actions).

CHARACTERISTICS OF A SENIOR HIGHER—GRADES 10–12

PHYSICAL
1. He is outgrowing his awkwardness.
2. He has an attractive, grown-up appearance.
3. His appetite is usually great.
4. His physical habits are being formed.
5. He is usually concerned about his sexual nature.

MENTAL
1. His reasoning powers are reaching new heights.
2. He likes argument and debate.
3. He is very creative and idealistic.
4. His judgment is improving.
5. His imagination is usually under the control of reason and judgment.
6. He is usually subject to suggestion.

SOCIAL
1. He belongs to a clique or exclusive social group.
2. He is attracted to the opposite sex (though not always).
3. He is very much interested in personal traits and outward appearance.
4. He wants social approval.
5. He is trying to find his place in society.
6. He usually has an increasing desire to help others.

EMOTIONAL
1. His emotions are still intense.
2. He now has more of an ability to control his emotions.
3. He may be moody.
4. He wants security.
5. He likes excitement and entertainment.

SPIRITUAL
1. His religion is personal.
2. His religion is one of action.
3. His religion is emotional.
4. His doubts may increase about his faith.
5. He can now appreciate the abstract and the atmosphere of worship.

quoted one of their poets to make a point! He then said, "I even found an altar with this inscription: TO AN UNKNOWN GOD. Now what you worship as something unknown I am going to proclaim to you" (v. 23). Understanding one's audience is the first step to successful ministry.

GOALS AND OBJECTIVES
How do we meet the needs of our youth?

How do we meet these needs in our teaching ministry within the home, church, and school? Our goals for youth ministry fall into two categories: (1) goals for the individual and (2) goals for the institution (home, church, or school) to facilitate teaching.

The following profile describes a discipled student. It motivates teachers and parents to ask, "What should each teenager be like after completing our youth ministry?" Each child matures differently in each area, so leaders need to use this as a guide to give direction for planning and programming.

GOALS FOR THE INDIVIDUAL'
PROFILE OF A DISCIPLED STUDENT

The following qualities should characterize a student who has been faithful in the youth ministry and who, on graduation from high school, will:
    a. Live each day with a realization of God's presence and leading.
    b. Think for himself, be able to make his own decisions under the guidance of the Holy Spirit.
    c. Verbally share his faith in Jesus Christ with his friends and those with whom he comes in contact.
    d. Share with other Christians what he knows about God and living as a Christian.

I. THE DISCIPLED STUDENT'S PROGRESSIVE COMMITMENT TO CHRIST.
  A. These principles and attitudes should guide the student to make decisions concerning his life-relationship with God:
    1. On his own seeks direction from God in making all decisions (Ps. 119:9-11; Prov. 3:5-6).
    2. Through the Holy Spirit should be responsible for his own growth and be willing to take the necessary steps to apply what he learns.
      a. Spiritual leadership of others (John 14:26; 1 John 2:27).
      b. Personal character (spiritual, mental, physical, social, emotional) (Luke 2:52; 2 Peter 3:18).
    3. Has a self-sacrificing, obedient mind-set, desiring to live for Christ, and not self (John 15:10, 14; Rom. 7:4; Gal. 2:20; Phil. 2).
  B. These characteristics of the student's spiritual life relate to the Lord:
    1. Demonstrates consistent self-sacrificial obedience to God in willingness to give of himself in these areas (Matt. 5:16; 1 Cor. 6:20).
      a. Consistent Bible study (2 Tim. 2:15).
      b. Memorization of Scripture (Ps. 119:11).

    c. Consistent communication with God (Eph. 3:20; 1 Thes. 5:17; 1 Peter 3:15).

    d. Meditates on Scripture (Pss. 1:2; 119:15).

      2. Demonstrates a reliance on the Holy Spirit when (Eph. 5:18):

        a. Making decisions (Prov. 3:5-6; Rom. 12:2).

        b. Sharing a subjective and/or objective testimony about God (John 9; Acts 1:8).

        c. Studying the Bible (John 14:26; 1 John 2:27).

  C. These characteristics describe the student's continued growth in the Lord:

    1. Consistent love (Matt. 22:37-38).

    2. Consistent obedience (John 14:21; 15:10, 14; Acts 5:29).

    3. Consistent trust (Prov. 3:5-6).

    4. Consistent respect (Ps. 2:11; Ecc. 12:13).

    5. Consistent humility (1 Peter 5:6).

    6. Consistent stewardship (Mal. 3:8-10; 1 Cor. 16:2).

II. THE DISCIPLED STUDENT'S PROGRESSIVE COMMITMENT TO OTHER CHRISTIANS (The "body of Christ")

  A. These principles and attitudes should guide the student when making decisions concerning his relationship with other Christians:

    1. Consider others as more important than himself (Rom. 12:3; Phil. 2:3-8).

      a. With the significant people in his life (family, peers).

      b. During adverse circumstances (1 Peter 2:11-12).

    2. Realize that God is the One who exalts (1 Peter 5:6).

  B. The following characteristics mark the student's spiritual life as it relates to other Christians:

    1. Humbly seeks instruction (teachable spirit) Pss. 25:4-5; 32:8; Prov. 2:3-5; 3:5-6).

      a. From God (Bible, prayer) (Ps. 119:105).

      b. From others (chain of counsel, books) (Prov. 10:17; 12:15; 15:22; Acts 2:42).

      c. Takes criticism well (Prov. 10:17).

    2. Practices self-disclosure, builds close relationships (Matt. 22:39; Acts 4:32).

    3. Takes time to help others with their:

      a. Life with Christ (Gal. 6:1-2; Col. 3:16; 2 Thes. 3:15).

      b. Personal ministries (1 Tim. 1:2; Titus 1:4).

    4. Teaches others to live the Christian life as he does, developing second and third generation leadership (2 Tim. 2:2).

    5. Willing to develop these ministry skills (Phil. 1:1; 1 Tim. 4:12).

      a. How to teach (2 Tim. 2:2).

      b. How to use spiritual gift(s).

      c. How to lead others.

III. THE DISCIPLED STUDENT'S PROGRESSIVE COMMITMENT TO THE WORK OF CHRIST IN THE WORLD

  A. This principle should guide the student when making decisions concerning the work of Christ in the world (Matt. 28:19-20; Acts 1:8; 1 Peter 3:15). Relying upon the enabling of the Holy Spirit, the student will take the initiative to communicate, in a verbal and nonverbal manner, the love of Jesus Christ to other students at all ministry programs as well as in daily contacts on campus and in the community.

B. The following characteristics of the student's spiritual life relate to the work of Christ in the world:
   1. Consistently living a life of example (Matt. 5:13-16; 1 Tim. 4:12).
   2. Knows how to help a new Christian grow in his spiritual life (Rom. 12:3; Eph. 4:11-13).
   3. Knows how to share with others his faith in Jesus (1 Peter 3:15).
C. The student should have this type of relationship with the world:
   1. A good reputation on campus (1 Tim. 3:7).
   2. A deep concern about the lives of non-Christian friends (gives of self) (Heb. 13:2).

One dynamic way for a local church or school to tailor this process is to have the junior and senior high leaders spend a day together brainstorming needs and goals for each area listed under "Goals for the individual." What profiles your discipled students? What would you include or delete? What goals do you consider realistic for the learners in your youth ministry?

The church and the home also require goals. The question must be asked, "How will the discipled student develop?" These three major goals with specific objectives for leaders working with youth can help you assess the strengths and weaknesses of your youth ministry.

Youth ministry goals and objectives for home, church, or school can be divided into three areas: the student himself, the staff, and the parents. Evaluate your youth ministry in light of these goals and objectives.

GOALS FOR THE INSTITUTION
YOUTH MINISTRY[5]

PURPOSE
The purpose of a youth ministry is to assist students in developing their relationships with God, self, family, peers, and others by creating an environment in which learners can be evangelized and discipled so as to equip them to do the work of the ministry.

GOAL I—STUDENTS
To provide learners with a variety of experiences and opportunities

Objective 1. **Worship**—to provide opportunities for expressions of worship.
   2. **Instruction**—to provide group relationships for accountability and training.
   3. **Fellowship**—to provide regular opportunities for students to share life together.
   4. **Evangelism**—to present Jesus Christ to every young person.
   5. **Service**—to provide opportunities for students to serve the local body, missions, their community, and those in need.

GOAL II—STAFF
To seek, develop, and train adult staff to evangelize and disciple students

Objective 1. **Recruit staff**—so that the teacher:student ratio is 1:6-8.
2. **Staff training**—to provide continual training and refresher opportunities for staff.
3. **Organizational structures**—to design, organize, and administer the youth ministry.
4. **Staff meetings**—to establish regular staff meetings for training, planning, sharing, and evaluating.
5. **Staff evangelism**—to involve staff in personal evangelism with students.

GOAL III—PARENTS
To provide training, counseling, encouragement, and godly models for parents

Objective 1. Develop staff/parent relationships and rapport.
2. Discern specific needs of parents and design a strategy to assist them.

Once we establish biblical goals for youth ministry, they will set the direction for programming. What kind of programming should be developed for teaching youth?

PROGRAMMING AND CURRICULUM
How do we program, schedule, and teach to meet our learners' needs?

Our program should be based on how youth learn. The two foci should clearly be (1) evangelism—reaching out to youth, leading them to a commitment to Jesus Christ as Saviour and Lord, and (2) discipleship—leading them to grow in the Word of God, equipping them to share their faith.

Programming for youth should include these guidelines:

1. *Modeling.* Paul told the members of the Corinthian church, "Follow my example, as I follow the example of Christ" (1 Cor. 11:1). Teachers and parents must model Christlike attitudes and behavior. They must also model the spiritual truth they teach. The watchwords in youth ministry still are, "Don't tell me; show me." For youth leaders and teachers this means activities must take place both inside and outside of the church or school context. By joining a few students for lunch, participating with them in sports, and welcoming them at home, the teacher can really model what it means to be a godly man or woman.

2. *Learning.* James writes, "Do not merely listen to the Word, and so deceive yourselves. Do what it says" (James 1:22). Learning must be active. Anytime youth learn passively, learning diminishes. The right

learning activities with youth can help bring them from the point of knowledge of the Word to motivation to obey what it says.

Teachers and parents colearn with youth. Each leader must grow, maturing in the Lord Jesus Christ. Youth will quickly label as a hypocrite any teacher who does not grow along with them!

3. *Thinking.* For youth still moving from concrete and literal thinking processes to the abstract, we need to teach biblical truth in the context of deep, personal relationships. In our Lord's ministry almost every context of teaching began with a relationship. He taught His disciples by sitting down with them. They observed Him; they ate together; He observed their ministry; and He encouraged them.

Our Bible teaching ministry must be put into firsthand experiences for our teens. When you teach a theological truth, give personal illustrations of God at work today! In your teaching, share the praises and the pitfalls. Teenagers need to see their teachers as humans.

4. *Evangelizing.* Teachers and parents must be involved in evangelism. Here the modeling aspect dominates. Anyone can *teach* evangelism—proclaiming the Gospel so that the lost trust Jesus Christ as Lord and Saviour. Becoming active in aggressive evangelism is another matter.

Our Lord's last command found in Matthew 28:19 states, "Therefore go and make disciples." The "go" actually means "as you go" or "while going." He is saying that one must take every opportunity to share the Good News.

5. *Multiplying.* The end product of a proper youth ministry will be learners who win others to Christ, building them in the faith, and sending them out to do the same. Model, learn, think, and evangelize for the purpose of multiplication—bringing others to find Jesus Christ as Saviour and Lord.

6. *Large and small groups.* Teens need identity with both large and small groups. Relationships, however, are best developed in the small group where the ratio is one teacher to eight or ten students. Large groups can be used for sharing, music, etc. The heart of Bible study should be done in small groups. This means recruitment and training of more leaders, but the end product (the discipled student) makes it all worthwhile.

7. *Building students.* Some young people have great ability to lead others. Develop a teaching ministry that will direct the lives of your students toward leadership. For example, train a group of senior highs to lead a small group Bible study. Encourage them to reach out to their friends by establishing one on or near the campus. Give them love and appreciation when they attempt to reach out to peers in their sphere of influence. Growth will take place in the *individual* and also in the *small group.*

8. *Building relationships.* Because teens are relational in their thinking, we need to develop personal relationships with them. Allowing youth to see teachers and leaders in ministry and to take part as they are able will help disciple them. The resulting relationship will help both teacher and learner, now and in the future.

9. *Building excitement.* Teachers and leaders should get excited about the things that concerned Jesus! Attendance figures, finances, and programs are all crucial to youth ministry. They are, however, peripheral. We encourage students to attend, to give, and to get involved in the programs for one purpose—to become disciples of the Lord Jesus Christ. The goal of teaching youth is basic and biblical—that every teenager might *know Jesus Christ and make Him known in his own life.*

10. *Building an environment. Individualization* is the key word in helping students grow to maturity in Jesus Christ. What does the environment reflect? How do youth move toward becoming leaders and multipliers?

Dann Spader, in his "Sonlife Strategy of Youth Discipleship and Evangelism" seminars (a ministry of Moody Bible Institute), encourages students to progress up the pyramid that is shown below.

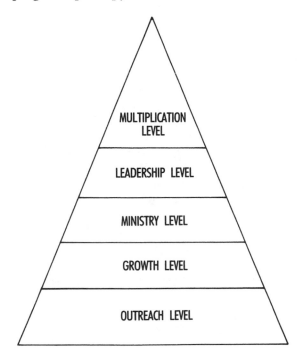

The teaching ministry of the home, church, or school should reach out to youth to come and listen. Some will respond and grow. Others will mature and learn how to lead others. Most classes may include a handpicked few who will become key leaders. This pyramid has been used very successfully by Reinhardt Bible Church where Youth Pastor Steve Johnson programs to move students toward a ministry of multiplication. As you look at the chart, "Programming for Youth Ministry," evaluate your own ministry with youth.

As teachers and leaders implement the strategy for reaching and teaching youth, there must be a plan that will help develop excellence in the instruction of God's Word. Help teachers make use of the entire teaching session and make every minute count for spiritual growth. Also take into account all of the guidelines mentioned earlier in this chapter. For a complete discussion, please refer to the section in chapter 10, "Youth/Adult" in "Understand the Teaching Schedule."

Certain specific programs can develop youth, moving them from outreach phases to becoming leaders of leaders.

1. *Outreach level.* A large variety of programs can be planned to reach out to youth in church, school campus, and community. Retreats, large group meetings, special parties/events, concerts, and camps can bring in non-Christians, give them a positive experience in a Christian atmosphere, and move them toward understanding and acceptance of the Gospel message.

2. *Growth level.* This level moves each learner toward Christian growth and maturity. Sunday School, retreats, Sunday evening meetings, mid-week Bible studies, etc. prove excellent for encouraging each learner to grow in God's Word.

3. *Ministry level.* Special training sessions can be scheduled to assist specific youth to learn to minister in many areas. Some will enjoy audiovisual and media production. Some will enjoy planning for drama. Others will enjoy putting together the monthly newsletter. Still others will want to shepherd their peers through a Bible study. Some youth may desire to teach a children's Bible class on Sunday or during the week. These students need to be given opportunity and encouragement.

4. *Leadership level.* A youth group will have a few at this level, designed to develop leaders within the group. One exciting method of developing leaders is to recruit those at this level to go as counselors-in-training on a week-long session of a children's summer camp. They will be ready to learn and lead.

5. *Multiplication level.* A group may have a few high school students who are ready to lead the leaders—to be trainers of leaders. More college students and adults fit into this category. Stretch those who are at this level in a multiplication ministry.

Programming should be based on the needs of youth along

PROGRAMMING FOR YOUTH MINISTRY*

STUDENT MATURITY LEVEL	PRODUCT	CHALLENGE
LEADER OF LEADERS	**MULTIPLICATION LEVEL** — Designed to use high school and college students to be leaders in youth ministry.	COME AND LEAD LEADERS
LEADERS	**LEADERSHIP LEVEL** — Designed to develop leaders within the group. — Tennessee Trek (Leadership Training during weeks at camp)	COME AND LEARN TO LEAD
COMMITTED	**MINISTRY LEVEL** — Designed to develop student leaders: AV, drama, newsletter, shepherds. — Ministry Team	COME AND MINISTER TO OTHERS
CONVINCED	**GROWTH LEVEL** — Designed to move student toward growth through classes, large groups, Bible teaching, electives. — Prime Time (Sunday AM) — Summer Retreat — High School Hour — Overtime (Sunday PM)	COME AND GROW
CURIOUS • Fun Seekers • Non-interested • Secular	**OUTREACH LEVEL** — Designed to bring in non-Christians, give a positive experience, allow them to get close to Christ or accept Him as Saviour and Lord. — Ski Trip (December) — Spring Retreat (April) — Life Line (large group meeting)	COME AND LISTEN

TEACHING YOUTH MEANS THAT LEADERS MINISTER TO THEM WHEREVER THEY ARE!

with specific goals to meet those needs. With the proper guidelines, strategy, teaching plan, and programming ideas, youth can develop into growing, serving leaders.

METHODS AND MATERIALS
What methods and materials do we use?

Teaching youth presents rewards and challenges. Today's teens have a fast lifestyle, filled with entertainment and self-indulgence. How do we compete with home video and laser shows?

What methods can be used for teaching junior and senior highs? Nine categories of methods and materials can assist in making Bible study come alive for youth. These methods can apply to teaching times other than Sunday morning.

1. *Art activities.* These activities encourage learners to express themselves through making bumper stickers, cartoon strips, montages, collages, and charts.

2. *Creative writing.* Writing is an excellent way to get learners into a passage of Scripture. Have them actually get into the character or be at an event. Such activities might be writing an acrostic, an abridged edition, a contemporary parable, graffiti poster, or a prayer.

3. *Discussion activities.* These stimulate learners both mentally and verbally. Agree/disagree, brainstorming, buzz groups, neighbor-nudge, picture-response, and debate are but a few that can be used successfully.

4. *Drama activities.* These activities will often bring out the "actor" in learners. Use interview, role play, or skits. Let them videotape their own "TV show." Use drama to motivate and involve your students.

5. *Music activities.* Most youth love music. Capture that enthusiasm by using some of these in teaching: commercial jingle, song writing, and listening to the words of a popular song.

6. *Oral presentation.* Bible reading, choral reading, the one-minute sermon, a monologue, or a panel can get learners involved verbally and mentally.

7. *Puzzles and games.* Learning should be fun! This group of activities will help students identify and remember points of the Bible passage: acrostic puzzle, crossword puzzle, scrambled verses, and secret message puzzle.

8. *Research activities.* These take more than reading and repeating. Some students want to get involved in an in-depth study of a passage, a book, the life of a Bible character, or a "hot" issue. Activities include: book report, survey, field trip, inductive study, research/report.

9. *Miscellaneous activities.* These don't fit any of the other eight groups. They feature: displays/exhibits, models, quizzes, and service projects.

These methods will work well in a Bible teaching ministry if you observe several guidelines:

1. *Start gradually.* Don't jump into the first teaching session with 4,987 different learning activities! Teach as you normally would and incorporate one or two activities, evaluating the learners' response.

2. *Give clear instructions.* Good directions prove crucial if the activity is to succeed. When possible, have the instructions written on a chalkboard, chart, or overhead projector.

3. *Choose a leader and recorder for each group.* For an activity to succeed, there must be a leader. Leaders can be peers, college students, or parents. Plan ahead to make activities work so that learners can grow.

4. *Give realistic time limits.* Always predetermine the length of time for any group activity. Stopping a group right in the middle of an exciting activity may sour them for next week's session.

5. *Encourage students.* Let them know that you have confidence in them. Visit each group, being ready to answer a question or make a suggestion.

6. *Let them do it alone.* It is not the job of the teacher to do for the student what he can do for himself. Allow them to succeed and, on occasion, fail.

7. *Provide the resources.* Make sure that all the needed equipment and materials are in the room and readily available.

8. *Sharing results.* Always plan time for students to share their finds or products. *Process is the most important part of using learning activities.*

9. *Be affirming.* Show that you appreciate their hard work. It will not only mean much to those who participated but it will also model for those who sat back and just watched.

ORGANIZATION AND ADMINISTRATION
How do we organize to make the ministry effective?

For a detailed discussion of organization and administration for youth ministry, please see the section by the same title in chapter 7. The discussion covers (1) recruiting and training of leaders, (2) facilities, and (3) curriculum. Keep in mind that youth need 10-15 square feet of space per person for proper educational facilities.

EVALUATION
How do we evaluate our ministry to youth?

Evaluation holds importance for ministry to youth. Are we accomplishing our goals? Are we helping to develop our discipled students? These eight questions can be used for evaluation of a teaching ministry for youth. As you read each one, evaluate the ministry of your church or school.

1. Do learners have strong, transparent models of the Christian faith? What changes need to take place? What staff training needs to take place?

2. Do teaching sessions provide active learning? Does the teaching portray leaders growing in the Christian faith? What changes need to take place? What emphasis should be given for future teacher training?

3. Does the teaching encourage thinking that is relational in process? Do teachers share firsthand experiences in the classroom? What changes need to take place?

4. Do teachers motivate learners to apply biblical truth? Does the program provide the motivation for multiplication? Do learners receive instruction on how to evangelize? Are they being motivated to spiritually multiply themselves on the campus? What changes need to take place to make this happen?

5. Do teachers build students so that they will lead peers to Jesus Christ? What should be done to make this happen?

6. Do teachers build relationships so that students can see leaders as growing Christians and disciple-makers? How can this happen?

7. Do teachers build excitement about the primary responsibilities of the Christian life—developing disciples who can then become disciple-makers?

8. Does the environment provide for individual growth? Are learners being motivated to move toward growth and leadership? What must change to allow this to happen?

Evaluation can be devastating or it can challenge a person to trust God for growth in an area of weakness. Evaluate with love and care. Let teachers and leaders know that the purpose is to help, not hinder.

Teaching young people means helping individuals grow in Christ. Remember the biblical directives God has given us and the educational cycle that can help us meet the challenge. Remember too that God is the One who empowers us to do the task. Youth ministry not bathed in prayer is just an exercise in futility! Trust our great God to achieve the impossible in your class! Trust God to heal and restore teens you don't know how to handle. Last, trust Him to help you become the leader that He has chosen for this special challenge—teaching His kids!

ENDNOTES

1. Doug Stevens, *Called to Care.* Grand Rapids: Zondervan Publishing House, 1985, p. 13.

2. Pastor Steve Johnson, Minister to Youth, Reinhardt Bible Church, Dallas, Texas.

3. Pastor Dennis Larkin, Minister to Youth, Pantego Bible Church, Arlington, Texas.

4. "Goals for the Individual—The Profile of a Discipled Student" was developed through many long weekends together by dedicated church staff and volunteers at Pantego Bible Church, Arlington, Texas, summer 1983.

5. "Goals for the Institution" was developed by Pastor Dennis Larkin, Youth Minister at Pantego Bible Church, Arlington, Texas.

6. "Programming for Youth Ministry" is adapted from Dann Spader's "Sonlife Seminar" by Pastor Steve Johnson, Minister to Youth, Reinhardt Bible Church, Dallas, Texas.

BIBLIOGRAPHY

Adelson, Joseph. *Handbook of Adolescent Psychology.* New York: John Wiley and Sons, 1980.

Aleshire, Daniel O. *Understanding Today's Youth.* Nashville, Tenn.: Convention Press, 1982.

Benson, Warren S., and Mark H. Senter. *The Complete Book of Youth Ministry.* Chicago: Moody Press, 1987.

Bimler, Richard W. *The Youth Group Meeting Guide.* Loveland, Colo.: Group Books, 1984.

Borthwick, Paul. *But You Don't Understand.* New York: Oliver Nelson, 1986.

Bradshaw, Charles. *You and Your Teen.* Elgin, Ill.: David C. Cook, 1985.

Bundschuh, Rich and Annette Parrish. *How to Do Bible Learning Activities, Grades 7–12—Book 2.* Ventura, Calif.: Gospel Light Publications, 1984.

Burns, Ridge. *Create in Me a Youth Ministry.* Wheaton, Ill.: Victor Books, 1986.

Campbell, Ross. *How to Really Love Your Teenager.* Wheaton, Ill.: Victor Books, 1983.

Dobson, James. *Preparing for Adolescence.* Santa Ana, Calif.: Vision House Publishers, 1979.

Elkind, David. *All Grown Up and No Place to Go.* Reading, Mass.: Addison-Wesley Publishing Company, 1984.

Erikson, Erik. H. *Identity: Youth and Crisis.* New York: W.W. Norton and Company, Inc., 1968.

Glenbard East *Echo. Teenagers Themselves.* New York: Adama Books, 1984.

Green, Kenneth. *Insights: Building a Successful Youth Ministry.* San Bernardino, Calif.: Here's Life Publishers, 1983.

Koteskey, Ronald L. *Understanding Adolescence.* Wheaton, Ill.: Victor Books, 1987.

Reed, Ed, and Bobbie Reed. *Creative Bible Learning for Youth, Grades 7–12.* Ventura, Calif.: Gospel Light Publications, 1977.

Rice, Wayne. *Junior High Ministry.* Grand Rapids: Zondervan Publishing House, 1978.

Richards, Lawrence O. *Youth Ministry: Its Renewal in the Local Church.* Grand Rapids: Zondervan Publishing House, 1985.

Roadcup, David, ed. *Methods for Youth Ministry.* Cincinnati: Standard Publishing, 1985.

Stevens, Doug. *Called to Care.* Grand Rapids: Zondervan Publishing House, 1985.

Stewart, Ed, and Neal McBride. *How to Do Bible Learning Activities, Grades 7–12—Book 1.* Ventura, Calif.: Gospel Light Publications, 1982.

Stone, J. David. *The Complete Youth Ministries Handbook.* Nashville, Tenn.: Abingdon, 1979.

Willey, Ray. *Working with Youth.* Wheaton, Ill.: Victor Books, 1982.

Yaconelli, Mike, and Jim Burns. *High School Ministry.* Grand Rapids: Zondervan Publishing House, 1986.

9. TEACHING ADULTS IN THE CHURCH

Kenneth O. Gangel

"Baby-boomers" we call them—Americans born between 1946 and 1964. Seventy-six million of them live across the fifty states. There are 60 million single adults in America and over 2 millions "POSSLQs," a term the Census Bureau now applies to "Persons of the Opposite Sex Sharing Living Quarters." By 1995 the number of Americans between the ages of 35–55 will have risen by one third. Single parent families accounted for 11 percent of all families in 1970; that figure doubled to 21 percent in 1981; and demographers expect it to reach 50 percent by 1990.

Teaching adults in the church today is certainly different from what it was twenty years ago! But few churches have understood that difference and fewer still have responded to it effectively. The 1990 population spread will generally approximate the following divisions and numbers: 19 million children under five; 33 million children between the ages of five–thirteen; 13 million senior high teens fourteen–seventeen; 65 million young adults ages eighteen–thirty-four; 83 million middle adults aged thirty-five–sixty-four; and 29 million senior adults over sixty-five.

To put it another way, over the forty years between 1950 and 1990, the number of people *under eighteen* will rise about 35 percent while the number of people *over eighteen* will rise by 68 percent. Adult education commands our attention—now and in the future.

But a greater question remains than that raised by population statistics; is adult education biblical? Apart from the teaching role of parents at home, no aspect of Christian education could be easier to defend. Teaching children and youth demands our best, and this chapter in no way diminishes that strategic ministry. But essentially the Bible is an adult book written by adults for adults with purposes of adult education in mind. Perhaps we can find no more definitive expression of adult education in the church than the words of Paul to a young pastor named Titus:

> You must teach what is in accord with sound doctrine. Teach the older men to be temperate, worthy of respect, self-controlled, and sound in faith, in love, and in endurance. Likewise, teach the older women to be reverent in the way they live, not to be slanderers or addicted to much wine, but to teach what is good. Then they can train the younger women to love their husbands and children. . . . Similarly, encourage the young men to be self-controlled. . . . Teach slaves to be subject to their masters in everything, to try to please them, not to talk back to them. . . . These, then, are the things you should teach. Encourage and rebuke with all authority. Do not let anyone despise you (Titus 2:1-4, 6, 9, 15).

Paul's commands in Titus 2 all aim at adult education of various ages and types of people. One understands immediately that unless Pastor Titus carries out his role of adult education, the ministry at Crete would be ineffective—a lesson we can well learn in the church today. Five specific groups are identified; older men, older women, young women, young men, and slaves. For each we read specific objectives and a brief overview of content. The goal of adult education at Crete was to produce self-controlled, godly Christians who were eagerly doing good while waiting for Christ's return (vv. 12-14).

The Greek text of this chapter contains eleven words related to instruction; the English text (NIV), fourteen such words. The first and last verses both strongly emphasize the importance of teaching adults.

Our purpose centers on grasping what is different about adult education and how to reorganize and reorient church education programs to accommodate this important dimension of ministry.

UNDERSTANDING HOW ADULTS ARE DIFFERENT

Adults *are* different. Different not only from each other but also from other age-groups we commonly teach in the church. They are different in their view of self, much more aware of personal needs and the immediacy of learning. Educational settings for adults need to be psychologically, physically, and environmentally adult. That usually leads to methods which emphasize informality, opportunities for participation, and an immediate dynamic relevance of content. But more of that later.

Adults are also different from children and youth in life experiences, having stored up a wealth of background which they bring to every learning situation. This enables us to draw on them as resources, not just students to be informed. It means they should have opportunities to diagnose their own learning needs rather than always having content imposed on them.

Their difference demonstrates itself in what we might call readiness to learn. Adults bring to the learning task much greater self-direction and willingness to "option" on issues. Motivation for adult education relates inseparably to what we might call "ownership"—adults must clearly understand that learning experiences relate and were not contrived just to keep educational machinery functioning.

Finally, adults differ in their perspective of time; they are possessed by a definite "now" orientation. Perhaps that is why Paul wrote that Titus ought to himself demonstrate and teach others to "live self-controlled, upright, and godly lives in this present age" (v. 12). Adults (particularly younger and middle adults) seem more "present-age" oriented than any other age-group. The educational implication emphasizes immediate practicality and specific problem-solving in the educational task.

LEARNING DISTINCTIVES

One could list almost endless "distinctives" of adult education but I have chosen two which need to be mastered and practiced by every teacher of adults.

ADULTS LEARN BY THEIR OWN INITIATIVE.

Their learning is, in effect, "self-directed." Children and young people perceive themselves as being dependent persons who constantly expect adults to make their decisions both at home and at school This changes, particularly in the senior high years, but we can assume it as a fair generalization of childhood and early teen years. We constantly work at "motivating" children and teenagers to learn and that motivation is quite commonly external.

With adults that approach simply will not work. In adult education we must come to a genuine unleashing of internal desire to learn, which provides the proper basis of motivation to begin with.

ADULTS WANT TO KNOW THE IMPORTANCE OF LEARNING ANY GIVEN SUBJECT.

Since learning for them serves as a means rather than an end, they resent learning situations which treat them like children. This relates back to that broad base of life experience mentioned earlier as well as their difference in self-concept. Sometimes we need to teach adults to relearn how to learn since formal schooling has conditioned them to a dependent procedure.

151

GOAL DISTINCTIVES

One could argue that since all Christian teaching aims toward bringing people to maturity in Christ, general goals do not vary among the age-groups. Perhaps if we used the word "purpose," we could make such a statement. With preparation of learning goals and teaching objectives, however, more specific orientation becomes necessary. Certainly we can correctly say that the learning goals related to any given class of adults look backward at the developmental and learning distinctives just discussed and look forward to the age-groupings which will form the next portion of this chapter.

Simply stated, the developmental task approach to education views the learning process not so much as a long, slow, but regular climb (such as might be pictured on a cost-of-living chart), but rather as a series of stair steps, rather steep at times but "interspersed with plateaus where one can speed along almost without effort."[1] Since the learning process continues from the cradle to the grave, it includes all adults, thereby making satisfactory, productive adulthood dependent on an understanding of the developmental task approach to learning. As an individual grows both in size and age, he discovers new physical, emotional, and psychological resources to meet tasks of increased difficulty. The tasks themselves arise not only from physical sources but also from cultural pressures and from the value system of the person.

In preparing to teach adults we must take into consideration the three types of learning recognized and described by Bloom, Krathwohl, and associates—*cognitive, affective,* and *conative.* Cognitive objectives deal with mental processes and identify what the adult learner should know, comprehend, apply, analyze, synthesize, and evaluate. Such objectives emphasize remembering or reproducing something which has been learned. They focus on solving intellectual problems or reordering information which has been given to the student. This area seems clear to most teachers since most classroom teaching tends to gear primarily toward cognitive objectives.

The affective domain, however, is considerably more fuzzy. Affective objectives emphasize a feeling tone, an emotion, an attitude or degree of acceptance or rejection on the part of the student. Obviously Christian teachers should be greatly concerned about this dimension of their ministry.

The third type of learning, described in secular education is generally referred to as "psychomotor," which emphasizes some muscular or motor skill, manipulation of materials and objects or hand-eye coordination. Some types of learning within Christian education fall into that category but some of us have chosen to substitute the term "conative" which deals with skills based on performance abilities. To put it almost too simply, *cognitive* deals with what the student knows, *affec-*

RELATIONSHIP OF 3 LEARNING
DOMAINS TO OBSERVED BEHAVIOR

COGNITIVE	AFFECTIVE	CONATIVE
Learner is able to interpret meaning of STOP sign	Learner feels it is important to be a safe driver and values his/her role as a good citizen	Learner has developed habit of stepping on brake to observe STOP sign

OBSERVED BEHAVIOR
Learner stops car at stop signs
even when other cars or officers are not around

tive with how he feels, and *conative* with what he can do. Espich and Williams pull these together in the illustration of a person who approaches a stop sign while driving a car.[2] Again, psychomotor forms the third category, but conative describes a skill as well as a mechanical response. The word "conative" is simply the adjectival form of "conation," a noun describing "the act of attempting" with the second meaning even more to the point—"to act purposefully."

In the first rectangle, the learner interprets the meaning of a stop sign as a command to stop his car. In the Affective Domain the learner feels it is important to be a safe driver and a good citizen by stopping. In the Psychomotor Conative Domain the learner has developed an unconscious habit of stepping on the brake when he wants to stop. Target Behavior? The learner stops his car at stop signs even when no other cars or policemen are around.

For over 30 years I have taught adults in colleges, seminaries, churches, conferences, seminars, and a host of other situations. I have had to force myself to balance these three goal distinctives by thinking of the way learning goals and teaching objectives flow out of the needs of the student. It doesn't come easily but it is imperative to teach adults.

One more thought. You will notice that I have not frequently used the word "behavioral" while talking about objectives, even though that term has earned popularity. In reality, the word "behavioral" is so broad that it can cover cognitive, affective, and conative. We dare not stop with just the knowledge and comprehension levels of the cognitive domain. As Leroy Ford puts it, we must take our students from the state of "So what?" to the state of "Aha!"[3]

UNDERSTANDING ADULT AGE-GROUPINGS

This area brings out the most arbitrary analysis of how adults should be taught. Some Sunday Schools do not concern themselves with age-groupings at all but rather sex groupings—classes for men and classes for women. Others argue that the age-groupings must have a definitive ten-year span with classes for those in their 20s, 30s, 40s, etc. Keep in mind here that our goal focuses not on how adults should be divided in Sunday School, but rather on how we understand them with respect to their needs within certain generalized age brackets. Even at that, the choices appear arbitrary. We will look at young adults as being eighteen–thirty-five; middle adults aged thirty-five–sixty; and senior adults over sixty. Few people will be happy with that kind of categorization but some boundaries must be selected to acquaint us with the characteristics of the three basic age-groups so that we can meet their needs in a local church teaching ministry.

YOUNG ADULTS—EIGHTEEN–THIRTY-FIVE.

Essentially almost any church contains five groups of young adults who call for attention. There are those we refer to as the *college and career group,* post-high school adults over the age of 18 who have had no relationship to marriage and may not for many years. The second group we'll just call *young couples,* newly marrieds, usually in their 20s, most likely still involved with education or career, but separate from that first group because they are married.

The third group we can label *new parents,* a term which speaks for itself. Here again the new parents might still be in college or graduate school, certainly one of them (if not both) is involved with a career, but they differ from the first two groups because they have one or more children. The fourth group almost automatically takes us up the chronological age ladder as we identify *parents of teens.* This group would actually overlap into the middle adulthood area, but many folks under the age of thirty-five find themselves parents of teens and so the category must be included here. Finally, the very popular category of *singles* which we'll deal with in a later section of this chapter is a special need group.

The age period must be superimposed on the category grid to understand and minister effectively to young adults. However, we must not "box" adults into any particular one of the five categories just because they fall into a certain age-group. For example, a single adult is a single adult whether she's eighteen or thirty-three; and new parents could be nineteen or twenty-nine or even thirty-nine. While the career choice group gets younger the college group gets older. All of these variations help us understand the flexibility that must be applied to recognizing and dealing with young adults.

How can we understand these people? One advantage points out that all of us have been (or are) in this age category, and that much more recently than we were children or youth. Personal experience provides a strength. Erikson's research suggests that "intimacy" offers the key word for this age-group, a period of vast transition and no small heartache.[4] With high school friendships gone and college ties broken, newly marrieds may be down to one "best friend." Their transition into the adult world causes them to ask, "Is this really what I expected?" They experiment with adult roles and lifestyles which may differ greatly from those of their parents. Only a modicum of career commitment shows, especially during the decade of the 20s. Overall statistics indicate that the average American changes jobs seven times and careers three times during his adult years.

Robert J. Havighurst, famous for his work on developmental tasks, suggests eight such tasks for early adulthood to which I have added two which seem particularly relevant to Christian adults:[5]

1. Selecting a mate.
2. Learning to live with a marriage partner and achieving a fusing of two lives into one.
3. Starting a family; having the first child successfully.
4. Raising children with accompanying adjustment to the expanding family, the whole new life of a family, and the psychological problems involved.
5. Managing a home.
6. Getting started in an occupation.
7. Taking on civic responsibilities.
8. Finding a congenial social group.
9. Accepting one's place in the local church.
10. Learning to assume Christian leadership and discipline with respect to oneself, one's family, and others.

MIDDLE ADULTS—THIRTY–FIVE-SIXTY.

Someone said middle age is when you've met so many people that everyone reminds you of someone you've met before. Now policemen look like teenagers and one meets young adults he knew as small children. In Daniel Levinson's much celebrated work on adulthood, he talks about a settling down time in the late 30s followed by the mid-life transition (crisis) in the early 40s.[6]

The rosy optimism of youth behind and the harsh realities of the final years not yet on them, middle adults generally tend to find life quite satisfying. However, since chronological age does not guarantee increasing emotional maturity, the danger exists that crisis will bring disillusionment and bitterness. Security jumps in as the key concern and middle adult males tend to be very career-oriented, which can sometimes cause problems at home. Mothers busily care for children who have become teenagers. They're about to enter adulthood, so both parents must prepare for the transition from parenthood to grand-parenthood.

Some refer to the middle adult as a "belonger" who affiliates with numerous fraternal, political, social, and religious organizations, spending time and resources to further their causes. The later years of the period have been often designated as a "dangerous age" or "the second storm in stress." During this time physical vigor begins gradual decline and each adult must consider philosophical adjustment to a lighter program of living in order to avoid what may become a disconcerting emotional state. Resistance to change will likely interfere with maturation of values, interests, and concepts.

Levinson sees five major transitions occurring about ages twenty, thirty, forty, fifty, and sixty. The "mid-life transition" of the early 40s brings middle adults (particularly men) face-to-face with mid-life crisis forcing appraisal of the past and preparation for a seemingly uncertain future.

It may be helpful to list some of the development tasks of middle adulthood as we did for young adults:

1. Learning advanced job skills.
2. Changing careers.
3. Planning for retirement.
4. Returning to careers (women).
5. Adjusting to aging parents.
6. Relating to one's spouse as a person.
7. Finding new interests.
8. Keeping out of a rut.
9. Compensating for physiological changes.
10. Developing a realistic time perspective on life.

SENIOR ADULTS—SIXTY AND OVER.

In the last decade of middle adulthood (fifty-five–sixty-five), there comes to both men and women an increased awareness of mortality, bringing with it a "mellowing" but not much flexibility in theology or lifestyle. In many ways maturity has finally arrived as these "genuine adults" no longer perceive parents as causing their problems or spouses as exercising undue control over their lives. Senior adulthood offers a challenge in our day and will continue as a major target for church ministry well into the next century. One million of those baby-boomers will reach the age of 100, and after the year 2000, there will be more "old people" than "young people" in the United States for the first time in the history of the country. Mancil Ezell, expert on curriculum and instruction for the Southern Baptist Convention, uses the word "celebration" to describe senior adults. He suggests that the key tense is the *present* as these folks have finally arrived at a level of life toward which they have been moving and working for over six decades.[7]

People in this category have earned the respect and dignity which the Bible certainly accords elders. Meanwhile, however, physical strength declines; but in most cases, the word "deterioration" is simply incorrect.

The church must affirm senior citizenry because we live in a society that puts a premium on youth. We tend to look at retired people in the light of what they *have* been or *have* accomplished rather than what they *are* or perhaps still *will* accomplish. The result to the older person is a feeling of having been shelved, and the body of Christ should provide a balanced view.

The wise church educator avoids any implicitly negative names or terms for senior adult groups. Even something like "The Golden Years" conjures up visions of retirement centers, wheelchairs, and Medicare.

The church can respond to senior adult ministry by developing both intellectual and interpersonal relationships. It is foolish to believe that adults can no longer learn; learning ability does not wear out. The *rate* of learning may decline but the *capacity* remains constant. We must all cultivate this capacity and encourage our senior adults to recognize that they need to exercise their minds. Like an atrophied muscle, the ability to learn tends to weaken only because it has not been used.

Most important for church education is a recognition that the Bible pays deep respect to older people. Both within families and the wider society God permits no scoffing or demeaning of "old people." We must adopt a program based on the guidelines of Scripture which elevates and celebrates the significance of folks in this age-group. As David Moberg notes, "Spiritual nurture is the number one task of the church in its work with the aging. But other ministries, rightly conducted, will aid in performing that task and increase the effectiveness of the church."[8]

One more time, a list of developmental tasks, here adapted from the work of Malcolm Knowles.[9]

1. Adjusting to retirement.
2. Finding new ways to be useful.
3. Understanding Social Security, Medicare, and other retirement programs.
4. Adjusting to reduced income.

157

5. Learning to live alone.
6. Relating to grandchildren.
7. Understanding the aging process.
8. Keeping morale high.
9. Keeping up personal appearance.
10. Preparing for death.

Rather than shunting off our senior citizens, or in some way belittling their contribution to the church's task, we should help them make uncommon demands on the church. In a very real sense, the opportunity to have a voice and role in the church's ministry has been *earned.* Our culture shames itself by catering to teenagers who have no idea what the church ought to be doing (encouraging their participation and seeking their advice), while bypassing people in whom the Spirit of God has been working for 50 years or more.

UNDERSTANDING HOW ADULTS LEARN

Much of this has been introduced earlier in the chapter under the general umbrella "Understanding How Adults Are Different." But further specificity would be useful, particularly with respect to the learning theories of andragogy. We have already spoken of Erikson, Havighurst, Levinson, and Knowles. Were this an entire volume just about adult learning theory we would add a discussion of Boelen's Five Stages and Roger Gould's Seven Stages, describing how various theories of adult learning all contribute to our overall understanding. But the major prophet of adult education has been Malcolm Knowles with his emphasis on *andragogy*—the theory and practice of adult education.

The term was first coined by German school teacher Alexander Kapp in 1833 and found its way through European educational systems until by 1954, Professor T.T. ten Have was lecturing and writing on andragogy in the Netherlands. In 1966, the University of Amsterdam introduced a doctorate in andragogy. Knowles entered the scene in 1950 with a book entitled *Informal Adult Education* followed by numerous other titles including his definitive, *The Modern Practice of Adult Education,* published by Association Press in 1975.

Knowles is clearly a developmentalist and refers to andragogy as a "process model" focusing on what happens *during* learning rather than on the content. Since Knowles will offer us no theological perspective, evangelical educators need to balance a proper emphasis on content (the authority of the inerrant Word of God) without losing touch with Knowles' helpful thoughts on process.

According to Knowles, andragogy unfolds in seven steps.
1. The establishment of a climate conducive to learning. The

objective of this first step serves to maintain a physical and mental atmosphere which encourages participation and learning at all levels.

2. Creation of a mechanism for mutual planning. Here we encourage the student to involve himself with the teacher in determining the mode of communication which will best lead to joint participation in the process.

3. Diagnosis of the needs for learning. Both individual needs and corporate needs must be addressed, both "felt" and fulfilled.

4. Formulation of program objectives. This step helps determine the content of material which will meet the needs identified in step 3.

5. Design of a pattern of learning experiences. Once we determine what the needs are and how teacher and student will mutually seek to meet them, a vehicle must be chosen to make those goals attainable.

6. Conducting of learning experiences with suitable techniques and materials. Here we add implementation of the learning procedure.

7. Evaluation of learning outcomes. During this final step we observe how the implementation and reception of both process and content actually "worked."

Perhaps it should be noted here that in his early works Knowles argued andragogy in *contrast* to pedagogy (the teaching of children). He has more recently mellowed his views to the presentation of andragogy as simply *another model* of assumptions about learners which should be used alongside pedagogy.

All this sounds very much like the educational cycle which some of us having been using for a long time (see chaps. 7–8). The adult education uniqueness, however, stresses individual responsibility, self-initiation, immediacy, and practicality of learning outcomes.

Finally in this section of our chapter I should say just a word about *synergogy,* a more advanced approach to adult learning built on the principles of andragogy. Synergogy is "learner-centered teaching which applies the principles of andragogy to peer group learning situations." It differs from other teaching approaches because it replaces authority figures with learning design and enables learners to become proactive participants who exercise responsibility for their own learning. The key is to pull learners together rather than to compete, to use the learners' "colleague affiliations" to enhance motivation.

Synergogy offers learners meaningful direction through learning designs and instruments. The teacher structures the process of learning by providing a framework of orderly steps to acquire knowledge, attitude, and skills (cognitive, affective, and conative). Numerous examples of the process exist, the most simple of which is the "team effectiveness design."

In the TED model the teacher assigns individual preparation

common to all members of the class (a reading assignment, interviews, video viewing). He then creates an adequate instrument to assess knowledge, probably a multiple choice exam which identifies key learning segments and concepts. The test is administered and teams of students pulled together.

Their discussion targets group agreement and in this process, the group regulates itself. The goal is a team score better than the individual scores, thereby indicating that joint effort (cooperation rather than competition) resulted in a better learning process than individual effort alone.

Eugene Trester spells it out when he says:

> Many educators who are interested in adult biblical learning are beginning to realize that for optimum learning to take place, they themselves need to acquire skills in facilitating the basic processes of adult learning. Educators have known for a long time, but are only recently really coming to practice the ancient insight, that learning, not teaching, is the heart of education. Novice teachers often need years of classroom experience before they can manage shifting the focus away from themselves as the teacher and attend to the needs of the learners. Increasing numbers of adult biblical educators are becoming convinced they need preparation, a certain amount of unlearning, a good knowledge of the theory and a rich experience with facilitating adult interdependent learning.[10]

UNDERSTANDING SPECIAL NEED GROUPS AMONG ADULTS

In an article in *Leadership* magazine, David Mains expressed the desire of most pastors and teachers of adults I know.

> I want my preaching to communicate specific responses to genuine needs felt by real people. And I find they respond favorably to such down-to-earth preaching anchored in their world. They don't particularly want more ideas. They aren't enamored with brilliant analysis or formal essays. I can't even assume that they have a great love for theology or a vast reservoir of biblical knowledge.
>
> I always ask the question: "What practical suggestions can I give to help people respond to what is said?" That's a watershed question. If I adequately address that question, my listeners will appreciate what they hear. And they'll be helped by it.[11]

Obviously multiple "special need groups" surface among adults in almost any church. We will look at just four and even those ever so briefly.

SINGLES.

Consider four types of singles: those who have never been married (either by choice or by circumstance); those who have been married and whose spouse still lives (representing either divorce or separation); those who have been widowed; and those who might be called "spiritual singles," Christians whose partners do not know the Lord. Great diversity marks these four groups of people but our ministry must focus on their *similarities*, particularly their similarities of need. In this section of our chapter we'll treat single parents apart from singles though many of the needs are comparable if not identical. What do our singles need?

They need *acceptance*. Only as people who fight the burden of loneliness recognize their acceptance by the Heavenly Father and by His people can they move on to seek and receive acceptance from others outside the body and, especially, acceptance of themselves.

Singles also need a *strong sense of self-worth*. Donna Peterson writes:

> Many Christian singles seem to struggle to find a positive identity. It is paradoxical that Christians, who believe that they are made in the image of God and that Jesus Christ loved them so much that He died to redeem them, have a poor self-image. Instead of developing their sense of self-worth as children of God, they feel inferior because they have not married. . . . The church, the place for Christian fellowship and encouragement, sometimes seems to alienate the single person because of its emphasis on marriage and the Christian family.[12]

Singles need a *sense of belonging*. Loneliness and insecurity are dispelled not only by a sense of belonging but also by the genuine *reality of belonging* both in attitude and act. Too often singles ministries in local churches create a social subculture which functions almost apart from the main body of the congregation. Integration into the body not only provides an antidote to the problem of feeling that one does not belong, but it is the biblical pattern of the New Testament church!

SINGLE PARENTS.

Nearly half the children born in the '70s will spend time living in one-parent homes before age eighteen. By 1990, one half of all children in American schools will be leaving and returning to one-parent homes every day. For traditional two-parent families in which both parents are believers, the church must never become a substitute for

God-ordained parental ministry. It serves rather as a supplement to what the Father wants the parents to do.

In the case of single-parent families, however, a certain amount of surrogate parenting is necessary and the body of Christ can help provide it. One major need here is freedom from stress. Most of the things we have talked about in relation to the loneliness of singles can become elements of *psychological and emotional stress* of much greater dimension for single parents. These are complicated by what might be called *domestic stress.* Family pressures build, especially in the homes of single parents, because their children struggle with adjusting in school and peer relations. *Financial stress* also comes about because of limited income and the necessity to work full time, sometimes during afternoon or evening hours, which makes effective parenting most difficult. *Social stress* creates problems as single parents ask themselves whether they ought to be dating, remarrying, or even spending so much time with their married friends. To these stressful, needy people, the body of Christ must bring a sense of security and peace; we must deal with the practical issues of their lives in real and helping ways.

DIVORCED.

Obviously many single parents can be classified as "singles" and many divorced adults as single parents. But not all, so divorce becomes a separate problem to be dealt with in a slightly different light by the local congregation. Dr. Albert Solnit, Director of the Yale Child Study Center in New Haven, Connecticut, suggests that divorce presents one of the most serious and complex mental health crises facing children in the 1980s. Over a million children a year suffer the dissolution of their families, and this plague has affected the church as it spreads across the nation and the world.

Without arguing different views on or about the rightness or wrongness of divorce, let us confine ourselves here to how we minister to adults who find themselves in this situation. Certainly forgiveness figures prominently. Assuming repentance and a willingness to follow the will of God, the body of Christ dare not be judgmental nor condemning. Divorced people must be restored to fellowship in the body, though some congregations may have specific restrictions with respect to certain offices.

The pastor particularly should make himself available to divorced people, representing the symbolic response of the body in a somewhat official way (Gal. 6:1-5). Finally, some kind of care group needs to be established, most likely made up of divorced people themselves. Relationships, group dependency, and prayer support can all come out of this kind of ministry.

Of crucial importance here is the attitude of the body. David Lambert, himself a single parent, asks, "Where is the church in all this?

Single parents hear themselves talked about a lot in sermons these days. It's one of the 'cutting edges' of Christian ministry. But for most single parents that's just a tease."[13]

Lambert argues that awareness offers only the beginning of help. Attitude and response in everything from financial assistance to loving acceptance becomes essential in ministering to divorced people in the local congregation.

FAMILIES.

One of the major goals of adult education strives to strengthen and build families, thereby reproducing the cycle of Christian education from the earliest instructional efforts in the preschool departments to senior adult classes which deal with grandparenting. Sunday School classes and other church educational experiences must focus on the real issues parents and children face in the late twentieth century. They must be aware of studies like those conducted by Yankelovich in which parents themselves enumerate the kinds of study groups which would interest them:[14]

1. Parenting and handling the attendant problems, 34 percent.
2. Teaching children about sex, 31 percent.
3. Handling problems of discipline, 36 percent.
4. Dealing with drug use among children, 49 percent.
5. Convincing children not to smoke, 37 percent.
6. Understanding new classroom teaching methods, 42 percent.
7. Teaching children about religion, 32 percent.

The obligation of children to parents and the obligation of parents to children has been obscured in modern-day society and needs to be biblically reaffirmed by the church. Pulpit preaching, special Sunday School classes, weekend seminars, family camps, and every possible means should be enlisted to develop a serious ministry of family life education in the church. We must teach our parents to be effective in modeling, in ministry, and in multiplication. The first two are obvious; the third should be.

Those who work professionally in Christian education often speak of teaching as "a ministry of multiplication." Since every parent is a teacher, parenting is also (indeed, more so) a ministry of multiplication. Obviously parenting includes physical reproduction but it also ought to feature spiritual reproduction. Christian parents need to rear children who possess Christian values and general commitment to Jesus Christ and His church. Our educational programs for adults should have those goals squarely up front.

Is the ministry of teaching adults in the church anachronistic—a leftover dream from an earlier day? Or is it a newborn baby wishing to be nurtured more effectively? According to a Church Data Service survey conducted by Denver Seminary, only 78 percent of the adults who attend church also attend Sunday School, at least every other week.

Meanwhile, Lyle Schaller reports that more adults attend Bible studies today than 20 years ago. Harold Westing recommends that adult Sunday School classes aim at the needs of adults at any given period in their lives, much as we have described them in this chapter. He argues for "classes with common goals," "friendship classes," "periodic electives," "promoting fellowship," "cell groups," and the process of "constantly starting new groups."

Adult education faces an exciting future. But only if educational leaders are willing to make it an area of significant concentration in their ministries. That kind of focus is not an option; it is a necessity. As Westing argues, "Your church can still have a growing adult Sunday School if its leaders are willing to adjust to our changing society."[15]

ENDNOTES

1. Robert J. Havighurst, *Developmental Tasks and Education*. New York: Longmans, Green & Co., 1948.

2. James E. Espich and Bill Williams, *Developing Programmed Instructional Materials.* Belmont, Calif.: Fearon, 1967, p. 5.

3. Leroy Ford, *Design for Teaching and Learning.* Nashville, Tenn.: Broadman Press, 1978, p. 360.

4. Eric Erikson. *Identity: Youth and Crisis.* New York: Norton, 1963.

5. Havighurst, pp. 72–98.

6. Daniel Levinson, *The Seasons of a Man's Life.* New York: Knopf, 1978.

7. Mancil Ezell, unpublished conference notes, Scripture Press Ministries Seminar on Adult Education.

8. David O. Moberg, "What the Graying of America Means to the Local Church," *Christianity Today* (Nov. 20, 1981), p. 33.

9. Malcolm Knowles, *The Adult Learner: A Neglected Species.* Houston: Gulf, 1973.

10. Eugene Trester, "Biblical Andragogy," *The Bible Today* (Sept. 1982), p. 293.

11. David Mains, "From Applications to Action," *Leadership* (Fall 1986), p. 65.

12. Donna Peterson, "Life Is for Singles Too," *Voices* (Winter 1981), p. 6.

13. David Lambert, "Coming Up Short," *Moody Monthly* (October 1987), p. 17.

14. Daniel Yankelovich, et al. *Raising Children in a Changing Society.* Minneapolis: General Mills, 1977.

15. Harold Westing, "Comeback in the Classroom," *Moody Monthly* (July/August 1987), p. 26.

BIBLIOGRAPHY

Bradshaw, Charles O. *Faith Development: The Lifelong Process.* Elgin, Ill.: David C. Cook Publishing Co., 1983.

Clements, William M., ed. *Ministry with the Aging.* San Francisco: Harper & Row, 1981.

Crawford, Dan R. *Single Adults: Resource and Recipients for Revival.* Nashville, Tenn.: Broadman Press, 1985.

DeBoy, James J., Jr. *Getting Started in Adult Religious Education.* New York: Paulist Press, 1970.

Elias, John L. *The Foundations and Practice of Adult Religious Education.* Malabar, Fla.: Kriegen Publishing Co., 1982.

Foltz, Nancy T. *Handbook of Adult Religious Education.* Birmingham, Ala.: Religious Education Press, 1986.

Knowles, Malcolm. *The Adult Learner: A Neglected Species.* Houston, Texas: Gulf Publications, 1973.

_____. *The Modern Practice of Adult Education.* Association Press, 1975.

Knox, Alan B. *Helping Adults Learn.* San Francisco: Jossey-Bass Publishers, 1985.

Peterson, Gilbert A., ed. *The Christian Education of Adults.* Chicago: Moody Press, 1985.

Sell, Charles A. *Transition.* Chicago: Moody Press, 1985.

Stokes, Kenneth, ed. *Faith Development in the Adult Life Cycle.* New York: Sadlier, 1983.

Vogel, Linda Jane. *The Religious Education of Older Adults.* Birmingham, Ala.: Religious Education Press, 1984.

Wilbert, Warren N. *Strategies for Teaching Christian Adults.* Grand Rapids: Baker Book House, 1984.

10. CHOOSING AND USING CREATIVE METHODS
Robert Joseph Choun, Jr.

Jesus Christ, the perfect Teacher, is our model for choosing and using creative methods. In fact, Horne states, "In a way not surprising but confirmatory of our previous impressions, Jesus embodies those qualities of the Teacher commonly set up as ideal."[1]

Jesus used a variety of methods to get people actively involved in the learning process. He combined His words with His works.

1. Jesus said, "While I am in the world, I am the light of the world" (John 9:5). Jesus then healed the man who was born blind. The man's response was, "I was blind but now I see!" (v. 25)

2. Jesus said, "I am the resurrection and the life. He who believes in Me will live, even though he dies; and whoever lives and believes in Me will never die. Do you believe this?" (11:25-26) Jesus then raised Lazarus from the dead (vv. 43-44).

3. Jesus said, "I am the bread of life. He who comes to Me will never go hungry, and he who believes in Me will never be thirsty" (6:35). Earlier in the chapter, Jesus had fed the 5,000 (vv. 1-14).

Jesus' methods moved His listeners from simple knowledge of the facts to proper attitudes and actions. The Master Teacher knew that learning is change—from the old life to the new.

Jesus used the following methods in His teaching and preaching ministry:

1. Object lessons (John 4:1-42)—using familiar "water," to help the Samaritan woman understand the unfamiliar "Living Water."
2. Points of contact (1:35-51)—using opportunities to build relationships with people, Andrew, John, Peter, Philip, and Nathanael.
3. Aims (4:34)—to move people to action.
4. Problem-solving (Mark 10:17-22)—to move people to un-

166

derstand and apply Jesus' words.

5. Conversation (v. 27)—to move people to obedience.
6. Questions—As recorded in the Gospels, Jesus asked more than 100 questions for the purpose of provoking people to think and to seek the truth.
7. Answers—Jesus used His answers to move people from where they were to where they needed to be in order to grow spiritually. Jesus encouraged people to discover the truth.
8. Lecture (Matthew 5–7; John 14–17)—Jesus made use of discourse to instruct and convince the people in the truth.
9. Parables (John 10:1-21; 15:1-10)—Jesus taught by illustrating spiritual truth with familiar situations.
10. Scripture—Jesus quoted extensively from the Old Testament to teach people God's truth.
11. The teachable moment (4:5-26)—Jesus took every opportunity to make an ordinary situation a "teaching situation."
12. Contrast (Matt. 5:21-22, 33-34, 38-39, 43-44)—Jesus contrasted His kingdom with worldly standards, giving the listener a choice for obedience.
13. Concrete and literal examples (6:26-34)—Jesus used the concrete to teach abstract truths such as trust, greatness, hospitality, discipleship, etc.
14. Symbols (26:17-30; John 13:1-20)—Jesus used symbols, such as the Passover before His death and washing His disciples' feet, to teach great lessons.
15. Large and small groups (Matt. 5–7; John 14–17)—Jesus taught large groups (the crowds, the multitudes) and small groups (the disciples).
16. Individual teaching opportunities (John 3:1-21; 4:5-26)—Jesus took the initiative in reaching out to individuals, helping them understand who He was and what He was going to do.
17. Modeling (Matt. 15:32; Luke 18:15-17)—Jesus, the Master Teacher, was the Truth and modeled what it meant to be a Man who loved God the Father.
18. Motivation (Matt. 16:24-27; 20:21-28; Mark 1:16-18)—Jesus motivated His followers to action. He sparked a response from within the person to godliness and obedience to the Father.
19. Impression and expression (Matt. 4:19-20; 7:20)—Jesus used Himself to impress and motivate His followers to act and obey. Jesus was God in the flesh, yet He helped His disciples decide for themselves.

20. Himself (28:19-20)—Jesus possessed the qualities of a great teacher: a global vision, understanding of man, mastery of all knowledge, ability in teaching, and a life that was an example to those whom He taught.

In your teaching ministry, how can you choose and use proper and exciting teaching methods that will challenge people to action, obedience, and growth? Consider five areas when choosing and using creative teaching methods.

UNDERSTAND THE CRITERIA

There are ten criteria that should be understood before teaching any age-level.

LESSON AIMS AND OBJECTIVES.

What are your lesson aims and objectives? What do you want your learners to KNOW, FEEL, and DO based on the lesson from God's Word? Your class session should contain a balance between the student's knowledge of God's Word, a proper attitude toward what it has to teach, and the willingness to apply the teaching to his life.

NUMBER OF LEARNERS.

A large class should be divided into small groups. Will each small group need a group leader? Will leaders need printed instructions? How much time will be given to small group work? How much to the assembled class?

SIZE OF CLASSROOM.

Assess your classroom carefully. How large is the classroom? Can you divide the class comfortably into smaller groups? Would it be best to ask for another classroom to facilitate your teaching methods?

ALLOTTED TIME.

How much time do you really have for your teaching session? If you have one hour or longer, you can incorporate many learning activities, providing time for exploration and discovery of the Scripture. If time is short, reevaluate the minutes you devote to large group activities.

EQUIPMENT AND FACILITIES.

Evaluate your classroom facilities and equipment. Would small tables help foster a warmer, more intimate atmosphere in the teaching session? Do you have access to visuals and audiovisual equipment? Must large items of furniture or equipment be moved out in favor of increased floor space?

RESOURCES AND CURRICULUM.

Evaluate your teaching resources and curriculum; gear both to the age-level of your learners. Involve students in the teaching/learning process and provide many creative methods to motivate them to obedience to our Lord.

LOCATION OF THE ROOM.

Is your room located in a quiet area of the building or next to a nursery filled with crying babies? Does the morning sun shine through the windows, preventing everyone from seeing the projection screen? Locate rooms in spaces conducive to learning.

AGE OF LEARNERS.

Review the suggested schedule for the age-level of your learners. Each age-level requires a special schedule. Teaching young children (see chap. 7) is much different from teaching adults (see chap. 9). Remember the age-group characteristics and needs of your learners. Attention span, literal-concrete vs. abstract thinking, verbal and motor skills, all play a very important part in your choice of methods.

CLIMATE OF THE GROUP.

How long have these people studied together as a class? If they've been together for six months or longer and have had monthly socials together, they will probably share on an intimate level. People relatively new to each other will not want to share on a deep level. Evaluate the level of trust, confidence, expectation, and commitment before selecting a method.

TEACHER(S).

Are you the only teacher? If so, you do all of the planning for the teaching sessions. If, however, you have one or more people teaching with you, meet together at least monthly to pray and plan for the upcoming month's or quarter's class sessions. Team teaching can be an exciting method in itself. Teachers can model relationships for class members (1 Cor. 11:1).

UNDERSTAND THE LEARNING PROCESS

Knowing how people learn and teaching accordingly can help them respond to God's Word with growth and obedience. What learning process should a teacher follow?

APPROACH   EXPLORE   DISCOVER   ASSUME RESPONSIBILITY

APPROACH.

The approach activity is designed to get the learner thinking about and involved in the session theme. For young children this involves learning activities that give each child experiences relative to the focus from God's Word. Elementary children begin with an activity to build readiness for the Bible study. Youth and adults usually enjoy an activity that challenges them to think and verbalize their thoughts on a specific topic. An approach activity can begin when the first learner walks into the room, thus using every minute for the teaching session.

EXPLORE.

Allowing learners to explore God's Word can be extremely rewarding. Exploration activities require extra preparation, but the investment pays off. Young children are asked to explore the "God's Wonders" table where they will be learning through nature activities. Letting children participate in Bible study keeps their interest and creates the excitement of exploration of something new. Youth and adults also need to explore and make observations for themselves to see God's Word through a new perspective.

DISCOVER.

Learners not only need to explore God's Word but also to make observations and discoveries. Imagine a young child discovering what it was really like for the blind man in John 9:1-41. "I can't see," the blindfolded little boy complains as he moves around the room, not knowing where his next step will lead him. The blindfold removed, he responds, "I can see! I can see!" The teacher whispers, "How do you think the blind man felt after Jesus healed him?" That experience will remain with a learner much longer than the simple fact, "Jesus healed the blind man" as told by a teacher. With the right guidance and encouragement, youth and adult learners can make excellent discoveries from God's Word and contribute them to the rest of the class.

ASSUME RESPONSIBILITY.

Jesus, in His teaching sessions, encouraged people to move toward maturity. He was constantly directing His followers to obedience. In Mark 10:17-23, Jesus told the rich, young ruler, "Go, sell everything you have and give to the poor, and you will have treasure in heaven. Then come, follow Me." James 1:22 says, "Do not merely listen to the Word, and so deceive yourselves. Do what it says." Taking the time in class to help students apply God's Word to life assists in the growth process. Every effective teacher works for change in the life of each class member.

UNDERSTAND THE TEACHING SCHEDULE

Learners at each age-level have specific characteristics and special needs. Challenge each learner in light of his development: physical, mental, social, emotional, and spiritual. Implement the teaching/learning process differently for each age-group.

EARLY CHILDHOOD (BIRTH THROUGH AGE SIX).

Research studies show that a child develops approximately 50 percent of his or her intelligence by the age of four, another 30 percent by eight, and the final 20 percent by seventeen.[2]

Young explorers spend every minute discovering themselves and their world. They can learn through a schedule of activities and creative methods designed specifically for their age-level.

Play occupies an increasingly large place in the child's life. A child plays spontaneously. You don't have to teach him how to play or provide him with special toys. The urge comes from within. A child learns, develops, and builds knowledge through play. Play reflects children's understanding of the world and is therefore a constant testing of the world.[3]

The Bible teaching schedule for young children should include:

1. Bible learning activities (30–45 minutes). BLAs allow learning to begin as soon as the first student arrives. They also provide for the child's constant need for activity and play. BLAs stimulate the child's interest, guiding it toward the focus for that teaching session. A choice of several BLAs give him the freedom to select an activity and to accept the responsibility for his decision. BLAs provide opportunities for the guided conversation needed to weave scriptural truths into everyday activities. Lastly, BLAs provide for the small group experiences that young children need for proper social development.

2. Worship time (10–15 minutes). Children move to a large group for worship time. Here, the child participates in additional activities focused on the theme from God's Word. Teachers lead children in music, prayer, repetition of the memory verse, finger fun, large muscle activities, action songs, acknowledgment of birthdays, and the offering. Teachers not involved in the direct leadership of worship time sit on the floor in the midst of the children.

3. Bible story and activity time (10–15 minutes). Our main objective in telling Bible stories is not to have children remember the small details. We want the Bible to speak to the child about his life at home, in his neighborhood, and at church.

Bible story time is a small group activity in which a teacher has the same group of children throughout the year. Preserving the small group helps build those vital teacher/student relationships.

Use creative methods to tell the story. The worst method that can be used this week is the same method that was used successfully last week. Though very young children enjoy some repetition, older children find it monotonous.

Activity time reviews and reinforces the truth found in the Bible story. Coloring pages, simple projects, guided conversation, and questions can help move the young child toward understanding and applying the truth from God's Word.

4. Until parents come. A wise teacher will always have games and songs available for young children until their parents arrive. Combining songs with the "clean-up game" encourages cooperation. Order resources from your curriculum publisher or your local Christian bookstore.

CHILDREN (GRADES 1–6).

Each minute of your Sunday morning schedule should contribute effectively to the learning experience of the child. Just as all the pieces of a puzzle interlock to produce one picture, so should every part of your schedule fit cohesively into an overall purpose.[4]

1. Bible study (total of 30 minutes). The child's Bible study time divides into three sections for proper involvement, comprehension, and application.

a. Readiness activities (approx. 10 minutes). Set up readiness activities before the first child walks into the classroom. As children arrive, they choose one of several activities, each one providing information which will aid in their understanding of the Bible story. Children can work on one or more activities in the time provided.

b. Bible story (approx. 10 minutes). The Bible story can be told live by the teacher, or played on audio or video tape. The readiness activities should be woven into the story, providing geographical, historical, archeological, or cultural backgrounds for the events. An example would be using a crayon resist technique on poster board to have the handwriting appear on the wall as in Daniel 5, "Belshazzar's Feast."

c. Life application (approx. 10 minutes). This section is designed to encourage children to live God's way. Activities, discussion, and decisions should all help children in discovering the relationship between Bible truths that they have been studying and their day-to-day experiences. Planned questions, along with the use of a student guide, can help put God's Word into the hearts, minds, and actions of these learners.

2. Bible learning activities (total of 20–30 minutes). BLAs review and reinforce the Bible story and the truths taught. These activities involve small groups that work with art, music, creative writing, drama, Bible games, and other skills. Whatever the activity, children work on their level of ability. The same class that produced the crayon resist for Daniel 5 could also put together a "frieze" (mural) depicting all the events in that same chapter. Later, it could be displayed on the walls of the classroom so that the teacher and children could "walk through" the story of Daniel and the events of his life. This frieze could also be displayed in the church narthex so that parents could see the progress made by their children.

3. Bible sharing (total of 10–15 minutes). This part of the hour includes activities that all focus on the theme from God's Word that has just been studied. Music, prayer, memory verse, teacher/learner testimonies, and the offering point the children toward the Lord and what His Word has meant to each one.

4. Until parents come. Waiting for parents to arrive can be a problem in children's ministry. Having Bible games and several songs available can be helpful. Resources can be secured from your curriculum publisher or your local Christian bookstore.

YOUTH/ADULT (GRADES 7–12 / COLLEGE AND ABOVE.)

1. Fellowship time (early arrivers until lesson begins). Youth and adults need close fellowship. They enjoy their peer groups and the activities that accompany these meaningful relationships. Fellowship begins when the first learners arrive. Sometimes this means talking, praying, or sharing light refreshments. Fellowship time should encourage warmth and acceptance within the group. The class should be a place where youth and adults feel comfortable and loved by other class members. This time also provides a welcome for visitors.

2. Approach (10 minutes). The approach activity focuses the learners' attention on the session topic or theme. It might be a discussion question, a neighbor-nudge, a graffiti poster, a puzzle, or one of more than a hundred different methods. Class members rarely come to class with a learner's attitude. They have gone through an entire week of events and trials since last Sunday. The approach activity can get them thinking about the topic or theme.

3. Exploring God's Word (30–45 minutes). The exploration and discovery of God's Word through various creative methods can be meaningful for each learner. This section of the teaching session focuses on getting the learner into God's Word instead of simply sitting and hearing a lecture.

The youth/adult teacher should consider these steps when preparing a lesson for these age-groups.

    a. Determine the purpose of your lesson. What are your goals?

    b. What is the main idea from God's Word that you want to teach? Keep it simple enough to remember.

    c. List two to five subpoints for the lesson. How can the Scripture be divided to be easily taught?

d. Vary the techniques and lesson organization.

e. Prepare visuals to clarify the lesson (overhead transparencies, charts, maps, illustrations, etc.).

f. Consider time allotted for the class session. Allow time for teacher input and learner participation.

g. Plan for learner involvement. Use methods such as worksheets, listening sheets, handouts, small group discussion, summarization, questions, and demonstrations.

h. Plan for transitions between sections of the teaching session. What will happen to move class members from the approach activity to the exploration of God's Word?

i. Check your plans. Does the lesson consider the age-group characteristics and needs of your learners?

j. Practice the lesson before a mirror or with a tape recorder. How will the learners react to the teacher's speech and gestures?

4. Conclusion/decision (10–15 minutes). Once learners have been challenged with God's Word through various teaching methods, they are ready for the last crucial step. That step encourages youth and adults to conclude what God's Word has said to them and apply it. Teachers often forget this step in teaching youth and adults. Students who know God's Word may not automatically apply it.

One class, after studying Joshua 1, wrote their fears on index cards. After small group prayer, each person went to the front of the room and dropped the index card into the flames in a barrel, signifying that God had heard the prayer and would answer.

CHOOSE APPROPRIATE METHODS

Once the teacher has understood the criteria, the learning process, and the teaching schedule for the age-group, creative methods can be chosen. Specific references in the bibliography contain hundreds of methods for each age-level.

Six guidelines are crucial to the selection of creative teaching methods:

1. Make sure that the method or activity matches the learners' level of ability and maturity.
2. Provide several choices of activities to stimulate interest in the learner.
3. Provide variety to keep learners' interest and prevent boredom.

4. Include clear directions to ensure learner success.
5. Include planned questions that assist the learner to think through the levels of knowledge, comprehension, and application.
6. Include guidance and encouragement that sustain the learner's interest and motivation.

EVALUATION

The teacher is not finished until evaluation has been completed. Evaluation should take place as soon after the class session as possible. The teacher might even ask a class member to help answer these eight questions.

1. Did all methods and activities help accomplish the aims?
2. Did my instructions seem clear to everyone?
3. Did the summarization and conclusion tie all of the session elements together?
4. Did my methods coordinate with the lesson?
5. Did I prepare my materials on time?
6. Did the questions stimulate thinking on the levels of knowledge, comprehension, and application?
7. Did activities provide for learners of varied abilities?
8. Did I plan for the use of several groups (depending on my class size)?

What other questions would you ask your class?

Properly applied, creative teaching methods serve as valuable tools. Improperly used, they can be reduced to flashy effects that dazzle rather than enlighten. The needs of the learners must be the foremost consideration because they indicate which Bible truth would be most vital to their current development The teaching goals for the learners' response to the lesson, along with the other factors considered in this chapter, will guide teachers in the selection and use of the best methods for that particular lesson. If a method fails to produce the expected results, store it away for another occasion when a different lesson or learners may provide a better application. Too novel or outlandish a method may obscure the lesson, but the perfect pairing of message and medium can instill new knowledge, alter attitudes, and change lives.

CHOOSING AND USING CREATIVE METHODS

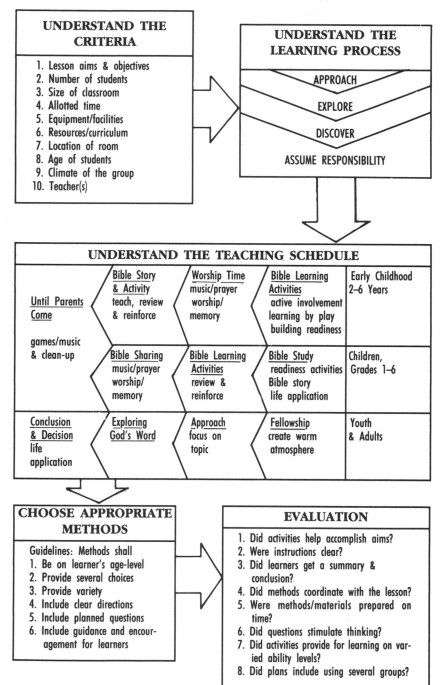

UNDERSTAND THE CRITERIA

1. Lesson aims & objectives
2. Number of students
3. Size of classroom
4. Allotted time
5. Equipment/facilities
6. Resources/curriculum
7. Location of room
8. Age of students
9. Climate of the group
10. Teacher(s)

UNDERSTAND THE LEARNING PROCESS

APPROACH

EXPLORE

DISCOVER

ASSUME RESPONSIBILITY

UNDERSTAND THE TEACHING SCHEDULE

Until Parents Come games/music & clean-up	Bible Story & Activity teach, review & reinforce	Worship Time music/prayer worship/ memory	Bible Learning Activities active involvement learning by play building readiness	Early Childhood 2–6 Years
	Bible Sharing music/prayer worship/ memory	Bible Learning Activities review & reinforce	Bible Study readiness activities Bible story life application	Children, Grades 1–6
Conclusion & Decision life application	Exploring God's Word	Approach focus on topic	Fellowship create warm atmosphere	Youth & Adults

CHOOSE APPROPRIATE METHODS

Guidelines: Methods shall
1. Be on learner's age-level
2. Provide several choices
3. Provide variety
4. Include clear directions
5. Include planned questions
6. Include guidance and encouragement for learners

EVALUATION

1. Did activities help accomplish aims?
2. Were instructions clear?
3. Did learners get a summary & conclusion?
4. Did methods coordinate with the lesson?
5. Were methods/materials prepared on time?
6. Did questions stimulate thinking?
7. Did activities provide for learning on varied ability levels?
8. Did plans include using several groups?

176

ENDNOTES

1. Herman Harrell Horne, *Teaching Techniques of Jesus.* Grand Rapids: Kregel Publications, 1978, reprint of 1920 edition, p. 206.

2. Susan Striker, *Please Touch.* New York: Simon and Schuster, Inc., 1986, p. 16.

3. Donna Harrell and Wesley Haystead, *Creative Bible Learning for Children—Birth to 5 Years.* Ventura, Calif.: Gospel Light Publications, 1977, p. 41.

4. Barbara J. Bolton and Charles T. Smith, *Creative Bible Learning for Children—Grades 1–6.* Ventura, Calif.: Gospel Light Publications, 1977, pp. 107–08.

BIBLIOGRAPHY

Bausch, William J. *Storytelling: Imagination and Faith.* Mystic, Conn.: Twenty-Third Publications, 1984.

Beaty, Janice J. *Skills for Preschool Teachers.* Columbus, Ohio: Charles E. Merrill Publishing Company, 1984.

Beechick, Ruth. *Teaching Juniors.* Denver, Colo.: Accent Books, 1981.

————. *Teaching Primaries.* Denver, Colo.: Accent Books, 1980.

Bolton, Barbara J. *How to Do Bible Learning Activities Grades—1–6.* Ventura, Calif.: Gospel Light Publications, 1982.

Bolton, Barbara J. and Charles T. Smith. *Creative Bible Learning for Children—Grades 1–6.* Ventura, Calif.: Gospel Light Publications, 1977.

Gangel, Kenneth O. *24 Ways to Improve Your Teaching.* Wheaton, Ill.: Victor Books, 1982.

Goldman, Ronald. *Religious Thinking from Childhood to Adolescence.* New York: The Seabury Press, 1964.

Griggs, Patricia. *Creative Activities in Church Education.* Nashville, Tenn.: Abingdon Press, 1974.

Griggs, Donald. *Translating the Good News through Teaching Activities.* Nashville, Tenn.: Abingdon Press, 1973.

Hall, Miriam J. *New Directions for Children's Ministries.* Kansas City, Mo.: Beacon Hill Press, 1980.

Harrell, Donna and Wesley Haystead, *Creative Bible Learning for Children—Birth to 5 Years.* Ventura, Calif.: Gospel Light Publications, 1974.

Horne, Herman Harrell. *Teaching Techniques of Jesus.* Grand Rapids: Kregel Publications, 1974 (reprint).

Howard, Walden, ed. *Groups That Work.* Grand Rapids: Zondervan Publishing House, 1967.

Klein, Karen. *How to Do Bible Learning Activities, Ages 2–5.* Ventura, Calif.: Gospel Light Publications, 1982.

LeBar, Lois E. *Family Devotions with School Age Children.* Old Tappan, N.J.: Fleming H. Revell, 1973.

LeBar, Mary E. *Children Can Worship.* Wheaton, Ill.: Victor Books, 1976.

LeFever, Marlene D. *Creative Teaching Methods.* Elgin, Ill.: David C. Cook, 1985.

Leypoldt, Martha M. *40 Ways to Teach in Groups.* Valley Forge, Pa.: Judson Press, 1967.

Marlowe, Monroe and Bobbie Reed. *Creative Bible Learning for Adults.* Ventura, Calif.: Gospel Light Publications, 1977.

Montessori, Maria. *The Absorbent Mind.* New York: Delta Books, 1967.

Newson, John and Elizabeth. *Toys and Playthings.* New York: Pantheon Books, 1979.

Reed, Ed and Bobbie. *Creative Bible Learning For Youth—Grades 7–12.* Ventura, Calif.: Gospel Light Publications, 1977.

Reid, Clyde. *Groups Alive—Church Alive.* New York: Harper and Row Publishers, 1969.

Richards, Lawrence O. *Creative Bible Study.* Grand Rapids: Zondervan Publishing House, 1971.

————. *Creative Bible Teaching.* Chicago, Ill.: Moody Press, 1970.

Stewart, Ed, Neal McBride, Sherry Lindvall, and Monroe Marlow. *How to Do Bible Learning Activities—Adult.* Ventura, Calif.: Gospel Light Publications, 1982.

Stewart, Ed and Neal McBride. *How to Do Bible Learning Activities—Grades 7–12.* Ventura, Calif.: Gospel Light Publications, 1978.

Striker, Susan. *Please Touch.* New York: Simon and Schuster, Inc. 1986.

Zuck, Roy B. *The Holy Spirit in Your Teaching.* Wheaton, Ill.: Victor Books, 1984.

11. USING YOUR PERSONAL COMPUTER IN TEACHING

Stuart S. Cook

Scanning her class during one of those precious quiet moments, Jennifer Thompson pondered the plight of prior generations of teachers who labored without the aid of personal computers. Just last night she used her computer to edit and print the class notes for today's afternoon class. Earlier she had compiled two tests with answer sheets using the school's computer and testing software. Later the same computer would allow automatic scoring and analyzing of the completed answer sheets and would record each student's score in an electronic gradebook. As Ms. Thompson surveyed the quiet scene she saw Jason, a slow reader, intently concentrating on the interactive reading lesson being handled by the classroom computer.

Not only did computer technology allow this teacher to complete teaching tasks more efficiently and effectively, it also enabled her to provide individualized instruction that would have been impossible prior to the advent of this instructional blessing. Many inspiring possibilities abound for teachers who learn to exploit computers in their teaching.

WHAT IS A PERSONAL COMPUTER?

A computer is a high-speed electronic device with the ability to accept instructions and data as input, analyze the data based on the instructions provided, and dispense information to a variety of output devices. You do not have to understand how the computer analyzes data as long as you know what input the computer requires in order to produce the desired output. A personal computer (PC) may be called a microcomputer, a computer built around a microprocessor. Generally small enough to sit on a desktop and possibly small enough to fit in a brief-

179

case or purse, the PC services one person at a time and performs functions that relate to the individual's work.

Computers are used in nearly every aspect of every industry in the modern world. Personal computers continue to shrink in size and price while growing more powerful and easier to use. People who thought they could not afford or understand how to use a personal computer a few years ago may be using one every day now and wondering how they ever managed without it.

The availability of computers to the average person has occurred rapidly over the past several years. As with most of the technologies we enjoy in the twentieth century, developments came slowly at first, then accelerated rapidly in the second half of the twentieth century. The slide rule was invented in 1630, followed by Pascal's adding machine in 1642. The first machine to utilize punched cards (the main input medium for mainframe computers until the mid-1970s) was Jacquard's punch card loom, invented in 1801. Babbage's "analytical engine" along with Ada Lovelace's programs in 1834 formed the first programmable computer, a mechanical rather than electronic computer. Two other prerequisites to modern computers followed in the middle 1800s: the invention of Boolean logic in 1854 and the typewriter in 1868.

The introduction of the electronic computer in the middle of the twentieth century heralded the beginning of the modern computer age. The evolution of computer technology is generally seen as occurring in four stages or generations (see Fig. 1). The first generation of electronic computers, introduced in 1946, had as their key component the vacuum tube, slow and unreliable by modern standards.

The "Whirlwind," one of the first vacuum-tube computers, occupied an entire building but could process only 20,000 arithmetic operations per second, about what a sophisticated hand-held calculator can process today.[1] The expression, "bugs" in a program, originated with vacuum-tube computers, because insects would fly into the com-

Figure 1

THE COMPUTER GENERATIONS

Computer Generation	Beginning Date	Major Innovation	Computer Designation
First	1946	Vacuum tube	Mainframe
Second	1959	Transistor	Mainframe
Third	1965	Integrated circuit	Minicomputer
Fourth	1977	VLSI	Microcomputer

puter and short-circuit one of the vacuum-tubes. This problem necessitated frequent shutdowns and occasional loss of data.

The beginning of the second generation of computers was signaled by the introduction of the transistor in 1959. Transistors are smaller, faster, more reliable, and use less power than vacuum tubes. As a result, second generation computers were smaller, much faster, and much more reliable than their first generation counterparts. First and second generation computers are referred to as "mainframe" computers, denoting large, fast, multiuser machines that require special environmental controls and trained operators to keep them running.

Integrated circuits, invented in 1965, gave birth to the third generation of computers. The development allowed computers to grow still smaller and faster. We call third generation computers "minicomputers."

The fourth generation of computers, known as "microcomputers," began in 1977 with the introduction of Very Large Scale Integration (VLSI), a process that allows integrated circuits containing tens of thousands of components to be packed onto a single silicon chip. VLSI resulted in microprocessors, complete computer processors imprinted on a single chip. This further miniaturization made the complete microcomputer system small enough to occupy part of an individual's desk or even be transported in a briefcase. Quite a change from the first generation of computers that had to be housed in separate buildings! This generation of personal computers that is now available for teachers to use in their teaching.

WHAT COMPUTERS DO AND DON'T DO

Computer technology has advanced so rapidly that many people are in awe of the machine itself. Computers seem to be able to do anything from playing chess to guiding a manned space flight. But can computers think? Do they possess intelligence? Well, yes and no.

The machine itself does not possess the capacity to reason. That it may appear to do so depends on the sophistication of the software that runs it. The term "software" connotes the set of instructions given the computer to guide its operations. The computer always does exactly as told. It cannot make decisions about what instructions to follow; it always follows the instructions given it by a human programmer. To be sure, the computer does not always do what we thought we told it to do; but it always acts on the instructions it has received (unless, of course, it is broken).

As computers get faster and remember more instructions (more memory), the sophistication of the software written for them is greatly increasing. Therefore, computers handle tasks today that we only dreamed about a few years ago. We even hear terms such as "artificial intelligence," an expression which refers to the concept that the computer can be given software that copies or models the procedures humans use to solve problems. But the intelligence must still be supplied by humans.

DOES THE COMPUTER BELONG IN THE CLASSROOM?

The existence of a new technology does not automatically mean that this new tool should be used in teaching. Nevertheless, computers are being used in teaching, as in virtually every aspect of modern life. The question is not, "Will we use computers in teaching?" but, "How will we use computers in teaching?" Shortly after the introduction of microcomputers Christopher Evans predicted that the microcomputer would result in the decline of the professions, particularly medicine and education.[2] He foresaw the computer replacing the classroom teacher in many instructional functions. To date this prediction has not materialized.

I believe that the microcomputer's greatest contribution to education is not to replace the teacher but to enhance his work. This enhancement can take place in two general areas. The first consists of using the computer as a *tool* in carrying out normal teaching duties; the second involves using the computer as a *tutor,* a teaching machine which delivers instruction, drills students on basic skills, or serves as a resource for inquiring minds. These two applications form the outline for the remainder of this chapter.

THE COMPUTER AS A TOOL

Software abounds to aid teachers with many of the tedious, mundane, and difficult tasks they perform on a regular basis. In addition, using a computer may reduce the time some tasks take, allowing the teacher to include more time for creativity in preparation for teaching.

Preparation of instructional materials can be strengthened with the use of computer technology. Virtually any task that can be carried out using a typewriter can be done more quickly, easily, and reliably with a computer using word-processing software.[3] Word processing software allows the teacher to create and edit complex documents without the need of retyping when revisions are needed.

In addition, special features of most word-processing software such as, automatic underlining, bolding, italics, centering, right margin justification, footnotes, endnotes, columns, spell-checking, etc., make the use of the typewriter completely obsolete for document preparation. Armed with word-processing software, you can crank out worksheets for students, class notes, exams, and many other types of instructional documents.

Your creative juices will flow as you explore ways to create visual aids for instruction using graphics software. Many excellent programs allow the teacher to prepare graphic visuals for use in student notes or as masters for production of overhead transparencies or slides. If you have a color monitor attached to the microcomputer, you can make a color slide of the screen's image and use it as a teaching visual.

At the time of this writing, the hottest topic in the microcomputer world is desktop publishing. Because of advances in computer technology, especially the introduction of laser printers, teachers can produce nearly typeset-quality visuals, newsletters, or even books with a microcomputer, desktop publishing software, and a good laser printer. Desktop publishing combines the features of word processing and graphics. Many programs allow the teacher to combine graphs, charts, even pictures into text created with a word processor. The results usually please both teacher and students.

RECORD-KEEPING.

Recording, averaging, and reporting grades strike many teachers as one of their most time-consuming and least satisfying tasks. Computer software can help. A class of software called electronic spreadsheets makes any numerical task that can be conceived of as rows and columns of numbers (such as a grade book) much easier.

Figure 2 displays a portion of a spreadsheet used as a grade book. Notice that we number the rows and letter the columns for easy reference. The individual averages and the descriptive statistics for each assignment (mean, standard deviation, high and low) are computed automatically by standard functions of the spreadsheet. Electronic spreadsheet software offers many of the same advantages as word processing software. It allows the teacher to enter, edit, compute, and report information without having to retype or calculate the information by hand.

The key to the usefulness of electronic spreadsheet software is its ability to accept formulas as entries in addition to numerical values and labels. Thus the spreadsheet can be set up to accept the values of scores earned on a series of assignments and tests and automatically compute the final average based on a formula that the teacher entered. This feature relieves the teacher of hand-calculating averages. The completed spreadsheet awaits your entering data and requesting printed reports. Reporting the information is done easily with flexible printing commands included in the spreadsheet software.

	A	B	C	D	E	F
1						
2		**GRADE BOOK FOR THEOLOGY 101**				
3						
4						
5	NAME	TEST 1	TEST 2	PAPER 1	PAPER 2	AVERAGE[a]
6						
7	DAHMS, DJ	85	88	89	92	88.9
8	FOUTS, DM	86	87	72	93	84.1
9	HALL, ME	90	95	80	88	87.4
10	HILL, SG	77	80	88	90	84.8
11	HOLTE, BD	95	94	86	90	90.6
12	JOHNSON, BG	99	96	85	97	93.6
13	JOHNSON, E	100	99	90	96	95.6
14	LEY, DP	65	78	82	88	79.6
15	MARTINI, WR	90	92	90	93	91.3
16	NORTH, JG	88	89	66	90	82.2
17	O'BRIEN, WD	84	88	90	87	87.5
18						
19	MEAN	87.2	89.6	83.5	91.3	87.8
20	S.D.	9.5	6.2	7.6	3.1	4.6
21	HIGH	100.0	99.0	90.0	97.0	95.6
22	LOW	65.0	78.0	66.0	87.0	79.6
23						

Figure 2—SPREADSHEET AS A GRADE BOOK

TEST CREATING, SCORING, AND ANALYZING.

Software is available for making the process of testing students much easier. Creating tests can be a tedious process. Test creation software allows the teacher to accumulate a collection of test items on related topics and then combine them into several different forms of the same test or to create several tests with different emphases.

Depending on the sophistication of the software, you may be able to select items with different difficulty, different format (true-false, matching, multiple choices, completion, essay), and other criteria. This type of software is particularly helpful if you use similar tests on numerous occasions. You can create alternate forms of the same test with the items in a different order to prevent students from becoming familiar with the exact test layout.

Paper and pencil tests generated by computer (or the old-fashioned way) may be scored and analyzed using computer technology. Input devices such as the marked-sense reader can scan an objective format answer sheet coded by the student with a soft lead pencil. Each student's answers can then be saved on a magnetic disk and used as input for a test analysis and reporting program.

In this system, the teacher receives a printed report detailing each student's performance as well as an analysis of item difficulty and the overall class performance on the test. For objective format test items, this system can save an enormous amount of time in the laborious task of scoring and analyzing a test.

EVALUATION AND SELECTION OF SOFTWARE.

In this section on the computer as a tool I want to suggest several types of teaching functions that can be enhanced with the use of computer software. I do not name specific software or hardware products. When you are ready to select software, the following steps should help:

First, carefully define the task you want to perform using the computer as a tool. Only when you know what your requirements are will you be in a position to evaluate a product.

Second, shop around to see what products you may secure in the general area you are interested in, whether word processing, graphics, desktop publishing, record-keeping, testing, or some other area. If you find a lot of features you didn't know you needed, go back to the first step and evaluate if you really need them.

Third, evaluate the cost and features of the software available to accomplish your tasks and select the product you feel will do the best job within the budget you have planned. Don't be taken in by software that has some "really neat" features that you do not need. You may be paying extra money for "bells and whistles."

THE COMPUTER AS A TUTOR

The ease with which a PC can store and utilize instructions prepared ahead of time by a programmer makes it capable of delivering instructions to students. Once you define effective interaction, the teaching session can be programmed and used repeatedly with the computer acting as tutor. This prospect does not eliminate the need of a teacher, but it does change the role of the teacher somewhat. By removing the necessity of individual drill with students, the machine as tutor frees the teacher to perform tasks better suited to humans.

Recent studies demonstrate the superiority of individual tutoring over conventional classroom instruction. The average achievement of students who received tutoring was better than the achievement of 98 percent of the students in the conventional classrooms.[5]

Individual tutoring often seems too expensive for all but the

185

wealthiest individuals. It is out of the question as an alternative for public or private education. However, the personal computer in the classroom could serve as a cost-effective alternative for at least some of the students' daily instructional time.

The first teaching machine was introduced by Sidney Pressey, a professor at Ohio State University in 1926.[6] Called the "Pressey Testing Machine," it was advertised as the machine that "tests and teaches." The concept, still foundational to programmed instruction, centers in the student gaining immediate knowledge of the results of his answer to a question. Correct responses are reinforced and incorrect responses are not.

In 1954 B.F. Skinner demonstrated a machine for teaching arithmetic.[7] This machine improved on Pressey's concept by not just testing the student (with learning as a byproduct) but presenting new information to the student in a planned sequence. The result was a complex skill built as the student progressed through a series of simpler subtasks. The machine presented material to the student and gave him opportunity to practice the skill a step at a time. Skinner reports that at this time he began to speak of "programmed instruction."

Programmed instruction became an educational fad in the '60s but faded because of the lack of an adequate delivery system. The introduction of the personal computer in the late '70s provided the basis for a programmed instruction delivery system sufficiently complex to create a realistic learning environment. The state of programmed instruction on computers, known as Computer Assisted Instruction (CAI), is still in its infancy.

A good deal of available instructional software suffers from poor design and programming. Most studies of the effect of CAI in comparison with traditional teaching methods show mixed results. Clearly, the state of computer technology and the sophistication of CAI software await further improvements before bringing about revolutionary improvements in the effectiveness of instruction. However, improvements in instructional hardware and software occur daily, and soon the computer as tutor will become a routine part of every person's educational experience.

APPROACHES TO THE COMPUTER AS TUTOR.

At least four major instructional models have been implemented using CAI software.

First, in drill and practice software, the student, having received instruction on a certain subject, sharpens his skill with the subject matter by interacting with the computer. He encounters arithmetic problems, spelling words, or foreign language vocabulary, for example, then formulates and enters the correct response. He receives immediate knowledge of the results of his response and opportunity to correct wrong answers until he has mastered the skill. This mode of instruction has been disparagingly referred to as "The World's Most Expensive Flash Card."[8] Kohl and others feel that the computer has too much potential to "waste" it on such trivial pursuits. Despite this opinion, drill and practice remains the primary instructional use of computers in schools today.[9]

Even if drill and practice software simply provides an electronic flash card, if the student gets individual practice time with feedback that he could not get because of the time pressures on the teacher, that practice offers a valuable use of instructional time. In addition, drill and practice software is becoming more sophisticated, including features that not only analyze the student's answer and give feedback, but analyze the pattern of incorrect answers and diagnose learning problems that are preventing the student from mastering the material. The diagnosis can be passed on to the teacher or can be used to lead directly into instruction delivered by the computer to help alleviate the learning problem.

Second, CAI software referred to as tutorial closely implements what is expected of a tutor. Tutorial software presents new information to the student, allows him to interact with the material (in some cases permitting the student to ask his own questions of the tutor), determines his progress in mastering the material, and structures learning experiences based on the progress of the student. This strategy presents a considerable challenge to computer programmers, considering that the program must be developed with students in general in mind and not just one particular student.

Tutorial software that adequately models a human tutor has not yet become available. All tutorial software currently available falls short in one or more of the functions that a student would expect of a human tutor. Nevertheless, we are making progress and software is available that allows the student to work with the CAI program and materials on other media to learn new material at his own pace, and learn it well.

The third category of instructional software includes simulations and games. This software presents the student with a situation that simulates real-life situations (past or present) or, in the case of some games, brings to life a fantasy. The student is faced with a problem plus certain rules and resources for solving the problem. He learns by implementing a solution to the problem and being shown how well his solution works. The program then lets him continue his search for adequate solutions to the problem. Should he continue to fail in his search for solutions, the program may present hints or display reasons why his solutions are not working.

Simulations can be used to teach history. For example, the student may be presented with a description of the resources available to the Union and Confederate armies at the Battle of Gettysburg. He might be given the choice of which army to lead and then be given the first decision he must make about deploying his forces, etc. The computer program analyzes his choices and presents the results of the first part of the battle using a simulation model or algorithm that is part of the design of the software.

The student then analyzes how well his initial strategy worked and uses that information in following decisions. This type of interaction (assuming the accuracy of the simulation model) provides a "hands-on" experience with a subject that otherwise may seem distant and unreal to young students of history.

Simulations proliferate in situations where real life presents too expensive or too dangerous a situation for an inexperienced student. For example, elaborate computer simulations find extensive use in training airline pilots. Pilots spend hours in simulators before being allowed to take the controls of a real 747. The simulator looks, feels, sounds, and responds like a real airplane but even the worst mistakes by the student result only in embarrassment rather than in disaster!

Simulations and educational games require more time in programming and more elaborate hardware than do drill and practice and tutorial programs. Therefore, they are fairly scarce among the offerings of CAI software vendors. Nevertheless, they hold promise as an effective model of computer-based instruction.

The fourth model of CAI envisions the computer program as a resource that the student may access with his own goals in mind. In the first three models, the instructor determined the goals of the software and the parameters regarding how the student would interact with the software. Viewing the computer as a resource that the student may utilize as needed puts the student in control of his learning to a greater extent, providing his means and methods to gather and use information.

One example of the computer as a resource comes from the realm of artificial intelligence (AI), a term which refers to computer software written to simulate the way humans solve problems. One type of AI software, called the expert system, includes facts (statements that represent what is known about a certain subject) and rules (ways in which the facts are related).[10]

An expert system containing information about any subject could be developed by "knowledge engineers" (programmers who develop AI applications). The student can sit down with the completed expert system and enter into a dialogue regarding its subject matter. In the dialogue the student uses normal English and the expert system responds in English sentences. We call this type of interaction with the computer natural language interface, one of the trademarks of programs utilizing artificial intelligence methods.

THE TEACHERS INVOLVEMENT IN SELECTION AND
CREATION OF CAI SOFTWARE.

You may choose from among three levels of involvement in determining what computer software you will use in your classroom.

Software or courseware (a term that refers to software that is closely tied to lesson, unit, or course objectives) may be selected by the educational administration under which you serve and used as a textbook or other element of the curriculum. At this level, you must simply learn to use the software that is presented.

You may participate in selection of "off the shelf" software. Here you must be able to articulate the course objectives and determine what software would be appropriate for use in helping to accomplish those objectives. You must then be able to review and evaluate appropriate software to determine which programs would be most useful. Periodicals that deal with computers in education contain reviews of educational software that should be helpful in evaluating software even before you are able to see it firsthand.

Software evaluation follows two lines of investigation. First, you should look at the instructional design of the software. It may display pretty color pictures and play the school *alma mater,* but if it uses poor instructional techniques, it probably will not help your students attain instructional objectives. Answering these eight questions about the instructional design of educational software will help you weigh its quality:[11]

1. Does the software require the student to interact with the program rather than become a passive observer?
2. Do student responses serve instructional goals?
3. Do students have to respond to the important parts of the problems?
4. Is most of the screen content necessary for the response?
5. Does each screen ask students to discriminate between at least two possible responses? (Something other than "Press Space Bar to Continue, Press ESC to Quit"!)
6. Can students see their progress as they work through the program each session?
7. Are students mostly successful as they work through the program? (Rather than being frustrated from failure)
8. For series or lessons to be used repeatedly: Does the program adjust according to the achievement level of the student?

Second, the technical or programming quality of the software should be evaluated. Questions such as these will help you determine how well the design was implemented:

1. Will students find the program easy to use?
2. How well does the software use features such as graphics, color, and sound?

3. Does the program operate consistently as it should?
4. Does the documentation allow the teacher to understand and explain to the students how the program should be used?

The third level of involvement in the selection and creation of instructional software places the teacher in the role of CAI author. Many teachers feel that they do not have the time or knowledge to create software for instructional use. But with advances in the tools available to help a CAI author in the creation of programs, this appears within reach of more teachers.

CAI programs may be created using an authoring system or authoring language. PILOT (Programmed Instruction for Learning of Teaching) is one of the best known of the microcomputer-based authoring languages. The teacher can use PILOT to create tutorials or drill and practice programs with a minimum of programming knowledge.

Related to authoring languages are shells. A shell provides instructional activities for which you supply the academic content. For example, Shell Games by Apple contains the procedures to display a matching game and several other learning techniques. The teacher simply specifies a collection of matched-pairs such as Thomas Edison—light bulb; Eli Whitney—cotton gin; etc. The shell uses this content to display a matching game, each time rearranging the two lists to avert boredom. Shells require little or no programming knowledge.

The teacher who wants to create original software that cannot be produced with an authoring language or shell can make use of programming languages. BASIC, Pascal, C, and Prolog represent the variety of languages available for microcomputers. Learning a programming language may not be for everyone (though at least one author includes the ability to write a computer program in his definition of computer literacy),[12] but for those who enjoy creating unique solutions to often difficult problems, computer programming can be a lot of fun.

Computer technology has begun to make a significant impact on teaching by providing teachers a tool and a tutor. Ever more exciting developments lie ahead in the use of these and related technological advancements in teaching.

ENDNOTES

1. "Evolution of a Technology," *Perspective: Digital Equipment Corporation's Computer Newsletter* 4 (Number 1) p. 2.

2. Christopher Evans, *The Micro Millennium.* New York: Viking Press, 1979, pp. 111–29.

3. Some tasks, such as filling in infrequently used forms and typing a single

mailing label may be accomplished more simply on a typewriter.

4. Note that this is a weighted average. Each test counts 20 percent and each paper counts 30 percent of the final grade.

5. Benjamin S. Bloom, "The 2 Sigma Problem: The Search for Methods of Group Instruction as Effective as One-to-One Tutoring," *Educational Researcher* (June/July 1984) pp. 4–16.

6. Sidney L. Pressey, "A Third and Fourth Contribution toward the Coming 'Industrial Revolution' in Education," *School and Society* 36 (1932) p. 934.

7. B.F. Skinner, "Programmed Instruction Revisited," *Phi Delta Kappan* (October 1986) p. 104.

8. Herbert Kohl, "The World's Most Expensive Flash Card," in *Intelligent Schoolhouse* edited by Dale Peterson. Reston, Va.: Reston Publishing Company, 1984, pp. 28–32.

9. Dale Peterson, ed., *Intelligent Schoolhouse*. Reston, Va.: Reston Publishing Company, 1984, p. 11.

10. Computer languages such as Prolog and LISP are designed to work with facts and rules to develop artificial intelligence applications.

11. Adapted from Julie S. Vargas, "Instructional Design Flaws in Computer-Assisted Instruction," *Phi Delta Kappan* (June 1986) p. 744.

12. Arthur Luehrmann, "Computer Literacy: The What, Why, and How," in *Intelligent Schoolhouse* edited by Dale Peterson. Reston, Va.: Reston Publishing Company, 1984, p. 55.

BIBLIOGRAPHY AND RESOURCES

Books

Alessi, Stephen M. and Stanley R. Trollip. *Computer-Based Instruction: Methods and Development.* Englewood Cliffs, N.J.: Prentice-Hall, Inc., 1985.

Bedell, Kenneth. *Role of Computers in Religious Education.* Nashville, Tenn.: Abingdon Press, 1986.

Bozeman, William C. *Computers and Computing in Education: An Introduction.* Scottsdale, Ariz.: Gorsuch Scarisbrick Publishers, 1985.

Bright, George W. *Microcomputer Applications in the Elementary Classroom: A Guide for Teachers.* Boston: Allyn and Bacon, Inc., 1987.

Brownell, Blaine A. *Using Microcomputers.* Beverly Hills, Calif.: Sage Publications, 1985.

Chan, Julie M. and Marilyn Korostoff. *Teachers' Guide to Designing Classroom Software.* Beverly Hills, Calif.: Sage Publications, 1984.

Clemens, Eldon Von. *Using Computers in Religious Education.* Nashville, Tenn.: Abingdon, 1986.

Clements, Douglas H. *Computers in Early and Primary Education.* Englewood Cliffs, N.J.: Prentice-Hall, 1985.

Culp, George and Herbert Nickles. *An Apple for the Teacher: Fundamentals of Instructional Computing.* Brooks/Cole Series in Computer Education. Monterey, Calif.: Brooks/Cole Publishing Co., 1983.

Evans, Christopher. *The Micro Millennium.* New York: The Viking Press, 1979.

Landa, Ruth Kaplan. *Creating Courseware: A Beginner's Guide.* New York: Harper & Row, 1984.

Lanthrop, Ann and Bobby Goodson. *Courseware in the Classroom: Selecting, Organizing, and Using Educational Software.* Menlo Park, Calif.: Addison-Wesley Publishing Co., 1983.

Maffei, Anthony C. *Classroom Computers: A Practical Guide to Effective Teaching.* New York: Human Sciences Press, 1986.

Olds, Henry F. *The Computer as an Educational Tool.* New York: Haworth Press, 1986.

Pantiel, Mindy and Becky Petersen. *The Junior High Computer Connection.* Englewood Cliffs, N.J.: Prentice-Hall, 1985.

Peterson, Dale, ed. *Intelligent Schoolhouse: Readings on Computers and Learning.* Reston, Va.: Reston Publishing Co., 1984.

Sloan, Douglas, ed. *The Computer in Education: A Critical Perspective.* 2nd ed. New York: Teachers College Press, 1985.

Vockell, Edward L. and Robert H. Rivers. *Instructional Computing for Today's Teachers.* New York: MacMillan Publishing Company, 1984.

Walker, Decker F. and Robert D. Hess. *Instructional Software: Principles and Perspectives for Design and Use.* Belmont, Calif.: Wadsworth Publishing Company, 1984.

Periodicals

Byte Magazine
Computing Teacher
Creative Computing
Electronic Learning
Journal of Computer-Based Instruction
T.H.E. Journal (Technological Horizons in Education)
Educational Technology

Special Interest Groups

The Christian Computer Teacher Association of Texas
The Journal of Educational Computing
3001 Golden Avenue
Bay City, TX 77414
(409) 244-5526

Chime, the newsletter of the Clearinghouse of Information on
Microcomputers in Education
College of Education
Oklahoma State University
108 Gundersen
Stillwater, OK 74078
(405) 624-6254

Christian Computer News
Christian Computer Users Association, Inc.
1145 Alexander, S.E.
Grand Rapids, MI 49507

12. AUDIOVISUAL SUPPORT FOR YOUR TEACHING
Donald P. Regier

A pilot guides a jumbo jet to a smooth landing at the Los Angeles International Airport. As he taxis to a stop, he glances at the lights of the cars on the freeway. Now he has to drive home in that traffic! Then he remembers. He's not in L.A. He's in a flight simulator in Dallas/Ft. Worth. He has just demonstrated to his flight instructor that he really can fly the plane, and though the trip was not real, the learning was. The philosophy of his flight academy has been confirmed: we learn by doing.

You learn to fly a plane by flying a plane; you learn to teach a Sunday School class by teaching a class. You learn the geography of the Holy Land by visiting the Holy Land; but sometimes an audiovisual substitute is safer and more cost-effective.

A flight simulator is a rather exotic substitute, at the cutting edge of technology. But any good audiovisual tool can, to a certain degree, do what a simulator can do. Audiovisuals provide substitutes for reality when the real experience would be too dangerous, or when it is removed by time or space. Something that happened 2,000 years ago on the other side of the world can be brought into our experience today through audiovisual media. Bible stories once obscure to us can come to life as we both hear and see them. Invisible spiritual realities can be made "visible" on a projection screen. As we interact with the audiovisual substitute, it becomes a part of our experience. We learn because all of our senses get involved in the process, and we learn by doing.

WHAT IS AUDIOVISUAL SUPPORT?

"Audiovisual" refers to the presentation of aural and visual information at the same time. Within this definition we find a wide range of possibilities. In the simple audiovisual aids concept, media merely support the traditional classroom. Familiar tools like filmstrip and overhead projectors have long been used to reinforce and enhance what the teacher is saying.

But many educators believe that the technology has outgrown the visual aids idea. In the instructional technology concept, audiovisual media can actually replace the teacher as students work alone, at their own pace, interacting with audio and video machines.

In the '60s and '70s, during the heyday of the visual literacy movement, some educators advocated a new approach to education in which media played a dominant role. Said media guru Marshall McLuhan, "We must invent a new metaphor, restructure our thoughts and feelings. The new media are not bridges between man and nature: they are nature."[1]

And more new media have been added since then. The microelectronic revolution has affected the way audiovisual materials are produced and presented, so that today the AV enthusiast finds the array of available tools expanded by microcomputers, video disks, cable television, satellites, and phone modems.

As the audio and visual methods of learning became fused into one, "audio visual" became "audio-visual" and now through usage has lost its hyphen altogether. And the continually changing language of the audiovisual field reflects its rapid development. Wilbur Schramm notes that "audiovisual aids" became "audiovisual instruction" and then "instructional technology," "each change indicating a broadening and deepening of the concepts involved."[2]

Mark Hendrickson points out that "this theory of education takes media far beyond the audiovisual aids concept (i.e., media are only an aid in the traditional classroom). To these educators, when media are properly understood and used in instruction, they become an integral part of a revolutionary approach to education." He further comments that "when this approach is adopted, instructional media may not only supplement the teacher, but may in some cases, if the objectives actually warrant it, *replace* the teacher."[3]

Can we really find good reasons for this exalted view of the media? Consider the following.

WHAT CAN AUDIOVISUALS DO?

Audiovisuals can stimulate interest. The human eye is attracted by motion, by brightness, and by color. Even the simple act of turning on an overhead projector creates involuntary attention in an audience because it creates motion, color, and brightness at the front of the room. The wise communicator will capitalize on this teachable moment and turn the involuntary attention into voluntary. Appropriate visuals capture and hold attention.

Audiovisual enthusiasts point out that learning takes place through all the five senses, and using media simply takes advantage of more than one sense at a time. This forces more involvement and hence more interest. One study indicates that we learn:

1 percent through taste
1.5 percent through touch
3.5 percent through smell
11 percent through hearing
83 percent through sight[4]

Says Terry Hall, "If showing and telling rate 94 percent, a solid A, should we be content to use these two senses exclusively? No—that's like picking up a book with only two fingers. We can lift it, if it's not too thick, but we have a far better grip on it with all five fingers. The more we appeal to all five senses of our audience, the more effective will be our teaching."[5]

If audiovisual materials did no more than create interest, we could probably justify them on that basis alone. But there are other values.

AUDIOVISUALS CAN SPEED LEARNING.

When a major airline flight academy switched from traditional teaching methods to flight simulators, they reduced their training time by one third to one half. Realizing that most church education experiences influence a person for only a very small fraction of the week, we would do well to maximize that time by using time-saving methods such as visuals. Where factual material is concerned, we can teach more in less time. Then we have more time for the application of truth to life.

AUDIOVISUALS CAN PREVENT MISUNDERSTANDING.

Over Sunday dinner I asked my five-year-old what the Sunday School lesson had been about. "Oh, about whales," he responded. "Really! What did the whales do?" "Oh, they gave water to hundreds of camels, oxen, and sheep." "Really! How did they do that?" "Well, they just opened their mouths and the water came out." I finally guessed that the lesson had been about the wells that the patriarchs dug in biblical times. I also guessed that the teacher had not used any visual aids.

This true-life Sunday School adventure demonstrates a point. Teaching without visual support can create a serious problem of verbalism, or misunderstanding of meanings, so that when a teacher says "wells," it comes out as "Wales" or "whales" to the child. Ten years later when my son and I traveled in Israel he discovered that cattle didn't drink from whales but from wells. Years of misunderstanding could have been prevented by an appropriate picture at the right time!

AUDIOVISUALS CAN IMPROVE RETENTION.

Studies revealed that the use of media can significantly affect how much we remember as shown in the following chart.[6]

Methods of Communication	Recall 3 hours later	Recall 3 days later
Telling when used alone	70%	10%
Showing when used alone	72%	20%
When a blend of telling and showing is used	85%	65%

Some teachers, realizing the educational values of audiovisual media, proclaim this as the only way to teach. "A lecturer is one who talks in other people's sleep," they say. While spoken tongue-in-cheek, the sentiment suggests that one should never lecture. They forget that AV is only one method among many.

Long ago Edgar Dale warned of the danger of being so dazzled with the new media of instruction that we cannot see clearly.

Aware of the impressive results achieved through the use of films, recordings, or television in schools, colleges, industry, and government, some of us may conclude that earlier teaching methods were "all wrong," "wasteful," "inefficient"; that textbooks should be discarded and the principles of education completely overhauled. Such an extreme attitude is unjustified by the facts. Moreover, it reflects a wholly unrealistic view of the new media.[7]

To assert that audiovisual media can improve learning does not mean that other methods of teaching are inferior. Obviously one can learn more from a good lecture than a bad film.

AUDIOVISUAL SUPPORT IN CHRISTIAN EDUCATION
CHRISTIANITY AND COMMUNICATION ARE INSEPARABLE.
We can know God because He has made Himself known. He has

197

communicated with His creation. Much of this communication has been sensory and without words.

"The heavens declare the glory of God," says the psalmist in Psalm 19, "the skies proclaim the work of His hands." A literal translation of verse 3 reads, "They have no speech, there are no words; no sound is heard from them." Yet this is one of God's great communications to man; so compelling, in fact, that men who have rejected this evidence of God's eternal power and divine nature are without excuse (Rom. 1:20).

"In the past God spoke to our forefathers through the prophets at many times and in various ways" declares Hebrews 1:1. These "various ways" are by no means limited to the spoken word. The prophets used a wide variety of visual methods, sometimes even communicating God's message without words, as in Ezekiel 4. God directed the prophet to construct a working model of the city of Jerusalem to depict its destruction at the hands of the Babylonian invaders. He dramatized the siege by lying on his left side for 390 days and on his right side for 40 days more. This audiovisual aid communicated its message without words.

The Old Testament tabernacle with all its intricate detail visually demonstrated the way of approach to God through the shedding of blood. Each piece of furniture pictorially communicated its truth.

"But in these last days He has spoken to us by His Son," continues the writer to the Hebrews. The Son, the Master Teacher, provides our ultimate example of how to teach. "He didn't line up the chairs in rows," quips Ted Ward. He did teach with a blend of words, visual metaphor, and word pictures. He illustrated His message with common, everyday objects. Even His miracles offered a visual proof of His message. We might have expected this in the light of Proverbs 20:12: "Ears that hear and eyes that see—the Lord has made them both."

COMMUNICATION AND MEDIA ARE INSEPARABLE.

The manual for a chaplain's media program says it well: If we communicate at all, we use some method or medium. We can no more decide not to use media than we can decide not to communicate (even if we are only communicating the idea that we don't want to communicate). The decision to lecture, using words alone, is really a media decision. The question, therefore, is not whether we should use media, but rather what kind of media to use.[8]

CHRISTIANS SHOULD USE THE COMMUNICATIONS MEDIA OF OUR DAY.

One humorist has noted that "the Word became flesh, and then the theologians put it back into words again." But God has always spoken in a language that people understand. Today, media represent one of the dialects of our culture, understood worldwide.

But while great potential exists for instantaneous and cross-cultural communication, there is also grave danger. Christian educators need to think seriously about the role of the teacher and his tools in the teaching/learning process. Anol W. Beahm notes that "though Christians have always had access to the Holy Spirit, it took the printing press to allow Christians to have access to Scripture. Now the high tech revolution will allow Christians to have instantaneous access to all the resources of the Christian tradition."[9]

Beahm warns that we need to ask some hard questions:

> If new technologies are adopted by churches, what, if any, changes will develop in the role of the teacher? In a church that uses satellite earth stations, cable TV, and videotapes to have "expert" Bible teachers in Sunday School classes, there may be a noticeable change in how local teachers view themselves and are viewed by the congregation.[10]

We must remember that though machines may do a better job of teaching certain factual information, they do not communicate. People do. There must always be a place for the teacher in Christian education.

NOT ONLY SHOULD CHRISTIANS USE MEDIA: THEY SHOULD PRODUCE IT.

The need for a Christian voice in the media marketplace has been expressed by John R.W. Stott:

> Christians should seek to penetrate the world of the mass media and to equip themselves as television script writers, producers, and performers. We can hardly complain of the low standard of many current programs if we take no constructive initiatives to provide alternatives which are not only technically equal if not better, but more wholesome as well.[11]

Today, a wide-open door stands before the communicator who wants to reach this culture. It is a door to people's minds through their eyes, their ears, and all of the five senses. By beginning with even the simplest of audiovisual materials, the Christian teacher can step through that door.

TWO TYPES OF AUDIOVISUAL MEDIA

Audiovisual materials can be divided into two categories: "speaker-support" and "stand-alone."

Speaker-support materials are used to enhance a presentation by a live speaker. Primarily, these include the traditional tools of the audiovisual aids movement, ranging from non-projected visuals like flannelgraph and object lessons to projected overhead transparencies and slides. The aids may range from a simple object to a complex multi-image format, but the focus is on the speaker. Our discussion will center on the production and use of two of these tools: overhead transparencies and 35mm slides.

Stand-alone materials can replace the presenter. Sometimes called "canned AV," these materials include filmstrips, films, videotapes, video disks, and any other media that contain the entire content and presentation. The teacher does not have to be present for these materials to do their job.

After viewing a flashy "canned" multi-projector slide show with stereo sound, the would-be audiovisual producer may feel a strong urge to "go and do likewise." Productions of this nature look like they would be fun to produce. They are. One of the attractions of the audiovisual field is that amateurs can become involved with little or no training. For someone with limited experience, however, such a project can become overwhelming due to the complexity of the equipment and procedures. Better to start small and build up to the big projects.

Why not begin your creative efforts with speaker-support materials like overhead transparencies and 35mm slides. What might begin as a hobby can easily become a new way to teach, and even a life vocation!

PRODUCING AV MATERIALS—YOU CAN MAKE YOUR OWN

Every Christian teacher delights to find creative methods of communicating old truths in new ways. Audiovisual materials provide one of those new ways, opening a door of opportunity for creative expression. AV brings rewards to the teacher both in communication success and in artistic fulfillment.

But mention the word "creative," and the average teacher moans, "Oh, I'm not creative. I can't draw."

It isn't so strange that we should equate creativity with the visual arts. God, the Creator, produced a world bursting with visual stimuli; so rich, in fact, that He holds man responsible to learn about Him from the work of His hands. "They are without excuse" who reject the witness of God's creative work, His great visual aid.

We are His creatures. From our Father we inherit the desire and ability to create. Our fall into sin has complicated the creative process, and too often we find the creative urge frustrated. We look on ourselves as people utterly lacking in creativity.

But creative frustration often stems from inappropriate expectations. We need to remember that we are not God; we cannot create "ex nihilo." Only God creates out of nothing.

Creativity, as practiced by God's created ones, has been defined as "making something new out of something old" or "arranging old things in new ways." When we remember that "there is nothing new under the sun," we are liberated from the feeling that all our work must be original. Teachers don't have to be artists to create effective visuals.

So, if you haven't picked up a coloring crayon since the third grade, take heart; you may not have to. Help is as near as your art store. Practice Wallace Wood's Rules of Drawing:

1. *Never draw what you can copy.*
2. *Never copy what you can trace.*
3. *Never trace what you can cut out and paste down.*

You don't have to be a visual artist. You don't even have to be able to trace to make a visual that communicates in a creative way. New and exciting resources are available that enable the teacher to make his or her own visuals. Let's look at a few.

CREATIVE RESOURCES
LET THERE BE CLIP ART!

Camera-ready "clip art" has evolved to meet the need for copyright-free illustrations for visuals, ads, newsletters, book covers, brochures, and other presentations. Typical clip art includes line illustrations, symbols, borders, textures, and cartoons. Check your Christian bookstore for the latest books of clip art. Take a look at the bookshelf at your local art supplies dealer as well. They probably stock books from Dover Press, one of the leading sources of copyright-free art. Other excellent sources include Dynamic Graphics, Inc., 6000 North Forest Park Drive, P.O. Box 1901, Peoria, IL 61656-9979; and The Church Art Works, 381 State Street, Salem, OR 97301. These subscription services bring the lastest art to your desk on a regular basis. For the price of one or two pieces of custom art, you can have scores of illustrations delivered to your church, school, or home.

LET THERE BE LETTERING!

Hand lettering is acceptable for many visual presentations, but may look "home-made." You can improve it by saving large newspaper and magazine headlines and tracing over them. Or you can check out some of the commercially available aids which can make the difference between amateur and professional. Just because your work *is* amateur doesn't mean it has to *look* like it. Here are some of the lettering possibilites.

1. Typesetting. This is the quickest but most expensive way to add professional lettering to your visual. Visit a local type house and ask for instructions on how to mark up your copy for typesetting. You will get back professional copy which you will then need to cut up and paste into position on your visual "master" or original.

2. Typewriter. Typed lettering will work for projected visuals if the type is large enough. When making an overhead transparency, you will want to bear in mind that minimal size for legibility is 24 point (or 1/4" high on capital letters). If your typewriter will not meet these specifications, plan to enlarge your lettering with a photocopier or graphic arts camera. If you type within a 3" x 4" area and then enlarge to fill a normal 8 1/2" x 11" page, your lettering should be quite readable when projected on a screen.

3. Templates or stencils. For low-cost lettering with an almost-professional look, visit your art store and investigate some of these inexpensive tools.

4. Lettering machines, such as Kroy, produce lettering on strips of sticky tape which are then applied to the visual master before making the transparency or slide. These machines are operated by turning a large wheel to select a letter, then pressing an enter key. More sophisticated models are operated from a keyboard.

5. Dry transfer or rub-on letters. You put these down one letter at a time, but the quality can equal the most expensive machine typesetting.

LET THERE BE ART AIDS!

Have you ever tried to draw a straight line with ink and a ruler? Or worse, a circle with ink and a cereal bowl? You laugh, but maybe that was when you decided you couldn't draw! You don't have to. Geometric shapes, boxes, borders, lines, arrows, and more are available in easy-to-use cut-out-and-stick-down form with an adhesive backing. Of note is the Formatt Library of Shapes, available at art stores. These helpful art elements can be adhered to a paper master and then reproduced on clear plastic film with a photocopier or other transparency maker. Or they can be photographed to make a slide.

LET THERE BE COMPUTER GRAPHICS!

With a graphics-oriented computer, you need none of the above, because a computer can do it all. Lettering, drawing, even painting in color can be done with a keyboard and a digitizing device. Consequently, the professional audiovisual producer now faces real competiton from people who could never draw. The emerging "techno-artist" is a new breed of communicator who understands not only graphics but computers. We could suggest a new rule for Wallace Wood: *Never cut out and paste down what you can create with a computer!*

New laser printers have greatly increased the quality of personal computers. Printing at resolutions of 200 or 300 dots per inch, these "near-typeset-quality" machines have all but eliminated the "jaggy" images formerly associated with low-cost computer graphics. Even if you cannot yet afford a laser printer, you can probably find one to share. "Networking" has made possible the simultaneous use of one printer by many computers. Also, some "quick print" businesses offer laser prints at reasonable prices. Just walk in with your disk and leave with a high resolution master or transparency.

Concerned that you cannot afford to make your visuals this way? Here's the good news—as sophistication goes up prices are coming down. Less than ten years ago, a sophisticated graphics computer cost $250,000. Obviously only the larger corporations could justify the expense. Today, churches and schools, and even individuals can afford nearly the same degree of sophistication. Keep your eyes on the used market too. As people upgrade to the newer machines, they either give the old ones to the kids or dump them on the used market at reduced prices.

The use of projected visuals in business and industry has grown dramatically in recent years, due primarily to the capability of computers to produce them. As the "information age" gathers momentum, communicators are eager to present their message visually as well as verbally. Annual reports, product introductions, and sales pitches are marked by sophisticated visuals that show as well as tell. AV must be successful or shrewd business people wouldn't spend billions of dollars annually on audiovisual materials, services, and equipment.

What a challenge to those of us who communicate the Good News, and whose audience includes some of the same people exposed to excellence in visual communication all week! Should they get anything less at church?

TYPES OF SPEAKER-SUPPORT VISUALS
TEXT.

The simple "word slide" has power to grab attention, particularly when embellished with typography or graphic detail.

Take the outline of your lesson or sermon and make a word visual for each main point. Too-small lettering persists as one of the most common mistakes in visual production, so you should remember to make the type "big and bold" for maximal effect.

A basic "word visual" can be used to introduce an idea.

The "big and bold" style and diagonal slant make this visual more dramatic. Adding color would increase its appeal even more.

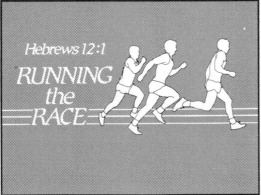

The addition of graphic elements makes the word visual more interesting.

REALISTIC PICTURES.

Pictures present a visual record made "on location" for presentation to people who may be far away. Popular 35mm slides demonstrate this type of visual with low cost and ease of production. Large format overhead transparencies of real scenes can be made from 35mm slides, but their cost may be prohibitive.

This realistic photo has been enhanced with a caption.

GRAPHIC SYMBOLS.

Symbols represent something in a simpler form than a photograph might. When people understand a symbol, it can even communicate across cultural and language barriers. Why is it that we hear in many languages but see in only one?

This symbol visual can be understood by everyone.

CARTOONS.

Cartoons inject humor into a presentation. It's amazing what people can swallow while they are laughing!

This cartoon takes a light approach to what might otherwise be a dull subject.

CHARTS AND DIAGRAMS.

These represent reality with the use of drawings, lines, rectangles, circles, and arrows to depict origins, developments, sequences, comparisons, contrasts, etc. The flow of church history can be graphically illustrated with a time line. "Law and Grace" can be contrasted with a chart. Many Bible teachers use charts to visually represent portions or entire books of the Bible.

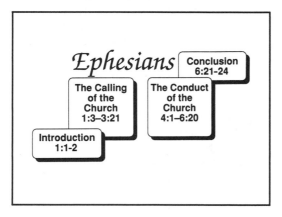

This Bible chart synthesizes the entire Book of Ephesians.

DESIGNING SPEAKER-SUPPORT VISUALS

One of the creatively stimulating aspects of AV is the fact that the individual teacher can design his or her own visuals. These principles of design can help your visuals communicate better.

MAKE IT SIMPLE.

The story about Michelangelo creating a horse sculpture by beginning with a large block of marble and "chipping away everything that's not a horse" is more than a good punchline. It's a rule to follow! A common flaw in many visuals is the inclusion of too much information, so that the picture looks like the Declaration of Independence on a dime. Like Michelangelo we should "chip away everything that's not a horse." Eliminate every element that doesn't contribute to the message of the visual. Remove all the clutter so that the visual is easier to look at and to remember.

C.I. Scofield, better known for his popular study Bible, recognized the danger of including too much in a visual. In a letter dated 1912, he wrote, "one immutable principle runs through all teaching by eye-gate = simplicity, simplicity, simplicity. . . . The vice of charts as usually made is the attempt to tell everything."[12]

In this "cluttered" visual, the teacher has included too much information out of fear of omitting something important. This kind of detail is appropriate for books that are to be read at leisure, but not for visuals in presentations. The details certainly won't be remembered. "If in doubt, leave it out."

Less is more.

MAKE IT UNIFIED.

"Unity," says Maitland Graves, "is the cohesion, consistency, oneness, or integrity that is the prime essential of all composition. Composition implies unity; the words are synonymous. To say that a composition lacks unity is a contradiction of terms. If it does, it is not a composition."[13] If you mix several different art styles and type faces together without design, you will probably create a disorganized, disunified mess.

This visual lacks harmony and unity because the various elements are not consistent in style.

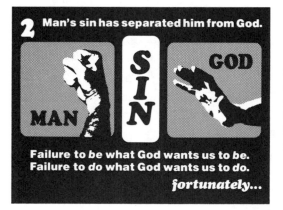

Repetition of similar shapes creates a feeling of oneness and harmony. Everything seems to fit together in this unified composition.

© 1988, DON REGIER.

MAKE IT INTERESTING.

Variety is the No-Doze of AV shows. Make your visual more exciting by using opposites of shape, size, and color value.

MAKE THE FOCAL POINT DOMINANT.

The visual should incorporate a focal point at which the eye comes to rest. The entire diagram points to this main idea. Using color helps to enhance a focal point. Remember that warm, bright colors (yellow, orange, red) are most likely to get attention. One need not cover the entire visual with a rainbow of colors, just highlight the focal point!

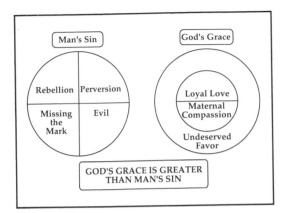

Too much similarity results in a boring design.

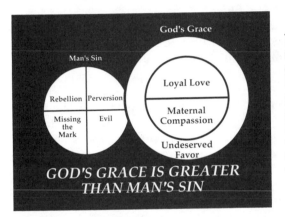

The same diagram is more interesting when one element, the circle, is larger than others. Color opposites or "complements" also help to show the contrast between concepts. In this visual we see enough repetition for unity, but enough variety to make it interesting.

Sometimes you may want to color the entire background in subdued hues while the focal point stands out in stark black and white.

The eye begins reading this visual at the upper left corner (the way we read) and ends at the lower right. Color reinforces the impact of the focal point.

209

These simple principles may not improve the content of your visual, but they will prevent poor art technique from standing in its way.

HOW TO MAKE VISUALS

There are many methods for making inexpensive visuals, and the exciting line-up of computers and printers increases the options. In the interest of presenting both low cost and professional quality, we will suggest only one method of creating thermal overhead transparencies and only one approach for 35mm slides. These are procedures that have been tested and proved by many audiovisual users.

MAKE A MASTER ON PAPER.

Our method begins with a master (original) on paper, which you can either make "the old way" with traditional graphic arts materials, or "the new way" with a graphics program in your computer (most of the suggestions below will still apply). A paper master is essential because, unlike transparencies created directly on plastic, you can correct your mistakes before you commit them to film. Further, the master gives you something to file for future retrieval and updating. After the master is made, you can transfer it to overhead transparency film, photograph it on 35mm film to make a slide, or even videotape it with a home video camera.

Specifications for masters.

1. Size. The master should be constructed in the proper proportions or "aspect ratio" for your medium. Start out with 8 1/2" x 11" paper, and mark out the margins with a non-reproducible blue pencil. Working within an area 7 1/2" by 10" is ideal for overhead transparencies or video because the ratio of short dimension to long is 3:4; that is, the short side of the visual is three units while the long side is four

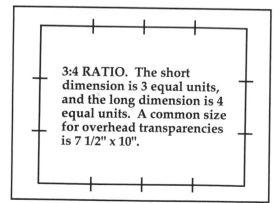

3:4 RATIO. The short dimension is 3 equal units, and the long dimension is 4 equal units. A common size for overhead transparencies is 7 1/2" x 10".

Use the 3:4 ratio for overheads, filmstrips, and video.

units. Anything placed outside this boundary is likely to be covered over by the transparency frame.

If you plan to turn your visual into a 35mm slide, use a ratio of 2:3. An area of 6″ x 9″ is a good working size for your slide master. This size is suggested for standardization only. Actually, with slides, the original can be anything as small as a postage stamp or as large as a house. Remember that you can enlarge a small object by moving the camera closer. Without costly equipment this kind of versatility is not available in overhead transparencies.

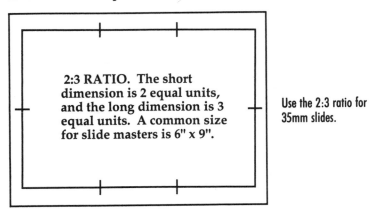

2:3 RATIO. The short dimension is 2 equal units, and the long dimension is 3 equal units. A common size for slide masters is 6″ x 9″.

Use the 2:3 ratio for 35mm slides.

2. Lettering size. A visual doesn't "aid" learning if the audience can't read it. *Everything must be designed for the viewer furthest from the screen and for the worst viewing conditions.* How many times have you lost interest in (or become frustrated by) a presentation that you simply couldn't read?

Working on an 8 1/2″ x 11″ master, use type no smaller than 24 point. This is equivalent to 1/4″ high capital letters. Anything smaller will probably not be visible in the back row of your class. Of course, larger type aids legibility and interest. The bigger the better!

3. Pasting Up. Clip art, borders, boxes, and other elements can be pasted to the master with rubber cement, spray glue, waxers, or other methods. Glue sticks are especially convenient. Edges of the pasteup will not show because most graphic arts films reproduce only black images and not shades of gray. However, it is good practice to trim edges as neatly as possible.

MAKE A THERMAL TRANSPARENCY
HOW THE THERMAL PROCESS WORKS.

Thermal ("dry-heat" or "heat-transfer," or "infrared") transparencies can be created in a few seconds using a machine like an infrared transparency maker.

Infrared light produces thermal transparencies. Black images on the paper original attract the heat of the lamp and burn it into the sensitized film. The resulting transparency can be a black image on a clear background, black on a color-tinted background, or any color on a clear background. (Reversal films are also available, producing clear images on a black or colored background, but consistent results are hard to obtain.)

To reproduce with the thermal method, all elements on the master must contain carbon. So you should use India ink, press-on letters, even soft lead pencil. Felt-tip pens and ball point pens will not work! If your master contains any such non-reproducible elements, you will first need to make a photocopy. Most photocopy toners are carbon-based.

AN ALTERNATVE TO THE THERMAL PROCESS.

Some overhead transparency users simply make the final transparency on the photocopy machine and bypass the thermal copier altogether. Just make sure to use film sheets designated for your particular copier. Check the manufacturer's specifications to avoid damage to the machine. If you elect to use your photocopier instead of a thermal machine, you can still add color with any of the methods suggested.

MAKING CORRECTIONS.

Before proceeding with the thermal transparency, correct all mistakes on your master. The best correction method is to position the error over a piece of scrap paper. Cut through both pieces of paper with an artist's knife or X-acto knife. Turn the master over, remove the mistake, and tape the scrap paper into the hole left in the master. Be sure to put the tape on the back side of the master.

The film manufacturer's instructions will tell you the proper orientation, but usually, the film notch goes in the upper right-hand corner.

IMAGING THE FILM.

Now you are ready to make the transparency. Place a sheet of film over the original, running both film and master together through the transparency machine. The proper speed can be determined by trial and error, but once determined, should not change. Peel the imaged transparency from the master.

ADD COLOR.

Use black on clear film so that all elements will stand out. Put on color with one or more of the following methods.

Pressure-sensitive films. You can add color with adhesive films, such as Letraset Project-A-Film. Make sure the film you use has been designed for projection; that is, it must be transparent. Cut out a piece slightly larger than needed. It has sticky backing and will adhere to the transparency (or to a sheet of inexpensive clear film that you have placed on top of it). With an X-acto knife, trim the color to the correct size and peel off the excess. Cut only on the black lines of your image, and avoid cuts and scratches on the clear areas which will show when projected.

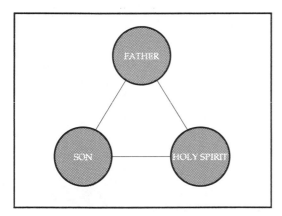

Add color to highlight important details.

Colored plastic sheets. Another method of adding color is quite inexpensive, yet effective. Tape a transparent report cover (available in several colors from a bookstore) over your transparency. With an X-acto knife, cut out all of the areas that you want to highlight. They will be emphasized in stark black and white, and the color will cover the entire background.

Color thermal film. You can separate the various elements of your master, creating individual masters which can each be imaged on a separate sheet of color thermal film.

MOUNT THE TRANSPARENCY.

Just as you frame a fine painting before you hang it on a wall, so a transparency should be framed before you present it to an audience. A

Add color to the background by using inexpensive, colored plastic sheets. The focal point is highlighted.

frame will give the finishing touch, block off light around the edges, add rigidity, and provide a border for writing notes.

Lay the frame down on a flat surface. Place the transparency face down on the frame. With transparent tape, secure the corners of each layer. Note: If you have used color adhesive film or a report cover with holes cut in it, it is best to seal these in by taping a sheet of clear inexpensive plastic over the back. After securing the final layer, add tape all the way around the frame to keep out dust and dirt.

A keystoned image.

Keystoning is corrected by slanting the screen.

USING YOUR TRANSPARENCIES IN CLASS.

Overheads are easy to use. It's just about as difficult to use an overhead projector as it is to as operate the average desk lamp. However, a few hints will improve your use of the machine.

Set up ahead of time. Spend a few minutes before class making sure that the lenses and glass surfaces are clean, that the projected

214

image is centered on the screen and in focus. Some tripod screens have a built-in "keystone eliminator." Use it to tilt the bottom edge of the screen back to avoid a "keystoned" image (ceiling-mounted screens should be mounted several feet out from the wall to permit tilting).

When you want to transfer attention from the teacher to the screen, turn on the projector with the visual already positioned. This helps avoid needless confusion and gives your presentation a more polished look. After using the visual to support your comments, turn it off and position the next visual on the projector. Do not leave the lamp on during transparency changes; this creates unnecessary distraction at the front of the room.

Overheads let you maintain eye contact. Turning one's back on a class to write on a chalkboard may spell disaster in some unruly situations. The overhead allows the teacher to face the class at all times and to create an intimate learning environment. To emphasize a point, rather than turning to face the screen, use a pointer on the projector stage while facing the audience.

Overheads can be used in full room light. Because of the great intensity of the projector, you need not dim the lights for viewing overhead transparencies. Do make sure that there are no room lights directly over your screen; they will "wash out" the projected image.

MAKE A HIGH-CONTRAST SLIDE

The same kind of paper master you use to produce an overhead transparency can be used to make a 35mm slide. The only difference is in the aspect ratio of 2:3; the slide is not quite so tall as the overhead transparency.

Also, you do not need to be concerned about carbon in the ink; any solid black image on white paper will reproduce well.

But why use slides? "If the Lord had intended for us to use slides," you are thinking, "He never would have given us the overhead projector!"

There are several advantages to using slides—important ones like portability and low cost. A slide projector can easily fit under an airline seat, and the slides can be slipped into a pocket. High-contrast slides cost much less than overhead transparencies because of their extreme miniaturization.

"But you can't show slides in a lighted room!" complain those whose only experience has been viewing poorly exposed travel slides in a poorly darkened room. Oh, yes you can, if they are *high-contrast slides!* Because of the clear film base and dense image area, a properly exposed slide will deliver maximal light to the screen, so that speaker-support slides can be used in a lighted classroom.

A high-contrast positive   A high-contrast negative

EQUIPMENT.

Here is what you will need to make fantastic yet inexpensive slides.

A single-lens-reflex camera (SLR). Since we are dealing with close-up photography, we must be able to visualize in the viewfinder exactly what the final image area will be. A regular camera with a viewfinder separate from the lens that takes the picture will not show what the film will see. A single-lens-reflex camera uses the same lens both for viewing the picture and for taking it.

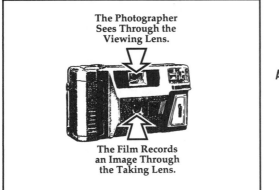

A viewfinder camera

The normal 50mm lens will be adequate if your masters are no smaller than 6″ x 9″. For shooting smaller originals, buy an inexpensive set of close-up filters that can be attached to the front of the lens.

A copystand with floodlights. These items can be purchased from a camera dealer. The best lights to use are the 250 watt ECA

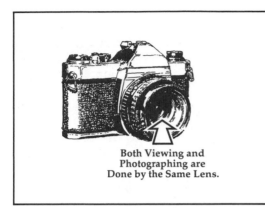

Both Viewing and
Photographing are
Done by the Same Lens.

A single-lens-reflex
camera

lamps. They will work for all of your copystand work—even color slides (when used with daylight slide film and an 80A conversion filter).

Kodak Precision Line film LPD-4 (150') for positive images (black on white), and Kodalith Ortho film 6556, Type 3 (100') for negative images (white on black from a black-on-white original). If you only want one kind of film, get the negative; it will produce more exciting images against a black background.

A bulk film loader. Buy two if you use both the negative and the positive films.

Reusable film cartridges.

A developing tank.

A 15-watt red safelight and a room that can be darkened. If you can't provide a permanent darkroom, a rest room offers a good substitute because of the availability of plumbing. Keep all your supplies on a rolling cart so the room can easily be returned to its normal purpose.

Kodalith Developer. This dry packaged developer makes one

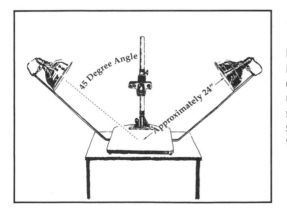

45 Degree Angle

Approximately 24"

Photographic flood lamp reflectors are mounted at a 45 degree angle to prevent unwanted reflections and hot spots. Make sure that the sockets are rated for 250 watts.

gallon of part A and one gallon of part B, which are mixed in small, equal quantities just before use. Once mixed, the working solution will only last for four hours or four rolls of film.

Kodak Rapid Fixer. This solution makes the image permanent.

35mm slide mounts.

Printer's opaque and a sharp-pointed brush for touching up flaws.

Dr. Martin's Synchromatic Transparent Water Colors. These color dyes, available from an art store, will add brilliant color to your negatives.

Here are two sources for most of the supplies listed above: Porter's Camera Store, Inc., Box 628, Cedar Falls, Ia 50613; and Spiratone Inc., 135-06 Northern Blvd., Flushing, NY 11354-4063. Write for a catalog.

LET'S GO THROUGH THE PROCESS STEP-BY-STEP

1. *Load the film,* following the instructions packaged with the bulk film loader.

2. *Determine the correct exposure* by conducting a test (you will not be using the camera's built-in exposure meter, so don't bother to set the film speed). Begin at the largest lens setting (the smallest number, probably f/2) and photograph one of your masters at each numbered aperture setting as well as between each setting (half-stops). The shutter speed will remain a constant eight seconds for positive slides (use the "B" setting and a stopwatch), and one second for negatives.

3. *Load the developing tank.* After you put the lid on the tank, you can perform the remaining steps in full room light.

4. *Mix* five ounces of developer part A with five ounces of part B and stir. It is extremely important that the developer not be contaminated by fixer. Always wash your hands and utensils before handling the developer.

5. *Develop for 2 3/4 minutes.* Pour the developer into the tank and agitate constantly. After 2 1/2 minutes, pour the developer back into a bottle (it can be reused for up to four hours). When 2¾ minutes have elapsed, pour in the fixer.

6. *Fix* for at least two minutes, agitating frequently. The fixer can be saved and reused until it begins to smell bad.

7. *Rinse* in room-temperature running water for about ten minutes. After the rinse process, the film can be removed from the tank.

8. *Dry the film* by hanging it on a line, or force it dry with a hair dryer.

9. *Examine* the strip of film with a magnifier to determine the best exposure. This will become the standard exposure for all similar masters.

10. *Add color* (best on negatives) with Dr. Martin's Synchromatic Transparent Water Colors. Don't worry about overlapping on the black background; it is totally opaque. Apply to either side of the slide with a cotton swab. The secret is to spread the color and then immediately wipe the area with the dry end of the swab to eliminate streaks.

You can add multiple colors by carefully masking the slide with transparent tape to protect what you don't want to color. Yellow is one of the most dramatic colors because of its contrast with the black background, but don't forget that white is a good color too!

11. *Touch up* any flaws or pinholes with a pointed artist's brush (examine the slide with a magnifier over a light table).

USING SLIDES IN TEACHING
PROPER SCREEN SIZE.

This is determined by the size of the room or the distance to the furthest viewer. Divide the distance by a factor of six. This will give you the correct screen width. For example, a thirty-foot distance from the furthest viewer to the screen requires a screen width of five feet.

These screen-size requirements apply to all projected media, including overhead projection.

REAR-SCREEN PROJECTION.

Where this is available, it places the projector behind the speaker. The slides are projected through a translucent screen, and the speaker can walk in front of the screen without casting a shadow on it.

Rear projection also allows for more room light, but that is usually not a problem with high-contrast slides. Remember, they can be shown in a lighted room.

REMOTE CONTROL.

Extension cords can be added to the standard remote controller so that the projector can be located behind the audience where it will be less distracting. Wireless remotes are available so that the teacher can roam anywhere in the room!

PROFESSIONAL TECHNIQUES.

Slides allow the teacher to progress smoothly from visual to visual without shuffling through a pile of overhead transparencies. With two projectors and a dissolve control your slides will fade on and off. When you want the screen to go blank, simply advance to a black slide or "slug," which you can make by mounting some of your left-over film leader in slide mounts. Some newer projectors have a shutter that automatically shuts when no slide is in the gate.

YOU CAN EVEN WRITE ON SLIDES!

Projecting on a white chalkboard (instead of a regular projection screen) provides the option of using liquid chalk markers to add or highlight information while you teach. White bathroom paneling converts the front wall of any classroom to a "teaching wall!"

WHAT NEXT?

Now that you have some experience with producing speaker-support visuals, you may be anxious to continue developing your skills. This true story tells what one teacher did.

Danice taught a class of fifth-grade girls in a church where nothing was new. These kids had heard all the Bible stories before, and now she was supposed to teach them the Book of Daniel. How could she keep their interest? How could she get them involved in the process so they could learn by doing?

Sunday number one: chapter 1. Ho-hum. "Now I want you girls to draw a black-and-white picture of this morning's lesson." So, what else is new?

Enter high-contrast slides. During the week, the teacher put the children's drawings on a copystand and photographed them. From some, she made positive slides. Other drawings were recorded on negative film.

Sunday number two: "You've read the book; now see it on the screen." "Hey, *I* drew that picture." "Let's draw some more pictures of this week's story."

Interest picked up. The kids got involved in the communication process, telling the story of Daniel in an international language: audiovisual media.

When the pictures were drawn, and all the slides were made, Danice colored them. She quickly wrote a script summarizing the book, recorded it on a cassette tape, and added music from a sound library. For a nice professional touch, she programmed the tape so that it would run two slide projectors, the pictures dissolving on and off at various dissolve rates.

She showed the finished presentation not only to her class, but to the entire church (many parents were there) on a Sunday evening. She even took it to Southeast Asia on a summer missions trip sponsored by her church! You'll never guess what she taught the believers on the other side of the world! Or the two classes of adults that she taught the next fall! Creativity! AV! You *can* create your own audiovisual materials!

ENDNOTES

1. Marshall McLuhan, "Five Sovereign Fingers Taxed the Breath," in *The Electric Anthology,* ed. Don Allen. Dayton, Ohio: Pflaum Publishing, 1975, p. 2.

2. Walter A. Wittich and Charles F. Schuller, *Instructional Technology: Its Nature and Use.* New York: Harper and Row, 1979, p. xvi.

3. Mark Hendrickson, "High Tech: Its Progress, Problems, and Potential for Use in the Local Church," *Christian Education Journal.* Glen Ellyn, Ill.: Scripture Press Ministries, 1985, Vol. VI, No. 2, p. 9.

4. Terry Hall, *Dynamic Bible Teaching with Overhead Transparencies.* Elgin, Ill.: David C. Cook Publishing Co., 1985, p. 8.

5. Hall, p. 8.

6. Hall, p. 8.

7. Edgar Dale, *Audio-Visual Methods in Teaching.* New York: Holt, Rinehart and Winston, 1954, p. 3.

8. *Multiple Choice: Rescue from Media Mediocrity.* Maxwell AFB, Ala.: USAF Chaplain Resource Board, p. 1.

9. Anol W. Beahm, "High Tech in Christian Education: Cure or Curse?" *Christian Education Journal.* Glen Ellyn, Ill.: Scripture Press Ministries, 1985, Vol. VI, No. 2, p. 20.

10. Beahm, p. 18.

11. John R.W. Stott, *Between Two Worlds.* Grand Rapids: William B. Eerdmans Publishing Company, 1982, p. 75.

12. C.I. Scofield, Letter to Lewis Sperry Chafer, August 5, 1912, unpublished.

13. Maitland Graves, *The Art of Color and Design.* New York: McGraw-Hill Book Company, 1951, p. 90.

BIBLIOGRAPHY

Benedict, Joel A. and Douglas A. Crane. *Producing Multi-Image Presentations.* Tempe, Ariz.: Media Research & Development, Arizona State University, 1973.

Branch, Tom. *The Photographer's Build-It-Yourself Book.* New York: American Photographic Book Publishing, 1982.

Bruno, Michael H., Manager—Graphic Arts Research, Corporate Research Center. *Pocket Pal.* New York: International Paper Company, 1973.

Douglias, Philip N. *Communicating with Pictures.* Chicago: Lawrence Regan Communications, Inc., 1979.

Dwyer, Francis M. *Strategies for Improving Visual Learning.* State College, Pa., 1978.

Gillis, Don. *The Art of Media Instruction.* Dallas, Texas: Crescendo Book Publications, 1973.

Graves, Maitland. *The Art of Color and Design.* New York: McGraw-Hill Book

Company, 1951.

Jensen, Mary and Andrew. *Audiovisual Idea Book for Churches.* Minneapolis: Augsburg Publishing House, 1974.

Jones, George William. *Landing Rightside Up in T.V. and Film.* Nashville, Tenn.: Abingdon Press, 1973.

Lesser, Gerald S. *Children and Television: Lessons from Sesame Street.* New York: Random House, 1974.

McKim, Robert H. *Experiences in Visual Thinking.* Monterey, Calif.: Brooks/Cole Publishing Company, 1980.

Pandolfi, Ralph. *The Utilization and Effectiveness of Multi-Image.* Tampa, Fla.: Association for Multi-Image International, Inc., 1983.

Planning and Producing Slide Programs. Eastman Kodak Company. Rochester, N.Y.: Eastman Kodak Company, 1975.

Stecker, Elinor, *High-Contrast Images.* Tucson, Ariz.: H.P. Books, 1982.

The Joy of Photography, by the Editors of Eastman Kodak Company. Rochester, N.Y.: Eastman Kodak Company, 1980.

Uchelen, Rod van. *Say It with Pictures.* New York: Von Nostrand Reinhold Company, 1979.

Wileman, Ralph E. *Exercises in Visual Thinking.* New York: Hastings House, 1980.

13. MEASUREMENT AND EVALUATION
Stuart S. Cook

As Dave approached Dr. Dixon's office door he wondered how he had done on his semester project. Dave appreciated the professor's willingness to allow students to submit a creative assignment in lieu of the term paper, and had created a set of maps depicting the spread of Christianity under the Roman Empire.

"Come on in," was the professor's reply to Dave's soft rap on the door.

"I came to pick up my project," said Dave hopefully. "Have you graded it?"

"Yes," replied Dr. Dixon, glancing up from the dusty volume he was perusing and pointed to a stack of materials balanced precariously on the filing cabinet.

After locating his set of maps, Dave began to leave. But as he looked over the project he noticed no grade indicated anywhere. So he approached Dr. Dixon's desk and said, "I don't see a grade on here."

Dr. Dixon reached out for the project and looked it over quickly. "That was a B," he said.

Neither greatly thrilled nor disappointed, Dave turned to leave the office when he remembered Dr. Dixon has mentioned in class he liked to keep some projects occasionally to show future classes. So he swung around and asked, "Oh, by the way, did you want to keep my project?"

Dr. Dixon, now tiring somewhat from Dave's interruption of his reading, said, "Well, let me see it again." After 30 seconds of quizzical examination, Dr. Dixon asked, "Just exactly what is this?" Following Dave's brief exegesis of his project, Dr. Dixon assured him he could take it along, which he did. And somehow Dave managed not to slam the door on the way out.

Can we blame Dave for feeling cheated by the grading game?

How could the professor evaluate a project as a "B" when he didn't even know what it was? No wonder many people fear evaluation, including students and teachers, who often feel threatened by testing and grading or fail to see its value.[1] Nevertheless, testing and grading, if done well, contribute significantly to the quality of education.

THE NEED OF MEASUREMENT AND EVALUATION

In education, as in any enterprise, failure to assess progress invites disaster. Evaluation helps us determine the progress of individual learners toward the goals of instruction. Information on student learning can be used to inform decisions about instructional strategies, curriculum choices, advanced placement, and other instructional and administrative issues. Without the information that comes from testing, many decisions educators make would be subject to serious error.

THE KEY TO MEASUREMENT AND EVALUATION

The key to educational measurement lies in matching measurement to the instructional goal.[2] Once the goals of instruction have been clearly delineated, the rest of the instructional process falls into place. When it comes to testing, you, the teacher, must answer one basic question: "To what extent have the students mastered the instructional goals?"

Testing may be as simple as giving the student the opportunity to demonstrate under the proper conditions that he can do what the objectives of the course said he should be able to do. If the test matches the objectives, it will provide useful information about the effectiveness of the instruction for individual students and the class as a whole.[3]

The importance of clear objectives for good evaluation cannot be overemphasized. Fuzzy objectives lead to fuzzy tests. Because of unclear objectives and ambiguous tests students often fear or hate testing.

EVALUATING COGNITIVE LEARNING: TEACHER-MADE TESTS

The bulk of the contact that students have with tests is based on what we'll call teacher-made tests. These tests measure a limited quantity of material, such as a chapter or unit in a textbook, one week's spelling words, etc. Teachers often construct such tests from scratch or adapt test items from the teacher's manual. They are usually fairly short (generally one class session), cover a limited amount of subject matter, and will be scored locally (by the teacher or by some mechanical means).

The teacher's role in this type of testing is to create or select and modify test items, put the test together, score and analyze it, and assign grades. We'll deal with these parts of the process in the following sections.

CREATING THE TEST: OBJECTIVE TEST ITEMS.

Objective test-item formats usually found in teacher-made tests include true-false, multiple choice, matching, and completion. Each of these has certain advantages and disadvantages and applies to testing certain types of objectives.

True-false items. A true-false item consists of a statement about the course content that can be evaluated by the student as being either true or false. True-false items can test achievement of objectives that require recall of factual information. Though true-false items should be straightforward and a good means of testing recall of information, students often dislike them, mainly because teachers tend to misuse the format. Several guidelines can help you to create true-false items:

Make sure you select a clear and unambiguous method for marking items as true and false. One such method presents the item with the letters T and F printed after the item number and before the statement. The directions instruct the student to circle T if the statement is true, F if the statement is false. For example, see items 1 and 2.

Directions: For items 1 and 2, circle T if the statement is true; circle F if the statement is false.

1. T F Genesis is the first book of the Bible.
2. T F Exodus tells the story of how Joseph saved his family after being sold as a slave to Egypt.

This method of marking true-false items averts the problem of a student making a T with a little line somewhere down the stem (arguably either a T or F) when unsure of the answer.

Write statements that are definitely true or definitely false. If the statement expresses an opinion, then attribute the opinion to its source and ask the students to confirm (true) or deny (false) that the opinion and the source belong together. For example, item 3 expresses an opinion; it is neither definitely true or false:

3. T F Every passage in the Bible should be interpreted using the same rules of interpretation.

A better item would attribute the opinion to a source.

3. T F According to our text, every passage in the Bible should be

interpreted using the same rules of interpretation.

Avoid using the words *always, never, all, every,* or *only.* Alert students know that statements containing these words are rarely true. All the student has to do is to think of one exception to disprove the statement. This guideline indicates that the example used above can be further improved by eliminating the word "every." A still better re-wording of the statement would yield the following item.

4.   T   F   According to our text, when we read the Bible we should follow the rules of interpretation consistently, regardless of the portion of the Bible we are reading.

Use relatively short, simple sentences that do not contain double negatives. The purpose of the item is not to trick students, but to provide clear statements that they can readily understand and evaluate in light of their knowledge of the subject.

Do not take statements directly from the text and present them as true-false items if the immediate context of the text is necessary to understand the statement. This guideline reminds us the Christian teacher is the student's friend, not his enemy.

Try to have about the same number of true and false items. False items are more difficult to write and may be neglected in the final offering of test items, so check yourself to be sure you are creating a balance of both true and false statements.

Multiple-choice items. A multiple-choice item consists of three parts: the stem, the correct or keyed option, and some distractor options. The stem presents a problem to the student in the form of a complete question or an incomplete statement. The correct option (key) provides the correct solution to the problem. The distractors present plausible substitutes to the key for someone who does not know the correct option.

The directions for multiple-choice items usually instruct the student to select the *correct* answer. However, when multiple-choice items are used to test higher levels of learning, the directions may instruct the student to select the *best* answer. In the former case, there will be only one correct answer. In the latter case, there may be more than one answer that correctly solves the problem, but the key provides a clearly superior response to any of the distractors. Teachers should use caution in constructing multiple-choice items utilizing the best answer approach. They should be sure that one answer is clearly superior to the others.

Multiple-choice items may be used to assess the achievement of instructional objectives at the knowledge (recall) level or higher. Multiple-choice items also offer the best objective item format for testing objectives that involve understanding, application, or higher skills.

The problem presented in the stem of the multiple-choice item may require the student to recall information (knowledge level) or it may require the student to demonstrate understanding of material, to apply a concept to a new situation, or perform any number of intellectual tasks. This flexibility makes the multiple-choice item one of the most popular of the objective item formats.

There are certain guidelines to follow in constructing multiple-choice items.

Provide a clear method for the student to indicate his choice. The simplest method allows the student to circle the letter corresponding to his choice. If you use a mark-sense system, the student would indicate his answer on the answer sheet only and not on the test booklet.

Write the stem of the item so that it concisely states the problem with all the essential information to determining the solution. Avoid item stems that do not present a problem. For example, the following item has a stem that just gets the sentence going, but does not clearly state a problem.

1. The Bible
   a. is a great book.
   b. is about Islam.
   c. contains 65 books.
   d. was written in Hebrew.

I have difficulty knowing what instructional objective the item is attempting to assess. Let's suppose the objective was "to know (recognize) the original language of the majority of the Old Testament." Then the item may be improved as follows.

2. The language in which the bulk of the Old Testament was written is
   a. Aramaic
   b. Greek
   c. Hebrew
   d. Latin

Here the stem of the item clearly requests the student to recall something. The alternatives present him with four choices from which to select his solution to the stem's request. This example also illustrates another guideline:

Arrange the key and distractors in some logical order. Here the choices are arranged alphabetically. Dates or numbers could be arranged from smallest to largest, books of the Bible according to canonical order, etc.

If the stem consists of an incomplete statement, make sure to supply grammatically correct continuations of the stem as options.

The key and distractors should be of about the same length. Most test writers tend to make keys slightly longer than distractors. This disparity of length becomes a clue to the students.

Make all distractors plausible responses. Check length, grammar, and vocabulary to be sure that *to someone who does not know the correct answer* all the distractors appear to be possible.

As with true-false questions, avoid use of the words *all, every, never, none.*

Avoid use of "all of the above." Test-wise students will identify it as a distractor by locating just one other distractor. If they cannot be sure of the falsehood of any of the other choices they will guess that it is the key.

Use "none of the above" with caution. This option can be useful in certain situations, but it must be used carefully. Be sure not to use it always as a distractor, or test-wise students will learn to view it as a throwaway option.

Matching items. Matching items offer a variation of the multiple choice format that can be useful when a series of stems may require the same or similar options. Matching items have the advantage of using the key from one item as a distractor for another, avoiding the problem of creating three wrong answers for each item. Matching items consist of a list of descriptions or short stems and a list of options to match to the descriptions. Matching items are generally used to test achievement of objectives at the knowledge level. Consider the following sample:

Directions: Match the inventor with the invention by placing the appropriate letter from the inventor column in the space to the left of the number in the invention column. Each name may be used only once.

Invention	Inventor
____ 1. Telephone	A. Alexander Graham Bell
____ 2. Cotton gin	B. Henry Bessemer
____ 3. Light bulb	C. Thomas Edison
____ 4. Airplane	D. Guglielmo Marconi
____ 5. Wireless	E. Eli Whitney
	F. Orville Wright

This example portrays several key guidelines for constructing matching items.

Both the list of descriptions and the list of options should be fairly short, homogeneous in nature, and titled. A list of homogeneous options provides a set of plausible distractors for all the descriptions.

Each description in the list is numbered (each is a separate item in the test), while the options are lettered, as in the multiple-choice format.

Options outnumber descriptions when the student uses each option only once. This prevents the last item from being a giveaway. However, a short list of options which the student may select from repeatedly provides a useful format when a few distractors go with a larger list of descriptions. Be sure to specify in the directions whether or not the options may be used more than once.

The options follow some logical arrangement, in this case alphabetical.

Completion items. Completion items resemble the stem of a multiple-choice item. The difference lies in the fact that the student must recall rather than simply recognize the correct answer. Recall is more demanding than recognition. This distinction should be kept in mind when writing instructional objectives. If the objective calls for recall, none of the three formats already discussed will work. The completion format furnishes the only objective items that require recall of information.

Completion items should clearly state a problem and provide sufficient information that there will be one correct response. The response to a completion should be one word if possible. If a phrase is required, it should be short and concise. Several guidelines may be mentioned for completion items.

Avoid indefinite statements that may have several correct answers. For example, the item "Romans was written in _____."
could be answered with "A.D. 57" (the date), "Corinth" (the place), "Greek" (the language), or other creative answers a student might concoct. If the objective was for the student to know the date Romans was written, the following item would be an improvement: "Romans was written in the year A.D. _____." Now the student faces an unambiguous problem with only one correct answer.

Generally one blank is enough for each completion item. Consider the following item: "The _____ book of the Bible was written by _____." Better item: "The first book of the Bible was written by _____."

The blank should appear at or near the end of the sentence. If it is appropriate, use a question rather than an incomplete sentence for the item on the test.

Essay items. Many educational objectives require the student to demonstrate learning by making a longer and more complex written response than may be accomplished with objective test items. Essay items provide a procedure for testing such objectives. Essay items occur in two types: restricted-response and extended-response. The difference lies in the length, cognitive level, and complexity of the response requested.

Restricted-response essay items pose a problem that may be solved with one or two paragraphs, whereas extended-response items require several paragraphs. Typically, extended-response items require students to evaluate, to organize material, and to select viewpoints. These skills fit in the synthesis and evaluation levels of the cognitive taxonomy. Restricted-response items are more likely to be appropriate for objectives in the knowledge, comprehension, application, and analysis levels of the taxonomy. Because of their length and complexity, extended-response items may be better suited for a term paper or take-home test than for a test to be completed in class.

Essay items have certain advantages over objective items. (1) They are relatively easy to construct, compared to multiple-choice items. (2) They allow assessment of higher cognitive skills more directly than with multiple-choice items. (3) They reduce the possibility of guessing. (4) They emphasize communication skills.

However, they also possess certain drawbacks. (1) They present difficulties for consistent scoring. (However, this problem can be limited if the procedures discussed later on are followed.) (2) The time saved in creating the items is dwarfed by time needed to score the items, especially with a large class. (3) While an essay test excels in assessing depth of knowledge, breadth suffers. Because essay items take longer to complete, the test contains fewer items (and objectives). The most logical solution to this problem consists of using both objective and essay items in most tests.

The following guidelines will help you in using essay items:

Write out the item and the scoring criteria before administering the test. The scoring criteria indicate exactly how the item should be scored. Consider the following example:

Objective: The student will be able to explain three purposes for Paul's writing the letter to the church in Rome and give internal support for them. Purposes and verses are:
  (1) To prepare the way for his coming to Rome and his proposed mission to Spain (1:10-15; 15:22-29).
  (2) To present the way of salvation to a church he had never visited (1:16-17).

230

(3) To explain the relationship between Jew and Gentile in God's overall plan of redemption (14:1-6).

Test Item: In your own words, list three purposes for Paul's writing the letter to the church in Rome. For each purpose, provide at least one verse or section of verses in Romans to support the purpose (1 point per purpose, 1 point for supporting verse up to 6 points; no penalty for spelling, punctuation, or grammar).

Scoring Criteria:
>1 point for each of the purposes listed.
>1 point for a correct verse listed with the purpose.
>No penalty for spelling, punctuation, or grammatical error.
>No extra credit for more than one verse or section of verses listed for a purpose.
>Extraneous information will be ignored.

Notice that scoring criteria provide some objectivity to the scoring.

Tell the student the criteria for scoring. The example shows a parenthetical explanation of how the response will be scored. This information helps guide the student as he formulates his response. This guideline illustrates that you should tell the student what you expect of him as often as possible. Students complain about tests because they must guess what the teacher wants. Clear objectives presented to the student during instruction and clear questions and scoring criteria in tests will help to make the test an opportunity for the student to demonstrate his knowledge and understand—not play a guessing game.

The following guidelines relate to scoring essay items:

Score the items without knowing the identity of the student. Cover the names before scoring the essays to avoid the "halo effect."

Score each essay item for all students before moving on to the next item. This procedure will allow the teacher to score the items more efficiently (you will keep the criteria in mind easily after a few papers) and more consistently (better chance of applying the criteria fairly from one student to the next). If you feel you may have applied the criteria differently as you went though the stack of papers, go back and score them again.

ANALYZING TEACHER-MADE TESTS.

Every test should be analyzed to determine the class mean and standard deviation. The mean tells the teacher the score around which the scores of the class members tended to cluster, or the point of "central tendency." Based on your knowledge of the class and your feeling about the difficulty of the test, you should have some idea where you expect the mean to fall. Unexpectedly low means indicate the test was more difficult than you intended or the class had not mastered the material as well as you thought. If the test was more difficult than you thought, you may raise the mean by adding points to every score.

The standard deviation indicates the degree to which the individual scores differed from each other. The larger the standard deviation, the more divergence in the results. You will get a feel for what standard deviation to expect as you give a few tests to your class. Low standard deviation indicates an easy or difficult test with most of the scores clustered tightly around either a very high or a very low mean. A larger-than-expected standard deviation indicates the class was more spread out in their knowledge of the material than anticipated. This may indicate a need to review the material again.

You don't need to worry about learning the formulas for calculating mean or standard deviation. Inexpensive hand-held calculators with statistical functions can compute these statistics for you. Microcomputer spreadsheets also contain built-in functions for calculating mean and standard deviation. (See chapter on computers.)

Often tests (especially multiple-choice tests) are analyzed by examining item difficulty and item discrimination. Discussion of those topics may be found in standard textbooks on testing.

GRADING TEACHER-MADE TESTS

Assigning grades goes beyond calculating the percent correct on a test. Grading involves assigning a qualitative evaluation to a numerical test result. When a student scores 85 percent correct on a test, we must ask, "How good is that?" The answer begins with another question: "Compared to what?" The key word for grading is comparison. Though many comparisons for grading have been suggested, only two make sense for most applications: (1) comparison to other students, and (2) comparison to established standards.

You will use the mean and standard deviation to derive grades comparing one student to another. You first establish groups using these two statistics. Then you assign qualitative labels to the groups, such as A, B, C, etc. For example, consider a test with mean of 78 correct and a standard deviation of 7 with scores expressed as percent correct. A distribution of these scores might be represented as in Figure 1.

Frequency		2	5	13	15	12	9	
Score	57	64	71	78	85	92	99
S. D.	-3	-2	-1	0	1	2	3

Figure 1
DISTRIBUTION OF TEST SCORES

One scheme that could be used would be to assign the group from one standard deviation below the mean (71) to one standard deviation above the mean (85), the middle grade in the scoring scheme. If the scheme goes from A to F, members of this group receive a grade of C. Other grades would be 86 to 92: B; 93 to 99: A; 57 to 63: F; and 64 to 70: D. Figure 2 presents these grades in tabular form.

Scores	Frequency	Percent	Grade
93-99	9	16.1	A
86-92	12	21.4	B
71-85	28	50.0	C
64-70	5	8.9	D
57-63	2	3.6	F
Total	56	100.0	

Figure 2
SCORE DISTRIBUTION AS A TABLE

The categories can be manipulated to suit the given situation. For example, in graduate school a range from A to C would cover nearly all students. This approach to grading takes into account the concept that the test is not perfect. It may have been too hard or too easy for the class. Since we base grading on the performance of the class on the exam, the relative performance, not the absolute performance, of the student is evaluated.

This approach works well if the distribution of achievement in the class fits the theoretical model implied in the grade-assignment procedure. However, a student of average ability placed in a class of exceptionally bright students may receive low grades rather than average grades if compared to the performance of the class as a whole. Clearly this is not fair to him. Some alternative comparisons should be used in situations such as this.

The second means of establishing grades compares the performance of a student with some fixed standard. Typically schools have established ranges of percent correct to correspond to certain letter grades. For example, 90-100 = A; 80-89 = B; etc. The grading process is simple. The teacher computes the percent correct for a student and looks up the corresponding letter grade on a chart. This system works because of its simplicity and apparent fairness, since the same standard is applied to everyone taking the test.

This system suffers from some disadvantages, however. First, the standard is difficult to validate. When the student asks why 92 earns him a B = instead of an A −, the teacher may not have a very sensible answer. Second, this system assumes that every test conforms perfectly to the quality standards. For the system to work it needs a way of adjusting scores on unexpectedly easy or difficult tests.

As the preceding paragraphs illustrate, grading has a subjective element. Evaluation requires more than transforming a numerical grade to a letter grade. You need a certain amount of intuitive insight and flexibility to make grades report student progress on achievement accurately and fairly for everyone.

EVALUATING COGNITIVE LEARNING: INTERPRETING AND UTILIZING STANDARDIZED TEST RESULTS

We make most decisions about student achievement on the basis of teacher-made tests. However, results of standardized tests provide additional insight in assessing the progress of students.

NORM-REFERENCED AND CRITERION-REFERENCED TEST INTERPRETATION.

Standardized achievement tests are tests geared to specific grade levels and/or school subjects that have been developed and tested carefully and widely so that many helpful comparisons can be made. Standardized tests enable the teacher to compare a student's achievement with that of his own class, his grade-level at his own school, all students of his grade in the United States, all students of his grade in Christian schools. Test interpretation that incorporates comparisons between one student and a certain group of students is referred to as norm-referenced test interpretation.

In addition, you can compare the individual student's understanding of a subject with the typical expectations of a student at his grade-level. We call test interpretation that incorporates comparisons between one student's achievement and complete understanding of the subject criterion-referenced test interpretation.

Both norm-referenced and criterion-referenced test interpretations may be reported in standardized test results. We use the former in evaluating the student's achievement in comparison to other students. We use the latter in diagnosing the individual strengths and weaknesses of the student's achievement.

TEST VALIDITY AND RELIABILITY.

Validity and reliability refer to qualities of the text that make it useful for a given application. Validity refers to the quality of a test whereby it is an appropriate instrument for a given purpose. A valid test measures what it is supposed to measure.

Reliability refers to the quality of a test whereby it measures whatever it measures consistently.

Validity and reliability information on all standardized tests is available in the test instruction booklet. Be sure to consult the manual to make certain that the test being used is appropriate for its purpose and that it will yield consistent results when used repeatedly.

TEST SCORE REPORTS.

Test publishers can provide a variety of reports of test scores. Standardized achievement tests include several subtests. The test analysis reports the results of each subtest separately and in combination for the total score. For each test score several types of scores may be reported.

Raw score. The raw score stands for the number of items answered correctly. You don't try to interpret the raw score all by itself.

Grade equivalent. The grade equivalent score (GE) represents the score as a grade in school in years and months. (The school year divides into 10 months.) Thus a GE of 4.8 means fourth grade, eighth month—the student scored as an average student in fourth grade, eighth month would on this test. If the student who took the test was in third grade at the time, the GE indicates that the student has done above average work for a third-grader; however, it says nothing about his achievement of fourth-grade material.

Test analysts invented grade equivalent scores to simplify score reporting. However, since they tend to confuse more people than they help, they should yield to other score formats.

Percentiles. Percentile scores or percentile ranks are a score transformation based on comparison with a norm group or comparison group. If Johnny has a raw score of 43 on the math computation subtest and this raw score has a percentile rank of 89, this means that 89 percent of the people in the comparison group scored below 43 on the math computation subtest.

Percentiles have a certain intrinsic appeal. They avoid the confusion of grade equivalents and present information in a form with which people are somewhat familiar. If a student scores above the 50th percentile, he has done better than half the people in the comparison group—he scored above average.

However, they do have certain drawbacks. (1) People often mistakenly interpret percentile rank as percent correct on the test. (2) They invite more precise interpretation than appropriate. What should we make of the difference in achievement of Johnny's percentile rank of 89 and Suzie's percentile rank of 92? Probably not much. Because no test has perfect reliability, test scores need to be given a less strict interpretation than we might like to give.

Stanine. Stanine represents a transformed score that has a mean of 5 and a standard deviation of 2. Stanine stands for standard nines, because the whole range of possible test scores is divided into nine scores.

Stanines bestow the benefits of an easily understood interpretation of raw scores. "On a scale of 1 to 9 your child scored 8." Stanines possess a certain elegance in their simplicity. They also avoid the percentiles' problem of overinterpreting the results. Since they divide the entire range of scores into 9 parts rather than 99, they supply less temptation to overemphasize small differences in achievement. Their advantages make stanines the score transformation of choice for most applications.

Testing and grading remain unlikely candidates for a teacher's (or student's) favorite activities. Yet with some understanding and skill, you can become a good maker and interpreter of tests and a worthy grader.

SOURCES FOR INFORMATION ON STANDARDIZED ACHIEVEMENT TESTS

Educational Testing Service
Information Services Division
Publication Order Services
Department I-101
Princeton, NJ 08541

Scholastic Aptitude Test (SAT).

Many helpful booklets on testing.

The Psychological Corporation
757 Third Avenue
New York, NY 10017

Metropolitan Achievement Tests.
Stanford Achievement Tests.
Test Service Notebooks.

The Riverside Publishing Co.
8420 Bryn Mawr Avenue
Chicago, IL 60631

Iowa Tests of Basic Skills.

ENDNOTES

1. For a helpful discussion of problems and solutions to testing in college see Ohmer Milton and John W. Edgerly, *The Testing and Grading of Students,* 2nd ed., *Change* Magazine, 1977.

2. The terms *purpose, goal, objective, aim, standard,* and *goal-indicator* have been used in a variety of ways in educational literature. No effort to distinguish among these terms is made in this chapter.

3. The idea that the test matches the objective is referred to as content validity. See Tom Kubiszyn and Gary Borich, *Educational Testing and Measurement: Classroom Application and Practice.* Glenview, Ill.: Scott, Foresman, and Co., 1984, and Robert F. Mager, *Measuring Instructional Intent: or Got a Match?* Belmont, Calif.: Fearon Pitman Publishers, Inc., 1973.

BIBLIOGRAPHY

Ahmann, J. Stanley and Marvin D. Glock. *Evaluating Student Progress: Principles of Tests and Measurements,* 6th ed. Boston: Allyn and Bacon, Inc., 1981.

Allen, Mary J. and Wendy M. Yen. *Introduction to Measurement Theory.* Monterey, Calif.: Brooks/Cole Publishing Co., 1979.

Buros, O.K. *Eighth Mental Measurements Yearbook.* Lincoln, Nebr.: University of Nebraska Press, 1978.

Burrill, Lois E. *How a Standardized Achievement Test Is Built.* Test Service Notebook 125. New York: Harcourt, Brace, Jovanovich, Inc., n.d.

Clegg, Victoria L. and William E. Cashin. *Improving Multiple-Choice Tests.* Idea Paper No. 16. Kansas State University, Center for Faculty Evaluation & Development, 1986.

Diederich, Paul B. *Short-Cut Statistics for Teacher-Made Tests,* 3rd ed. Princeton, N.J.: Educational Testing Service, 1973.

Ebel, Robert L. *The Uses of Standardized Testing.* Fastback No. 93. Bloomington, Ind.: Phi Delta Kappa Educational Foundation, 1977.

Katz, Martin. *Selecting an Achievement Test: Principles and Procedures,* 3rd ed. Princeton, N.J.: Educational Testing Service, 1973.

Kubiszyn, Tom and Gary Borich. *Educational Testing and Measurement: Classroom Application and Practice.* Glenview, Ill.: Scott, Foresman and Company, 1984.

Lyman, Howard B. *Test Scores and What They Mean,* 4th ed. Englewood Cliffs, N.J.: Prentice-Hall, 1986.

Mager, Robert F. *Measuring Instructional Intent: or Got a Match?* Belmont, Calif.: Fearon Pitman Publishers, Inc., 1973.

_____ . *Preparing Instructional Objectives.* 2nd ed. Belmont, Calif.: Fearon Pitman Publishers, Inc., 1975.

Making the Classroom Test: a Guide for Teachers, 3rd ed. Princeton, N.J.: Educational Testing Service, 1973.

Milton, Ohmer and John W. Edgerly. *The Testing and Grading of Students,* 2nd ed., *Change* Magazine, 1977.

Mitchell, Blythe C. *A Glossary of Measurement Terms.* Test Service Notebook

13. New York: Harcourt, Brace, Jovanovich, Inc., n.d.

Multiple Choice Questions: A Close Look, 2nd ed. Princeton, N.J.: Educational Testing Service, 1973.

Nunnally, Jum C. *Psychometric Theory,* 2nd ed. New York: McGraw-Hill Book Company, 1978.

Perrone, Vito. *The Abuses of Standardized Testing.* Fastback No. 92. Bloomington, Ind.: Phi Delta Kappa Educational Foundation, 1977.

Popham, W. James, "Instructional Objectives: Two Decades of Decadence." Paper presented at the annual meeting of the American Educational Research Association, San Francisco, April 16-20, 1986.

Riegel, Rodney P. and Ned B. Lovell. *Minimum Competency Testing.* Fastback No. 137. Bloomington, Ind.: Phi Delta Kappa Educational Foundation, 1980.

Wilson, Ruth. *Criterion-Referenced Testing.* Test Service Notebook 37. New York: Harcourt, Brace, Jovanovich, Inc., 1980.

Part Three

CRUCIAL ROLES
in Christian Teaching

14. THE TEACHER AS LEADER
Howard G. Hendricks

Leaders are fast becoming an endangered species. Wherever one goes—across America or around the world—he discovers the screaming need for leaders.

Unfortunately, as John Gardner perceptively suggested in the 1960s, young Americans were being infected with an antileadership virus which greatly exacerbated the problem.

Our leadership deficit is evidenced in several determinative areas.

WE NEED LEADERS IN OUR HOMES
God's fulcrum is the family. It is, therefore, a startling historical fact to contemplate that no society has ever survived the disintegration of its family life. In the United States today the domestic fabric is unraveling like a cheap sweater. Working wives and absent, passive husbands are hallmarks of our age.

Pierre Mornell, California psychiatrist, confesses:

Over the last few years I have seen in my office an increasing number of couples who share a common denominator. The man is active, articulate, energetic and usually successful in his work. But he is inactive, inarticulate, lethargic and withdrawn at home. In his relationship to his wife he is passive. And his passivity drives her crazy. In the face of his retreat, she goes wild.[1]

Unfortunately, the fragmentation of the family is not limited to America. In seventy-plus countries which I visited, Christian leaders—

241

national and missionary—all testify to the breakdown of the family as one of their greatest unsolved problems.

WE NEED LEADERS IN OUR CHURCHES

The average church in America is operated by 15–20 percent of its membership. More people spectate than participate. Very few churches can afford to have a sign out on their front doors, "No Help Wanted."

We need to be very careful not to blame God for the deficiency. God is still in the process of dispensing gifts (1 Cor. 12:4-6), but we are not in the process of developing gifts. The primary task of a Spirit-gifted person given to the church is to equip the saints for their work of ministry (Eph. 4:7-16).

WE NEED LEADERS IN OUR SOCIETY

Arnold Toynbee, noted historian, in assessing the flow of history, concluded that the rise and fall of societies has depended almost exclusively on the quality of their leaders.

In America the crisis of leadership pervades every segment of society. It involves the revelations in business of inside trading on Wall Street, the alarming increase of substance abuse in athletics, the lack of integrity among Presidential candidates, and even the immorality and consumptive lifestyles of religious leaders. No province of our national life escapes the cancer of corruption.

Eugene Peterson places a burr in our mental saddle with these words:

> The puzzle is why so many people live so badly. Not so wickedly, but so inanely. Not so cruelly, but so stupidly. There is little to admire and less to imitate in the people who are prominent in our culture. We have celebrities but not saints. Famous entertainers amuse a nation of bored insomniacs. Infamous criminals act out the aggressions of timid conformists. Petulant and spoiled athletes play games vicariously for lazy and apathetic spectators. People, aimless and bored, amuse themselves with trivia and trash. Neither the adventures of goodness nor the pursuit of righteousness gets headlines.[2]

The moral microbes are eating the heart out of the body politic. It is disintegrating from within. The pedestals are empty.

But why is it so difficult to find leaders when every segment

242

desperately needs them? Much of the blame can be laid at the door of the classrooms of America.

This chapter suggests that in the midst of the malaise, one of the greatest hopes for the new generation of leaders resides with the teacher. The art of leading can be taught and potential leaders can be developed, provided the educational system does not abort the educational embryo.

Henry Brooks Adams capsulizes the thrust with these words: "A murderer takes life, but his deed stops there; a teacher affects eternity; he can never tell where his influence stops."[3]

Why is the teacher so essential to the development of quality leaders? For three reasons at least: (1) the people for whom he performs his tasks—young, plastic minds that are like wet cement; (2) the position which he holds—one of visibility and influence; and (3) the person that he is—authentic or phony, godly or godless—will leave his permanent mark.

THE DEFINITION OF A LEADER

Charles Kettering said, "A problem well defined is a problem half solved." In order to refine our subject we need to define it.

Here's my working definition of a leader: a person who knows where he is going and is able to persuade others to go along with him. That is, he has clear-cut objectives and he is a motivator. He is not only enamored of ideas but of individuals; he is task- as well as person-oriented.

We see these components clearly in the life of Christ and the Apostle Paul. "For even the Son of man did not come to be served, but to serve [objective], and to give His life as a ransom for many [motivation]." In 1 Thessalonians 2:8, Paul explains: "We loved you so much that we were delighted to share with you not only the Gospel of God [objective] but our lives as well, because you had become so dear to us [motivation]."

A teacher is primarily a person with transparent objectives and transformative motivation. If he does not know where he is going, how can he lead others? If people do not follow him, he is not a leader.

HE MUST BE A PERSON OF INFLUENCE.

Leadership is more than a position, it is power; it is not a role but a responsibility; it is not a title but a function.

People in all walks of life, when evaluating the most influential people who impacted their lives, invariably describe a teacher. Someone who significantly and permanently shaped the direction of their lives, often the choice of their specializations. It had little to do with subject but everything to do with significance.

This is why we can say that teaching often consists of a few teachable moments. Good teachers often hear, "You changed the whole course of my life."

Interestingly, the influence is often not immediate but long-range. That's why patience is an essential garment in a teacher's wardrobe. Like the farmer, he/she plants the seed, later to witness the harvest. As in Jesus' day, "The Society of the Thankless Nine, Local 281" is very much alive in our day (cf. Luke 17:11-19).

A teacher's influence may be negative or positive, but influence he has. Who of us cannot identify with Houston Peterson in his grabbing description:

> We must recoil from the graveyard of books and authors killed by inept pedagogy. Who has not had an entire subject, such as history or mathematics, ruined for him? Who has not been driven permanently away from Shakespeare or Wordsworth or Emerson by heavy-handed scholarship or misguided dissection? The epithets of crime are not inappropriate here, for again and again one hears students speak of being "robbed" by one professor, or of having a subject "killed" by another.[4]

Teachers must be people who serve. The servant leader is the Jesus model.

In capsulizing His life our Lord said, "But I am among you as One who serves" (Luke 22:27). The Christian teacher develops himself to the highest level possible—personally and professionally—and then he gives it all away.

Unfortunately today, servant leadership is a buzz word. It suffers more at the hands of its friends than its enemies and has been raped of its biblical nuances.

While it is true that teachers also serve, they serve best by leading. Servant leaders are not passive but active; they are not waiting for something to happen but causing something to happen. We all embrace the concept but fail to understand exactly what is involved. It embraces more than acts; it is an attitude that pervades all that we do.

The teacher exists for the student—not for the administration, his colleagues, or the constituency—though he has an important responsibility to all three. He teaches more than a subject; he teaches individuals. If the student has not learned, the teacher has not taught. His highest fulfillment comes in pouring his life out like a drink-offering for his students. He lives to serve them.

Financial compensation is not his greatest concern. Like the Saviour he can say, "I have food to eat that you know nothing about"

(John 4:32). His pay is his fulfillment—the satisfaction of having built into the life of another human being with an eternal impact. He is a member of "The Order of the Towel" (cf. 13:1-17), the greatest educational fraternity entitled. He must be a person of character.

Fred Smith summarizes the issue well:

> Leadership as we have seen, is both something you *are* and something you *do*. But effective leadership starts with character. When leaders fail, more often it is a result of a character flaw than lack of competence.
>
> The aim of any Christian is to mature, to conform more and more to the image of Christ. This character development is especially important for leaders. And it's a process, not a plateau where we sit down to rest. Leaders who last don't stop growing; they continue to stretch themselves.[5]

God is into character, not credentials. He is not impressed with what we do but with who we are becoming, because that is always the product of what *He* does. When the Holy Spirit outlines the qualifications of a leader in 1 Timothy 3 and Titus 2, He instructs that the majority of these qualities are reflections of godly character development. They focus on being rather than doing; on what kind of a person we are. But why so demanding? Because a leader is so determinative. He must generate respect.

Like all of God's creatures, teachers reproduce after their kind. The results endure. The thinking they produce will be around for a long time. So, Paul reminds us, "Be careful how you build!"

The greatest crisis of leadership today is a crisis of character. Key Watergate witness John Dean describes the all-too-familiar process of ethical waffling:

> To make my way upward, into a position of confidence and influence, I had to travel downward through factional power plays, corruption and finally outright crimes. Slowly, steadily, I would climb toward the moral abyss of the President's inner circle until I finally fell into it, thinking I had made it to the top just as I began to realize I had actually touched bottom.[6]

Our generation requires men and women of integrity, people who are authentic. The New Testament never advocates for Christian leaders a model of perfection, but progression (cf. 1 Tim. 4:15).

Mark Hatfield, in his excellent chapter, "Maintaining Integrity Under Pressure," calls attention to the words of Peter Drucker that "quality of character doesn't make a leader, but the lack of it flaws the entire process."[7]

The quality of the teacher is the key to future leadership. His pupils either lay bricks or build cathedrals.

THE DISTINCTIVE CONTRIBUTION OF TEACHERS

Teachers shape young people's thinking, attitudes, and behavior during the most formative period of their lives. Leaders are often formed in the process of intensive exposure to one or more significant educators, not all of whom serve in classrooms. Some of the most significant teachers in any generation frequently do not bear that title.

Teaching leadership is essential but not easy. Our society communicates to youth a sense of powerlessness, of dispensability. John Gardner assesses the situation:

> Our young people are born into a society that is huge, impersonal and intricately organized. Far from calling them to leadership, it appears totally indifferent. It does not seem to need them at all. Far from creating the confidence that young leaders require, it is apt to create puzzlement and a sense of powerlessness. It is very hard for young people today to believe that any action on their part will affect the vast processes of their society.[8]

For the Christian young person the problem intensifies when the world asks, "Why bother? Why involve yourself in such a costly commitment?"

> There is plenty to enjoy without involving yourself in all that. The past is a graveyard; ignore it; the future is a holocaust; avoid it. There is no payoff for discipleship; there is no destination for pilgrimage. Get God the quick way; buy instant charisma.[9]

If leadership is to flourish there must be conditions in which it can emerge. Certainly the teacher is the ideal one to create the most favorable climate in which it can flower. What the teacher can do to create a new breed of leaders will be determined by two seminal ingredients.

THE TEACHER'S EDUCATIONAL PHILOSOPHY.

This chapter does not intend to explicate a philosophy of education. Nevertheless, such is essential if one expects the learning environment to be conducive to the development of leaders.

The life of learning is not done *to* us but developed *in* us. For this reason, the essence of teaching must embrace the understanding that it is not what the teacher does but what the student does as a result.

Two questions stand at the core of a well-formulated philosophy of education: (1) What is teaching? and (2) What is learning? If teaching is causing people to learn, then one's prior concern must be, How do students learn?

Learning, to be most effective, demands that the student be active, not passive; participators, not spectators. While we know very little about the true nature of leadership, we do know that leaders are not passive onlookers.

Christian education, as presently conceived, is entirely too passive, too inactive. Christianity is the most revolutionary force on earth—it radicalizes people—and yet most often it is set in concrete.

Leaders are not reproduced in soporific settings. Jeremiah asks this penetrating question: "If you have raced with men on foot and they have worn you out, how can you compete with horses?" (12:5)

The quality of the teacher is the key to quality education. People learn to lead by spending time with people of proven leadership ability. If a teacher is infectious and models leadership, he has the best shot at reproducing leaders. You can't teach leadership; but you can develop leaders.

THE TEACHER'S EDUCATIONAL PRACTICE.

Philosophy always precedes and results in practice. Effective teachers balance their teaching between analysis and action, between abstract theory and realistic practice. Many a scholar seems careless about the teaching process because it interferes with his primary interest; namely, his subject. Courses often lead to a degree but not an education.

Three ingredients bias us to action in teaching.

It must be geared to process. Teachers should cease to be performers and become learners. They should be people who can do things better but, more importantly, they should be people who can equip others to do it better. When process is one's primary goal he does not limit others by his own limitations. He launches the student on a journey which may, and often does, go far beyond his own.

Henry Adams underscores the need for learning: "What one knows is, in youth, of little moment; they know enough who know how to learn."[10]

The saying is true, "Give me a fish and I eat for a day; teach me to fish and I eat for life."

One needs to understand that schooling and learning are very different. Eugene Peterson explains:

In schooling persons count for very little. Facts are memorized, information assimilated, examinations passed. Teachers are subjected to a supervision that attempts to insure uniform performance, which means that everyone operates as much alike as possible and is rewarded insofar as the transfer of data from book to brain is made with as little personal contamination as possible. In schooling, the personal is reduced to the minimum: standardized tests, regulated teachers, information-oriented students.[11]

Quality teaching requires time. In an age of instant everything educators dare not buy into the system. Our task as teachers is to equip our students for that perpetual learning process. Teachers usually erroneously see themselves as dispensers of information rather than developers of life. Schools do not spawn leaders; life does.

It must be geared to people. Learning is a most intricately personal process. It cannot be mass-produced. Churchill expressed it well: "I love to learn; I hate to be taught."

Learning corresponds to this analogy:

Like pilots whose navigational systems sometimes fail, leaders fly blind with alarming frequency. Although leadership theory abounds (one book summarizes more than 3,000 studies), much of it is based on a fetchingly simple—but dangerously flawed—premise. Human beings, it postulates, are like chessmen or tin soldiers. They can be relied on to move in predictable ways, responding to outside stimuli much like Pavlov's salivating dogs. But the theorists have failed to take into account an essential part of man's humanness—his penchant for maddening inconsistency. They have to face the troubling fact that unlike the phenomena of chemistry or physics—where water always boils at 212 degrees Fahrenheit—humans often behave in unexpected ways.[12]

This is what generates excitement and demands creativity in teaching. Learners are as different as snowflakes, voice, and fingerprints. One recoils at the contemporary attempt to standardize education.

Since learning is so interactive, *who* the teacher is determines *what* the teacher does. Students are not merely interested in what you know and how you got there but primarily in who you are.

Modeling, therefore, becomes of prime importance in the practice of teaching. But most teachers are too far removed from the students they are attempting to impact. You cannot communicate across a chasm. You impact in direct proportion to involvement.

I have long been convinced that four walls are often the greatest preventive to efficient learning. Sometimes the greatest learning takes place *outside* the classroom in informal settings.

The art of teaching is the art of being fully human. Teachers can afford to be vulnerable because students often view their mentors in terms of where they are, not in terms of the process required to get there.

It must be geared to life. Life is incredibly messy, unpredictable, and constantly changing. It cannot be tied in neat little packages. It does not present itself the way we are taught in schools. It invariably does not compete with the ivory-tower musings with which we were confronted.

At times we as teachers not only do not know the answers, we don't even know the problems. We were trained in an age which no longer exists. This explains why students often complain, "My education answered the questions no one is asking, but the questions that are destroying men's lives, we never got around to discussing."

Realistically, there is only one way to obviate this transparent deficiency—teach people a process of decision-making—the ability to think and solve problems, to question more answers.

Andrew LePeau surfaces the need in a Christian context:

We call people to "make a decision" for Christ, yet too often we believe that is the last decision they have to make as Christians. Our Christian lives are full of decisions and crossroads. How will I confront Mary about her incessant sarcasm? What will I do to help Jim while his dad is in the hospital? How much time should I spend studying, how much at church and how much with family this semester? If we try to spoon-feed those in our care, they will never get the practice of dealing with such problems themselves. They will remain immature.[13]

Christian teachers must create learning environments in which students are not only free to ask life-related questions but are encouraged to do so. Perhaps the greatest problem requiring solution is the lack of self-worth on the part of present-day students. No one epitomizes that kind of teaching better than Marva Collins.

Marva Collins, like many excellent teachers, left the traditional classroom. *Unlike* many excellent teachers, she did not turn away from education. Rather, she made positive use of the energy that could, instead, have been dissipated through anger and frustration. She brought to fruition a dream that must have lain dormant through the years when she wrestled with a fail-

249

ing educational system that was impeding development of youthful human potential.

She chose not to join the ranks of those who merely argued about appropriate educational theory in the safe and antiseptic halls of academia. She decided to act on the courage of her convictions and to test some of the tenets of common wisdom (or common sense).

Mrs. Collins abandoned empty questions like, "Why can't Johnny read?" She refused to get enmeshed in platitudes like, "Back to basics." She eschewed high-sounding theories of motivation, cognitive attribution, and the like.[14]

The ultimate goal of the teacher is to produce a self-learner committed to overcoming any learning disability and developing a lifelong learning curiosity, self-discipline, and intellectual honesty. That is transformative teaching.

THE DEVELOPMENT OF LEADERS

According to many thoughtful observers the most compelling issue in the remainder of the twentieth century is leadership development. It is a universal imperative.

John Gardner sounds the alarm in his historical reminder:

At the time this nation was formed our population stood at around 3 million. And we produced out of that 3 million perhaps six leaders of world class—Washington, Adams, Jefferson, Franklin, Madison, Hamilton. One could name others, but let's leave it at six. Today our population stands at around 240 million, so we might expect 80 times as many world class leaders—480 Jeffersons, Madisons, Adams, Washingtons, Hamiltons, Franklins. Where are they?[15]

He is convinced they are among us. "Out there in the settings we are all familiar with are the inactivated leaders feeling no overpowering call to lead and hardly aware of the potential within."[16]

But the question nags: How can the teacher awaken and develop them? Two areas will be probed, each of which bristles with potential: (1) the principles to be employed; and (2) the possibilities to be explored.

PRINCIPLES TO BE EMPLOYED.

Our Lord's creation of a leadership pool is undoubtedly the best example of workable and transferable principles to overcome a shortage of leaders (cf. Matt. 9:37-38). Jesus took a group of ordinary men with widely diverse personalities and backgrounds and galvanized them into a leadership team that was irrepressible.

How did He do it?

By careful selection. Difficulties in assessing leadership potential stem from the very nature of leadership. Promise of greatness and desirable attributes are often deeply buried and do not surface with limited exposure.

In Luke 6:12-16 we see our Lord in the process of choosing His men. Three criteria are employed, all of which are usable by any teacher: (1) He bathed His choices in prayer. Jesus spent an entire night seeking the Father's mind. John 17:6, 9 informs us these were those the Father had given Him. (2) He chose individuals with proven characteristics. Jesus had extensive and intimate involvement with these men—at least a year, some think more—living and ministering together. (3) Jesus opted for diversity in His choices. He handpicked a radical and a redneck, extroverts and introverts, natural leaders and those we seldom hear from.

Teachers need to have their antennae sensitized to pick up signals of significance in terms of emerging potential for leadership.

By intensive association. Mark 3:14 informs us that Christ chose men with a twofold objective: (1) "that they might be with Him"; and (2) "that He might send them out to preach." The order is instructive: association before communication; isolation before involvement. On twelve separate occasions in the Gospels Jesus took the initiative in getting time alone with His men.

You can impress people at a distance but you can only impact them up close. Teachers need to intensify their interpersonal relations with their students. Leadership is caught not taught.

By consistent modeling. The disciples saw our Lord in action—teaching, healing, debating, serving—because God's method is always incarnational. It was with our Lord's coming to earth (John 1:14) and also with the Apostle Paul's lifestyle (Phil. 4:9). In fact, Paul urged the Corinthians, "Follow my example, as I follow the example of Christ" (1 Cor. 11:1).

Most teachers are too insulated from their students to impact them. Students only see them in formal and controlled situations. You don't pick up a leader's heartbeat that far removed.

By creative training. Mark 6:6-13 is a case study in leadership development. Our Lord did several things: (1) He demonstrated what He wanted His disciples to do; (2) He instructed them as to how they were to do it—including negative and positive suggestions; and (3) He sent them out in teams of two to participate in ministry.

Jesus was never limited in His use of methods to develop people, but He never depended on them to accomplish His objectives. Gardner correctly observes:

> Little by little, preoccupation with method, technique and procedure gains a subtle dominance *over* the whole process of goal seeking. How it is done becomes more important than whether it is done. Means triumph over ends. Form triumphs over spirit. Method is enthroned. Men become prisoners of their procedures, and organizations that were designed to achieve some goal become obstacles in the path to that goal.[17]

Jesus achieved that for which He aimed—life change, not legalistic conformity. He instilled vision, goals, trust, and meaning in His followers. To accomplish those goals, the Saviour—great developer of people that He was—employed a total training model. He told them, showed them, put them in action, and then evaluated their performance. What a model of mentoring at its best.

By personal dedication. In John 15:16 Jesus informed His disciples that He had chosen them "to go and bear fruit—fruit that will last." What confidence that must have generated. After the Resurrection He assured the disciples, "As the Father has sent Me, I am sending you" (20:21). What courage that must have engendered. In the Great Commission Jesus said, "All authority in heaven and on earth has been given to Me. Therefore go and make disciples" (Matt. 28:18-19). What continuity that must have provided.

Teachers are often guilty of hogging the show. Every time they do anything for their students that they are capable of doing themselves, they are producing pedagogical paraplegics.

By realistic expectation. Someone said, "If you believe in me, it is easier for me to believe in myself." Jesus' expressed expectations dramatically impacted His disciples.

The first time our Lord met Peter He said, "You are Simon son of John. You will be called Cephas" (John 1:42). That's the before and after of Peter's life—a thumbnail sketch of his entire pilgrimage. What a challenge! In Luke 22:31-32 He said, "Simon, Simon, Satan has asked to sift you as wheat. But I have prayed for you, Simon, that your faith may not fail. And when you have turned back, strengthen your brothers." What a comfort!

How a teacher perceives his students may determine what they become—a problem or a potential in terms of leadership.

The principles elucidated above are easy to state and understand but the process of internalizing them is a lifetime challenge.

POSSIBILITIES TO BE EXPLORED.

By developing interests. Leaders are perpetual learners. It is their essential fuel. Unfortunately, most educational exposure is a process of producing technicians, not leaders.

> Leaders have always been generalists. Tomorrow's leaders will very likely have begun life as trained specialists, but to mature as leaders they must sooner or later climb out of the trenches of specialization and rise above the boundaries that separate the various segments of society. Only as generalists can they cope with the diversity of problems and multiple constituencies that contemporary leaders face.[18]

I believe that the best preparation for leadership is a liberal arts education which broadens and deepens the student's reservoir of resources.

The teacher's task is to stretch the minds of his students—to introduce them to new areas of interest, problems to be solved, challenges to be embraced. Paul urged, "If God has . . . put you in charge . . . take the responsibility seriously" (Rom. 12:8, TLB).

By providing insights. Probably the greatest of these is self-knowledge. One cannot manage others until he learns to manage himself. Understanding oneself includes not only the effect others have on us but the impact we have on others as well.

By middle-age most people are accomplished fugitives from themselves. Their self-image is in the algebraic minus quantity, their fear of the future is paralyzing. Winston Churchill, however, was 66 when he rose above the nonleaders who had so disastrously been in charge of his country.

Teaching and leading are processes of introducing the person to himself. In so doing he comes to understand his strengths and his weaknesses. In his leadership role, consequently, he can lead on the basis of his strengths and staff on the basis of his weaknesses. If such insight is not gained, he spends the rest of his life trying to prove something or functioning as a square peg in a round hole.

Warren Bennis and Burt Nanus concluded that leaders share four areas of competency: (1) the management of attention; (2) meaning; (3) trust; and (4) self. The fourth area of competency includes viewing oneself positively and inspiring positive feelings in others.[19]

There is no effective leadership without communication. Most leaders, however, focus on the wrong end of the communication process; namely, what they are saying, thinking, or feeling. Becoming receptor-oriented is the most freeing skill to be learned. What are the hearers saying, thinking, or feeling? That's the ultimate insight in communication.

By encouraging involvements. Opportunities outside the classroom need to be explored—activities that provide a laboratory for the testing of leadership skills; for example, sports, writing, dramatics, public service, Christian missions, cross-cultural ministries, etc. In addition, Outward Bound and other wilderness experiences provide opportunity to build self-confidence and team skills. As has been said, "There are some things you can't learn from others. You have to pass through the fire."

Above all, young people should be given opportunities to observe leaders at close range and identify with positive leadership role models. Some may even experience a mentoring relationship—formally or informally. Internships are highly educative in developing leaders.

Work assignments provide a healthy dose of reality and an opportunity to use skills and evaluate gifts.

All of the above are maximally profitable when coupled with personal evaluation. Honest feedback is priceless.

CONCLUSION

Plato expressed it clearly: "What is honored in a country is cultivated there." Not until teachers gain a new vision of how determinative they are in raising a crop of leaders will there be any significant change in the chronic crisis of governance. Those responsible for our future more than any other must raise the intensive search for new leadership to a much higher priority.

If leadership is to flourish, there must be an environment conducive to its emergence and individuals committed to its development: an environment that is receptive, not hostile with alienating structures; and individuals that commit people to action, convert followers into leaders, and leaders into agents of change.

The present-day challenges and the laser pace of change require great ideas and great individuals to implement them. We need to clone men with David's focus, of whom it is said, "For when David had served God's purpose in his own generation, he fell asleep" (Acts 13:36). May his tribe increase!

ENDNOTES

1. Pierre Mornell, *Passive Men, Wild Women.* New York: Ballantine Books, 1979, p. 1.

2. Eugene H. Peterson, *Run with the Horses.* Downers Grove, Ill.: InterVarsity Press, 1983, pp. 11–12.

3. Henry Brooks Adams, *The Education of Henry Adams.* New York: Time, Inc., 1964, Vol. II, p. 73.

4. Houston Peterson, *Great Teachers.* New Brunswick, N.J.: Rutgers University Press, 1946, p. xvi.

5. Fred Smith, *Learning to Lead.* Waco, Texas: Word Books, 1986, p. 47.

6. John W. Dean, *Blind Ambition.* New York: Simon and Schuster, 1976, pp. 30–31.

7. Cited by Harold Myra, ed., in *Leaders.* Waco, Texas: Word Books, 1987, pp. 27–28.

8. John Gardner, *Leadership Development.* Washington, D.C.: Independent Sector, 1987, p. 6.

9. Eugene H. Peterson, *A Long Obedience in the Same Direction.* Downers Grove, Ill.: InterVarsity Press, 1980, p. 16.

10. Adams, p. 89.

11. Eugene H. Peterson, *Working the Angles.* Downers Grove, Ill.: InterVarsity Press, 1987, pp. 65–66.

12. John K. Clemens and Douglas F. Mayer, *The Classic Touch.* Homewood, Ill.: Dow Jones-Irwin, 1987, p. 79.

13. Andrew T. LePeau, *Paths of Leadership.* Downers Grove, Ill.: InterVarsity Press, 1983, p. 84.

14. Melvin P. Sikes, *A Conversation with Marva Collins.* Austin, Texas: Hogg Foundation for Mental Health, The University of Texas, 1982, p. 2.

15. Gardner, p. 24.

16. Gardner, p. 7.

17. John Gardner, *Self-Renewal.* New York: Harper and Row, 1963, p. 58.

18. John Gardner, *Leadership Development.* Washington, D.C.: Independent Sector, 1987, p. 7.

19. Warren Bennis and Burt Nanus, *Leaders: The Strategies for Taking Charge.* New York: Harper and Row, 1985, pp. 26–28.

BIBLIOGRAPHY

Adams, Henry Brooks. *The Education of Henry Adams,* Vol. II. New York: Time, Inc., 1964.

Bennis, Warren and Burt Nanus. *Leaders: The Strategies for Taking Charge.* New York: Harper and Row, 1985.

Clemens, John K. and Douglas F. Mayer. *The Classic Touch.* Homewood, Ill.: Dow Jones-Irwin, 1987.

Gardner, John. *Leadership Development.* Washington, D.C.: Independent Sector, 1987.

————. *Self-Renewal.* New York: Harper and Row, 1963.

Habecker, Eugene B. *The Other Side of Leadership.* Wheaton, Ill.: Victor Books, 1987.

Hendricks, Howard G. *Teaching to Change Lives.* Portland, Ore.: Multnomah Press. 1987.

Kouzes, James M. and Barry Z. Posner. *The Leadership Challenge.* San Francisco: Jossey-Bass Publishers, 1987.

LePeau, Andrew T. *Paths of Leadership.* Downers Grove, Ill.: InterVarsity Press, 1983.

Myra, Harold, ed. *Leaders.* Waco, Texas: Word Books, 1987.

Peterson, Eugene H. *Working the Angles.* Downers Grove, Ill.: InterVarsity Press, 1987.

Peterson, Houston. *Great Teachers.* New Brunswick, N.J.: Rutgers University Press, 1946.

Sanders, J. Oswald. *Spiritual Leadership.* Revised Edition. Chicago: Moody Press, 1986.

Sikes, Melvin P. *A Conversation with Marva Collins.* Austin, Texas: Hogg Foundation for Mental Health, The University of Texas, 1982.

Smith, Fred. *Learning to Lead.* Waco, Texas: Word Books, 1986.

15. THE TEACHER AS DISCIPLER
James R. Slaughter

A study of the New Testament makes it clear that the ministry of discipleship is a responsibility which every Christian should assume at some point in his walk of faith. Jesus' last words on earth were spoken to His followers who had gathered around Him on the mountain:

> Therefore go and make disciples of all nations, baptizing them in the name of the Father and of the Son and of the Holy Spirit, and teaching them to obey everything I have commanded you. And surely I will be with you always, to the very end of the age (Matt. 28:19-20).

The two-pronged ministry of discipleship includes both evangelism (winning, baptizing) and equipping (building, teaching). The Scripture exhorts all who know Christ to share their faith (1 Thes. 1:8; 1 Peter 2:9-10; 3:15) and to help other believers grow in their Christian experience (Rom. 14:19; Col. 3:16). This winning-building task belongs not only to the professional minister, but also to the Christian layman. God calls Christians in all walks of life to be disciple-makers as evidenced by the ministry of Aquila and his wife Priscilla (Acts 18). Though a tentmaker by trade (v. 3), Aquila was keenly aware of his responsibility as a discipler, and both he and his wife ministered as such to the eloquent but insufficiently instructed Apollos (vv. 24-26). Christians today in every walk of life must be no less keenly aware of the call for them to make disciples. Coleman puts it well when he writes:

> The Great Commission is not a special calling or a gift of the Spirit; it is a command—an obligation incumbent upon the whole community of faith. There are no exceptions. Bank presidents and automobile mechanics, physicians and schoolteach-

ers, theologians and homemakers—everyone who believes on Christ has a part in His work (John 14:12).[1]

No Christian has a more promising opportunity for discipleship ministry than the teacher. The teacher has a ready-made audience (his students) with whom he associates regularly (usually on a daily or at least weekly basis), an audience made up of people who look to him as a source of truth and a guide for relating that truth to life. The goal of every teacher-discipler is to enable his student-disciples to become more like Jesus Christ through the winning and building process. The Apostle Paul states this purpose clearly: "We proclaim Him, admonishing and teaching everyone with all wisdom, so that we may present everyone perfect in Christ" (Col. 1:28).

God allows every Christian teacher to be a part of that process whereby the Holy Spirit brings a student more closely into conformity with his Saviour "to become mature, attaining to the whole measure of the fullness of Christ" (Eph. 4:13).

THE ELEMENTS OF THE TEACHER-DISCIPLER'S MINISTRY

Those who teach Bible in a Christian school or college may clearly understand how their ministry includes the process of discipleship. After all, they are teaching biblical material. Their curriculum, if not specifically books of the Bible, is certainly Bible-related, and the association is clear. However, for those called to be teacher-disciplers but who teach secular subjects, the relationship may not be quite so obvious. How does a teacher disciple his students while teaching them English, trigonometry, or physical education? How can the application to spiritual life be made apparent?

The following five principles of discipleship are useful in virtually any teaching situation, regardless of its orientation. They are useful generically because they focus not on *content* but on *context*—that is, on developing an environment in which teachers nourish relationships with students so that spiritual growth takes place.

THE ELEMENT OF CONSECRATION

(the teacher-discipler as shepherd).

The word "consecration" means dedicate to God, to set something or someone apart for use by the Lord. Moses and Solomon consecrated the tabernacle and temple in ancient Israel, along with all their furnishings, setting them apart for God's use (Lev. 8:1-11; 1 Kings 8). The priests of Israel themselves lived lives consecrated for service to the Lord, and they consecrated the sacrifices they offered to God on behalf of His people (Lev. 8:12-36).

The New Testament combines the ideas of priest and sacrifice into one entity in the life of the believer. Every believer functions as a priest in the Lord's service, commissioned to offer "spiritual sacrifices acceptable to God through Jesus Christ" (1 Peter 2:5). In Romans 12:1-2 the apostle spells out more precisely the nature of the sacrifice to be offered by the believer-priest: "Therefore, I urge you, brothers, in view of God's mercy, to offer your bodies as living sacrifices, holy and pleasing to God—which is your spiritual worship."

The priest himself offers his very life as the sacrifice. Not a lifeless sacrifice as in the Old Testament era, but a live sacrifice useful to God on a continual basis. The sacrifices of the Old Testament priests of Israel were offered and consumed (either burned or eaten by the priest and his family as the Torah allowed). But the New Testament believer-priest (himself the sacrifice) continues daily in his walk with and service to the Lord.

This commitment to be a living sacrifice is incumbent on every Christian student but must reside first in the life of the teacher-discipler. He in turn will encourage and exhort his student-disciples to offer their lives as living sacrifices. Such a commitment on the part of the teacher necessitates a regular, vital, devotional life, including the regular study of the Word of God. Jesus Himself articulated clearly, "If you hold to [continue to be immersed in] My teaching, you are really My disciples" (John 8:31). Only as the teacher enriches himself in the Word of God as a disciple can he hope to impart to his students the reality of the need to consecrate their own lives to God, and the need to cultivate their own devotional experience.

As a disciple-maker the teacher approaches the teaching process in the context of consecrated living. Teaching leads to assimilation of academic material, but this material must be used however possible to bring glory to the Saviour. Paul exhorts believers in 1 Corinthians 10:31: "So whether you eat or drink or whatever you do, do it all for the glory of God." Although the specific context concerns behavior which may cause a brother to stumble, the principle clearly applies to all endeavors of life. The Christian disciple must be consecrated, set apart for God, holy in everything he does, whether eating or drinking, writing or making change, building a bridge or delivering a speech. The disciple does everything for God's glory.

A Christian teacher communicates the importance of consecration in a number of ways. He brings a distinctly biblical-theological orientation to the class through his own testimony and lifestyle. He may want to include Bible reading and/or prayer before the class period begins simply to commit the time to the Lord for His blessing and use. The teacher may want to have his students sing a hymn or Christian song at some time during the class period in order to draw their attention to spiritual things. The song may express a biblical truth, or may in some way communicate how material being studied may be used in service of Christ.

At all times, the teacher-discipler should keep in the forefront of his mind the importance of communicating to and, if possible, discussing with, his students their own consecration to Christ, including the progress of their devotional lives, or perhaps even their need for Christ as Saviour if they are not yet believers. In addition, he must demonstrate the application of classroom learning to their everyday service for Christ, the noblest of tasks, whether he teaches mathematics, home economics, United States government, or Bible 101. A teacher's first priority must be his own consecrated life. Then their godliness should be the first issue he seeks to address with the student-disciples in his class. As shepherd of his students the teacher must constantly work to expose them to biblical truth and challenge them to consecrated, set-apart living.

THE ELEMENT OF AFFECTION
(the teacher-discipler as friend).

Unfortunately there often exists an unhealthy distance between a teacher and his students. The student may stand somewhat in awe of his teacher's knowledge, ability, and experience, and may be anxious with respect to their relationship. A worse situation develops when the teacher remains aloof, formal, and impersonal, or when he communicates in some way a sense of superiority to his students. The teacher must seek to close the relational gap between himself and his students if he wishes to disciple them effectively.

In order to close the gap the teacher initiates the element of affection so crucial in discipleship ministry. Not only does he shepherd his students, but he becomes a friend who loves them, cares for them, and accepts them. In many respects the teacher's ministry of discipleship hinges on his commitment to this element of the process. A disciple-maker can offer the right content, model consistently, integrate material properly—do all the things a discipler does; but if he fails to love his disciples his ministry will bear no fruit.

The Gospel of John impresses its readers with the depth of Jesus' love for His own disciples: "It was just before the Passover feast. Jesus knew that the time had come for Him to leave this world and go to the Father. Having loved His own [disciples] who were in the world, He now showed them the full extent of His love" (13:1).

Following this testimony, the Lord tangibly expressed His love for the disciples as He washed their feet (vv. 2-11). He then called them to have that same love for one another: "A new command I give you: Love one another. As I loved you, so you must love one another. All men will know that you are My disciples if you love one another" (vv. 34-35). In Romans 12:10, the Apostle Paul commands all believers to "be devoted to one another in brotherly love," and in 1 Corinthians 13 describes true love. Affection has an essential part in discipleship ministry and must be initiated by the teacher himself.

As we disciple our students we will want to be aware of two basic aspects of the element of affection: (1) the aspect of *caring* for our students, and (2) the aspect of *accepting* our students. Both aspects enable us to communicate the love of Jesus Christ and to close relational gaps between ourselves and the people in our class. A teacher-discipler cares for his students by showing *concern, consideration,* and *appreciation* for them. His concern when they are under stress may be manifested by listening carefully and seriously when a student shares a problem. Praying together when a student shares a need also demonstrates the teacher's loving care, as does a follow-up telephone call, card, or letter. The teacher may be a resource of helpful information or suggestions as an outgrowth of his own expertise. Caring for one's student-disciple also takes the form of exhortation ("Why not do this?"), encouragement ("You can do this!"), and confrontation ("Why didn't you do this?"), depending on the need.

We manifest care for students through consideration in addition to concern. It shows up through such things as setting reasonable, attainable course objectives and requirements, and taking care to limit the assignment of homework and other outside responsibilities. We also show consideration in the classroom by treating students with dignity and respect. Belittling does not belong in biblical education, and certainly has no place in discipleship ministry.

As teacher-disciplers we also care for our students by showing them appreciation. This can easily be accomplished through a spoken word of thanks or praise for a job well done. Sincere appreciation is catching and, when modeled regularly by the teacher, can become a shared activity among members of his class.

Note in this matter of appreciation that the use of insult humor always destroys the effectiveness of discipleship ministry. It devastates relationships and must be avoided. Someone may think he can make a friend by the use of insult humor but in reality he makes enemies by creating tension in the relationship. Avoid it at all costs.

Accepting the student constitutes the second aspect of the element of affection. This aspect involves accepting both the person and the person's feelings. God has fabricated each person uniquely in his mother's uterus (Ps. 139:13-16). He fashioned each human being with certain tendencies, strengths, and weaknesses. He has given each one a personality which makes him special, and various talents and gifts for ministry which make him the kind of person God wants him to be. The teacher is responsible to know his students—the uniqueness of each one, how each one contributes by using his gifts, where his strengths and weaknesses lie. One student may be expressive and outgoing; another, quiet and analytical.

The teacher-discipler must not be guilty of requiring one student to be like another. As discipler the teacher must accept his student with the strengths and limitations God has given him, and challenge the student to be, in his own way, the best he can be for Jesus' sake. Caring and acceptance add up to the element of affection, an indispensable part of the teacher's discipleship ministry.

THE ELEMENT OF DEMONSTRATION
(the teacher-discipler as model).

The old adage, "Actions speak louder than words," applies as well to discipleship as to any other context. Though words may be important in communicating what we believe, what we do usually carries much more weight than what we say. The teacher greatly enhances discipleship training in the classroom when he models traits of the mature Christian. Like the other elements of discipleship, demonstration occupied an important place in Jesus' ministry to the Twelve, and the New Testament consistently upholds His model to those who wish to grow in Christian stature. Following His ministry of service in the washing of the disciples' feet Jesus remarked: "Now that I, your Lord and Teacher, have washed your feet, you also should wash one another's feet. I have set you an example that you should do as I have done for you" (John 13:14-15).

Paul in Philippians 2:5-7 exhorts every believer, "Your attitude [of humility] should be the same as that of Christ Jesus; who . . . made Himself nothing, taking the very nature of a servant, being made in human likeness." Jesus was never content with simply telling His disciples how to live the Christian life—He showed them how to do it; He modeled it; He demonstrated it. The Scripture commands Christian husbands to love their wives "just as Christ loved the church" (Eph. 5:25), and exhorts all believers to "accept one another, then, just as Christ accepted you in order to bring praise to God" (Rom. 15:7). In other words, we best train others to live godly lives not by telling them how, but by showing them how; and as the Christian life is modeled by the discipler, the discipler himself begins to catch on and exhibit Christian behavior.

Often Jesus' method of discipling involved an inductive approach with students. His disciples would observe Him, His attitude, His actions, His habits, and His priorities. The Master would interpret His behavior for them and encourage them to follow His lead. He would show, tell, and encourage—they would see, understand, and do. Jesus' life emphasized the importance of this approach with His first-century disciples, and as modern teachers we must practice it with our present-day student-disciples. Forms of Christian behavior which Jesus demonstrated to His disciples, and which the teacher would do well to model for his students, include prayer, Scripture memory, social responsibility, love for the brethren, and concern for unbelievers.[2] It appears that Jesus' modeling of His vital prayer life prompted the disciples to exhort Him, "Lord, teach us to pray" (Luke 11:1), and afterward, His explanation of how it should be done. Similarly, the teacher motivates his students to be people of prayer when he himself prays regularly with them and for them, and when he sustains a rigorous prayer life in which they see prayer answered.

Jesus made great use of Scripture quotations in His ministry (cf. Matt. 5:27-28; 12:18-21; 13:14-15). Perhaps Peter's extensive use of Scripture (Acts 2:17-21, 25-28; 1 Peter 1:24-25; 2:6-10; 3:10-12) was motivated and cultivated through Jesus' model in the discipleship process. The teacher-discipler also models the use of Scripture truth in his own life, and shares from memory passages which have been particularly meaningful.

As Jesus modeled the importance of being civically responsible in such things as paying taxes (Matt. 22:15-22) and submitting to authority (John 18:10-13), the teacher likewise has a great opportunity to influence his disciples by modeling civic responsibility. Such things as paying taxes, voting regularly, and being willing to serve as a juror when called all speak volumes to disciples who watch to see if their leader practices what he preaches. Praying for government leaders can also be demonstrated (1 Tim. 2:1-2) as can obedience to the law (Rom. 13:1-7; 1 Peter 2:13-17), including driving the speed limit and stopping at stop signs. Willing submission to authority and responsibility to fulfill civic duty are Christian traits to be demonstrated by the teacher-discipler for the growth of his students.

Love for Christian brothers and concern for unbelievers were both consistently demonstrated by Jesus to His disciples. His prayer for the Twelve, His instruction and protection of them, His defense of them, and His provision for them are well attested by the New Testament. It has already been affirmed that they loved one another because Jesus had first demonstrated His great love for them (cf. 1 John 4:7-21).

In addition to loving His brothers, Jesus manifested a compassionate love for the unbeliever as well. Each unbelieving person was worthy of His time and consideration whether the well-respected teacher of Israel (John 3) or the little-known and immoral woman of Samaria (John 4). The Saviour cared deeply for both, and this concern was a shocking revelation to His disciples (v. 27). Love for the lost was an ever-present expression of Jesus' heart, and so should it be for every Christian teacher. Discussing with students about sharing their faith, praying together for unbelieving friends and relatives, rejoicing as they come to faith, and praying as a class for pockets of unreached people by country or continent all model a love for the lost which is motivating and attractive to the student-disciple.

As a teacher one must think constantly about what he does as well as about what he says. As Horne remarks, "It is a pedagogical truism that we teach more by what we are than what we say."[3] This idea communicates the essence of the element of demonstration in the ministry of the teacher-discipler.

THE ELEMENT OF MINISTRATION
(the teacher-discipler as servant).

The Christian teacher also disciples his students by serving them and thus helping them in turn to become servants. From beginning to end, the life of Christ reveals that the Christian life is not a life of receiving but a life of giving.

No passage of Scripture illustrates this fact more clearly than Mark 10:32-45. The passage describes a solemn occasion from Jesus' perspective. He and His disciples travel toward Jerusalem where He will be delivered into the hands of Roman authorities to be put to death. He explains this fact in verses 32-34 but the disciples fail to understand. They have misconstrued the time frame of His ministry and believe Jesus will soon usher in the Kingdom Age, a thousand-year earthly reign of Christ in a virtually perfect environmental setting. He focuses on thorns and crosses; they focus on thrones and crowns. James and John ask Him for special positions and favors in the kingdom. What crass selfishness! But interestingly the Lord doesn't rebuke them for their request. He simply communicates that true greatness is not attained by a high position in society, but by assuming a lowly position as servant. He says to His disciples:

> You know that those who are regarded as rulers of the Gentiles lord it over them, and their high officials exercise authority over them. Not so with you. Instead, whoever wants to become great among you must be your servant, and whoever wants to be first must be slave of all (vv. 42-44).

In God's eyes servanthood marks true greatness, and characterizes the true disciple. Jesus Himself perfectly models servant-leadership and the reality of this truth. He continues to explain, "For even the Son of man did not come to be served, but to serve, and to give His life as a ransom for many" (v. 45).

If the Lord Jesus put such an emphasis on servanthood, can the present-day teacher-discipler emphasize it less? Students do not usually learn best from a teacher who enjoys exercising authority over them. Students learn best from the teacher who gives his life away in service to them—the teacher who closes the relational gap by ministering to them. This kind of teacher often sees himself as a student among students.

Taking up this theme the Apostle Paul defends his ministry by arguing that the most important credentials for ministry are not academic credentials but service credentials (2 Cor. 3). The point is not that degrees are unimportant in education, but that degrees alone, without a servant's heart, do not insure that effective ministry will take place.

The teacher-discipler serves his students. Most Christian teachers would not quarrel with this idea, at least in theory. But serving only when it is convenient, or when we receive proper recognition and thanks for our services, means serving on our own terms. He does not mind being a servant; he just does not want anyone to treat him like one. But doesn't Jesus teach us to put aside our own desires in order to meet the needs of others?

When the teacher-discipler serves his students on their terms, sacrificing himself to meet their needs, true discipleship takes place. It may mean investing precious time before and after class talking with students about an assignment or answering questions raised by a text. Serving your student-disciple may mean meeting with him in your office to counsel him and pray with him through a difficult home situation even though you had designated that schedule slot as "research time."

Serving students may take the form of having them in your home as guests if a need should arise, or caring for their children in an emergency. In being served by his teacher the student learns the importance of having a true servant's heart. He comes to understand the value and productivity of servanthood and its impact in the life of others, and perhaps will take opportunities to give himself to others as his teacher has done for him.

THE ELEMENT OF INTEGRATION
(the teacher-discipler as unifier of truth).

Students often find it hard to see the forest for the trees. So involved with details of assignments, they fail to see the whole picture; so intent on analysis, they neglect synthesis; so concerned with particulars, they are not aware of the overall pattern of God's truth. The teacher-discipler helps every student formulate a Christian worldview, that is, a biblical view of life. In so doing, he enables the student to relate accurately his academic studies to a biblical framework. To the teacher belongs this task of integration; at least this is where it must begin.

The student tends to see everything in pieces, and his experience in education seems diverse and fragmented, a collage of unrelated

material in which any touchpoint or commonality is purely coinciden-
tal. The teacher helps the student take the fragments of his educational
collage and form them into a unified whole with Jesus Christ at its
center. Both universally and personally, our world revolves around
Him; thus everything we study must find its ultimate purpose in service
to Him. The Bible teaches that God has revealed Himself to man in two
different spheres: (1) through the revelation of the Scriptures (special
revelation) and (2) through the revelation of the creation (natural revelation). In Psalm 19:1 David writes of God's natural revelation, "The
heavens declare the glory of God; the skies proclaim the work of His
hands." In verse 7 David discusses God's special revelation, "The law of
the Lord is perfect, reviving the soul; the statutes of the Lord are trust-
worthy, making wise the simple."

God's truth is revealed in both creation and the Scriptures so
that both spheres together form a unified reservoir of truth for the
believer. Important in discipleship is the teacher's task of demonstrating
for his students how secular subjects may be related to biblical truth. In
fact, he must assume the responsibility of showing that all subjects
should not be interpreted as "secular" at all, but part of a Christian
worldview based on a biblical framework. Gaebelein reminds us of the
misleading distinction between sacred and secular, and the need to see
all subjects in light of a biblical purpose. He suggests, "We have fallen
into the error of failing to see as clearly as we should that there are
areas of truth not fully explicated in Scripture and that these, too, are
part of God's truth. Thus we have made the misleading distinction
between sacred and secular, forgetting that . . . 'where the truth is, in so
far as it is truth, there is God.' "[4]

The teacher may instruct his students that the precision of
mathematics constitutes a work of God who Himself may be described
as precise and true. He has created an orderly universe which operates
according to precise physical laws (Ps. 19). Newton discovered the law
of gravity put into effect by God and now used by man to subjugate the
creation at God's command (Gen. 1:28). The formula for finding the
hypotenuse of a right triangle exists not as Pythagoras' truth but God's
truth expressed by Pythagoras in mathematical terms for use by man in
the mathematical sciences. Therefore, mathematics finds both its ultimate source and purpose in God. Man has received mathematical laws
from God and uses them scientifically to bring glory to the Creator.

Literature can be used for expressing biblical values and Christian thinking, and may be taught so as to emphasize godly principles of
life. The teacher-discipler may wish to compare the values expressed in
various kinds of literature in order to point out discrepancies or agreement with biblical teaching.

God's all-embracing truth includes another important medium—music. And what components of truth do we find in music? Again, Gaebelein says it well: "Are they not honesty of expression, sincerity in the sense of avoidance of the cheap and contrived? Surely they also include such elements as simplicity and directness."[5] Truth about God can be expressed mightily in music, both secular and sacred, through its honesty and integrity. The teacher may find occasion to bring his students to grips with the truth of God as it is expressed through the chords of a musical composition.

Other subjects such as philosophy, government, world history, physical education, and biological sciences must be addressed by the teacher who seeks to impart to his students a Christian life view. Teaching affects behavior. Christian teaching helps a student live Christianly in an unchristian world, reflecting the presence of Christ in his life. As Lockerbie says, Jesus Christ is the "Cosmic Center,"[6] the center of creation, and everything created finds its focus in Him.

As the Apostle Paul writes to the Colossians, "For by Him all things were created . . . all things were created by Him and for Him" (Col. 1:16). Primarily for this reason the teacher instructs his student-disciples with respect to the integration of "sacred" and "secular." The student must see that all disciplines fit together in a unified whole with Christ as center, and that this integrated whole forms the framework for faith and life.

God calls all Christians to make disciples, and Christian teachers are no exception. Indeed they have a unique opportunity to mold the development of their students regardless of the discipline they teach. The teacher disciples his students by acting as their shepherd (the ministry of consecration), as their friend (the ministry of affection), as their model (the ministry of demonstration), as their servant (the ministry of ministration), and as their unifier of truth (the ministry of integration). Through the work of God's Spirit these elements of discipleship are assimilated by the student-disciple, becoming a part of his own growth process in sanctification. Teachers who impart to their students these important aspects of Christian living are privileged to enjoy an experience beyond which there is no nobler call.

ENDNOTES

1. Robert E. Coleman, *The Master Plan of Discipleship*. Old Tappan, N.J.: Fleming H. Revell Company, 1987, p. 10.

2. Jesus also used the tool of demonstration to teach His disciples such things as obedience to God's will (John 12:27), trusting God for daily provision (6:1-4), mercy (8:2-11), forgiveness (Luke 23:34), and the reality of resurrection life (John 20:26-31).

3. Herman H. Horne, *The Teaching Techniques of Jesus*. Grand Rapids: Kregel Publications, 1964; reprint ed., 1974, p. 143.

4. Frank E. Gaebelein, *The Pattern of God's Truth*. Chicago: Moody Press, 1954; reprint ed., 1973, pp. 21–22.

5. Frank E. Gaebelein, *The Christian, the Arts, and Truth,* ed. D. Bruce Lockerbie. Portland, Ore.: Multnomah Press, 1985, p. 166.

6. D. Bruce Lockerbie, *The Cosmic Center*. Portland, Ore.: Multnomah Press, 1986.

BIBLIOGRAPHY

Boice, James Montgomery. *Christ's Call to Discipleship*. Chicago: Moody Press, 1986.

Bruce, A.A. *The Training of the Twelve*. Grand Rapids: Kregel, 1971.

Coleman, Robert E. *The Master Plan of Evangelism*. Old Tappan, N.J.: Fleming H. Revell Co., 1963.

Coleman, Robert E. *The Master Plan of Discipleship*. Old Tappan, N.J.: Fleming H. Revell Co., 1987.

Eims, Leroy. *The Lost Art of Disciple-Making*. Grand Rapids: Zondervan, n.d.

Hartman, Doug and Doug Southerland. *A Guidebook to Discipleship*. Irvine, Calif.: Harvest House, 1983.

Hendrix, John and Lloyd Householder. *The Equipping of Disciples*. Nashville, Tenn.: Broadman, 1977.

Henrichsen, Walt. *Disciples Are Made—Not Born*. Wheaton, Ill.: Victor Books, 1974.

—————. *How to Disciple Your Children*. Wheaton, Ill.: Victor Books, 1981.

Horne, H.H. *The Teaching Techniques of Jesus*. Grand Rapids: Kregel, reprint ed., 1974.

Howard, J. Grant. *Balancing Life's Demands*. Portland, Ore.: Multnomah Press, 1983.

Pentecost, J.D. *Design for Discipleship*. Grand Rapids: Zondervan, 1977.

Wilson, Clifford A. *Jesus, the Master Teacher*. Grand Rapids: Zondervan, n.d.

16. THE TEACHER AS BIBLE STUDENT
Roy B. Zuck

United States athletes competing in the 1984 World Olympics frequently used the slogan, "Go for the gold." Their goal was high: not just to receive a bronze or silver medal for their athletic achievements, but to receive a gold medal, the highest award possible. The words, "Go for the gold," have been used since those Olympics as a slogan to spur others on to attain high goals, to achieve something of great value to them.

No goal could be greater than going for the "gold" of the Scriptures. The Bible frequently refers to itself as gold or other precious commodities, such as rubies, thus underscoring the high value of its contents. For example David wrote, "The ordinances of the Lord are sure and altogether righteous. They are more precious than gold, than much pure gold" (Ps. 19:9-10). Psalm 119, that great psalm that extols the Word of God in almost every one of its 176 verses, includes this statement by the psalmist: "The Law from Your mouth is more precious to me than thousands of pieces of silver and gold" (v. 72). In the same chapter the psalmist wrote that he loves God's commands "more than gold, more than pure gold" (v. 127).

As students of the Word, Christian teachers should mine the gold of Scripture, digging "shafts" into the depths of the Bible, and sifting out the truths of the Scriptures for themselves. Daily exploration of the riches of the Word enriches their own lives—better enabling them to guide others in the same explorations.

WHY PAN FOR GOLD?
The Bible gives several reasons why every believer, and certainly Christian teachers, should be diligent Bible students.

269

First, the Bible helps us grow spiritually. "Like newborn babies, crave pure spiritual milk, so that by it you may grow up in your salvation, now that you have tasted that the Lord is good" (1 Peter 2:2-3). Without the intake of the Word, Christians become spiritually malnourished. Besides gold, food is another object to which the Bible compares itself. The Lord's commands are said to be "sweeter than honey, than honey from the comb" (Ps. 19:10). And 119:103 reads, "How sweet are Your promises to my taste, sweeter than honey to my mouth!"

Believers who are strong spiritually, growing and developing in their inner lives, are feeding on God's Word. The Apostle John spoke of the relationship of these two in 1 John 2:14: "I write to you, young men, because you are strong, and the Word of God lives in you, and you have overcome the evil one."

Second, the Bible guides us. When you buy a stereo system, lawnmower, or microwave oven, an instruction manual comes with it to tell you how to use it. Purchase an automobile and the driver's manual in the glove compartment explains the car's features and how to drive it and care for it. The Bible too is like a manual. It tells what life is like and how to make the best of it. As Irving Jensen wrote, "Have you ever thought of the Bible as being a manual that goes along with the 'product,' which is *you*? The Bible and you are meant to go together, to be inseparable. Both were brought into being by the same breath of God (Gen. 2:7; 2 Tim. 3:16). The Bible was given *for* you, to go *with* you. This is clearly God's design."[1]

In the Bible God tells us about ourselves, about Himself, about our present and our future. And it is written to guide us in the right direction, to help us make the right decisions. The psalmist wrote, "Your Word is a lamp to my feet and a light for my path" (Ps. 119:105), and, "The entrance of Your words gives light" (v. 130). God's "statutes" are the believer's "counselors" (v. 24).

Third, the Bible guards us against sin. The Bible has a cleansing effect on Christians. When they allow the spotlight of God's truth to shine on their lives, they see areas that need correcting and cleansing. David also wrote of this benefit from the Word: "By them is Your servant warned" (19:11). God's Word, the psalmist wrote, was hidden in his heart so that he "might not sin against" God (119:11). In the Upper Room Discourse, Jesus told His 11 disciples, "You are already clean because of the Word I have spoken to you" (John 15:3).

Like a mirror the Bible reflects our needs, and when a believer obeys what the Word commands, God blesses him (James 1:23-25). And when a believer sins, the Word can bring spiritual restoration. "The Law of the Lord is perfect, reviving the soul" (Ps. 19:7).

Fourth, the Bible goads us to spiritual maturity. "All Scripture is God-breathed and is useful for teaching, rebuking, correcting, and training in righteousness, so that the man of God may be thoroughly equipped for every good work" (2 Tim. 3:16-17). The word "teaching" suggests that the Scriptures help guide believers in the right direction. "Rebuking" is the Bible's ministry of calling attention to a believer when he gets off the track. "Correcting" or "restoring" speaks of the ministry of the Word in getting the believer back on track. And "training," a word referring to the nurturing of children, suggests helping a believer stay on the track after he has been restored to it.

As a Christian teacher allows the Holy Spirit to appropriate the Word of God in these four ways in his life, he is then "thoroughly equipped for every good work." The Greek word rendered "thoroughly" could also be translated "adequately," meaning in fit shape or condition. The Greek word rendered "equipped" suggests being adequately supplied for a task. The Greek papyri use this word of a boat supplied with two oars, and of an oil press in working order. In other words, as we appropriate the Word of God to our lives, we become adequately supplied for the work and service God intends for us.

Growth, guidance, guarding, and goading—four reasons for being a consistent and diligent student of the Scriptures.

Christian teachers must set the example for their students in Bible study. If teachers want their students to manifest the fruit of the Spirit (Gal. 5:22-23) and to be "filled with the fruit of righteousness" (Phil. 1:11), then the teachers too must do the same. If they want their students to get into the Bible for spiritual nurture, guidance, cleansing, and maturity, the teachers must be in the Word.

This underscores the fact that a teacher must first be a student. Effective teaching requires consistent learning. If a teacher stops studying, his teaching effectiveness drops. As he continues to read, research, think, interact, probe, and question, he keeps himself fresh and up-to-date on his subject. As he stretches his mental muscles, widens his intellectual horizons, and deepens his knowledge, he can better help his students do the same.

A tree without water dies; a muscle without movement atrophies; a person without food starves. Likewise a teacher who stops learning fails as a teacher. This is true of any teaching field, but especially of teaching the Bible and related subjects. A Christian teacher must continually drink at the streams of Scripture. He must perennially feed on the food of the Word. Without spiritual nourishment he has no strength by which to nourish others.

Unless we study and follow God's ways, we will find it difficult to lead others to do so. Unless our lives are in tune with the Word, we will have difficulty bringing others into harmony with God's precepts. Without spiritual possessions we have nothing by which to enrich others. To quench the intellectual and spiritual thirst of others, we ourselves must be drinking at the headwaters of God's truths.

The following portions of this chapter discuss ways of studying the Bible ("mining the gold"), principles for interpreting the Bible ("assessing the gold"), and ideas for applying the Bible ("investing the gold"). These three areas are essential for every teacher who wants to enrich his life with the wealth of the Word.

WAYS TO STUDY THE BIBLE: MINING THE GOLD

A variety of approaches may be used in studying the Bible. The following represent some of those ways.

BOOK SYNTHESIS.

When visiting an exhibit in an art museum, some people enter, walk through the museum hurriedly, glance at a few things here and there, and walk out. They may or may not decide to spend their time reading what others have seen in the pieces of art and what others think about them. Others, however, go in, spend time looking carefully at each painting and possibly asking questions of the artists or museum curators.

Bible study too is approached in one of two ways—either the casual, occasional glance or haphazard approach, viewing some things and overlooking others, or the more thorough approach, in which all is carefully observed. Any method of Bible study, and certainly book synthesis, requires careful and thorough observation.

Bible book studies approach the Bible as it was written—in books. The human authors, writing under the inspiration of the Holy Spirit, did not simply write a few verses here and there, one every day or so, and then throw them together in a hodgepodge fashion, eventually ending up with a complete book. As they wrote they had the big picture—the structure of the entire book—in mind. To the extent that we look for that same structure we get closer to what the Lord has in mind for us.

Also book synthesis provides a basis for chapter and verse analysis. It is important to see the Bible telescopically before viewing it microscopically. Martin Luther said he often studied the Bible the way he gathered apples. First he shook the whole tree to let the ripest fruit fall. Then he climbed the tree and shook each limb. Then he moved to the branch of each limb. Next he shook each twig, and finally he looked under each leaf. The whole tree suggests the entire Bible, the limbs suggest Bible books, the branches refer to chapters, the twigs refer to verses, and the leaves to the words.

Book synthesis also helps us keep the parts of the book in proper perspective. Some teachers yank verses out of context with no concern for why they appear in a given Bible book. Without synthesis this becomes a common pitfall in Bible study. For example, when Matthew recorded that Jesus told the Twelve not to go to the Gentiles but rather to the lost sheep of Israel (Matt. 10:5-6), he was writing in a book addressed to Israel about her Messiah. The Twelve were to take the message of the kingdom of heaven (v. 7) to the nation Israel.

The following steps may be followed in studying a Bible book.

Read the book at least twice. Read it as if you were seeing it for the first time. Trying to forget what you already know about the book will enable you to see some things you might otherwise miss. Read through the book at one sitting, without trying to soak up every detail. The purpose of this reading is to get a feel for the book, to sense the overview of what the writer said. Read it thoughtfully, using your imagination to picture what you read.

Look for background information. Note who wrote the book, to whom it was written, where it was written, when it was written, and under what circumstances. Not all these questions will be evident in every Bible book but many of them will be. For example Ephesians 1:1 states who wrote the book and to whom it was written, but only in the last chapter (6:20) do we learn that Paul was writing from prison.

Look for repeated phrases and words in the book. For example the fact that the word "better" occurs twelve times in the Book of Hebrews indicates that the author was emphasizing the superiority of Christ. The author's frequent use of the words "priest," "high priest," and "sacrifices" points to his emphasis on Christ's work as the believer's High Priest, who is superior to the priests of the Old Testament.

Divide the book into its parts. Look for major turning points or definite changes of pace, direction, or emphasis. The change may be geographical, as in the Book of Acts in which Jerusalem served as the location of the events that occurred in chapters 1–7; Judea and Samaria are the locales of the events in chapters 8–12; and the "ends of the earth" provide geographical indicators for chapters 13–28. These three are like concentric circles, starting with Jerusalem in the smallest inner circle, which in turn spell out Jesus' command in 1:8.

A book may be divided by the major persons in it. For example, in Genesis, chapters 1–11 highlight Adam and Eve, Enoch, and Noah; chapters 12–23 emphasize Abraham; chapters 24–27 highlight Isaac; chapters 28–36 emphasize Jacob; and in chapters 37–50 Joseph is the key figure.

In some books, the parts are literary. For example in Isaiah 1–39 the prophet emphasizes judgment, whereas the emphasis in Isaiah 40–66 is comfort. The Book of Romans may be divided by its doctrinal subject matter. Occasionally a book is divided by its questions, such as the Book of Malachi.

Find the purpose of the book. Sometimes we find the purpose of a book clearly stated as in, for example, Luke 1:4 or John 20:31. In many books, however, the purpose must be determined by various subject-matter clues in the book. For instance the emphasis on joy and rejoicing in the midst of suffering shows that in Philippians Paul purposed to encourage believers not to be defeated by suffering but to experience God's joy in it.

Feel its pulse. In studying a Bible book, we want to notice whether the book is primarily narrative or poetry, whether letters or prophecy. It helps to sense the "atmosphere" of the book. Galatians and Jude, for example, are argumentative in the sense of being defenses of the truth and opposing false teaching. First Corinthians offers correction; Romans is theological; Leviticus gives instruction; 1 and 2 Kings describe exciting narrative action; and the Psalms are reflective. Of course several of these "atmospheres" may exist in one book, but the point is to sense the primary thrust of the Bible book being studied.

CHAPTER ANALYSIS.

After getting the feel of a book, you can then study it in more detail. One way to do that is to study the book by chapters. Again several steps are helpful.

Read the chapter several times. The more you read the chapter the more you will see in it.

Divide it. Note where the chapter changes subjects. For example Psalm 1 shifts from the godly person in verses 1-3 to the wicked person in verses 4-6. In 1 Corinthians 6, Paul speaks of lawsuits in the first 11 verses and then changes the subject to immorality in verses 12-20.

Sometimes a single chapter will include a number of narrative events. It is interesting to look for these shifts in Mark 3, for example. A chapter may also be divided according to locations where the events took place. In John 2, Cana is the location for verses 1-11, Capernaum and Jerusalem are the sites in verses 12-13, and verses 14-25 speak of Jesus being in Jerusalem. In Job 1–2 the scene shifts from the earth (1:1-5) to heaven (vv. 6-12), back to earth (vv. 13-22), to heaven (2:1-6), and then to the earth (vv. 7-13). A chapter may also be divided according to the addressees, as in Ephesians 5. Verses 1-21 are addressed to all believers, verses 22-24 to wives, verses 25-31 to husbands, and 32-33 to all believers. Some chapters may be divided by the persons who are speaking. In Jeremiah 36 the speakers in sequence are the Lord, Jeremiah, Baruch, Micaiah, Jehudi, Baruch, the king, and the Lord.

View its structure. In this step in chapter analysis you look for numerous relationships. These include *comparisons* (e.g., how the Samaritan woman in John 4 was similar to Nicodemus in John 3), *con-*

274

trasts (e.g., how the Samaritan woman in John 4:1-42 differs from the official in vv. 43-54), *repetitions* (e.g., angels are referred to seven times in Heb. 1; Habakkuk mentions woe five times in 2:4-20; and the word "gospel" is mentioned by Paul six times in 1 Thes.), *connectives*— words that tie verses together (e.g., Eph. 2:4, 6, 8, 11, 13, 14, 18-19, 22).

Also look for movements or shifts within a chapter. These may include movement from the general to the specific (Gen. 1:1-2 is general, and vv. 3-25 are specific); movement from the specific to the general (James 2:1-13 is specific, and vv. 14-26 are more general); movement from cause to effect; movement to a climax (as in Amos 1–2 in which the prophet leads up to his "punch line" in which he finally addresses Israel after speaking of other nations; or as in the response of the Samaritan woman to Jesus in John 4 in which she progresses from referring to Him first as a Jew, then as one greater than Jacob, then as a Prophet, and finally as the Messiah); or movements in interchange (as in 1 Sam. 1–12, which speaks of Eli's sons and then Samuel, and then Eli's sons again and Samuel again).

The movement in a chapter may also be an expansion, as in Jesus' prayer in John 17, in which he prayed for Himself (vv. 1-5), for His disciples (vv. 6-19), and then for all believers (vv. 20-26). Still another form of movement may be from questions to answers, as in, for example, Malachi 3:7-16.

Look for answers to the questions of when, where, how, who, what, and why. The "when" question addresses the time elements in the chapter (the time of day, the time of year, or other time elements such as feast days). The "where" question addresses the geographical elements, and the "how" question addresses the way in which certain things were done. For example the Jewish officials opposed Jesus, as recorded in the Gospel of John, in various ways: by questions, attempts to stone Him, attempts to arrest Him, accusing Him of blasphemy, and finally by crucifixion.

Obviously the "who" question addresses the people referred to in the chapter. The "what" question pertains to events, statements, questions, commands, responses. The "why" question looks at why the people in the narrative did what they did or said what they said, or reasons for statements given in nonnarrative material.

Ask "I wonder" questions. This is helpful as a step in probing toward what is stated in the chapter. For example in John 2:6, these questions might be asked: I wonder why six waterpots were there at the wedding? I wonder why the waterpots were so large? I wonder about the custom of purification? Or in Mark 10, the Bible student might ask, I wonder why parents were bringing their children to Jesus? I wonder why the disciples rebuked the parents?

Summarize the point of the chapter. A good way to be sure you understand a Bible chapter is to summarize it in your own words. Some students do this by finishing the sentence, "This chapter is saying that. . . ." Still another way to summarize the chapter is to give it a brief caption in as few words as possible. For example Job 14 might be entitled "From the womb to the tomb." One challenging exercise calls for writing a caption for each chapter in an entire Bible book.

VERSE ANALYSIS.

Decide its kind. Is the verse a statement, a command, a question, or a wish? For example Ephesians 5:22 is a command, whereas the next verse is a statement.

Write the main thought. Here you state who is or should be doing what to whom. In John 3:16, "God" is the subject, "loved" the verb, and "world" the object. In Romans 3:23, "all" is the subject, and "have sinned" is the verb. In Proverbs 3:5, the subject (implied) is "you," the verb is "trust," and the object is "in the Lord."

Write out subsidiary thoughts. Various points in the verses add to the main thought, words that give additional information beyond the main subject and verb. In John 3:16 the words "that He gave His one and only Son that whoever believes in Him shall not perish but have eternal life" are subsidiary to the major point of the verse, which is that "God so loved the world." In Proverbs 3:5 the words "with all your heart" add additional information to the main point of the verse, that believers should "trust in the Lord." The words "just as in fact you are doing" in 1 Thessalonians 5:11 give additional subsidiary information beyond the major thoughts forming two commands, "encourage one another and build each other up."

Mark certain words in the text, including connectives (e.g., "therefore," "and," "for" in Eph. 4:25); underline repeated words and join them by a line; circle significant words (e.g., "foreigners," "aliens," "fellow citizens," "household" in 2:19); and write question marks by any words that are not clear to you.

Paraphrase the verse. Rewriting the verse, giving the sense of it in your own words, can help you grasp the thrust of the verse. An example occurs in the following paraphrase of 4:12: "This is for the purpose of preparing saints to serve the Lord which in turn will result in edifying the church."

Still another step calls for the Bible student to write many observations about the verse. In this step you seek to observe everything in the verse. These observations can be completions of the sentence, "This verse tells us that. . . ."

BIOGRAPHICAL APPROACH.

A study of people offers one of the most exciting and interesting ways to probe the Bible. Bible biographies present truth in action.

As we see God working in others' lives, we recognize He can work in ours as well. Victories and defeats, hopes and fears, struggles and triumphs, goofs and glories, ecstasy and agony, strengths and weaknesses—all these are seen in people in the Bible.

The following steps may be taken in studying Bible biographies.

Locate and read all the references to that person. When studying Naaman the leper, you need to read not only 2 Kings 5 but also Luke 4:27. In studying Elijah, you need to read not only 1 Kings 17–2 Kings 2, but also 2 Kings 9–10, 2 Chronicles 21:12, and references in Malachi, Matthew, Mark, Luke, John, as well as Romans 11:2 and James 5:17.

Observe and write down all the facts about that person. These facts may include information about his parentage, ancestors, and birth; his family; occupation; characteristics; crises; influence on others; associates; places traveled; death, and burial.

Write the order of events in his life.

List his strengths and weaknesses. These are interesting observations to note, for example, in the lives of Moses, Jonah, Peter, and others.

Write out one or more major principles (in one sentence each) illustrated in that person's life.

Write out one or more personal applications from the person's life. These should be action steps you will seek to take in view of what you have learned from that biographical study. Is there any example to follow, any sin to avoid, any prayer to voice, any quality to cultivate, any error to correct?

An advanced step in biographical study is to write a creative presentation on that person's life. This might take the form of a newspaper reporter's article, an editorial, a poem, a song, a letter, a question-and-answer interview, a short story.

PRINCIPLES FOR INTERPRETING THE BIBLE:
ASSESSING THE GOLD

When Philip spoke to the Ethiopian eunuch he asked him, "Do you understand what you are reading?" (Acts 8:30) This question pertains to hermeneutics, the proper interpretation of the passage being read. The eunuch's reading of Isaiah 53 did not guarantee that he understood the passage. Proper interpreting must build on adequate observing. In observation we ask, "What do I see?" In interpretation we ask, "What does it mean?"

Without proper attention to hermeneutics, the science and art of interpreting the Bible, people may arrive at novel, farfetched views of

Bible passages—interpretations that the Bible itself never intended. An awareness of basic hermeneutical principles in interpreting the Bible is essential in Bible study. Since the Bible is an ancient Book, a time gap exists between its original composition and today. We also have a space gap, in view of the distance between us and the places where Bible people lived. And a customs gap means there are differences between our way of doing and thinking and the way people in Bible times lived and thought. Also there is a language gap, since the Bible was written in Hebrew and Greek. In addition there is a spiritual gap since this book was written by and about God. Bible interpretation helps us bridge these gaps, making it easier to understand the Bible.

Space does not permit developing the subject of hermeneutics in detail; the reader is referred to books on the subject.[2] However, attention to the following hermeneutical principles can help Bible students arrive at proper interpretations and avoid false interpretation.

These hermeneutical principles are not laws imposed over the Bible. They simply reflect the steps we normally follow in reading any piece of literature. As a literary composition, the Bible falls under the same principles we use when reading any literary piece. In reading a newspaper, a novel, a recipe, a board report, or scientific study, (1) we note the historical setting and purpose of the writing, (2) we understand it in normal grammatical terms, (3) we acknowledge the cultural setting in which the writing was composed, (4) we understand words and sentences in their immediate context, and (5) we note the literary form of the writing.

HISTORICAL SETTING AND PURPOSE.

In studying a portion of the Bible, look for the historical and geographical situation and the purpose of the writing of that book or portion of a book. Sometimes a writer states the purpose of his book; other times we must assess his purpose by noting the problems he addresses, the subjects he repeats, and the issues he discusses. Noting the background and purpose can help prevent trying to make the text say something the author never intended, and it helps avoid reading something into the passage (eisegesis). We should read from the passage what is actually there (exegesis).

NORMAL GRAMMATICAL MEANINGS.

Taking the Bible in its normal sense lets the Word speak for itself as the initial readers would have understood it. This means that in Mark 5:1-20, for example, demons mean fallen angels, not false doctrines; and the swine means animals, not the subconscious mind.

This principle also means avoiding reading into the Bible mystical meanings, a practice common in the Middle Ages. In this allegorical approach, so-called "deeper" meanings were supposedly more spiritual meanings. Thus "Jerusalem" could mean the city, the soul, or even heaven. However, this approach to the Scriptures left the language of the Bible with no controls. If a word in a given context can mean several contradictory things, then Bible interpretation becomes totally subjective.

Therefore, in Bible interpretation it is important to note the meanings of words, the usage of words (in the same book, in Bible books written by the same author, or by other Bible writers), and how the word may differ from its synonyms and antonyms.

Thoughts are expressed through words. Therefore, if we are to determine God's thoughts as recorded in the Bible, we must study words and how they are associated grammatically in sentences. As Philip Melanchthon, the Protestant reformer and friend of Martin Luther, wrote, "The Scripture cannot be understood theologically unless it be first understood grammatically."[3]

CONTEXT.

Each verse or chapter must be understood in the light of its context. The Bible student must ask, What is the meaning of the words in view of the sentences and paragraphs that precede and follow it? A single word or even a sentence may have several meanings depending on the context in which it is used. Seeing how a writer or other writers use a word is helpful in determining its meaning. The English word "trunk" comes from the old English word "tronke" meaning box. But that understanding of the origin of the word does not indicate what a given writer means when he uses the word. He may have in mind any one of several meanings: the main part of a tree, the torso of the human body, the thorax of an insect, the shaft of a column, a large piece of luggage, the luggage compartment of an automobile, the part of a cabin of a boat that projects over the deck, the proboscis of an elephant, men's shorts, or a circuit between two telephone exchanges.

The Greek word *pneuma* ("spirit") is derived from *pneō* ("to breathe") but in the Bible the word "pneuma" only occasionally means breath. It has other meanings in the Bible such as wind, attitude, demons, angels, the Holy Spirit, emotions, the believer's spiritual nature, or the immaterial part of man apart from the body. The sentence, "He is over the hill," may mean that a man is on the other side of a small mountain or it may mean that he is getting old and has relatively few years in which to live. Only the context of the sentence indicates which meaning is correct. To take a meaning inconsistent with the context is to do violence to proper interpretation.

Often false interpretations arise from ignoring the context. For example, "Ask of Me, and I will make the nations your inheritance" (Ps. 2:8), does not mean that God will give entire nations in salvation to missionaries in return for their efforts. The context shows that this is speaking of the Messiah, who, God the Father said, will receive all the nations as His inheritance as He rules over them in the Millennium.

The context also helps determine the meanings of words. In Jude 3 "faith" means the body of truth, in Romans 3:3 it means faithfulness, in 1:17 it means trust or confidence in God, and in James 2:17, 19 it means intellectual assent. Even the word "salvation" may have several meanings: safety or deliverance from difficult circumstances (Ex. 14:13; Acts 27:20; Phil. 1:19), physical and/or emotional health (Luke 18:42), deliverance from the penalty of sin by the substitutionary death of Christ (John 3:17; Acts 15:11; 16:30), or final deliverance from the presence of sin (Rom. 5:9).

The word "law" may mean a principle, the Pentateuch, all the Old Testament except the prophets, or the Mosaic system. The meaning of "fire" in Matthew 3:11 is not spiritual dynamics, but rather judgment as indicated in verses 10, 12. When Jesus said, "Heal the sick, raise the dead, cleanse those who have leprosy, drive out demons" (10:8), He was not giving a command for all Christians because the context (v. 1) shows He was addressing only the twelve disciples.

Sometimes the scope and purpose of a Bible book as a whole must be seen in order to clarify certain words or phrases in the book. For example, 1 John 3:6-10 does not mean that a Christian never sins. First John 1:8-10 and 2:1 make this clear.

The context of parallel passages can help explain other words or ideas. The word "hate" in Luke 14:26 is clarified by the parallel passage in Matthew 10:37.

CULTURAL BACKGROUNDS.

Since the Bible was written about and by people who lived in cultures different from that of the Western world, it is important to know cultural customs to understand a number of passages properly. Jonah's lack of interest in going to Nineveh is better understood, though not excused, when we realize that the Ninevites were known for terrible atrocities to their enemies. When Boaz's closest relative gave his sandal to Boaz (Ruth 4:8-17), he symbolized releasing his right to the land he previously walked on.

The Laodicean church could well appreciate the statement in Revelation 3:16 that they were "lukewarm—neither hot nor cold" because cold water in aqueducts and hot water from hot springs were channeled in pipes to Laodicea from Hierapolis. By the time the water reached Laodicea it was neither hot nor cold and, therefore, undesirable. Spiritually the people were the same way. Bible dictionaries, encyclopedias, and commentaries can help explain many otherwise hard-to-understand Bible passages.

Normal grammatical interpretation does not rule out the use of figures of speech. Sometimes Bible passages seem difficult to comprehend because of figurative language. Statements such as, "The trees clap their hands," "Your blood be on your heads," "These men . . . are clouds without rain," "I am the bread," and others point up the importance of knowing the meaning of these strange expressions.

Figures of speech add zest to a language and help the reader/listener retain the idea. Figures of speech include similes (a comparison in which one thing explicitly, by using "like" or "as," resembles another); metaphors (comparisons in which one thing represents another though the two are basically unlike); hypocatastasis (a comparison in which the likeness is implied by a direct naming, e.g., "dogs have surrounded me," Ps. 22:16); metonymy (the substituting of one word for another, as in substituting the cause for the effect or the effect for the cause); synecdoche (substituting a part for the whole or the whole for the part); personification; hyperbole (an exaggeration, in which more is said than is literally meant, to add emphasis); litotes (an understatement or a negative statement to express an affirmation); irony (a kind of ridicule in the form of a compliment which is opposite of what is meant); rhetorical questions; paronomasia (using the same words or similar-sounding words to suggest different meanings); and others.

Once we recognize a figure of speech, the next step is to determine the purpose of the figure of speech. For instance in the clause, "All men are like grass" (1 Peter 1:24), the Bible student must think through the similarities between humanity and grass. A figure of speech may not always mean the same thing. The lion, for example, is a symbol of Satan in 5:8 but a symbol of Christ in Revelation 5:5.

Careful attention to these principles of interpretation can enable you to be a more accurate interpreter of the Bible.

APPLYING THE BIBLE: INVESTING THE GOLD

Application provides the capstone of Bible study, the peak of the process of mining the gold of the Scriptures. Without application, Bible study remains incomplete. As James wrote, "Do not merely listen to the Word. . . . Do what it says" (James 1:22). The Bible is not a museum piece to be exhibited or an antique to be examined. It is a guidebook for living. Like Ezra, we are to devote ourselves not only to the study of God's Word but also to the practice of it (Ezra 7:10). God gave His Word not simply for knowledge but for spiritual growth. Christians must "be careful to devote themselves to doing what is good" (Titus 3:8). Christians must know the Word of God so that through it they can know the God of the Word.

PRINCIPLES FOR APPLICATION.

Application must stem from a proper interpretation of the passage. As I wrote elsewhere:

Correct interpretation of the passage is basic to proper application. If a text is interpreted inaccurately, then the application will be faulty as well. Unfortunately many people go to the Bible for a "blessing" or for guidance for the day, and therefore they either build an application on an invalid interpretation or ignore the interpretive process altogether. In their intense desire to find something devotional or practical, many Christians distort the original meaning of some passages of Scripture.[4]

Personal response to a passage should be based on an understanding of the meaning of the text to its original audience in light of the purpose of the book. In interpretation you examine the *meaning* of the passage in its original setting, and in application you look at the *significance* of that meaning for current situations.

Application must be based on principles. Principles serve as bridges between interpretation and application. A principle summarizes a truth in the verse or chapter. Because of the cultural differences between Bible times and our times, it is important to bridge that gap by means of principles. First Thessalonians 5:18 clearly states that Thessalonian believers in Paul's day should be thankful in every circumstance of their lives. The principle for today is that Christians now should be thankful regardless of their circumstances. This easy transfer of truth makes God's message to the Thessalonian believers relevant for believers today.

However, Ephesians 6:5 presents a different problem. In Paul's day this verse meant slaves should obey their masters. But if a person is living today in a culture that does not have slaves, he faces the question as to how this passage relates to him. The answer seems to lie in the principle that Christian workers should follow the instructions of their supervisors. In Genesis 6:22 Noah obeyed God without visible reason for building an ark. But what do believers today have in common with Noah? Are we to build arks? No; instead the principle inherent in Noah's example is that Christians today should obey God's commands even when they, like Noah, have no visible evidence for doing so.

Application involves finding the elements the reader has in common with the original audience. When Paul told the Corinthians to refrain from eating meat sacrificed to idols to avoid bringing difficulty to other Christians (1 Cor. 8:7-13), he was speaking to a situation not current now. Therefore, in application we need to recognize that the element we have in common with the Corinthians is that actions causing others to sin should be avoided.

Proper application must include specific action/response. As you study the Bible, write down specific ways to apply the truth. Make your response a personal "I will" application with time limits.

"We should" applications are too general and do not have the firm commitment needed in applying the Scriptures. Rather than saying, "I should or will be more like Jesus," it is better to say, "I'll not lose my temper next time my children do something wrong." Or instead of saying, "I should or will love my wife more," it is better to say, "I will take my wife flowers."

Adding a time limit ("this Friday evening," "Thursday afternoon," "this weekend," or "by the end of this month") helps insure that the application is not delayed indefinitely. For example Paul wrote, "Do everything without complaining or arguing" (Phil. 2:14). A personal application-response of this verse might begin with the words, "I will not complain. . . ."

At the end of the time limit you wrote for your application, record whether you completed that application-response, and if not, what remains to be done. Of course these personal areas of determination and commitment need to be made in the strength of the Holy Spirit. As you approach the applicational step in your Bible study, seek the Lord's guidance regarding areas of your life where improvement is needed. Bathe your study in prayer, asking God to help you overcome weaknesses and to experience His blessings in your life.

ADDITIONAL IDEAS FOR STUDYING THE BIBLE

The following at-random suggestions are given as ways to keep moving ahead in your Bible study. Try one or more of these ideas and you may find increasing joy in studying the Word.

1. Read a book on inductive Bible study.
2. In your personal devotions each day read a corresponding portion of a Bible commentary.
3. Memorize a verse or paragraph.
4. Bombard a passage with numerous questions.
5. Keep a diary of your applications.
6. Take a correspondence course on a book of the Bible.
7. Attend evening classes in a Bible college or seminary, perhaps working toward a master's degree.
8. Teach the Bible. That is one of the best ways to learn the Scriptures.
9. Join a discipleship or Bible study group.
10. Read a passage in different versions.
11. Study Greek and/or Hebrew.
12. Purchase Bible study tools, such as Bible dictionaries, encyclopedias, concordances, commentaries.
13. Set up a file folder on each book of the Bible.

14. Read one chapter of Proverbs each day.
15. Experiment with new study approaches to the Bible.
16. Turn a passage into a first-person prayer. For example after reading Jonah 1, you might pray, "Lord, help me not to disobey You."
17. Share your discoveries in the Word with someone else and also share some of your application-responses.

To be an effective teacher of the Word of God, you first need to be an effective student of the Word. As you are enriched by the wealth of the Bible, you can more effectively help enrich the lives of others.

ENDNOTES

1. Irving L. Jensen, *Enjoy Your Bible.* Chicago: Moody Press, 1969, p. 10.

2. See the Bibliography for books on hermeneutics.

3. Martin Luther, cited by A. Skevington Wood, *The Principles of Biblical Interpretation.* Grand Rapids: Zondervan Publishing House, 1967, p. 80.

4. Roy B. Zuck, "Application in Biblical Hermeneutics and Exposition," in *Walvoord: A Tribute,* ed. Donald K. Campbell. Chicago: Moody Press, 1982, p. 26.

BIBLIOGRAPHY

Bible Study
Finzel, Hans. *Opening the Book.* Wheaton, Ill.: Victor Books, 1984.

————. *Unlocking the Scriptures.* Wheaton, Ill.: Victor Books, 1986.

Hall, Terry. *Getting More from Your Bible.* Wheaton, Ill.: Victor Books, 1984.

Henrichsen, Walter. *A Layman's Guide to Studying the Bible.* Grand Rapids: Zondervan Publishing House, 1985.

Henrichsen, Walter, and Gayle Jackson. *A Layman's Guide to Applying the Bible.* Grand Rapids: Zondervan Publishing House, 1985.

Jensen, Irving L. *Enjoy Your Bible.* Chicago: Moody Press, 1969.

LaHaye, Tim. *How to Study the Bible for Yourself.* Irvine, Calif.: Harvest House Publishers, 1976.

Lincoln, William C. *Personal Bible Study.* Minneapolis: Bethany Fellowship, 1975.

Traina, Robert A. *Methodical Bible Study.* 1952. Reprint, Grand Rapids: Zondervan Publishing House, 1980.

Vos, Howard F. *Effective Bible Study.* Grand Rapids: Zondervan Publishing House, 1956.

Wald, Oletta. *The Joy of Discovery*. Minneapolis: Bible Banner Press, 1956.

————. *The Joy of Teaching Discovery Bible Study*. Minneapolis: Augsburg Publishing House, 1976.

Warren, Richard, and William A. Shell. *12 Dynamic Bible Study Methods*. Wheaton, Ill.: Victor Books, 1981.

Hermeneutics
Fee, Gordon D., and Douglas Stuart. *How to Read the Bible for All It's Worth*. Grand Rapids: Zondervan Publishing House, 1981.

Henrichsen, Walter. *A Layman's Guide to Interpreting the Bible*. Grand Rapids: Zondervan Publishing House, 1985.

Mayhue, Richard. *How to Interpret the Bible for Yourself*. Chicago: Moody Press, 1986.

McQuilkin, J. Robertson. *Understanding and Applying the Bible*. Chicago: Moody Press, 1983.

Mickelsen, A. Berkeley. *Interpreting the Bible*. Grand Rapids: Wm. B. Eerdmans Publishing Co., 1963.

Radmacher, Earl D., and Robert D. Preus, eds. *Hermeneutics, Inerrancy, and the Bible*. Grand Rapids: Zondervan Publishing House, 1984.

Ramm, Bernard. *Protestant Biblical Interpretation*. 3rd ed. Grand Rapids: Baker Book House, 1970.

Ryken, Leland. *How to Read the Bible as Literature*. Grand Rapids: Zondervan Publishing House, 1984.

————. *The Literature of the Bible*. Grand Rapids: Zondervan Publishing House, 1974.

Smith, Bob. *Basics of Bible Interpretation*. Waco, Texas: Word Books, 1978.

Sproule, R.C. *Knowing Scripture*. Downers Grove, Ill.: InterVarsity Press, 1977.

Sterrett, T. Norton. *How to Understand Your Bible*. Rev. ed. Downers Grove, Ill.: InterVarsity Press, 1974.

Stott, John R.W. *Understanding the Bible*. Glendale, Calif.: G/L Publications, 1972.

Tan, Paul Lee. *Literal Interpretation of the Bible*. Rockville, Md.: Assurance Publishers, 1978.

Terry, Milton S. *Biblical Hermeneutics*. Grand Rapids: Zondervan Publishing House, n.d.

Virkler, Henry A. *Hermeneutics: Principles and Processes of Biblical Interpretation*. Grand Rapids: Baker Book House, 1981.

Part Four

VARIETIES
of Christian Teaching

17. TEACHING IN THE FAMILY

James R. Slaughter

This year millions of Americans will take a step which will change their own lives significantly, and profoundly affect the next generation: they will have children. How they raise their youngsters will have a greater impact on society than how they vote, what technologies they produce, the wars they fight, or the art they create. When someone suggested that the family is the hand that writes history he was not spouting sentimental rhetoric; he was plugged directly into reality. The family today provides the most basic training ground for tomorrow's teachers, pastors, physicians, scientists, politicians, sociologists, mothers, fathers—the family exerts the most direct influence on those who will shape tomorrow's ideologies. The most important educational contribution to the life of a child is not made by his school, his church, his Boy Scout troop, or his Little League team, but by his family.[1]

The student of the Scriptures discovers early in his study the crucial role the family plays in the history of Israel and the emerging Christian community. For both Israel and the church, the family provided an environment for nurture in which a child grew to be a godly, contributing adult. In the context of loving warmth, acceptance, and communication, the family became an educational tool for teaching a child about his relationship to God. Hebrew children, for example, were to learn about *Yahweh*'s grace and provision for them through the family's annual observance of Passover. Moses' instructions to the elders of Israel just prior to the last plague in Egypt include the following exhortation:

> Obey these instructions as a lasting ordinance for you and your descendants. When you enter the land that the Lord will give you as He promised, observe this ceremony. And when your children ask you, "What does this ceremony mean to you?"

then tell them, "It is the Passover sacrifice to the Lord, who passed over the houses of the Israelites in Egypt and spared our homes when He struck down the Egyptians." Then the people bowed down and worshiped (Ex. 12:24-27).

Joshua also emphasizes to God's people the important educational role the family plays in the spiritual nurture of their children. After the Lord miraculously enabled Israel to cross the Jordan River and enter the land of Canaan, their new leader issued this command to the twelve tribes:

Go over before the ark of the Lord your God into the middle of the Jordan. Each of you is to take up a stone on his shoulder, according to the number of the tribes of the Israelites, to serve as a sign among you. In the future, when your children ask you, "What do these stones mean?" tell them that the flow of the Jordan was cut off before the ark of the covenant of the Lord. When it crossed the Jordan, the waters of the Jordan were cut off. These stones are to be a memorial to the people of Israel forever (Josh. 4:5-7).

In these two passages Israel's leaders anticipate children's questions coming as a result of family participation in commemorative religious ceremonies. Hebrew children learned primarily through teaching in the family that God is omnipotent, merciful, gracious, and mindful of those who fear Him, a redeemer of His people.

In the New Testament we see similar indications of the important role the family plays in the spiritual education of children. The Apostle Paul wrote to his disciple and close friend Timothy: "I have been reminded of your sincere faith, which first lived in your grandmother Lois and your mother Eunice and, I am persuaded, now lives in you also" (2 Tim. 1:5).

Some suggest Paul won Timothy to Christ on an evangelistic journey but this is unlikely. Acts 16:1-2 indicates Timothy was already a believing disciple before Paul met him. Probably he was won through the teaching ministry of his grandmother and mother who, besides sharing their own faith with him, exposed him to the sound doctrine of God's Word: "And how from infancy you have known the Holy Scriptures, which are able to make you wise for salvation through faith in Christ Jesus" (2 Tim. 3:15).

The Scriptures reveal that from the earliest days of God's people the family has had more than simply physiological (procreative) and sociological (integrative) purposes. A key element in the biblical purpose of family is educational (communicative), an element through which the child is brought to grips with the reality of God and His Son Jesus Christ, and the ministry of the Holy Spirit. The child learns about God primarily in the context of family, and how he may know God through faith. In addition, the child learns how he should behave in society as a representative of God and God's people. Parents enjoy the greatest privilege and, at the same time, bear the greatest responsibility for the spiritual education and development of their children.

THE RESPONSIBILITY OF PARENTS TO TEACH THEIR CHILDREN

The Scriptures make it abundantly clear God gives parents the primary responsibility for the spiritual training of children. Local churches and Christian schools can reinforce the teaching of children at home but never should they be called on to supplant the family in this responsibility. A number of Bible passages set forth a biblical theology of parenting and explain the role of parents as teachers of their children.

Deuteronomy 6:4-9—the responsibility of parents to teach their children incisively.

We find the exhortation to parents in Deuteronomy 6 nestled within Moses' words to Israel just before their entrance into the Promised Land. Moses would not accompany them to Canaan but would die on the east side of the Jordan River shortly after delivering this address. These, therefore, constitute his parting words to the people he had loved and shepherded for 40 years. With this last opportunity to be with them he reminded them of the Law of God and their responsibility to keep it faithfully. He did not waste his breath on things not absolutely crucial to the well-being of God's people in the land. When they had forgotten everything else they should remember these things. Moses realized the weighty importance of teaching in the home, and took this valuable opportunity to bring parents to grips with their responsibility.

As we study the passage we discover two parts to Moses' exhortation to parents, two elements of the teaching process in the family. A devotional element comes first. The parent cannot impart adequately to his children truth not first made real in his own life. Therefore, before he teaches his children, he must himself have an experiential relationship with God which is cultivated and consistent:

> Hear, O Israel: The Lord our God, the Lord is one. Love the Lord your God with all your heart and with all your soul and with all your strength. These commandments that I give you today are to be upon your hearts (Deut. 6:4-6).

After reminding Israel of God's unity, Moses exhorted them to

291

love God passionately with every ounce of their being, in every area of their personhood. The word "love" is the Hebrew *ahab,* often used of the marriage relationship to reflect the passion expressed between a husband and wife.[2] Here it is used of the love one must cultivate for the Lord before he can teach his children adequately to love God. Parents cultivate a fiery, consuming love for God which motivates and controls every aspect of their beings—volitional (heart), spiritual (soul), and physical (strength).

In addition (and probably as a consequence of this love for God), the burden of parents' hearts must be obedience to the commands of God reiterated by Moses in his address. Before teaching their children adequately, parents must first cultivate their own devotional relationship to God. They develop a passionate love for God expressed in every aspect of their being, and always keep before them the responsibility of obeying God's commands. This close relationship to God on the part of the parents sets the stage for effective teaching of children in the family context.

Moses then addressed the second element of the teaching process in the family, the *instructional* dimension (vv. 7-9). Parents teach these spiritual commandments and exhortations to their children in a special way: "Impress them on your children." The word impress ("teach," NASB) comes from the Hebrew word, "to whet, sharpen." In Deuteronomy 6 it means to teach incisively. The parent cuts to the very core of the truth of spiritual things, going deeply to the heart of a matter without blurring or ambiguity. His teaching must be direct and clear, exposing his children to key spiritual issues. Parents accomplish this incisive teaching not only by planning formal times and places of instruction but through everyday experiences of family living. Instruction in spiritual things happens in a variety of family contexts and should permeate every corner of the family environment: "Talk about them when you sit at home and when you walk along the road, when you lie down and when you get up" (v. 7).

Here the author uses a figure of speech (opposites for emphasis) to communicate that teaching in the family is a constant part of homelife: from the time a child gets up in the morning till he goes to bed at night. The teaching done by parents may at times be planned, but more often than not it will happen casually as a parent talks to his child about spiritual things in the context of everyday experiences ("when you sit at home and when you walk along the road"). This exhortation does not exclude formal family worship times but broadens the perspective of family teaching to include less formal times as well.

The charge in verse 8 to "tie [these commands] as symbols on your hands and . . . on your foreheads," though interpreted literally in the past by conservative Judaism, is taken by most expositors to be a figure of speech emphasizing the need for godly living and obedience to God's commands to permeate, to motivate, to direct the parent's actions ("hands") and his attitudes ("foreheads").[3] Similarly, the injunction to write the commands "on the doorframes of your houses and on your gates" (v. 9) may refer to the necessity of maintaining a godly lifestyle both in the private sphere ("doorframes") and in the public sphere ("gates"). So all family life becomes a classroom in which godly parents instruct their children in spiritual things through the experiences of everyday living.

Proverbs 22:6—the responsibility of parents to establish their children in the right pattern of life.

The importance of Proverbs 22:6 as it relates to teaching in the family must not be underestimated. In this verse the parent-teacher observes yet another dimension to his responsibility of teaching in the family: "Train a child in the way he should go, and when he is old he will not turn from it."

The Old Testament uses the word "train" four times in addition to its use in Proverbs 22:6. Moses applies it twice to the dedication of a house (Deut. 20:5), and other historical writers use it of the dedication and establishment of the temple (1 Kings 8:63; 2 Chron. 7:5). The word really carries the sense of "inaugurate" which of course includes the ideas of both dedicating and establishing. The worshiper dedicates the object (house, temple, child), starting it off, establishing it, setting it forth, and at its beginning setting it apart to God for His purposes. Parents have the responsibility to "inaugurate" their children; that is, start them off right by dedicating them to the Lord for His purposes. This seems to be the sense of "train" as used in Proverbs 22:6.

The phrase translated "in the way he should go" literally means "according to his way." But how does a parent establish a child's way? Commentators propose different answers to the question, each having merit; deciding among them makes for a difficult task.[4] The word "way" in Proverbs refers to a person's manner of life, his lifestyle, and refers to both righteous and unrighteous living. In the context of Proverbs 22:6, "his way" most likely refers to the child's manner of life which results from his individuality and calling by God.[5] Thus the parent must know his child well, discerning his individual uniqueness, and start him out by dedicating him to the Lord for service as his own character and abilities enable him to serve.

The parent guides the development of the child enabling him to contribute to the Lord's work from his own sphere of ability and expertise. As a general principle (and not a specific promise), the child will, even as an adult, serve the Lord out of his unique capabilities and personhood as his parents taught him to do. As Gangel points out, this process "requires personalization, individualization, and a willingness to recognize that the rules of child-rearing change with each child who enters the home."[6] Each child is different and must be set apart to the Lord for different purposes and uses.

Ephesians 6:4—the responsibility of parents to raise their children in the discipline and instruction of the Lord.

The New Testament also makes clear the responsibility of parents to teach their children. In Ephesians 5–6 the Apostle Paul instructs Christians how to live well together in a way pleasing to the Saviour—the entire church (5:1-21); wives with husbands (vv. 22-33); children with parents (6:1-4); and slaves with masters (vv. 5-9). His command to fathers (the word can also mean "parents") begins with the negative injunction, "Do not exasperate your children" (v. 4), do not provoke or frustrate your children (cf. Rom. 10:19; Col. 3:21). The charge warns parents to guard against unreasonable demands, petty rules, or favoritism which bring discouragement, resentment, and bitterness.

Rather than angering their children, parents should "bring them up in the training and instruction of the Lord" (Eph. 6:4). They should nourish and provide for them, raise them lovingly and caringly. Such loving, caring nourishment includes discipline, a word which refers to child training, guiding, correcting, and developing spiritually. In addition, parental instruction includes a degree of admonition ("instruction"). Teaching in the house often takes the form of warning regarding the consequences of disobedience. The word "instruction" here has this sense of admonishing or urging the child to live righteously. Note that children obey "in the Lord" (v. 1) and parents instruct and admonish "in the Lord." The Spirit of Christ guides and permeates every motive and every action. The center of family relationships and the center of family teaching and learning is Christ Himself.[7]

THE CONTENT OF TEACHING IN THE FAMILY

After a parent recognizes his biblical responsibility to teach his children spiritual things he probably will ask himself, "What do I teach them? Where do I begin? What are they able to comprehend?" To determine what to teach their children, parents need some understanding of child development and age-level suitability of content. Parents can teach their children more effectively when they know what kinds of information a child can understand, assimilate, and apply at various stages in his development.

The growing child goes through four basic developmental stages: 1. infancy (birth to 2 years of age); 2. the preconceptual period (3 to 6 years of age); 3. the concrete conceptualization period (7 to 11 years of age); 4. the abstract conceptualization period (12 to 18 years of age). In each developmental stage the child is learning certain tasks unique to his particular age-level, and responds to instruction in a relatively predictable manner.

INFANCY.

The child enters life outside his mother's body with great intellectual potential but with very little developed intellectual ability. He is beginning to coordinate eyesight with physical movement, and to follow visually the movement of people and things around him. The necessary ingredients for thinking are in place but it will still be some time before he can think logically.

Some Spiritual Things Children from Birth to Two Can Learn
There are people who love them and who take care of them.
There are people they can trust.
Happy feelings are associated with Jesus.
The world is an interesting and beautiful place.
Going to church is a pleasurable experience.
The Bible is important.

THE PRECONCEPTUAL PERIOD (3 to 6 YEARS).

During this period of life the child expresses himself verbally and begins to explore his world in a new dimension. He is able to understand time, space, and number, but unable to group ideas together to form a resulting principle. Often he joins together unrelated facts which may confuse him and cause him to reach wrong conclusions. He tends to have a personal reference, that is, his world tends to revolve around himself. LeBar suggests for this reason that ideas presented to children during this period need to be quite personal in relation to them and their lives and how they should behave.[8] Therefore, biblical truth must be related to everyday experience as the child lives his life in the family context "when you sit at home and . . . walk along the road" (Deut. 6:7).

Some Spiritual Things Children of Three to Six Can Learn
God loves them.
God is all-powerful, knows everything, and is everywhere at the same time.
God takes care of them.
They can talk to God in prayer.
Jesus is God's Son.
Jesus once was a child like them.
Jesus died so they could live in heaven.
The Bible is God's Word.
The Bible tells them about God.
The Bible tells them how they should live.

Bible stories are true stories.

Bible verses can be memorized.

They should obey their parents.

When they obey their parents they obey God.

Their parents love them and want to help them.

The church is people who love Jesus.

They should meet with the church to sing, pray, and learn about God.

They should share with others.

They should forgive others even when others are unkind to them.

They should tell others about Jesus.

THE CONCRETE CONCEPTUALIZATION PERIOD
(7 TO 11 YEARS).

During this period of development the child grows increasingly more active and has a longer attention span (10 to 20 minutes). But instruction still must be varied and creative. The child at this stage becomes very inquisitive and should be encouraged to ask questions which make him think. He likes to collect things and enjoys games and puzzles. He reads and should be exposed to Christian literature for his own personal consumption, and also for participation along with the family. He memorizes easily, so Bible memory is profitable. The child needs to be taught right from wrong, and should be guided into establishing good devotional habits. He is able to understand the plan of salvation and needs the opportunity to receive Christ as Saviour if he has not previously done so. His questions must be answered clearly and honestly.

Some Spiritual Things Children of Seven to Eleven Can Learn

There is one God but He exists in three Persons: Father, Son and Holy Spirit.

The Holy Spirit comes into their lives when they receive Jesus as Saviour.

God sometimes permits bad things to happen.

God hates sin.

Jesus is God's Son who died on the cross for sin.

Jesus can forgive sins and give salvation to those who believe in Him.

Jesus rose from the dead and lives in heaven.

The Bible is a true Book.

The Bible answers their questions and offers solutions to their problems.

The Bible is God's Word and should be obeyed.

Home is a place where they can be happy.

They should ask their parents when they have a problem because parents want to help.

They can trust their parents and should accept correction from them.

The church is a fellowship of people who believe in Jesus Christ.

They should invite their friends to worship with them at church.

They should use their money, their time, and their special abilities to help the church operate properly.

Satan is a wicked angel who sinned against God.

Satan tempts Christians and tries to get them to sin.

Jesus will return to rule the world.

People who trust Christ as Saviour will live forever in heaven with God.

THE ABSTRACT CONCEPTUALIZATION PERIOD
(12 TO 18 YEARS).

Very real strains and adjustments take place during this time as the child begins his transition to adulthood. His attitudes, abilities, and personality continue to be shaped and his imagination takes on a new vividness and creativity. He thinks abstractly and can reason for himself much more cogently. He desires to make his own decisions and should be guided in doing so as much as possible. Thinking clearly and logically in the decision-making process becomes important in the transition to adulthood. The Spirit of God begins to move in his life to convict, comfort, and guide him. In this period, the parent helps the child to establish Christlike habit patterns, ideas, and ideals. Crucial parental contributions such as modeling, prayer, and personal counseling can make a great impact in this stage of development. Parents can provide the developing adolescent with security by communicating love, confidence, and support. Parents must also realize that God is revealing His plan for the child's life. God's plan may not always be exactly what the parents had in mind and their sensitivity to the way God leads their children during this period becomes extremely important.

Some Spiritual Things Children of Twelve to Eighteen Can Learn
God is perfectly loving and just.
God is eternal.
God is the blessed Controller of all things.
God answers prayer.
They should love God and trust Him with their lives.
Jesus is God's Son who existed eternally with God.
Jesus came into the world as a human being.
Jesus was born of a virgin.

Jesus was at the same time both human and divine.

Jesus was sinless in every respect.

Jesus died willingly for the sins of the whole world.

The Bible is inspired by God and without error in any part.

The Bible is given by God for practical instruction of believers.

They should read and study the Bible on a regular basis.

Their homes should be God-centered.

They are responsible to God for obeying their parents.

A spiritual home enriches the church.

They should be thinking of starting their own Christian homes someday.

The church now forms the body of Christ on earth.

They should serve their churches.

They should witness to their friends.

Christ will come in the air to receive His church.

Christ will one day establish His physical earthly kingdom.

The present heaven and earth eventually will be destroyed and replaced by a newly created heaven and earth.

It is often surprising to discover how much children can learn so early in their development. Teaching parents must remember to expose their children as early as possible to Christian attitudes and actions. From his earliest recollection a child should experience a warm and loving family environment established on a biblical pattern and directed toward exalting Christ in every endeavor. Through the consistent example of godly parents, the child should believe that things such as reading the Bible, praying together, and discussing spiritual principles are among the most natural experiences of family life.

THE METHODS OF TEACHING IN THE FAMILY

"How" parents should teach their children is every bit as important as "why" parents should teach their children and "what" they should teach them. Methodology provides the third essential ingredient to teaching in the family. By having some understanding of effective teaching methods the parent-teacher finds himself better equipped and more highly motivated to fulfill his responsibility in the home. Interestingly the area of methodology is often frustrating for a parent. More than any other factor it keeps him from accomplishing the work of teaching his children spiritual things. "Where do I begin? I'm untrained! What do I do?" are common pleas from parents who have a feeling of helpless inadequacy when it comes to their teaching roles in the family. Four methodological considerations can help take some of the fear and frustration out of family teaching.

TEACHING CHILDREN THROUGH MODELING.

Parents can use modeling in a highly effective way to teach children in the family. The godly example set by parents becomes the most powerful weapon in their pedagogical arsenal. Whether or not parents believe it is true, they exert the most influence on their child, not the child's school teacher, Girl Scout leader, coach, or even his pastor. The parent has the greatest opportunity to turn a child toward spiritual things and to help him become a godly person. Children most often turn to parents for help and guidance during times of stress. It is the parent whom the child most often observes when it comes to practical Christian living. The child sees his parents in a wide variety of situations exhibiting a broad range of feelings and moods: at church worshiping, at home relating to one another, cleaning the house, fixing the sink, helping with school homework, at the hospital waiting for the report on an illness or injury.

What does the child observe when he sees his parents in these various circumstances? What is their attitude? What is their behavior like? Does their focus remain Christ-centered? Is it consistently·so? Do they pray? Do they thank God? Are they kind? Are they generous? These traits of godliness can be transferred from parent to child through the modeling process.

But be careful; negative traits are also transmitted by example. Jesus Himself makes it quite clear: "A student is not above his teacher; but everyone who is fully trained will be like his teacher" (Luke 6:40). The student-child will become like his parent-teacher. Parents must live their lives in such a way that becoming like them means becoming like Jesus Christ.

In addition to modeling through a godly personal lifestyle, parents also model Christian marriage through their own relationship as husband and wife. Nothing does more to whet a child's appetite for having his own Christian home someday, nothing prepares him more adequately, than observing his parents relate to one another according to biblical principles of marriage. It is important for the child to see his parents loving each other unconditionally, expressing affection, encouraging, helping, forgiving one another, building each other up, not tearing each other down. He needs to learn firsthand from his parents how a husband loves his wife the way Christ loved the church, and how a Christian wife submits herself to her husband as to the Lord (Eph. 5:22-33). Obviously this presupposes that his parents understand the process and live it out in the home. Such an environment produces much more long-lasting and fruitful instruction than any marriage textbook.

PLANNED METHODS FOR TEACHING CHILDREN.

Planned family devotions (though usually more effective with preteens) can provide a unified and regular approach to spiritual teaching in the family. Many Christian families set aside one evening each week to enjoy reading the Bible together, praying, singing, and even acting out Bible stories. Parents who have made this method work suggest four essential characteristics of the effective family devotional time:

1 It must be regular. Regularity communicates the important priority you give to family worship in the home. Inconsistency and missed devotional times communicate just the opposite.

2. It must be applicational. Sessions must be designed to meet specific individual and family needs, being geared to real-life situations. Time must be spent illustrating and explaining how the biblical material covered might be put into practice day by day. Prayer and sharing must reflect current concerns and be related to present circumstances and needs.

3. It must be child-centered. The family devotion is primarily a time for communicating spiritual truth to children, though parents also derive benefit. Teaching must be age-level appropriate both in content and methodology, and must focus on ideas the child can understand and put to use in his own daily life.

4. It must be planned. Planning the family devotional time does not equate to being rigid and highly systematized. Rather it implies having well-thought-out goals and some plan for achieving them. The plan should be flexible and innovative, involving everyone present and taking advantage of any spontaneous development. The following is a list of practical "do's and don'ts" for those considering a family devotional time:

Do be innovative and imaginative. Try new ideas.
Do use recent translations.
Do make specific applications.
Do see the Bible happening now.
Do aim for quality, not quantity.
Do be vocal.
Do include singing.
Do act out Bible stories.
Do use questions and discussion.
Do use personal and individual illustrations.
Do use pictures whenever possible.
Do use humor.
Do include jokes.
Do take advantage of situations in the home for humor and applicational purposes.
Do use games.
Do use memorization.

Do frequently change the location of your worship.

Do read from the Bible whenever possible, not just from your devotional guide.

Do make the time child-centered.

Don't make your sessions too long.

Don't make your sessions too deep theologically.

Don't use your worship time as an ax-grinding session.

Don't use material which is unrelated to life.

Don't use the same procedure and methods every time.

Don't include so much reading that you have no time for discussion.

Another planned method of teaching children is *table grace*. Thanking God for His blessings in life communicates an abundance of biblical truth to children, and doing so at mealtimes offers an excellent opportunity for teaching in the family. Jesus Himself modeled this teaching method when He gave thanks before feeding the 5,000 (John 6:11), the 4,000 (Matt. 15:36), and at the Last Supper (1 Cor. 11:23-24). Thanks through table grace teaches children, among other things, that God is a loving Father who meets the needs of His children, that material blessings are gifts from God, and that God is pleased when Christians have thankful hearts. The father may wish to offer thanks on behalf of the entire family; he may delegate the privilege to another member of the family; or all may express in turn their own thanks to God. In any case, such prayer should be heartfelt and fresh, and offered in the leader's own words. Avoid prayer formulas; they tend to become ritualistic and devoid of meaning.

A final method of planned teaching is *bedtime prayer and Bible story reading*. Parents and children can share an extremely warm and meaningful quiet time at the end of a busy day. Often this situation finds a young child especially sensitive and receptive to instruction from his parents. Bedtime prayer and Bible reading can become a time fondly anticipated by both parent and child, one which is highly productive relationally, spiritually, and educationally. Read short stories from a Bible or Bible storybook written in a linguistic style easily understood by children. Prayers should be short, original, and directed toward current considerations and needs. Bedtime affords a great opportunity to involve children in the practice of conversational prayer.

SPONTANEOUS METHODS OF TEACHING.

In the context of family life, unexpected opportunities often arise to teach children important spiritual truths. Such unexpected but productive opportunities some have called "*teachable moments*" and consist of a shared experience between parent and child in which application of a biblical principle or insight can be made. Divine provision through answered prayer gives parent and child an opportunity to stop and thank God together. Bad news in the form of illness, injury, or death of a friend gives parents an opportunity to turn the faces of their little ones toward God for healing, comfort, and assurance.

Even the death of a pet can provide a teachable moment— unexpected, but spiritually fruitful in a child's life as the parent shares the fact that God sees, cares, and brings comfort in times of personal loss. Hearing a bird sing, watching autumn leaves fall, or observing a snail crawl across the sidewalk all translate into teachable moments for the parent who is quick to communicate the reality of the living Lord to his child.

Talking about *forgiveness* when a child has been hurt by a friend, about *faithfulness* when conflict arises between a promise to baby-sit and the last minute opportunity to attend a party, or about *trusting* when it comes to preparing for a biology examination are examples of grasping teachable moments. But the parent needs to be prepared and observant because these are times which are unannounced and can be gone before he knows it. A *shared thought* or *verse* or an *encouraging word* from the parent can be used by God to whisper in the ear of an impressionable young person, "I am real! I am here! I care!" This is the teachable moment; spontaneous, but highly effective for teaching in the family.

DISCIPLINE AND PUNISHMENT AS TEACHING TOOLS WITH CHILDREN.

Parents often have a difficult time understanding how to discipline their children correctly. But when carried out in a biblical manner, discipline becomes a family teaching tool which produces godliness. We often use the terms discipline and punishment synonymously, the symbol of enforcement being a swat on the bottom. However, the Scriptures make discipline and punishment two different issues. Hebrews 12:5-6 seems to divide this aspect of instruction into two different forms—one discipline, the other punishment or reproof: "My son, do not make light of the Lord's discipline, and do not lose heart when He rebukes you" (v. 5); and again: "Because the Lord disciplines those He loves, and He punishes everyone He accepts as a son" (v. 6).

The author goes on to affirm that God's discipline and punishment resemble a father's discipline and punishment of his son. In both cases they demonstrate the love of the father for the child, and the genuineness of the relationship between father and child. Discipline is the first stage of this teaching method and involves the setting of standards and cultivating of excellence in the child's life. Nurture enables the child to grow in holiness, to be conformed to the image of Christ by living within certain biblical boundaries. Punishment, on the other hand, occurs when the boundaries have been crossed, when the fences which circumscribe righteous living are torn down. Thus discipline precedes punishment and not vice versa. The parent who punishes without having first disciplined his child, who grabs for the rod before adequately seeking to guide behavior, is guilty of being both *unfair* and *unjust.*

Every parent is responsible to God for teaching his children through discipline and punishment, but he must remember that both are to be done in a spirit of love and concern, never out of anger or frustration. Both forms of instruction have different purposes, but both are carried out in the same spirit. The following may be helpful for the sake of comparison:

Discipline	*Punishment*
Purpose . . . to train for righteousness and maturity	to inflict penalty for an offense
Focus . . . future correct deeds	past misdeeds
Attitude . . . love and concern	love and concern
Result . . . security of the child	security of the child

When they discipline, parents should set reasonable standards for their children to maintain, and should guide them into a willing submission to Christ which is the highest form of discipline. When parents punish, their actions should be prompt, should be equal to the offense, and should be supported by both mother and father.

Instruction in the forms of discipline and punishment constitutes an important part of teaching in the family. To be effective it takes commitment and consistency from parents. Discipline seldom seems like a pleasant task but it yields great produce, for "no discipline seems pleasant at the time, but painful. Later on, however, it produces a harvest of righteousness and peace for those who have been trained by it" (Heb. 12:11).

There is no greater privilege for parents than to teach their children to know Christ and to grow in His grace. God wants parents to assume the responsibility of being the primary communicators of spiritual truth to their little ones. Modeling Christlikeness, planned and unplanned teaching times, and a biblical approach to discipline all are means at parents' disposal for teaching their children about the reality of Christ. Christian parents really have no option when it comes to teaching in the family. The responsibility is theirs and it is a great privilege. Parents can experience no greater joy than to see their children walking in the truth.

ENDNOTES

1. Jay Kesler, "Ministry to Youth and Their Families." Cassette tape, Pasadena,

303

Calif.: Fuller Theological Seminary, 1984.

2. For example, Genesis 24:67; Proverbs 5:19; Song of Songs 2:5; Hosea 3:1.

3. Compare C.F. Keil and F. Delitzsch, *Commentary on the Old Testament,* "The Pentateuch," vol. 1 of 10 vols., Grand Rapids: William B. Eerdmans Publishing Company, 1973, p. 324; Jack S. Deere, "Deuteronomy," in *The Bible Knowledge Commentary, Old Testament.* Wheaton, Ill.: Victor Books, 1985, p. 275.

4. For the three major views contrast Franz Delitzsch, *Commentary on the Old Testament,* "Proverbs," vol. 6 of 10 vols. Grand Rapids: William B. Eerdmans Publishing Co., 1973 ("his way" means according to the child's stage of development); Derek Kidner, *Proverbs,* The Tyndale Old Testament Commentaries. London: The Tyndale Press, reprint ed., 1972 ("his way" means with respect to his individuality and vocation); and Sid S. Buzzel, "Proverbs," in *The Bible Knowledge Commentary, Old Testament.* Wheaton, Ill.: Victor Books, 1985 ("his way" means the proper way, the path of wise, godly living).

5. Derek Kidner, *Proverbs,* The Tyndale Old Testament Commentaries. London: The Tyndale Press, reprint ed., 1972, p. 147.

6. Kenneth O. Gangel and Elizabeth Gangel, *Building a Christian Family.* Chicago: Moody Press, 1987, p. 39.

7. Harold Hoehner, "Ephesians," in *The Bible Knowledge Commentary, New Testament.* Wheaton, Ill.: Victor Books, 1983, p. 642.

8. Lois LeBar, *Children in the Bible School.* Westwood, N.J.: Fleming H. Revell Company, 1952, p. 138.

BIBLIOGRAPHY

Barth, Markus. *Ephesians 4–6.* The Anchor Bible. Garden City, N.Y.: Doubleday and Company, 1974.

Bruce, F.F. *Epistles to Colossians, Philemon and Ephesians.* The New International Commentary on the New Testament. Grand Rapids: Wm. B. Eerdmans Publishing Co., 1984.

Campbell, Ross. *How to Really Love Your Child.* Wheaton, Ill.: Victor Books, 1977.

————. *How to Really Love Your Teenager.* Wheaton, Ill.: Victor Books, 1981.

Curran, Dolores. *Who, Me Teach My Child Religion?* 4th revision. Minneapolis: Winston Press, 1982.

Delitzsch, Franz. "Proverbs." In vol. 6: *Proverbs, Ecclesiastes, Song of Solomon.* Translated by M.G. Easton. Commentary on the Old Testament. 10 vols., reprint ed., Grand Rapids: Wm. B. Eerdmans Publishing Co., 1973.

Dobson, James. *Dare to Discipline.* Wheaton, Ill.: Tyndale House, 1970.

————. *Dr. Dobson Answers Your Questions.* Wheaton, Ill.: Tyndale House Publishers, 1982.

Gangel, Kenneth O. and Elizabeth. *Building a Christian Family.* Chicago: Moody Press, 1987.

Hunt, Gladys. *Honey for a Child's Heart.* Grand Rapids: Zondervan Publishing House, 1969.

Keil, C.F. and F. Delitzsch. "The Pentateuch." In vol. 1: *Commentary on the Old Testament.* 10 vols. Grand Rapids: William B. Eerdmans Publishing Company, 1973.

Kesler, Jay, ed. *Parents and Children.* Wheaton, Ill.: Victor Books, 1986.

_____ . *Parents and Teenagers.* Wheaton, Ill.: Victor Books, 1984.

_____ . *Too Big to Spank.* Glendale, Calif.: Gospel Light, Regal, 1978.

Kidner, Derek. *The Proverbs.* The Tyndale Old Testament Commentaries. London: The Tyndale Press, 1972.

Maston, T.B. and William M. Tillman, Jr. *The Bible and Family Relations.* Nashville, Tenn.: Broadman Press, 1983.

Rekers, George. *Family Building.* Ventura, Calif.: Regal Books, 1985.

Sell, Charles M. *Family Ministry: The Enrichment of Family Life through the Church.* Grand Rapids: Zondervan, 1981.

Smalley, Gary and John Trent. *The Blessing.* Nashville, Tenn.: The Thomas Nelson Press, 1986.

Walvoord John and Roy Zuck, eds. *The Bible Knowledge Commentary:* Old Testament. Wheaton, Ill.: Victor Books, 1985.

Wonderly, Gustava M. *Training Children.* Lincoln, Nebr.: Good News Broadcasting Association, 1959.

Wright, H. Norman and Rex Johnson. *Communication: Key to Your Teens.* n.d.

18. TEACHING IN THE CHURCH
Michael S. Lawson

The church stands under the mandate of the New Testament to teach the Scriptures to its constituents. Therefore, the church's obligations differ substantially from informal Bible teaching settings. The church must continually strive to meet its biblical objectives. Whereas a home Bible study usually organizes itself around the felt needs of the group, the church must plan its teaching differently. Needs expressed by the congregation and those perceived by church leadership must blend together to form a stable and systematic curriculum.

KINDS OF CHURCH TEACHING

Churches offer a wide variety of teaching opportunities. The large teaching platform includes both formal and informal settings.

THE PULPIT.

The master teacher approach to teaching finds a home in the pulpit. Pastors teach the Scriptures as a part of their responsibilities. Even the words "pastors and teachers" come together in Ephesians 4 to apparently describe their office. Some pastors train people within their churches to speak during the regular worship services.

SPECIAL SEMINARS.

If attendance means anything, people enjoy this approach to teaching. For the most part, the style of teaching remains traditional while the content changes from seminar to seminar. However, Bruce Wilkerson has pioneered a creative and energetic approach to Bible survey called Walk-Through-The-Bible. Under his leadership, Bible facts combine with body motions to assist the short-term memory and involve everyone in the process. The intergenerational experience demonstrates what can be done with thoughtful and creative preparation.

306

PERIODIC CLASSES.

Churches need to instruct new believers, new members, and those who seek baptism (if baptism and church membership are not combined). Usually short-term in nature, the classes rely on people who have already made certain decisions. Teachers introduce Christians to the implications of their decisions along with the procedures they must follow. Because visuals can be recycled, churches could justify producing more expensive ones to assist the instruction. If we took these classes seriously, we could do our very best work since we have the opportunity to practice again and again.

INTENSIVE STUDY CLASSES.

Some churches have borrowed generously from the Bible college movement and established "Lay Institutes." This satisfies many people who want to know more about the Bible but never had an opportunity for formal study. Subjects and textbooks vary but the courses follow an academic model with outside reading and sometimes even homework assignments.

COUNSELING AND CONVERSING.

Many teachers underestimate the opportunities of informal settings for teaching. Yet on these occasions our words can strike directly at the problems people face. Wise teachers seek these settings in order to make precise applications. Students can avoid misunderstandings by asking for clarification immediately. Perhaps the ultimate extract of teaching awaits untapped in these interchanges.

GROUPING FOR TEACHING

Though not always necessary, we can group people in a variety of creative ways for effective teaching. Age remains the most common grouping criterion until people reach adult status where maturity, interest, or educational background gain more influence.

AGE.

Churches generally recognize four major age-divisions. Within each division (Early Childhood, Children, Youth, and Adult), many churches employ different arrangements to facilitate teaching. In Early Childhood, chronological age is the main issue. Even six-month intervals help because young children develop so rapidly. In the Children and Youth divisions, school grades serve grouping purposes well. Parents generally cooperate and accept these divisions with few exceptions.

Adults can complicate matters considerably within their division. Many churches have employed groupings such as chronological age, gender, and marital status with varying degrees of success. Singles commonly request their own group. Sometimes "the never married" prefer a group separate from the formerly married. Generally speaking, however, if adults group themselves, they tend to associate with others who have children of the same age considering their own general chronological age of secondary importance.

MATURITY.

The Bible clearly mentions maturity as a distinguishing mark of growing Christians. Defining it on paper seems tantalizingly easy when measured against the difficulty of sorting people according to their maturity. So we should not be surprised that maturity has not often been used to create artificial groups of adults. Who wants to admit he's an immature Christian? Who would prefer to associate primarily with immature Christians? If it has a place, someone needs to devise a good instrument for distinguishing people using this criterion.

INTERESTS.

Presently, few educators would permanently sort children or youth by interest groups, but would reserve this system exclusively for adults. Adults often sort themselves by attending those classes or learning opportunities that meet specific needs in their lives. As publishing houses service this growing market by producing more materials, teachers will be better able to accommodate the growing need for variety among adults.

EDUCATION.

American churches tend to organize roughly around socioeconomic lines. Typically, the higher the socioeconomic level, the higher the educational level. Attempts to alter this have largely been unsuccessful except for a few visionary inner-city churches. The quality of teaching required in a college-town church with highly educated constituents will certainly differ from churches composed of less-educated (though not necessarily less committed) adherents.

Reading comprehension illustrates the type of learning activities that may require more time in some settings. This fundamental skill sorts people quickly and affects dramatically their capabilities in classroom settings. Teachers need to adapt to various educational backgrounds or to group people accordingly.

CHURCH CALENDAR FOR TEACHING

Effective teaching in the church requires careful coordination of curriculum with the church calendar. A novice might look at the calendar and conclude the church year can be divided into four equal quarters. Not so; educational interruptions routinely clutter the annual church calendar.

Note the following list of days which draw people away from church. Remember, when people are absent, we lose continuity in the student's grasp of the curriculum.

SUNDAYS LOST DUE TO PLANNED ABSENCES.

1. Summer vacation	2–3 Sundays
2. Memorial Day	1 Sunday
3. Labor Day	1 Sunday
4. Independence Day	1 Sunday (if near weekend)

These five–six Sundays represent 10 percent of the calendar and they all occur essentially during the summer months. Of course, not everyone chooses all these dates nor leaves at the same time. But because of this erratic attendance pattern during summer, other dates become difficult to salvage for any continuing curriculum. Teachers wisely avoid curriculum that builds from week to week during the summer.

SUNDAYS LOST DUE TO SPECIAL EMPHASES.

1. Christmas	1–2 Sundays
2. Thanksgiving	1 Sunday
3. Easter	1–2 Sundays
4. Mission Emphasis	1–2 Sundays

These four–seven Sundays represent roughly another 10 percent of the calendar. They differ from the previous list because more people make a point to attend on these Sundays than other Sundays. But the effect is the same. The special emphasis removes these days from curriculum continuity.

SUNDAYS LOST DUE TO OTHER CAUSES.

How can we measure the Sundays affected by other factors? Are we foolish to assume that all other Sundays of the year are available for sophisticated curriculum planning? Certainly some of the following causes suggest interruptions will occur at least sporadically. Note the following normal life experiences:

1. Illness (of any family member)
2. Fatigue (decided to sleep in)
3. Weekend away (resort, friends, family)
4. Sporting event attendance

All of these affect teaching in the church directly since they interrupt consistency. The church must build periodic repetition and review into its curriculum to offset staggered attendance. As much as possible, series should last only 4–6 weeks since sustained attendance over any given quarter of the church year has become increasingly unrealistic. Sunday School publishers recognize this limitation and organize their quarter around two or three units of study. Specific churches may develop unique attendance patterns which would provide different alternatives.

STRATEGY FOR CHURCH TEACHING
MAINTAINING PARTICIPATORY METHODS.

Creative teaching requires varying the methods from week to week. All teaching methods fall into one of four major categories.

Audio. These methods depend almost exclusively on concentrated listening and assume a high degree of personal motivation on the part of the student. Only exceptional verbal skills can compensate if students lack interest in the subject. Most skilled teachers recognize this intrinsic weakness and seek to supplement their lessons with multiple methods. Lectures, storytelling, audio tapes, debate, panel, and symposium qualify for this category if they rely exclusively on student listening.

Audiovisual. These methods involve both auditory and visual stimulation. The combination catches and holds students' attention if used correctly. Unfortunately, many teachers fail to develop skilled use of visual media. Films, slide-tape, television, puppets, drama, or lectures combined with chalkboard, overhead, slides, charts, or flannelgraph enhance verbal communication.

Interactive. These methods may incorporate ideas from either or both previous categories. Here the students interact with the teacher, debater, or panel member. Many teachers misuse the term "discussion" to describe this activity. Actually, "question and answer" more accurately depicts what happens in most classrooms because attention focuses on the teacher. Interaction helps students who seek clarification or expansion of some point.

Participatory. These methods call on students to work with each other on some common problem. This goes against the typical school requirement to "do your own work." However, some recent research suggests that these methods promote better student learning and involvement.[1] Some successful businesses have seized on the creativity stimulated by people working together and require employees to cooperate on most if not all projects.[2]

Methods in this category require less initial motivation on the part of the student but produce the most enthusiasm for learning (given the voluntary nature of church teaching). The kinds of activities which can be employed appear limited only by our creativity. The International Center for Learning produced a book called *How to Do Bible Learning Activities* (Ed Stuart, et al.) for every major age-group, listing specific categories such as "Art Activities," "Creative Writing," "Discussion Activities," "Drama Activities," "Music Activities," "Oral Presentations," "Puzzles and Games," "Research Activities," and "Miscellaneous Activities." More recently, Marlene LeFever has written a book entitled *Creative Teaching Methods* (David C. Cook). Both of these excellent sources contain ideas to help you implement a participatory teaching style which heavily involves students in the learning process.

Ideally, any given class would combine something from all of these four categories. Mixing and matching these can provide an almost infinite variety for teaching. Too often, volunteer teachers simply cannot give the amount of time and effort required to study a passage sufficiently and then package it attractively in appropriate methods without specific resources. Evangelical publishing houses definitely provde exceptional materials to solve this problem.

MANAGING VOLUNTEER TEACHERS.

The key to effective teaching in the church unquestionably lies with the teacher. The curriculum, calendar, and class-hour management all depend on the wise implementation of a caring teacher. No educational program can rise above the teachers' commitment level to excellence in teaching.

Since most churches have a chronic need for more teachers, they usually set the entry requirements too low. Often mere interest in teaching qualifies a person to teach. Once in that position, even well-meaning teachers can fall victim to inflated egos and forget their need for continual training. Many Christian educators complain that their adult division teachers resist change and regularly avoid teachers meetings. This autonomous spirit hinders them from developing excellence in teaching.

Some thoughtful management strategies attached to the beginning of a teacher's ministry can condition them to different expectations.

Curriculum. Require all new teachers to use prepared curriculum for some period of time before they launch out on their own. Following the predigested procedures provides important structure for the future.

Team teaching. Require all teachers to plan and team teach a series with your most proficient teacher annually. Not only will the regular teacher see innovative techniques work but the class itself may exert pressure to move toward a more participatory style.

Multiple teachers. Whenever possible, use more than one regular teacher for each class. Rotating teachers get extra preparation time which can radically improve the quality of their teaching.

Be aware of teacher "fit." Not every qualified teacher can teach every class. A certain "chemistry" develops between a class and a teacher. Often a perfectly capable teacher simply does not fit a particular class. You can discover if positive potential exists by evaluating a new teacher in a short series without further commitment. If the class responds negatively, no one suffers embarrassment.

Task force. Assign a special task force to plan an annual teaching extravaganza. Carefully plan a two- or three-week series incorporating a large variety of methodologies. Rotate the team through different classes and agencies, providing relief for the regular teachers and fresh stimulation for the classes.

THE SUNDAY SCHOOL

The Sunday School has become the major educational agency of the church. Though many churches try to provide a variety of educational programs, the Sunday School maintains better attendance than any other and sometimes all the others combined. Because of its size and broad base, the Sunday School uses more teachers than any other agency and will be considered separately.

Because the church's main educational agency has "school" in its name people sometimes assume that it functions like a public school. But Sunday Schools differ from public schools in several significant ways. For instance, how many Sunday School classes can require homework from their students? Or, how many Sunday Schools can mandate attendance and involvement? Many implications emerge from the voluntary nature of Sunday School attendance.

In addition, the basic activities of the Sunday School differ from ordinary schooling. Class time cannot be devoted exclusively to academic pursuits because time for mutual encouragement and caring forms an essential part of the Sunday School's purpose.

This brings us to the fundamental difference. The goals differ. Schools in a general way claim to seek life change as a result of the information dispensed. But successful schools are still measured by the academic achievements and not moral integrity of their students. But in the Sunday School, life change is generic to the educational process. We seek to promote moral decisions based on accurate biblical information and encouraged by warm Christian fellowship. The successful Sunday School is measured by the Christlikeness of its students and not by their academic achievement. To achieve that goal, three concurrent themes must pervade the Sunday School class hour.

1. Fellowship
2. Information
3. Application

MAXIMIZING THE CLASS HOUR.

Most Sunday Schools normally operate about sixty minutes. Some churches employ an extended session which runs concurrent with double church services. Though some inherent disadvantages exist in this system, one glaring advantage shows up when you notice how the Sunday School time extends to seventy-five minutes. Since it's much easier to accommodate more time, and since comparatively few churches implement the extended session, we can use sixty minutes as the class hour standard for analysis purposes.

To accommodate stragglers the class hour for youth and adults usually follows this format:

MINUTES	ACTIVITY
10–15	Arrive & socialize
10–15	Announcements & prayer
30–40	Lecture or lesson

However, top educators who write Sunday School material for major publishing houses have suggested a little different format for a number of years. The revised plan avoids the waste of strategic time built into the former system. Most publishers propose something similar to the following:

MINUTES	ACTIVITY
10–15	Approach activity
10–15	Fellowship or lesson introduction and life need
10–15	Bible discovery/research
10–15	Application & discussion
5–10	Class business and announcements

These two formats bristle with philosophical differences. Notice that one relates to how the hour begins. In the second proposal, Sunday School begins when the first person arrives. Leaders plan the kind of activities which accommodate staggered arrivals. But while people socialize, the activity helps focus people's thinking on the general area of study for the day. When everyone realizes the class begins promptly with a fun yet meaningful activity, they try harder to arrive on time.

Coordinating the initial activity with the lesson is virtually impossible unless the leader has identified a specific lesson aim. This furnishes the basis for thoroughly integrating the class hour. Though numerous different aims can surface in any given passage of Scripture, the best teachers plan to focus on only one.

Lesson aims are generally written by completing a sentence in terms of what the student will do during the class hour. A good aim might look like this: "The student will summarize the reasons for God's judgment on Israel as proclaimed by Habakkuk." Or "The student will determine one way to minister to the needs of the underprivileged in our community in response to 'The Good Samaritan.'"

Following the opening activity, verbally introduce the lesson and give necessary information. If not overused or misused, brief lectures serve extremely well at this point. But be careful, two sermons in one morning represents poor educational strategy. The Sunday School hour needs completely different ways to involve students heavily in the learning process which do not just require them to listen.

After the introductory information, guide the students into *firsthand discovery* of the lesson. You must do more than report findings from your personal study. You must help each student to inquire directly into the passage during the hour. Most people simply will not do homework to prepare for class. For those who do not spend time studying the Bible for themselves during the week, this may furnish their only firsthand encounter with the Word of God. This is an excellent time to have people help one another by working briefly together on the same assignment.

Next, students should report their findings and interact with the teacher's thoughts and input. This summarization crystallizes the discoveries into workable information.

On completion, move the class into the final application phase. Here, activities can assist students to make personal suggestions about how to live out Scripture. Teachers who serve predigested applications rob their students of the wonderful opportunity to respond personally to God's Word.

Sometimes students may suggest farfetched ideas which are irrelevant to the passage. Tactful teachers insert alternatives at this point as they help students think more precisely. People make mistakes about the meaning and application of Scripture with or without the help of teachers. But, ideal Sunday School classes with warm accepting atmospheres can provide a proving ground for developing biblical perspectives and theologically sound thinking.

Prayer can conclude the application time. Not only should we remember the needs of absent class members but we need to ask for help from God to live out the applications we have verbalized.

Finally, conduct class business and dismiss. With this procedure

Date _____
Title _____

Group _____

LESSON PLAN

Specific Lesson Aim: _____

_____

_____

TIME:		ACTIVITIES	EQUIPMENT
_____	Intro: _____	_____	_____
	_____	_____	_____
	_____	_____	_____
_____	Approach: _____	_____	_____
	Life _____	_____	_____
	Need _____	_____	_____
	_____	_____	_____
	_____	_____	_____
	_____	_____	_____
_____	Discovery: _____	_____	_____
	_____	_____	_____
	_____	_____	_____
	_____	_____	_____
	_____	_____	_____
	_____	_____	_____
_____	Response: _____	_____	_____
	_____	_____	_____
	_____	_____	_____
_____	Summary: _____	_____	_____
	_____	_____	_____

Evaluation:

315

the teacher need not adjust to weekly variations in teaching time. Primary emphasis remains on the Scripture and interaction. Abbreviating announcements is better than abbreviating Bible study.

Previously, only the most creative and experienced teachers could follow a format like the one just described. Now, most major curriculum publishers provide numerous ideas to facilitate student involvement and creatively package the time. Teachers can select from among several biblically sound alternatives to guide and stimulate student thinking. No thoughtful teacher would use any curriculum word for word. But any teacher who tries to work independently of well-designed curriculum has overlooked a crucial, time-saving, and creative resource.

Examine carefully the blank sample lesson plan on page 315. Adapt it to your own curriculum by adjusting the main ingredients. Remember to work toward specific lesson aims, creative time management, and multiple teaching methods.

ENDNOTES

1. Pauline B. Gough, "The Key to Improving Schools: An Interview with William Glasser." *Phi Delta Kappan,* May 1987, pp. 656ff.

2. Thomas J. Peters and Robert H. Waterman, Jr., *In Search of Excellence.* New York: Warner Books, 1982, pp. 235–78.

BIBLIOGRAPHY

Adams, Jay E. *Back to the Blackboard.* Phillipsburg, N.J.: Presbyterian & Reformed, 1982.

Bruce, Joyce and Marcia Weil. *Models of Teaching.* 2nd ed., Englewood Cliffs, N.J.: Prentice-Hall, 1980.

Coleman, Lucian E., Jr. *Understanding Today's Adults.* Nashville, Tenn.: Convention Press, 1982.

Dewey, John. *Experience and Education.* New York: MacMillan, 1973.

Gangel, Kenneth O. *24 Ways to Improve Your Teaching.* Wheaton, Ill.: Victor Books, 1982.

Gregory, John M. *The Seven Laws of Teaching.* Grand Rapids: Baker Book House, 1975.

Hill, Brian V. *Faith at the Blackboard—Issues Facing the Christian Teacher.* Grand Rapids: William B. Eerdmans Publishing Company, 1982.

Horne, Herman. *Teaching Techniques of Jesus.* Grand Rapids: Kregel, 1974.

Hendricks, Howard G. *Teaching to Change Lives.* Portland, Ore.: Multnomah Press and Walk Thru the Bible Ministries, 1987.

Jackson, Phillip W. *Life in Classrooms.* New York: Holt Rinehart and Winston, Inc., 1968.

LeFever, Marlene D. *Creative Teaching Methods.* Elgin, Ill.: David C. Cook, 1985.

Marlowe, Monroe and Bobbie Reed. *Creative Bible Learning for Adults.* Glendale, Calif.: Regal Books, 1977.

Merch, James Deforest. *Teach or Perish.* Grand Rapids: William B. Eerdmans Publishing Co., 1961 (out of print).

Richards, Lawrence O. *Creative Bible Teaching.* Chicago: Moody Press, 1970.

Stewart, Ed, Neal McBride, Sherry Lindvall and Monroe Marlowe. *How to Do Bible Learning Activities—Adult.* Ventura, Calif.: Gospel Light Publications, 1982.

Toffler, Alvin. *Learning for Tomorrow—The Role of the Future in Education.* New York: Random House Publishers, 1974.

Zuck, Roy B. *The Holy Spirit in Your Teaching.* Wheaton, Ill.: Victor Books, 1984.

19. TEACHING IN THE CHRISTIAN SCHOOL
David L. Edwards

The impact of Christian schools on American precollegiate education during the past two decades has been phenomenal. Based on its 1985–86 survey of private schools, the U.S. Department of Education estimates that the number of non-Catholic, religiously affiliated schools has increased by an estimated 520 percent.[1] From their former status as virtual scholastic nonentities, Christian schools collectively represent (after Roman Catholic parochial schools) the second-largest identified grouping of nonpublic schools in America. The report observes that "schools with the highest growth rates in enrollment in recent years— among religiously affiliated schools—have been evangelical, Calvinist, and Lutheran schools.[2]

The number of students these schools enroll has expanded comparably: by 1983 one fourth of all nonpublic elementary and secondary school pupils were studying in non-Catholic religious schools; that estimate would translate to over 1 ¼ million students, and the trend continues.

One consequence of this expansion is commensurate increase in the number of educators filling professional staff positions in such schools—127,000 according to one estimate. Christian schools have, of course, needed supervisory and administrative personnel in addition to classroom teachers. For the evangelical educator with a career ministry in view, teaching in a Christian school has become an option that ought legitimately, and perhaps necessarily, to be considered.

Opting to teach in a Christian school is not, however, merely choosing a different environment: Christian school education is qualitatively distinct in both philosophy and practice from its secular counterpart. Effectiveness in the Christian classroom requires a pedagogical approach radically altered from what is advocated in many college and university training programs, even some associated with evangelical

318

institutions. Comprehending the distinction between a teacher who is a Christian and a Christian teacher is not always simple; to implement that distinction in consistent classroom practice is even more challenging. This chapter will indicate some of the issues and concerns to be considered before deciding to commit to the ministry of teaching in a Christian school.

DISTINCTIVE PHILOSOPHY

No one teaches in a neutral milieu. Each school, in fact each classroom, evidences a specific approach to teaching. One's approach to teaching in turn reflects a set of assumptions and presuppositions about the nature and purpose of education generally. This philosophic commitment then dictates how the countless day-to-day choices implicit to classroom instruction will be made. Christian school education is predicated on the existence of a biblical conception of reality, truth, and morality as the basis for both curriculum content and instructional practice. It requires teachers to think through basic philosophical issues of teaching and learning, and to develop a premise for teaching compatible with the school's own educational philosophy and ultimately with the Word of God.

Forming and implementing such a philosophy is not the task of a moment, nor is it the inevitable consequence of a formal course in educational philosophy. Rather it is the Christian educators' perpetual challenge to refine a coherent world and life view that recognizes God as the ultimate source of all truth: truth as general revelation throughout the created universe, accessible to everyone; and truth as special revelation sovereignly mediated by God the Holy Spirit through Scripture.[3] Attempting to "Christianize" a secular philosophy by incorporating elements of doctrine or scriptural prooftexts will not suffice: the Christian teacher's hallmark must be a consistent perspective on teaching and all of life, with Christ as the "cosmic center."[4]

DISTINCTIVE PURPOSE

As the number of Christian schools increased, it is perhaps inevitable that a significant number would be established for invalid or, at least, inadequate reasons. The teacher evaluating career possibilities in Christian schools needs, therefore, to formulate a clear conception of why Christian school education is both appropriate and necessary within the context of a reasoned biblical life view. Disjunction between the teacher's philosophy and that of the school can result only in mutual dissatisfaction. Both share the obligation to determine in advance if the fundamental purposes for which the school exists and those embraced by the teacher are essentially alike.

When local public schools evidence characteristics unacceptable to Christian parents, one reaction may be to initiate an alternative. Diminished academic emphasis or standards, laxity in student discipline, perceived problems with drugs, curriculum content, or values—all of these have at times stimulated interest in a Christian school. The specific concerns are probably only symptoms of the persistent erosion of what Francis Schaeffer termed a "Christian consensus" in American society,[5] a consensus that preserved at least a modicum of propriety and ethics within our public institutions. Confronted with their declining influence in local policy development and philosophically alienated by liberal tendencies among professional school managers, parents grasped at the Christian school alternative. Perhaps the school might succeed where parents and churches were failing in instilling a better perspective toward "morality."

As valid as those parental concerns may be, Christian schools require a more substantial rationale for existence than the failures and deficiencies of public schools. Rather than as a reaction to negative features in secular education, Christian pedagogy ought to be anchored on the positive foundation of a thoroughly biblical conception of teaching as the communication of God's truth. Curriculum developed under the auspices of parents directly or through church sponsorship opens possibilities nonexistent in the finest secular system. In such a context the school provides students with the opportunity to develop a biblical view of life; to profit from the lifestyle modeling of mature Christian adults besides their own parents; to explore difficult issues within the secure limits of adherence to the ultimate authority of Scripture; to worship, serve, and study within a supportive spiritual community.

Organizationally Christian schools tend to follow one of three basic patterns: parochial, parent society, or board sponsorship. While the educational goals and objectives may be similar, the choice of operational structure influences and even dictates certain characteristic emphases within the school. It is, therefore, a significant variable among evangelical schools, one which the prospective staff member needs to understand.

A majority of Christian schools founded since 1970 have been parochial (church-sponsored) schools. Like the Roman Catholic and Lutheran school systems formed in earlier generations, these schools emerged from the ministry vision of a local church. Such churches typically view the Christian school as an integral part of their overall Christian education program, overseen by a designated church board. Parochial schools often share facilities with the Sunday School and other church ministries and thus receive a generous subsidy, reducing the costs borne by tuition. However, shared facilities impose definite limitations on all users and require a gracious spirit of universal cooperation to work effectively.

Parent sponsorship was more common for Christian schools founded prior to 1970, perhaps because churches commonly had little vision for day-school education outside those few denominations traditionally committed to parochial schooling. Without the protective, corporate umbrella of church sponsorship, parent-controlled schools typically organize as a legal association or society with the specific purpose of operating a school and auxiliary functions. While direct oversight of the school may be delegated to a representative and accountable governing board, control of the educational program and policies remains with parents to a much greater degree than with the parochial structure. Virtually all school costs, however, ultimately fall on the families enrolled.

A third mode for Christian day schools follows an organizational structure typical among independent schools and in Christian higher education. Here a corporate board assumes responsibility for establishing and maintaining the school: members are not necessarily parents, but the personal commitment required by service on the board is not common among nonparents. Such boards serve as trustees of the school's assets, pledged to continuing the declared intent of the founder(s). To maintain institutional integrity, board members tend to serve longer terms of office. They carefully select as new or additional members candidates firmly espousing the same educational purposes.

For the classroom teacher, arcane issues such as organizational structure may seem remote. Their impact on the teacher's professional role is considerable, though. Church sponsorship implies greater fiscal security; facilities and equipment are often superior; and there is no question of the "integral religious intent" of the school as an issue of law. For this security, however, the teacher may trade a measure of privacy since the room is used for nonschool functions. Sponsoring churches may require school staff to become church members and to participate broadly in nonschool church activities, such as, visitation and educational ministries. The vitality of church commitment to the day-school program often fluctuates with pastoral changes too.

In parent-controlled schools there is a clear correlation with the biblical mandate for parental responsibility in training and nurturing their children. But parents may have difficulty seeing where their delegation to school staff standing *in loco parentis* is bounded. Consequently, teachers are sometimes subjected to parental pressures that are not only at variance but even incompatible with each other and with school standards. The strength of the board-sustained school lies in its ability

321

to maintain fundamental integrity in doctrine and practice. However, insulation from the influences of school patrons may also remove them from sensitivity to the needs of staff. Retention of all authority within the scope of board membership may over time cause the school to lose contact with pedagogical "best practice."

DISTINCTIVE PREPARATION

A teacher exerts enormous influence over his students. As a direct consequence of his relative effectiveness in instruction the student is more or less equipped for future studies and for life itself. Students' affective responses to classroom experiences (and to the teacher) imprint academic likes and dislikes, some of which may lead to life-orienting decisions. The teacher's own values, beliefs, and preferences are conveyed to students in remarkably pervasive ways. In our Lord's words, a student "fully trained will be like his teacher" (Luke 6:40).

Since the teacher's impact is both extensive and intensive, preservice preparation must be pursued carefully and diligently. What should characterize the preparation of a well-qualified candidate for Christian school teaching? At least three essential areas of solid college or university level studies should be evidenced: training in Bible and theology, general studies, and professional theory and methods.

In truly *Christian* schooling, every curriculum subject is to be presented as integrated truth derived from God's general and special revelation. Teachers competent to achieve this end will be thoroughly informed in both dimensions. Personal study of the Word on the part of Christian school personnel is assumed, and the Bible knowledge accumulated through local church teaching can be a substantial asset. But formal study of Scripture—at the very least survey courses in Bible content and hopefully more extensive study—should be required. The ability to handle scriptural texts appropriately in teaching Bible as well as in applying its truths to other subjects demands some exegetical and hermeneutical skills as well. While some excellent curriculum materials for Christian schools have been developed, reliance on those resources leaves the teacher underprepared for the spontaneous student question as well as for expanding personal understanding. Facility in using standard research tools ought to be developed within preservice training.

Competence in scholastic content is required. Many undergraduate teacher training programs slight this, leaving the beginning teacher to supplement his inadequate grasp of concepts in math, science, or history by personal study. In a recent study of American public schools John Goodlad reported more than 10 percent of elementary teachers feeling "uncomfortable" with their level of competence to teach one or more subjects in the required curriculum. Even at the secondary level where specialization is typically assumed, nearly 4 percent of teachers surveyed considered themselves un- or underqualified for one or more of their assigned teaching responsibilities.[6]

Concern for the quality of American education generally has prompted numerous efforts to reform the process of training teachers. One crucial issue is the role of general studies in contrast to specialized or professional emphases. Since the Christian school often has fewer total faculty, yet aspires to high standards of scholastic achievement, its staff needs both versatility and competence. For these schools, at least, the ideal teacher would have a broad liberal arts core, its breadth supplemented with appropriate depth in one or more areas of concentration for secondary candidates.

Emphasis on biblical and liberal studies does not diminish the importance of developing pedagogical skills. Both in formal classroom studies and clinical experience the teacher-in-training should have a twofold purpose: to develop a repertoire of instructional skills, and to confirm the presence of those personal and spiritual endowments by which one is truly gifted for effective teaching. To attempt to teach with spiritual impact apart from that divinely imparted spiritual dynamic can only end in mutual frustration. The student-teacher's mentors should provide perceptive counsel regarding this essential qualification.

Satisfied that appropriate gifts have been endowed, it is important to continue discovering the teacher you will be. Teaching style is neither singular in character nor prescriptive in practice. Teachers employ a variety of strategies as effective instructors and classroom managers. What is essential is to discern those teaching and disciplinary methods that "fit" the teacher you intend to be; during your professional training courses, you will be introduced to several possibilities, but each individual must eventually decide for herself what works. Student teaching is an opportunity to make decisions with limited risks.

Children are remarkably adaptable to a variety of approaches to teaching, so long as the teacher is consistent. There is less flexibility granted teachers in some institutional settings than in others, however, and classroom effectiveness is greatly inhibited if school policies cannot be enthusiastically and freely endorsed. "Know yourself, and know the system!" might be good practical advice as you consider service in a Christian school.

DISTINCTIVE PRESSURES

Professional staff in a Christian school experience a number of distinct blessings in their work. The freedom to share one's beliefs and values freely within the classroom, to use Scripture as a source of truth for our students, the delight that comes with leading a student to faith in Christ, or seeing a major spiritual decision consummated as a direct outgrowth of some class or school activity—these are precious indeed! But there are also special pressures not usually faced by educators employed in secular settings.

One obvious source of pressure is financial. Though Christian schools have worked diligently at improving their financial bases, most teachers can still expect to make a significant contribution to the school's continuation by way of salary differential. That contribution may range from several percent up to nearly half. One study involving about 150 Christian schools indicated that from 1977 to 1982 the starting salaries in these schools remained consistently at or near 58 percent of the national average for public school beginning teachers.[7]

While the financial pressure may not be as keen for a single person or where there is a second income, new teachers ought not discount the tension that continual fiscal scarcity engenders emotionally, even spiritually. That tension can be employed by God's Spirit to increase faith and produce spiritual maturity; it can also become an instrument of the enemy engendering discouragement or discontent. The teacher considering Christian school employment must heed the biblical injunction to "count the cost" in several ways.

A more subtle form of pressure is exerted by well-intentioned evangelicals who question the propriety of the Christian school enterprise altogether. Their number is legion and their fidelity unquestioned. What about the legitimacy of their objections? Typically, two concerns surface: (1) Do Christian schools adequately prepare for life in "the real world"? and (2) How will we fulfill our responsibility for community witness if Christian schools prevail?

In actuality Christian schools don't guarantee an antiseptic environment. Human nature still flourishes even where admissions criteria are clear, and among children from Christian families. Christian schools deal with their share of misconduct, and their students must still make personal ethical choices and sometimes stand alone. Many find it at least as challenging to live "Christianly" on the Christian school campus as it would be in the public school.

The more basic issue, however, concerns what is meant by "the real world": is the culture more real that denies the legitimacy of non-relative truth? That systematically excludes the mention of Deity? That belies the religious foundations of our society? Those who advocate Christian schools strongly affirm that the "real world" is the one encompassed within their curriculum where God is honored and His truth sought.

And what of our duty to be light and salt before the unbelieving community? Do Christian families deny a mandate for witness by withdrawing from public schools? Answering this concern effectively requires a comprehension of the nature and purpose of public education.

Commenting on the socializing influence of American schools, education historian Diane Ravitch observes that:

> Integration and pluralism are both versions of assimilation. . . . Cultural pluralism has been discussed for most of this century, but usually in relation to white ethnic and religious groups that had a distinct cultural heritage and wanted to preserve it.[8]

"Assimilation" has been an implicit purpose for public schools since the rise of the common school movement in the nineteenth century. It was the task of schools to inculcate societal values and mores into the younger generation of immigrant Americans. The effectiveness of this effort, in fact, promoted the establishment of the first Roman Catholic schools: public schools of the 1800s were, in the opinion of at least one bishop, too "godless and Protestant" to be trusted with the education of his flock.[9]

Should evangelicals be less concerned over the assimilating aspirations of public education at the end of the twentieth century? The premises and values inherent in the state's approach to schooling cannot be shared by Christian families: their only defense is to counteract or withdraw.

DISTINCTIVE BENEFITS

Teachers in Christian schools also experience special joys and blessings from serving God in this context. People generally derive satisfaction from success in their work or profession, and the more intimate relationships among faculty and with parents that frequently emerge in the smaller community of the Christian school make it even easier for good work to be visible and appreciated. A chief benefit is that spiritual peace that comes with the assurance that God's calling and your service are identical.

Parents expect that students will be instructed in biblical truth across the curriculum. For the Christian teacher, there is a sense of freedom from the restraints of a secular classroom, and the ability to interact with students freely on the most crucial issues of life. The teacher should not assume that all parents have enrolled their children with full understanding of what "biblical integration" means or that all will entirely approve of institutional policies. But within the structure of a scriptural approach to learning there is recourse to an unfailing Authority.

The liberty to experience genuine fellowship with parents, students, and colleagues is a precious aspect of Christian school teaching. Faculty members experience mutual ministries of caring, counsel, and sharing with respect to all kinds of needs. Knowing that there is a level of commitment surpassing mere generosity makes it easier to endure whatever hardships may ensue. As teachers and administrators share concerns and pray for one another, the Spirit of God has often worked extraordinarily through the collective resources of the school family to meet needs.

According to a national survey conducted by Louis Harris and Associates, public school teachers experience major dissatisfaction with their role in educational decision-making. While nearly all teachers interviewed (97 percent) believed school districts should use team-management concepts, only half felt that their district currently implemented such an approach. Even in the areas closest to the classroom teacher (curriculum, pedagogy, student welfare, and discipline), teachers felt strongly that their influence on policy is inadequate.[10] By their structure, philosophic unanimity among leadership elements, and characteristic openness in communication, Christian schools increase the likelihood that teachers share responsibility for the educational decisions affecting them.

CONCLUSIONS

Teaching in a Christian school is above all a ministry. Formal training, professional credentials, articulation of a biblical philosophy of teaching and learning—these are all essential, but insufficient. Those who would serve there must know a strong sense of call, an understanding that it is not human choice alone that motivates. As with ministry in any other context it is often that pervading consciousness of God's appointment that alone sustains.

Coupled with a sense of call should come realization of divine gifting. The spiritual gift of teaching is manifest in diverse styles; effective teachers evidence it variously. The gifted teacher knows it best through exercising the gift and seeing the response of those who profit from it. By virtue of talent, inate ability, and training, a person can employ good instructional technique. To impart life-orienting truth, and to do it in the teaching of math, literature, or geography as well as in Bible class, requires the teacher to have the operational dynamic of spiritual enabling.

Christian schools are maturing. With increasing numbers there has been significant qualitative growth too. But Christian schools are not all elements in some monolithic whole: each school is a unique combination of strengths and weaknesses. Part of the process of selection on both sides should demand careful examination of mutual concerns. Schools as well as teacher candidates must measure up well for the partnership to succeed.

After the family, Christian schools may represent our most effective means for helping parents train sons and daughters in godliness. To serve God in such a way is no small privilege.

ENDNOTES

1. *Digest of Education Statistics, 1987 Ed.* Washington, D.C.: U.S. Department of Education, Center for Education Statistics, 1987, pp. 52ff.

2. Mary Frase Williams, "Private School Enrollment and Tuition Trends" in *The Condition of Education, 1986 Ed.* Washington, D.C.: Office of Educational Research and Improvement, Department of Education, pp. 182ff.

3. For helpful insights the reader is referred to Kenneth O. Gangel and Warren S. Benson, *Christian Education: Its History and Philosophy.* Chicago: Moody Press, 1983; Paul A. Kienel, ed., *The Philosophy of Christian School Education,* 3rd Ed., Whittier, Calif.: ACSI, 1980; and Frank Gaebelein, *The Pattern of God's Truth.* Chicago: Moody Press, 1968.

4. D. Bruce Lockerbie, *The Cosmic Center* (Rev. Ed.). Portland, Ore.: Multnomah Press, 1986.

5. Francis Schaeffer, *The Great Evangelical Disaster.* Westchester, Ill.: Crossway, 1984, pp. 183ff.

6. John I. Goodlad, *A Place Called School.* New York: McGraw-Hill Book Co., 1984, pp. 183–4.

7. James W. Deuink, *Christian School Finance.* Greenville, S.C.: Bob Jones University Press, 1985, p. 85.

8. Diane Ravitch, *The Schools We Deserve.* New York: Basic Books, Inc., 1985, p. 211.

9. Robert L. Church and Michael W. Sedlak, *Education in the United States.* New York: The Free Press, 1976, p. 162.

10. *The American Teacher 1986,* Metropolitan Life Insurance Co., 1987.

BIBLIOGRAPHY

Adams, Jay. *Back to the Blackboard.* Phillipsburg, N.J.: Presbyterian and Reformed Publishing Co., 1982.

Adler, Mortimer. *The Paideia Proposal: An Educational Manifesto.* New York: Macmillan, 1982.

Blamires, Harry. *The Christian Mind.* Ann Arbor, Mich.: Servant Books, 1980.

Byrne, Herbert W. *A Christian Approach to Education.* Rev. Ed. Milford, Mich.: Mott Media, 1977.

Chadwick, Ronald P. *Teaching and Learning: An Integrated Approach to Christian Education.* Old Tappan, N.J.: Fleming H. Revell, 1982.

Gaebelein, Frank E. *The Pattern of God's Truth.* Chicago: Moody Press, 1968.

Gangel, Kenneth O. and Warren S. Benson. *Christian Education: Its History and Philosophy.* Chicago: Moody Press, 1983.

Holmes, Arthur. *All Truth Is God's Truth.* Grand Rapids: Wm. B. Eerdmans, 1977.

Kienel, Paul A., ed. *The Philosophy of Christian School Education,* 3rd Ed. Whittier, Calif.: Association of Christian Schools International, 1980.

Knight, George R. *Philosophy and Education: An Introduction in Christian Perspective.* Berrien Springs, Mich.: Andrews University Press, 1980.

Lockerbie, D. Bruce. *The Way They Should Go.* New York: Oxford University Press, 1972.

Lowrie, Roy W., Jr. *To Those Who Teach in Christian Schools.* Whittier, Calif.: Association of Christian Schools International, 1978.

May, Philip. *Which Way to Educate?* Chicago: Moody Press, 1975.

Peshkin, Alan. *God's Choice: The Total World of a Fundamentalist Christian School.* Chicago: University of Chicago Press, 1986.

20. TEACHING IN THE CHRISTIAN COLLEGE
Kenneth O. Gangel

The end of the twentieth century is proving a difficult time for Christian higher education. From 1970 to 1985 liberal arts enrollment dropped two thirds, and the pool of high school graduates from which colleges draw students has been steadily shrinking.

Meanwhile, both students and parents seem to be losing confidence in that great American dream, the college diploma. The inexpensive community college now serves one half of all freshmen and sophomores attending postsecondary institutions in America. Colleges are restructuring their orientation toward older students, extension programs, and a much greater emphasis on vocational, career, and specialization tracts. In a knowledge explosion climate, however, many believe the generalist will fare better than the specialist. Dr. Kenneth Kantzer argues in *Christianity Today:*

> The highest and best vocational training, therefore, becomes a long-term, lifetime process. And the person who is best equipped to function effectively in the marketplace future will be the generalist who has not only learned his economic skills, but who is also equipped by his general education to be flexible enough to make moves from one vocation to another as the economic picture changes. For any youth in the eighties, the best preparation to make money is to get a broad cultural education in the arts and sciences.[1]

What kind of teachers can work with students under these changing conditions? What distinctives do evangelicals expect in the classrooms of their institutions of higher learning? Though obviously a glancing overview, this chapter will attempt to answer these crucial questions.

THE UNIQUE ROLE OF THE CHRISTIAN COLLEGE

A book in the higher education section of my library heralds the title, *College Ruined My Daughter.* The author, using the shock title as a reverse message, argues that it probably wasn't the college at all but the failure of the parents and the spiritual condition of the daughter when she went to college. Though debatable, the case does reflect what parents do expect from Christian colleges and their faculties—a reasonable *in loco parentis* role which affirms the Christian values and ethics their kids have learned at home and church for almost two decades. As Eugene Habecker reminds us, it becomes a question of trust.

> When one becomes a leader in an organization—any organization, whether a church, a college, a business—there are a variety of voices saying, "Trust me." In a college situation, for example, the faculty wants the trust of the administration and vice versa. The alumni want to trust the administration and vice versa, and so on down the line. Everybody wants to be trusted.[2]

Our approach to Christian colleges in this chapter will deal with Bible institutes, Bible colleges, Christian liberal arts colleges, Christian universities, and seminaries. The institutions differ one from another but the purposes of faculty and process of teaching are sufficiently common that we can treat them within the same frame of reference.

In reality, the Christian college represents a genuine piece of Americana. Spanning over 350 years, the history of higher education in America takes us back to the earliest purposes of our founding fathers.

> There is no question that the earliest colleges in America were Christian institutions. The Colonial Anglicans and Calvinists wanted a highly literate and college-trained clergy functioning in their churches and so established their colleges with that goal in mind. John S. Brubacher and Willis Rudy, in their authoritative history entitled *Higher Education in Transition,* clearly state that "Christian tradition was the foundation stone of the whole intellectual structure which was brought to the new world."[3]

In my writings in this field I have repeatedly emphasized a four-part definition of the Christian college which may bear repeating here: *A Christian college is a postsecondary institution of learning which takes seriously an evangelical doctrinal statement; classes in Bible and Christian ministry; a distinctively Christian philosophy of education and life; and the quality of spiritual life on campus.* Such a definition can apply to a Christian liberal arts college or university with the broadest of programs or to a small Bible institute or seminary with a single-purpose curriculum.

In fulfilling the definition a Christian institution finds its uniqueness by emphasizing at least three basic components: evangelical commitment (the serious view of a doctrinal statement with faculty and board compliance); ecclesiastical allegiance (a willingness to serve the body of Christ in general as well as the sponsoring denomination where appropriate); and educational quality (a willingness to submit the institution to analysis and approval by the appropriate professional accrediting and certifying agencies).

The unique curriculum of Christian colleges consists essentially of three parts; there must be biblical studies, vocational studies, and liberal arts or general education. Different types of Christian institutions disagree as to how the pie should be divided, with Bible colleges placing a much greater emphasis on Bible and theology, liberal arts colleges on the arts and sciences, and both forced into the modern-day emphasis on vocational studies.

These institutions stand essential to the body of Christ in the late twentieth century. They represent the source of our pastors, missionaries, and Christian leaders. Their faculties produce books which train and develop our church leaders and establish a Christian voice in society. Yet our colleges struggle today with denominational loyalties, increasing theological weaknesses, confusing goals, and mission statements, plus an unfortunate but real competition among themselves. The area of ultimate concern lies not with better public relations programs and lucrative educational advancement; it lies rather with more godly, more biblically literate, and more student-oriented faculty.

QUALIFICATIONS FOR CHRISTIAN COLLEGE TEACHING

Is there an ideal preparation for teaching in the Christian college? Probably not. But several types of experiences help and some are virtually mandatory. It would be useful for a faculty member to have had *experience* as a student in a Christian college. He will better understand his students and the motivation that brought them to such an institution. Undergraduate, graduate, and doctoral *degrees* from different institutions seem a good idea in higher education since it usually provides greater breadth for the faculty member. Internship, practical experience (in the pastorate, on the mission field, etc.), and the appropriate academic and general education are obvious factors.

Absolutely essential, yet often missing, is the theological dimension. We have already dealt with the issue of integration, but the out-

331

working of this process depends not on the institution's commitment but rather each faculty member's competence to make it work. Even a dedicated Christian who walks closely with the Lord in his personal life and faithfully attends church does not automatically integrate in his classroom. That requires *formal theological training* which will enable the teacher to harmonize a given academic discipline with the absolute and inerrant Word of God.

What qualities does an institution look for in a faculty member? Obviously the criteria mentioned above are primary, in addition to which almost any school would take into consideration: personality, age, general philosophy of life, recommendations from reference sources, scholarly publications, and membership in learned societies.

But we must be more specific. A Christian college teacher needs to be a true professional whose *self-motivated growth* keeps him on the cutting edge of his discipline. In reality he serves both as generalist and specialist. As a geologist or philosopher he must be a precise specialist in a given academic arena. In his broader Christian worldview he's a generalist. Such a blend enables the Christian teacher to apply biblical truth both to his academic specialty and to the current issues of the day.

Team cooperation is also crucial. Especially in the smaller college (and most Christian institutions are smaller colleges), the faculty member must relate positively to his colleagues both intra- and interdepartmentally. The academic community becomes a meaningful, mutual, and model society for the Christian student.

Alexander Astin bemoans the dominance of competition which detracts from professorial humanness.

> The most important thing for each of us to recognize is that there is much that we as individuals can do on our campuses, in spite of our tendency to believe that trying to change an institution is much like trying to move Mt. Everest. We can, for example, examine the way we teach our classes, treat our students, and treat our colleagues. And when we have an opportunity to participate in curriculum decisions, long-range planning, and similar kinds of group activities, we can take the initiative to introduce value questions such as "cooperation versus competition" into the deliberations.[4]

The Christian college teacher understands what *academic freedom* means in an evangelical context. The faculty runs the educational program of any respectable college and relations with both administration and board should be a part of that model society mentioned above. Yet in the Christian context academic freedom includes much more responsibility. Arthur Holmes writes:

> In order to avoid becoming a stumbling-block, the Christian educator needs to scrutinize his pedagogy, to organize his curriculum, even to restrict at times his own public utterances. Intellectual food that has been offered to idols may well be wholesome in itself, and may be helpful in the diet of a mature thinker, yet this fact is not always apparent to the weaker brother in the earlier stages of his development.[5]

For a number of years I have asked graduate students in my higher education classes what they remembered most about their "favorite" college and seminary professors. What qualities did they find outstanding in teachers they considered effective?

For one thing, students are looking for *availability* in their faculty. Seeing a high-profile professor only in a large lecture class doesn't get the job done in Christian education. That professor (and all professors) should be available to students outside of class.

Students also want to see *vulnerability*. They don't need concrete idols before whom to bow or literary lions who never make a mistake either in class or out. The genuinely transparent Christian teacher allows students to see the real person, a human being in formation by the hand of God, complete with flaws and failures. Only with such a person can students identify.

Dependability is a third quality students usually name in describing faculty who have impressed them. Almost a cliché idea, within the framework of Christian higher education it means that faculty will not let students down in areas of behavior, standards, and a meaningful commitment to excellence. The dependable faculty member comes to class prepared, organized, and over the years demonstrates a maturing depth of knowledge in both his subject matter field and its relationship to the Word of God.

Finally, students look for *flexibility* in their teachers. Rigid academic caricatures may still be popular on Ivy League campuses but are hardly suited to the overall goals of Christian education. The job description of the small-college faculty member changes with regularity and requires a willingness to flex within the academic community in order to meet the needs of the institution and its students.

A CHRISTIAN PHILOSOPHY OF TEACHING

As Benjamin Bloom has warned us regarding the word "learn," the word "teach" means many different things even within the educational profession. It virtually defies definition. The following teaching continuum diagram emphasizes that "teaching" can aim at behavior/conduct goals or knowledge/belief goals. The center of the continuum line represents the "heart of rational inquiry" while the dotted-line rectangle outlines the "region of intelligence" beyond which mechanistic machinations may occur but should never be appropriately labeled "teaching."

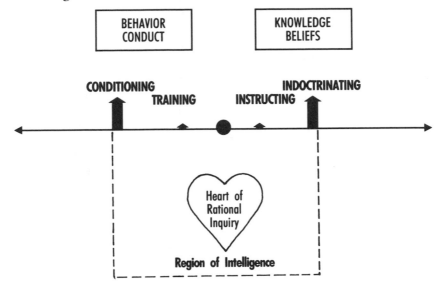

The heart of rational inquiry centers in the process of thinking, aiming at the *whys* rather than just the *whats* and *hows* of any particular subject matter. The implications of the model should strike us as both crucial and far-reaching. As on any continuum line, the distinctions are not clear and precise but each "species" of teaching blends into the next. Every point on the continuum may be equally a point of learning, but not every point on the continuum (nor every method of bringing about learning) equally relates to the heart of rational education and, therefore, the center of the concept of teaching.

The speed or accuracy of learning may not lead us to the best concept of teaching; *a theory of teaching rests on more than just the observation of how people learn.* The Christian college professor has committed himself to absolute truth and its resulting core curriculum, and also to the priority of the spiritual dimension of life. In the case of the first he finds himself moving away from the educational philosophy of the secularist by indicating that he cannot follow just any behavioral trail to positive outcomes.

In the second, he wonders about the limitations of behavioral objectives in dealing with the spiritual dimensions of life. To be sure, we may stumble on semantics here, but we must nevertheless insist that cautions are essential when designing objectives for Christian teaching at any level.

Excellence in Christian teaching depends on excellence in Christian teachers. In the final analysis we must focus not so much on the *process* as on the *professor*—not so much on the *classroom* as on the *candidate.* Perhaps one problem in developing a distinctly Christian philosophy of teaching is just plain carelessness. Once filled with sufficient content, we assume, surely anyone can teach. But after almost three decades I've found teaching rather like playing golf: a succession of bad habits slowly and painstakingly corrected. As you try to acquire the slice, the short iron shots go awry; concentrate on them and the putting disappears. The trick is to get it all together at the same time in the same place.

The famous Gilbert Highet who taught at Oxford and Columbia for forty years reminds us to constantly renew ourselves and our content for the magnificent task of teaching, a task which he sees as *creating,* not *repeating.*

> Everytime a teacher faces a class, he or she is creating something which did not exist before. Even if the pupils always belong to the same age group and social milieu, every class is an entity different from other classes in the past, every pupil in it is a novelty, and the whole thing is a new opportunity.[6]

There is a tradition of excellence among the shipbuilders along the Clyde, a reputation for unsurpassed quality. But recent decades have seen a decline. An old gateman in one of the yards lamented, "Once iron men came here to build wooden ships; today wooden men come to build iron ships." May such a complaint never be honestly launched against present and future generations of teachers in the glorious tradition of Christian higher education.

CONSTRUCTING LEARNING EXPERIENCES

College and seminary teaching contain challenges different from other kinds of teaching described in this volume. The importance of the syllabus, the emphasis on faculty trained at the doctoral level, the high degree of specialization and professionalization—all these and many more variables make this a distinctive kind of ministry. Yet the centrality of objectives stands in common with all teaching. *The efficiency of learning and the effectiveness of evaluation depend on and inseparately relate to the adequacy of educational objectives in any given class or course.* The educational cycle (chap. 3) begins with a recognition of needs which is translated into objectives when we define new patterns of behavior which will meet those needs.

Designing objectives is a part of *planning a course.* The well-constructed syllabus contains the course description, clear objectives, course requirements, criteria for grading, rationale for procedure, schedule or outline of topics, identification of textbooks, and up-to-date, adequate bibliography. *Effective teaching objectives at any level of education must be clear, specific, brief, flexible, and worded in terms of student outcomes.* In today's educational terminology we refer to them as "performance-related" or "competency-based." Constructing learning experiences includes *choosing a methodology.* Once student needs have adequately interacted with course content, objectives can be formulated and methods chosen. By then the teacher has asked himself several important questions:

(1) What do I want the student to learn?

(2) Why do I want the student to learn this?

(3) When he has learned it, what do I want him to do with it?

(4) When he has learned it, how long do I expect him to retain it?

(5) Is this objective "testable"?

(6) What provision will I make for various learning abilities, such as, rate, mode, and motivation?

Obviously objectives represent only one factor in the choice of methodology. The teacher must also consider time, facilities, the ability of students, and numerous other variables.

Constructing learning experiences for the Christian college classroom also involves designing *evaluation.* The teacher who signs a contract to teach agrees thereby to evaluate student learning. "Testing," a term somewhat more narrow than either "evaluation" or "measurement," describes the systematic procedure of comparing the behavior of two or more persons. Rather than complaining about testing and grading, or worse yet, mocking the procedure in the presence of students, Christian college teachers must take seriously this important and strategic dimension of their professional responsibility.

TEACHING THROUGH GROUPS

Be careful of extremes, warns Eble, because a teacher can go wrong in all the right directions—balance is a major key to effective college teaching. Also high on his list of effective teaching components are such things as variety, enthusiasm, and creativity.[7] All of that points to something other than a rigid adherence to lecturing in college and seminary classrooms. Obviously we can choose numerous creative methods apart from group work (interaction, case studies, role playing, demonstrations, etc.), but group processes bring to the classroom a certain dynamic which puts the focus on students rather than on the teacher. Students get involved and participate in their own learning process. Motivation tends to be much higher in development of student incentive. Outcomes, of course, are crucial as in all teaching methodology, but *the value of group work resides in the process*, especially in preparation for the "serving professions" where the graduate must work with people in some form of group involvement.

Obviously commitment to group process in the college or seminary classroom takes time and can be threatening to some teachers. On the other side of the desk, some students simply don't want process orientation. Though they can't explain it in detail, they've committed themselves to analytical learning styles.

Certain process dynamics occur in various kinds of classroom groups which we really achieve in no other way. The interaction of teacher with students, and students with students creates a participational environment impossible in the larger structure of the class, even with a teacher given to reasonably open discussion. Perhaps it's the informality, or maybe the fact that students grasp the rationale which led the teacher toward a commitment to process as well as content.

Virtually any size class can be turned into small group sessions assuming movable classroom furniture and a sufficiently knowledgeable teacher. Buzz groups, dyads, or triads can all work in classes of 150 students or more. Certain rules, however, do apply:

(1) Plan the class time carefully.

(2) Explain the roles of both leader and recorder in the group.

(3) Set a time limit for a group effort.

(4) If possible, float from group to group.

(5) Have the groups compare notes and prepare a summary.

But how effective are student group presentations? After nearly three decades I don't have a single answer to that question. They vary in quality from embarrassing to superb. Group effectiveness depends on the quality of student involvement in the group, a dynamic often created by the value "feel" a student picks up from the teacher. Are the groups just an add-on? Is he really committed to the values of the group effort, assisting groups in their preparation? Obviously the students most benefited on any given subject are those students in the group preparing that particular subject. They find great value in the preparation/planning/cooperation stage—even in the frustrating moments when they can't find the time to meet or don't agree on how to best present the material.

Group process in the college classroom demands time and some risk but, from the perspective of the authors of this volume (not just this chapter), stands absolutely essential in teaching students the technique of working with other people to arrive at group decisions and solve group problems. Astin argues strongly for such a cooperative view of college education which stands in opposition to the traditional competitive approach.

> America's greatest achievements as a society are attributed to our intense competitiveness; it is through "competitive spirit" that we have been able to achieve greatness as a society. Our free enterprise system certainly implies a competitive view: Individuals are given a maximum opportunity to compete with each other for the largest possible share of the resources and rewards in the society.
>
> This competitive world view has deep roots in the history of Western civilization. The rise of Darwinism, with its emphasis on competition among species and the survival of the fittest, provided a scientific framework within which to view the development of the human species. . . . Many of the issues that plague higher education these days can be better understood when viewed within this cooperative-competitive framework.[8]

If a cooperative approach to education (as represented methodologically in group process) can be considered important in secular education and the major university systems as Astin proclaims, how much more important in Bible colleges, Christian liberal arts colleges, and seminaries. At the very least students can gain awareness of how to operate in small groups within the framework of the local church.

RELATING TO STUDENTS

At this point the reader might want to review the chapter on adult education and the theories of andragogy. With a reasonable amount of aggressiveness, college educators must investigate the implications of andragogical theory for *student participation in determining both learning processes and products.* Answers suggested by some institutions include students on most faculty committees, greater opportunity for electives, a wider choice of assignments and in-class learning experiences, students pressed to determine and state their own objectives in learning and many other ways. The ultimate goal? Student participation in the learning process to the greatest possible extent.

How can a college teacher cope with the *wide variety of learning levels* in almost every class? Why include such a question under the subheading "relating to students"? Because the teacher who cares not for the latter will care nothing about the former. But the student-related teacher will vary his teaching methods, expand his grading methods, consider ability sectioning if possible, provide tutorial time when necessary, and provide out-of-class audio and visual materials to support classroom learning experiences.

Student-relatedness also finds form in *contract learning.* One could argue that a learning contract constitutes a teaching methodology, not a form of student-relatedness. But one can reasonably conclude that only the student-related teacher will commit to the contract process. Learning contracts can be variously defined. One authoritative source suggests that a learning contract is "a document drawn up by a student or a mentor or advisor that specifies what a student will learn in a given period of time and how. The contract is distinct from traditional courses or semester equivalence and is evaluated but not graded."[9]

The definition may be a bit narrow since the use of contracts has widened considerably since it was written; nevertheless, at stake here is the attitude of the teacher toward the student's role in the learning process.

Let's conclude our chapter with a return to the andragogical approach to teaching in the Christian college. The following simple quiz can serve as a self-evaluation tool for teachers of adults. If you teach college students or adults in any setting, try it out on yourself; then think about it in relationship to the college teachers you know.

AM I A PEDAGOGUE OR AN ANDRAGOGUE?
(A self-analysis for teachers of adults)
circle one

1. My students are independent and self-directed in the way they view their responsibility for the learning experiences of the class.　　1 2 3 4 5

2. My class sets a climate of mutuality and collaboration between/among students and teacher in the quest for truth.　　1 2 3 4 5

3. My syllabus is designed to use the experiences of the student as a resource for further learning.　　1 2 3 4 5

4. Classroom learning experiences are planned jointly by teacher and students.　　1 2 3 4 5

5. Class sessions take into consideration the social roles my students have already taken and/or those which are currently developing.　　1 2 3 4 5

6. Needs of the students, with respect to the context of any given course, are identified by the students themselves.　　1 2 3 4 5

7. The application of the content I teach is immediate; that is to say, the students are able to perceive and implement the learning in real life without any substantial delay.　　1 2 3 4 5

8. The learning objectives for my classes are jointly agreed on by teacher and students; i.e., they not only "own" my objectives but are encouraged to identify their own.　　1 2 3 4 5

9. I design the learning experiences of my courses to be problem-centered (solutions to practical life situations) rather than subject-centered (memorization of data).　　1 2 3 4 5

10. The actual class methodology leads students through experiences which relate content to life rather than cognitively adding content to content.　　1 2 3 4 5

11. I aggressively teach for *affective* (attitudinal) goals as
    well as *cognitive* (assimilation of content) goals.

    1 2 3 4 5

12. My tests and other required assignments reflect *conative*
    (skill, competency) as well as cognitive concerns.

    1 2 3 4 5

13. Evaluation and grading are inseparably linked with learning
    goals clearly announced at the outset of the class and
    emphasized throughout the term of learning.

    1 2 3 4 5

14. Student feedback in various forms is used to reorganize
    and improve the learning process.

    1 2 3 4 5

15. In my courses I emphasize process as well as product; i.e.,
    I teach the student not only what I have learned but the ways
    in which he can learn.

    1 2 3 4 5

16. As I enter each class I have with me a written set of learn-
    ing objectives which are clear, precise, and worded in terms
    of students skills and competencies.

    1 2 3 4 5

17. I base my teaching on a conscious awareness of student
    readiness: I am aware of what they know and don't know.

    1 2 3 4 5

18. The basis for my grading is broad; that is, in order to
    arrive at a final course grade I measure student learning by
    several means which vary in type and intensity.

    1 2 3 4 5

19. I encourage students to ask questions, provide ample opportunity
    for them to do so, and neither intimidate nor patronize with my
    answers.

    1 2 3 4 5

20. I take seriously the faculty evaluations filled out by my
    classes and conscientiously plan teaching improvements on the
    basis of that information.

    1 2 3 4 5

ENDNOTES

1. Kenneth S. Kantzer, "Can Christian Colleges Survive the Eighties?" *Christianity Today,* September 16, 1983, p. 10.

2. Eugene B. Habecker, *The Other Side of Leadership,* Wheaton, Ill.: Victor Books, 1987, p. 40.

3. Kenneth O. Gangel and Warren S. Benson, *Christian Education: Its History and Philosophy.* Chicago: Moody Press, 1982, p. 359.

4. Alexander W. Astin, "Competition or Cooperation?" *Change,* September/October 1987, p. 18.

5. Arthur F. Holmes, "Academic Freedom in the Christian College," *Bulletin of Wheaton College.* February 1964, p. 6.

6. Gilbert Highet, "The Need to 'Make It New,'" *The Chronicle of Higher Education,* June 21, 1977, p. 40.

7. Kenneth E. Eble, *Professors as Teachers.* San Francisco: Jossey-Bass, 1972, pp. 36–53.

8. Astin, p. 14.

9. William Mayville, "Contract Learning," *ERIC Research Currents.* December 1973, p. 3.

BIBLIOGRAPHY

Aleamoni, Lawrence, ed. *Techniques for Instructional Improvement and Evaluation.* San Francisco: Jossey-Bass, 1987.

Civikly, Jean M., ed. *Communicating in College Classrooms.* San Francisco: Jossey-Bass, 1986.

Eble, Kenneth E. *The Aims of College Teaching.* San Francisco: Jossey-Bass, 1983.

_____. *The Craft of Teaching.* San Francisco: Jossey-Bass, 1976.

_____. *Professors as Teachers.* San Francisco: Jossey-Bass, 1972.

Ericson, Stanford C. *The Essence of Good Teaching.* San Francisco: Jossey-Bass, 1985.

Gangel, Kenneth O., ed. *Toward a Harmony of Faith and Learning.* Farmington Hills, Mich.: Wm. Tyndale College Press, 1984.

Holmes, Arthur F. *All Truth Is God's Truth.* Grand Rapids: Eerdmans, 1977.

_____. *The Idea of a Christian College.* Grand Rapids: Eerdmans, 1975.

Katz, Joseph, ed. *Teaching as Though Students Mattered.* San Francisco: Jossey-Bass, 1985.

Knowles, Malcolm S. and Associates. *Andragogy in Action.* San Francisco: Jossey-Bass, 1984.

Lowman, Joseph. *Mastering the Techniques of Teaching.* San Francisco: Jossey-

Bass, 1985.

Malik, Charles H. *A Christian Critique of the University.* Downers Grove, Ill.: InterVarsity Press, 1982.

Meyers, Chet. *Teaching Students to Think Critically.* San Francisco: Jossey-Bass, 1986.

Sandin, R.T. *The Search for Excellence.* Macon, Ga.: Mercer University Press, 1982.

Stice, James, ed. *Developing Critical Thinking and Problem-Solving Abilities.* San Francisco: Jossey-Bass, 1987.

21. TEACHING IN THE COMMUNITY
Michael S. Lawson

Interest in Bible study outside the confines of the local church or under the direct supervision of the local pastor has dramatically increased. Accurate statistical research eludes us since informal groups rarely keep or publish formal rolls. But the number of parachurch groups focusing on Bible teaching continues to grow.

Whether these groups represent merely another symptom or a fundamental cause, the fact remains that evangelical Christianity in North America is becoming more homogenized. Christians now regularly cross denominational lines through Christian literature, camps, conferences, radio, television, seminars, special speakers, Sunday School conventions, parachurch organizations, and nonsectarian Sunday School curriculum. All of these contribute to an atmosphere conducive to Bible teaching in the community. Their continuing popularity provides convincing evidence that a real need exists.

Because of this homogenization, teaching in the community has theologically focused more on points of common agreement and less on denominational distinctives. Teachers and groups that work within the community but outside the church usually are more tolerant and less dogmatic. Their materials appear more acceptable to most evangelicals. Groups like "Bible Study Fellowships," "Precepts," and "Walk-Thru-the-Bible" contribute both to the homogenization process and to the increase in biblical literacy.

This increased interest in Bible study comes at a time when Christians in North America also seem to be facing increased moral problems. Even the most theologically conservative groups now feel the effects of immorality.

Teaching in a community in North America under the conditions previously described requires a different set of goals and objectives than those that apply in the local church. For instance, the local

344

church must address the issue of curriculum balance for both the spiritually young and spiritually mature. The church must also be sure to give adequate attention to educational systems which promote fellowship and service. Though these objectives may be desirable, they are not essential for teaching outside its walls.

In a community setting, Bible teaching curriculum can reflect needs felt by either the teacher or the group. The two can agree to the subject with no interference from the outside and perhaps no thought given to balance. Frequently, curiosity functions as the only criterion with groups selecting a Bible book or theme previously overlooked in their church setting.

Another contrast between teaching in the community and in the church worth mentioning is the calendar. Many community groups use the school year to determine their calendar. Traditional breaks occur during the Christmas holidays and spring break. Obviously, churches continue to meet throughout the year.

KINDS OF COMMUNITY BIBLE CLASSES

The kinds of Bible classes offered in the community vary greatly in format. Teaching styles and purposes distinguish them substantially from one another.

EVANGELISTIC CLASSES.

Some Bible teaching in the community specifically invites the non-Christian for evangelistic purposes. Church planting often begins this way and any number of parachurch groups offer classes of this nature. When a number of people experience conversion, then the purpose of the class must change or people must move to a different class. Often, because the group prefers to stay together, they redirect their attention to the immediate need for Christian nurture.

Maintaining a purely evangelistic Bible class provides unique challenges. Some leaders deliberately limit the duration of a class to a specific number of weeks. When it concludes, the evangelistic class recycles and maintains its original purpose. Simultaneously, other classes begin with nurture-oriented studies.

Precisely at this point, many questions emerge. Are community Bible classes the best way to nurture young Christians? Can a church meet a broader range of spiritual needs? Who decides which church? Will new converts move into a church? If they will move, should the church prepare special classes? If they do not move, how will other spiritual dimensions develop? These and other questions like them can complicate matters. If taken lightly, disaster may eat the fruit of our labor.

345

BOOKLET CLASSES.

Numerous publishing houses have provided Bible study booklets for quite some time. In addition, parachurch organizations often publish their own materials frequently oriented to new or young converts. Though relatively simple to use because of their fill-in-the-blank format, the booklets usually need the motivating power of a group or mentor to be sure the young believer completes the assignment. The local leader assigns a specific number of questions for each student to address between sessions.

Even a casual survey of this material discloses its basic thrust. *The Survival Kit, The Ten Basic Steps, Living in Christ,* and others mainly get the young Christian started with basic information and procedures of the spiritual life.

TAPE CLASSES.

The advent of the tape recorder may have revolutionized Bible study as much as the printing press revolutionized Bible reading. Most prominent Bible teachers are now available on cassette tape. In the not-too-distant past, groups frequently organized around a favorite teacher or a common subject interest. Not everybody could afford a tape recorder in those days! Now almost every home has several and many cars offer tape playing capabilities. Therefore, group study seems less important. Rather, individuals use the tapes for personal instruction.

The tape classes of the future will be video. The home video revolution surprised many modern technologists with its popularity. Consequently, reformatted old films dominate the home video market. However, some evangelical groups see new opportunities by providing Bible teaching in this new medium.[1] These same groups target church libraries as potential video warehouses for church members to use. Users invite friends to see and hear top evangelical leaders deliver their best material in the comfort of a home atmosphere. Though presently dominated by the lecture ("the talking head"), the technological possibilities will certainly catch on in evangelical production. These tools provide a new and appealing method for reaching friends and offering Bible teaching in the community.

NATIONALLY ORGANIZED CLASSES.

A growing number of Bible teaching groups aim at the whole community. Their highly trained teachers and specialized curriculum offer Bible teaching in some very interesting formats. These groups often carefully select their students. Unlike some groups which require almost nothing from the student and depend exclusively on personal motivation for enrichment and attendance, groups like Bible Study Fellowships and the Navigator 2:7 require definite accountability. From the beginning, students commit to Bible study as a priority for the duration of the course. Teachers regularly assign homework and limit participation if the assignment has not been completed.

LOCAL HOME BIBLE STUDIES.

Informally organized, this form of community Bible teaching remains prolific yet unstable. Some local people organize and teach these with varying degrees of biblical training. Some of these classes retain the same teacher for years and become rather ingrown. Others change teachers from time to time but attendance still depends largely on the teacher's personality. Almost all use the lecture as the primary format with some question-and-answer time as the only variation in method. While a few follow prescribed material, most simply proceed verse by verse through a book of the Bible. Since the teacher shares details of personal research, the studies revolve around the teacher.

GROUP DYNAMICS IN THE COMMUNITY

Unfortunately, Bible teaching in the community finds its greatest weakness at the point of its greatest potential. Because many informal and local groups tend to be small, discussion could be employed with extremely effective results. However, very few teachers really understand how to conduct a true discussion. Helping students process biblical information in relationship to their everyday lives threatens many teachers. Unpredictable, paradoxical, and even erroneous responses require spontaneous yet gentle handling. The uncertainty of this approach in addition to fewer effective models discourages many teachers from its use.

In defense, teachers sometimes dismiss discussion as a pooling of ignorance. Students who have been involved with a poor group experience agree with this evaluation. Or teachers claim to have a lot of discussion when in fact their practices more accurately resemble question-and-answer between the student and the teacher. Note the difference between a true discussion and question-and-answer in the following diagram:

QUESTION & ANSWER   DISCUSSION

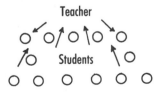

True discussions provide wonderful learning opportunities especially when done:

1. in a caring atmosphere
2. under competent leadership
3. with variety of material
4. among diverse participants.

As in no other setting, discussion provides an opportunity to verbalize beliefs and have them challenged. In spite of the proliferation of biblical information among Christians, the ability to accurately articulate their faith eludes most laymen. Having beliefs challenged by friends can stimulate that capacity like few other experiences. Truly provocative discussions spur critical thinking and reevaluation of reasons for beliefs. However, none of these productive processes occur if people become defensive and "sandbag" their positions. Avoiding this huge pitfall requires adept leadership.

For the most part, leading true discussions remains a lost art. Yet teachers can learn the necessary skills. If preaching and lecturing can be taught and learned, so can discussion-leading. Certainly as much work and preparation go into leading a good discussion but the dynamics are more complicated than preaching or lecturing. The preacher need only develop personal communication skills; the discussion leader must develop his own skills and maximize the contributions of all the participants. Good discussion leaders either consciously or instinctively understand how healthy groups move and how healthy leaders keep them moving.

HOW GROUPS MOVE.

Successful groups seem to move through three distinct phases. Each phase must occur sequentially or the group process breaks down and the participants feel frustrated. The vague sense of dissatisfaction often defies precise identification apart from careful analysis of the breakdown in the phases. Though not profound, these phases are essential to success.

Personalization. Good discussions require a friendly accepting atmosphere. The overworked (but still effective) coffee and doughnut time represents a traditional attempt to fill this need. A more effective procedure would combine the coffee and doughnuts with an activity focused on helping people meet and relate to one another. The activity should encourage people to move away from their usual acquaintances and form new groupings. Initial activities, such as, finding people with the same birth month, born in the same home state, or who have a child the same age help people learn information basic to group process. The mixer enables them to initiate new acquaintances without embarrassment since everyone participates.

Name tags help dissolve a major barrier to conversation which centers on remembering a person's name. Each group member wears a tag but visitors receive a different color for quick identification. After several weeks, name tags may only be needed when visitors come. The tag, whether simple or elaborate, should display the first name clearly in extra-large letters for easy identification from a distance. In lieu of a creative alternative, buy a pack of 3 x 5 cards and attach them with masking tape to avoid damaging garments. Note the following example:

With adequate time and good leadership, people learn to trust one another. Only when relationships deepen, do discussions take on a more sensitive nature. Remember the more sensitive the subject, the more people need to feel safe with one another. Subjecting our opinions to the scrutiny of others creates fear in the best of us.

In order to develop deep interpersonal relationships, the leader must set a tone of acceptance in the group. In fact, he may repeatedly need to help people disagree without being disagreeable. Hopefully, he will infect the members of the group with a spirit of understanding. Discussions can end abruptly with questions like, "You don't really believe that, do you?" A good leader should respond, "Of course he believes it, that's why he shared it. Would you like to share some good reasons why you don't believe it?"

The personalization phase includes getting acquainted, developing deeper interpersonal relationships, and setting a healthy tone for the group. The leader must structure activities in such a way that everyone participates in personalization. The quality of the second phase depends on the success of the first.

Participation. The leader assumes responsibility for stimulating good interaction among group members to promote discussion. Acting as a facilitator, his ability to ask good questions emerges as an art form. Though foundational to both the physical and social sciences, somehow teachers rarely develop sophisticated questioning skills.

Often, we equate teaching more with telling than questioning. Yet Jesus used questions extensively in His own teaching ministry. In fact, Herman Horne includes a chapter in his book, *The Teaching Techniques of Jesus*, on Jesus' use of questions. He introduces that chapter with these words, "Somehow at the beginning of this inquiry I sense that we are near the heart of the teaching methods of Jesus."[2] Horne's own book uniquely features an interrogative style. Question piles upon question, forcing the reader's mind to struggle rather than become complacent. He only interjects small bits of information when the reader needs a tiny bit of direction.

Thought-provoking open-ended questions require enormous amounts of time to write. So, most of us succumb to propositional declarations. However, Neighborhood Bible Studies feature studies on every book of the Bible and several character studies constructed around an almost unending series of pertinent questions. You may wish to purchase the series if for no other reason than to simply see great examples of how to construct thought-provoking biblical questions. Another outstanding publisher of this kind of material is Serendipity.

Can questions guide us to think more clearly and inquire more precisely about how to construct questions? Try these three.

First, ask yourself, "To whom is the question directed?" Questions may point in at least five different directions. (Can you think of others?)

1. Oneself—rhetorical
2. A specific member of the group—direct
3. The previous contributor—reverse
4. Any member of the group—relay
5. The group as a whole—general

Notice how the focus of attention shifts when we ask the same question in a different way about obedience to Jesus.

1. Why would I want to obey Jesus?
2. Jim, why would someone what to obey Jesus?
3. Jim, why would you want to obey Jesus?
4. Why would any of you want to obey Jesus?
5. Why would anyone want to obey Jesus?

Second, ask yourself, "What is the purpose of the question?" Formulating precise questions depends on understanding your specific purpose. Though not comprehensive, the following list stirs us to note how many possibilities exist. A question may be asked in order to:

1. Accumulate facts
2. Define terms
3. Clarify meanings
4. Explain clearly
5. Develop fully
6. Compare
7. Contrast
8. Relate to other subjects
9. Return to the subject

10. Change the subject
11. Involve
12. Arrive at conclusions
13. Summarize findings
14. Extract expected answers
15. Prejudice responses

(Can you think of illustrations for each of these? Can you think of other purposes questions might serve?)

When formulating questions for maximum participation phrases like "in your opinion" or "what do you think" give people the freedom to express themselves without fear of being wrong, embarrassed, or rejected. If the group senses any one of these, discussion may immediately cease. Carefully phrased questions reveal their purpose clearly and cause people to sense their response will be accepted.

Third, ask yourself, "Is the question really appropriate?" Unfortunately, a question appropriate for the age, background, and capacity of one group may not necessarily apply to another. Sometimes rephrasing the question or breaking it into several smaller questions really helps. Without changing the thought, we can rework the structure and sequence.

The question should match the purpose of the biblical passage. Even preachers can commit the crime of teaching a biblical truth which simply does not appear in the passage at hand. Can you think of times when you have wondered how a teacher found his idea in the passage being considered? Good commentaries can protect a beginning (or advanced?) teacher from this embarrassing error. When the passage fails to clearly support the inquiry, people get confused.

A really good question can also be inappropriate to the purpose of the discussion. If the discussion has a clearly stated purpose or direction, each question should be examined in light of that purpose. Will it move us toward the goal? Will it shed light on the subject? Will everyone benefit from an answer to this question? Will we get sidetracked onto a highly interesting but peripheral issue that deserves its own discussion at a later date? Do we need to probe one area before another in order to build on that information? Evaluative questions like these force us to think clearly about the purpose of the discussion.

Good questions can link together sequentially and lead logically through the lesson. A series of four or five key questions might guide a discussion for an entire class period. However, developing four or five leading questions can rack your brain. How would you estimate the time necessary to write leading discussion questions? While not precisely the same thing, some research suggests a trained person writing quality multiple choice test questions can produce somewhere between 5 and 15 in one day.[3]

Formulating and asking quality questions in a warm and accepting atmosphere creates extremely satisfying participation. But the group will still experience frustration until it enters the third phase.

Realization of purpose. Groups with well-defined purposes clearly understood by all participants seem to experience the most satisfaction. Discussions get criticized when they fail to accomplish anything. Too often, the group never intended to produce anything specific and, therefore, achieved its non-purpose.

A discussion can focus on any one of many purposes; possibilities are almost limitless. Consider these samples:

1. "For the next hour, we want to discuss how this passage affects the doctrine of inspiration."
2. "This evening we will explore what changes our lives would exhibit if we really believed the doctrine of the Atonement."
3. "Our purpose is to explore several workable explanations for Hebrews 6."

In any case, before and after the discussion, clearly state the purpose in terms understood by the group. Someone should summarize the efforts of the group at the end of the classtime. Everyone should evaluate how close the group came to accomplishing its stated purpose. Groups can tolerate failure to achieve a stated purpose but they need to see movement toward the goal. Groups that regularly realize their purpose enjoy continued participation in future discussions.

HOW LEADERS KEEP GROUPS MOVING.

Groups do not necessarily move through the three phases on their own. When movement stalls, the leader or someone in the group must do something to get the group back on track. George Henderson gives the following helpful summary of both positive and negative group behavior.

"*Initiating*—suggesting new ideas or a changed way of looking at the group problem or goal; proposing new activities.

"*Information-seeking*—asking for relevant facts or authoritative information.

"*Information-giving*—providing pertinent facts or authoritative information or relating personal experience relevant to the group task.

"*Elaborating*—building on a previous comment, enlarging on it, giving examples.

"*Coordinating*—showing or clarifying the relationships among various ideas, trying to pull ideas and suggestions together.

"*Orienting*—defining the progress of the discussion in terms of the group's goals, raising questions about the direction the discussion is taking.

"*Testing*—checking with the group to see if it is ready to make a decision or to take some action."[4]

On the other hand, numerous behaviors hinder the group. Group leaders must prepare themselves to deal graciously but firmly when these occur.

"Blocking—interfering with the progress of the group by going off at a tangent, citing personal experiences unrelated to the group's problem, arguing too much on a point the rest of the group has resolved, rejecting ideas without consideration, preventing a vote.

"Aggression—criticizing or blaming others, showing hostility toward the group or some individual without relation to what has happened in the group, attacking the motives of others, deflating the ego or status of others.

"Seeking recognition—attempting to call attention to oneself by excessive talking, extreme ideas, boasting, boisterousness.

"Special pleading—introducing or supporting ideas related to one's own pet concerns or philosophies beyond reason, attempting to speak for the 'grass roots,' 'the common man,' 'the underdog.'

"Withdrawing—acting indifferent or passive, resorting to excessive formality, doodling, whispering to others.

"Dominating—trying to assert authority in manipulating the group or certain members of it by 'pulling rank,' giving directions authoritatively, interrupting contributions of others."[5]

Leaders can discourage unwanted behavior by identifying it openly in the beginning. On the positive side, leaders who establish standards prior to the discussion do not offend individual members when enforcing them later on.

For sure, each participant should observe a specific time limit and violating the time limit should bring friendly but firm consequences. A leader might set the standard for time by saying, "I will feel free to interrupt if someone is taking up too much time (e.g., over three minutes). Remember, we want discussion, not a lecture."

SUMMARY

Who knows how long the open atmosphere in the community will last? Community Bible teachers should seize the wonderful opportunity to lead and guide the thinking of their students. Each of the different kinds of classes could benefit from large doses of discussion. While discussions rarely provide a teacher with the opportunity to impress others with his personal knowledge, they do create marvelous learning environments. Listening to and expressing beliefs may penetrate deep into the conscious experience of people.

Fortunately, educators have identified the necessary skills for leading discussions much more precisely today than even twenty years ago. Evangelicals have produced excellent books to inform and equip even the beginning teacher.[6] Most major barriers to discussions come from personal fears. Yet those of us who affirm the universal body of Christ can practice our faith through community Bible teaching. Our communities await our initiative and leadership.

ENDNOTES

1. One such group is Church Video Centers, Inc., 1750 Northwest Highway, Suite 250, Garland, Texas 75041.

2. Herman Harrell Horne, *The Teaching Techniques of Jesus*. Grand Rapids: Kregel, 1920, p. 45.

3. David Pratt, *Curriculum Design and Development*. New York: Harcourt, Brace Jovanovich, Inc., 1980, p. 234.

4. George Henderson, *Human Relations from Theory to Practice*. Norman, Okla.: University of Oklahoma Press, 1974, p. 203.

5. Henderson, p. 203.

6. An extensive and current Christian education bibliography is available through the Dallas Seminary book room, 3909 Swiss Ave., Dallas, Texas 75204.

BIBLIOGRAPHY

Auer, J. Jeffery. *Handbook for Discussion Leaders*. New York: Harper and Brothers, 1954.

Bonner, Hubert. *Group Dynamics*. New York: Ronald Press, 1959.

Coleman, Lyman. *Serendipity New Testament for Groups*. Grand Rapids: Zondervan, 1986.

Cooper, Polly. *How to Guide Adults*. Nashville, Tenn.: Convention Press, 1982.

Griffin, Em. *Getting Together*. Downers Grove, Ill.: InterVarsity Press, 1982.

Kunz, Marilyn and Catherine Schell. *How to Start a Neighborhood Bible Study*. New York: Neighborhood Bible Studies, 1966.

Knowles, M.S. *How to Develop Better Leaders*. New York: Association Press, 1955.

Knowles, Malcolm and Hulda. *Introduction to Group Dynamics*. New York: Association Press, 1959.

Kuhn, Margaret. *You Can't Be Human Alone*. New York: National Council of the Churches of Christ in the U.S.A., 1956.

Leypoldt, Martha M. *Forty Ways to Teach in Groups*. Valley Forge, Pa.: Judson

Press, 1967.

―――― . *Learning Is Change.* Valley Forge, Pa.: Judson Press, 1971.

Miles, Matthew B. *Learning to Work in Groups.* New York: Teacher's College, Columbia University, 1959.

Strang, Ruth M. *Group Work in Education.* New York: Harper, 1958.

Thelen, Herbert A. *Dynamics of Groups at Work.* Chicago: University Press, 1954.

CONCLUSION
MANDATE FOR THE FUTURE

Kenneth O. Gangel

"Opening the way and not conducting to the end," wrote Confucius some 500 years before Christ, "makes the learner thoughtful. He who produces such harmony, easy attainment, and thoughtfulness may be pronounced a skillful teacher."[1] Five centuries later our Lord modeled that description for 3½ years while teaching His disciples to do precisely the same.

The twenty-one chapters of this book attempt to describe teaching as it is and as it should be. On those observations serious Christian teachers must design classroom strategies for the future. How we should (or must) change the current wisdom depends on how well prevailing views correlate with timeless biblical truth. Ofttimes we find it difficult to relate God's Word to a process or function like teaching. Yet we dare never give up the search nor abandon the quest.

Ten years before the writing of this book Art Criscoe identified five trends in current teaching-learning methodology: (1) the systems approach, (2) individualized or self-paced instruction, (3) experiential education, (4) media-assisted instruction, and (5) extension education.[2] Dr. Criscoe was on target; all five have developed significantly over the intervening decade. Yet he dealt only with methodology.

In a broader sense we can expand the line of march with a scouting report which includes:

1. Continuing and increasing debates among evangelicals on the issue of integration: what it is and how we do it (see chap. 5).
2. Exponential development of mass, group, and individual computer-assisted learning (see chap. 11).
3. More and better audio, video, and even laser productions by both professionals (teachers) and amateurs (students).
4. Widespread understanding of synergogy and its application

356

in Christian classrooms.

5. An increasing passing-off of responsibility for learning to the learner—less telling, more guiding.

6. Expanded use of heretofore esoteric techniques, such as, case studies, gaming, and information mapping systems.

Youth for Christ, Intl. once used a catchy motto—"Anchored to the rock, geared to the times." So we find it with Christian teaching. Which would be the greater loss? A foolish question, ignored by intentional communicators. In the words of *the* Teacher, "You should have practiced the latter, without neglecting the former" (Matt. 23:23). Content and method offer no opportunity for severance.

Recent research published by the U.S. Office of Education points up our dependence on both biblical and secular sources. Just a few examples.[3]

1. Parents are their children's first and most influential teachers. What parents do to help their children learn is more important to academic success than how well-off the family is.

2. Teachers who set and communicate high expectations to all their students obtain greater academic performance from those students than teachers who set low expectations.

3. How much time students are actively engaged in learning contributes strongly to their achievement. The amount of time available for learning is determined by the instructional and management skills of the teacher and the priorities set by the school administration.

4. Teachers welcome professional suggestions about improving their work, but they rarely receive them.

Writing in the *Christian Education Journal,* Bruce Lockerbie reminds us that Christian teaching must be incarnational, not institutional; natural, not contrived; and developmental, not formulaic.[4] In order to do that, in order to be what the Master wants us to be throughout the remainder of our years, our teaching must conform to His directives. We dare not take aim, as someone has noted, "on a cloth askew, with a cue untrue and elliptical billard balls."

ENDNOTES

1. Book XVI—HSIO KI (Record on the Subject of Education).

2. Art Criscoe, "Current Trends in Teaching—Learning Methodology," *Search.* Fall 1978, pp. 41–51.

3. *What Works—Research about Teaching and Learning.* U.S. Department of

Education, 1986.

4. Bruce Lockerbie, "Epilogue," *Christian Education Journal.* Fall 1988, p. 83.

Kenneth O. Gangel is vice president for academic affairs, academic dean, and distinguished professor of Christian Education at Dallas Theological Seminary. He has also served at Calvary Bible College and Miami Christian College and holds doctorates from the University of Missouri and Mercy College. He has written more than 800 articles for journals and periodicals and is author or editor of over 20 books, including *Christian Education—Its History and Philosophy*, *Leadership for Church Education*, *The Christian Educator's Handbook on Adult Education*, and *Feeding and Leading*.

Howard G. Hendricks has served as professor and chairman of the department of Christian Education at Dallas Theological Seminary and is distinguished professor and chairman of the Center for Christian Leadership at the seminary. He holds degrees from Wheaton College and Dallas Theological Seminary and has written or edited numerous books, including *Teaching to Change Lives*, *Mastering Teaching*, *Living by the Book*, and *Heaven Help the Home*.